# TO RUN A CONSTITUTION

STUDIES IN
GOVERNMENT AND PUBLIC POLICY

Charles H. Levine, Series Editor

# TO RUN
# A CONSTITUTION

## THE LEGITIMACY
## OF THE ADMINISTRATIVE STATE

JOHN A. ROHR

UNIVERSITY PRESS OF KANSAS

Published by the University Press of Kansas (Lawrence, Kansas 66045),
which was organized by the Kansas Board of Regents and is operated
and funded by Emporia State University, Fort Hays State University,
Kansas State University, Pittsburg State University,
the University of Kansas, and Wichita State University

Library of Congress Cataloging in Publication Data

Rohr, John A. (John Anthony), 1934–
    To run a constitution.
    (Studies in government and public policy)
    Bibliography: p.
    Includes index.
    1. Administrative agencies—United States—History.
2. Public administration—United States—History.
3. Legitimacy of governments—United States—History.
4. United States—Constitutional history. I. Title. II. Series.
JK411.R64    1986        353.03′09        85-28867
ISBN 0-7006-0291-7
ISBN 0-7006-0301-8 (pbk.)

Printed in the United States of America
10   9   8   7   6   5   4   3   2

*For Paul and Mark*

The world is charged with the grandeur of God.
It will flame out, like shining from shook foil.

It is getting to be harder to *run* a constitution than to frame one.
—Woodrow Wilson

# Contents

# Preface

Men are not corrupted by the exercise of power or debased by the habit of obedience, but by the exercise of power which they believe to be illegitimate, and by obedience to a rule which they consider to be usurped and oppressive.

—Alexis de Tocqueville

The purpose of this book is to legitimate the administrative state in terms of constitutional principle. It is intended for two groups of readers: public administrators themselves and interested Americans who are the beneficiaries, victims, citizens, and authors of the administrative state. It contributes to a growing body of literature that defends the integrity of the Public Administration as an institution of government.[1]

In writing for the Public Administration community, my goal is to introduce both practitioners and students of Public Administration to the constitutional origins of our profession. Unfortunately, the word *introduce* is used with some precision. Constitutional law and history are sadly neglected in academic programs in Public Administration and in public-management training as well. Because public administrators at virtually all levels of government take an oath to uphold the Constitution of the United States, this neglect deprives the profession of the opportunity to consider an important normative foundation for its activities. An oath is a profound moral commitment. It seems fitting that those who take an oath to uphold the Constitution should be invited to reflect seriously on how the object of their oath grounds the agencies they manage. This book extends that invitation.

In writing for an interested public, my goal is to defend the compatibility of the modern administrative state with the plans of the framers of the Constitution. This is no easy task. Many administrative agencies combine powers of rule making, investigation, prosecution, and adjudication. Such a combination of powers is ill at ease in a regime anchored in the constitutional principle of separation of powers. Public Administration joins together what constitutional principle keeps apart. As a matter of public law, of course, this combination of powers has been upheld by the Supreme Court of the United States; but this book goes beyond questions of legal correctness in its effort to legitimate the administrative state. The book's focus is on the troubling questions of legitimacy that survive the resolution of a legal controversy. With constitutional issues, there are many such survivors, because the Constitution is more than a legal document; it is covenant as well as contract.[2]

To illustrate the point of legitimacy-beyond-legality, consider the American Nazi party, the Flat Earth Society, and *Hustler* magazine. All three are quite legal, but they lack legitimacy. We acquiesce in their presence as the price we pay for living in a free society; but we refuse to take them seriously as "legitimate" expressions of political action, scientific inquiry, or literary endeavor. Legitimacy means more than a grudging acceptance of the inevitable.[3] The word suggests at least confidence and respect and, at times, even warmth and affection. Alexander Hamilton spoke the language of legitimacy when, as Publius, he noted in *Federalist 27* the connection between sound Public Administration and widespread popular support.[4] His point was that a well-administered government would win the affection of the people. I suggest that we stand Hamilton's argument on its head and say that governmental institutions with weak legitimacy will not be well administered.[5]

That is, it is important to legitimate administrative institutions not only because they deserve to be legitimated but also to help them perform their appointed tasks more effectively. This is a significant issue of public interest even in an era of deregulation, cutback management, and "bashing the bureaucrat." I carry no brief for "bloated bureaucracies" and "Potomac puzzle palaces"—those darlings of irresponsible campaign oratory. I am not particularly interested in whether administrative agencies wax or wane; but I am quite concerned that they perform well whether their sphere of influence expands, contracts, or remains the same. Such changes in administrative practice as privatization, deregulation, and the 1978 efforts to politicize the civil service in the name of "reform" are flowers of a day when compared with the simple presence of the administrative state, which is massive and enduring.[6]

This book rests on the assumption that we live in an administrative state and will continue to do so for the foreseeable future. The Public Administration, as an institution of government, has withstood merciless bipartisan attacks during both the Carter and Reagan administrations. Like Glendower, presidents can call spirits from the deep; but like Hotspur, we know they will not come. It is futile to kick against the goad or to curse the fate that has cast our lot in a public order that ill fits our political traditions. The path of wisdom is to examine these traditions to see if they will yield principles likely to legitimate the administrative state in which we have lived for the past half-century and in which we shall spend the rest of our days. It is degrading for administrators to govern and for citizens to be governed by institutions that are deemed illegitimate—as Tocqueville noted in the passage cited at the beginning of this preface. As a matter of fact, however, the administrative state is perceived as illegitimate.[7] If the administrative state is both inevitable and illegitimate, our dignity as citizens of a constitutional republic is in jeopardy.

The plot thickens when one recalls that elected officials give forthcoming elections—sometimes as far as eighteen months away—as a reason for *failing* to act in such crucial matters as Social Security reform and an alarming deficit. And yet we are told that administrative agencies must be kept firmly under the thumb of elected officials.[8] This is a formula for inaction that betrays the vigorous government the framers of the Constitution envisioned.[9] The sad spectacle of elected officials pleading their accountability to the public to justify their failure to govern only strengthens the case for the administrative state.

When I speak of the "administrative state," I mean the political order that came into its own during the New Deal and still dominates our politics. It is the form of government that Dwight Waldo described so eloquently four decades ago in his political-science classic *The Administrative State*.[10] Its hallmark is the expert agency tasked with important governing functions through loosely drawn statutes that empower unelected officials to undertake such important matters as preventing "unfair competition," granting licenses as "the public interest, convenience or necessity" will indicate, maintaining a "fair and orderly market," and so forth.[11]

The administrative state is not confined to regulating industry. Its writ runs to defense contracting and procurement, military and diplomatic policy, and the institutions of mass justice that manage programs in public assistance, public housing, public education, public health, disability benefits, food stamps, and so forth. The administrative state is in reality the welfare/warfare state we know so well. Despite its warts and wrinkles, it has provided the underpinnings of the free, decent, and prosperous society most Americans have enjoyed for the past half-century. I want to legitimate the American administrative state because I believe it provides the stability to accommodate orderly change in a liberal democratic regime that is fundamentally just.

The time is right for an effort to legitimate the administrative state in terms of constitutional principle. In 1987 we shall mark the bicentennial of the Constitution of the United States. It is merely a coincidence, but surely a happy one for the Public Administration community, that 1987 will also mark the centennial of Woodrow Wilson's famous essay on administration, which is usually credited with marking the beginning of Public Administration as a distinctive form of governmental activity with its own norms, problems, and practices.[12] The American Society for Public Administration (ASPA) has wisely acknowledged this happy coincidence by establishing the Committee on Three Centuries of Public Administration: 1787–2087 and assigning it the task of "identifying, clarifying, and addressing high priority substantive issues to which we ought to be attending in ASPA as the field of Public Administration prepares to enter its second century as a profession and our third century as a constitutional democracy."[13]

With professional attention formally and officially turned to the Constitution and Public Administration, this would seem to be the acceptable time to examine the links between them. Not all is well in the field of Public Administration, just as all is not well in the Congress, the presidency, the courts, the media, the churches, the schools, and the business community. Each of these institutions continually engages in the never-ending task of reform, but only the Public Administration does so under a cloud of constitutional illegitimacy. This book is intended to dispel that cloud so that the Public Administration community and the public at large can address in a clearheaded fashion the pressing problems of improving administrative governance without unwelcome and unhelpful distractions about the legitimacy of the administrative state.

The argument of this book is presented more in the form of an essay than as a lawyer's brief or a mathematician's theorem. I do not begin with postulates and proceed rigorously to the inevitable Q.E.D. My argument might better be described as reaching its appointed end through the plodding but sure progress of two steps forward and one step back. The case against the constitutional legitimacy of the administrative state is not frivolous. Nor are the friends of the administrative state always helpful in the sorts of arguments they present to justify their positions. This is true of such champions of Public Administration as Woodrow Wilson, Frank J. Goodnow, Louis Brownlow, and even Franklin D. Roosevelt. I have tried to be fair in presenting the constitutional attacks on the administrative state as well as the inadequacies of many of the replies. The result is that my argument does no more than conclude that "on balance" the administrative state enjoys constitutional legitimacy. I do not establish my case "beyond all reasonable doubt," but I do believe that "the preponderance of the evidence" supports my position. This is enough, however, for the purposes I have stated above. I sound no clarion to mount the bureaucratic parapets. What I present is what I hope will be regarded as a serious and sober argument defending the rightful place of the administrative state in our constitutional heritage.

I began this Preface with the hope that legitimating the administrative state would enable it to perform more effectively. I shall close it with another hope—that legitimation will tame the excesses of the administrative state. Legitimation has a civilizing aspect about it. In grounding the nature and function of the administrative state in constitutional principle, we invite administrators to assimilate the salient values in the constitutional heritage. If they do this, they will find at the center of this heritage a profound belief in individual rights and in the securing of these rights as the great, overarching purpose of American government. If administrators look to this heritage to grant legitimacy to vigorous administration, they will find what they seek; but they will find much else besides. They will find principles capable of instructing them on how to avoid the worst excesses of the administrative state. To legitimate is to tame, to civilize.

Several sections of this book rely on articles of mine that have appeared in academic journals and collections of essays. I am grateful to the journals and publishers for permission to make use of selections from these publications:

"Civil Servants and Second-class Citizens," *Public Administration Review* 44 (Mar. 1984): 135–43.

"The Constitutional World of Woodrow Wilson," in *Politics and Administration: Woodrow Wilson and American Public Administration,* ed. Jack Rabin and James S. Bowman (New York: Marcel Dekker, 1983), pp. 31–49.

"Professionalism, Legitimacy and the Constitution," *Public Administration Quarterly* 8 (Winter 1985): 401–18.

"Administrative Decision-Making and Professionalism: The Role of the Constitution," *Review of Public Personnel Administration* 3 (Spring 1983): 61–70.

"Constitutional Foundations of the Administrative State," in *A Centennial History of the American Administrative State,* ed. Ralph C. Chandler (New York: John Wiley & Sons, forthcoming).

Throughout this book I frequently quote *The Federalist Papers* and leading Anti-Federalists. Quotations from *The Federalist Papers* are always taken from the text edited by Jacob E. Cooke and published by Wesleyan University Press of Middletown, Connecticut, in 1961. Anti-Federalist quotations are taken from Herbert J. Storing's seven-volume edition of Anti-Federalist writings published under the title *The Complete Anti-Federalist* (Chicago: University of Chicago Press, 1983). I am grateful to both of these publishers for granting me permission to quote their carefully edited texts.

The most pleasurable moment in writing a book comes at the end, when the author recalls with gratitude the many persons whose support and encouragement made it possible. My acknowledgments begin with a recognition of my continuing indebtedness to the late Herbert J. Storing, my teacher at the University of Chicago in the late 1960s. A substantial portion of my professional work in this book and elsewhere is the result of reflecting on his brilliant insights into the American constitutional tradition. His influence upon me, like his thought itself, is profound and abiding.

Charles Goodsell, my colleague at Virginia Polytechnic Institute; David Rosenbloom of the Maxwell School at Syracuse University; and Phillip Cooper of SUNY-Albany have rendered invaluable professional assistance by reading an earlier draft of the entire manuscript. Their frank and incisive criticisms have immeasurably strengthened the final version. Victor Rosenblum of the Northwestern University Law School, David O'Brien of the Department of Government at the University of Virginia, and Stanley Katz of Princeton's History Department read portions of this manuscript that related to my concern on how to integrate constitutional studies into the Public Administration curriculum. Their comments and bibliographical suggestions were most enlightening. This book would be much better if I possessed the wit and energy to follow all the suggestions of these six readers, who are hereby absolved of any implication in the book's errors and inadequacies.

Gerhard Casper, dean of the University of Chicago Law School; John Dawson, professor emeritus of Harvard Law School; Herman Belz of the University of Maryland's Department of History; and Paul Green, director of the Institute of Public Service at Governors State University, generously provided me with unpublished classroom notes, draft versions of articles in progress, and extensive published materials that were most helpful in my work. When Dean Casper's 1500-page set of notes on the separation of powers was lost in the mail (a casualty of the administrative state), he promptly and graciously sent me a second copy of this valuable collection.

Throughout the years that I have been working on this book, the faculty, students, and staff at Virginia Tech's Center for Public Administration and Policy have been most supportive of my efforts. In particular, I want to thank the center's director, Gary Wamsley, for his warm encouragement and intellectual leadership. Graduate students in a series of seminars have helped me refine my thinking on many points in this book. I am pleased to acknowledge my debt to my students for their patience as I formulated my ideas and for their comments when I expressed them. This debt is owed to many students, but I would be remiss if I failed to mention specifically the immediate and direct contributions of Lluana McCann, Richard Green, Larry Lane, and Susan Sparks. The manuscript in its several drafts was prepared for publication by Judi Hoover, who combines grace and efficiency in a most remarkable way; my lasting thanks to her.

I am indebted to many librarians for prompt, courteous, and correct responses to my endless queries. Chief among these is Janet Spahr of Virginia Polytechnic Institute. I am also pleased to acknowledge the generous support and cooperation I received from the National Archives staff in Suitland, Maryland; the Library of Congress; the Franklin D. Roosevelt Library in Hyde Park, New York; and the Bentley Historical Library of the University of Michigan.

I thank the National Endowment for the Humanities and the Earhart Foundation for substantial financial awards that gave me the time to think and read and write about the topics developed in this book. The stimulating semiannual discussions sponsored by the Committee on the Constitutional System have also helped me to think seriously about my topic. Recent national conferences of both the American Society for Public Administration and the American Political Science Association have presented forums in which I was able to present my research and receive valuable professional criticism.

My final word of thanks is reserved for my wife, Kathy, and my sons, Paul and Mark. While I was writing about how to run a constitution, Kathy addressed what Aristotle recognized as the more fundamental task of running a household. Quite un-Aristotelian, however, was her willingness to share with me, a technological primitive, her professional expertise as an engineer by initiating me into the mysteries of the word processor. My sons, aged eleven and nine, need not yet worry about running either households or constitutions. Their boyish ways of earnest play were my delight and diversion as I struggled through this book. They made quite real to me the noble efforts of the founding fathers of the Republic to "secure the Blessings of Liberty to ourselves and our Posterity." It is to Paul and Mark, in the hope of their lasting liberty, that I have dedicated this book.

John A. Rohr

*Blacksburg, Virginia*
4 July 1985

states and that this is one very important reason why the new Constitution should be approved. Prudently, he makes no mention of his earlier argument that superior federal administration is the only way in which popular esteem for the states might be weakened to the advantage of the new government.

The mask is dropped in *Federalist 46,* where Publius boldly asserts that if the people should ever "become more partial to the Foederal than to the state governments, the change can only result . . . from manifest and irresistible proofs of a better administration." To this he adds the normative consideration that this is only right because the people "ought not surely to be precluded from giving most of their confidence where they may discover it to be most due."

The argument culminates in *Federalist 68:* there the prosaic Publius turns to poetry to buttress his case for the importance of administration in the new government. Wisely, he rejects as "political heresy" the couplet from Alexander Pope:

> For forms of government let fools contest—
> That which is best administered is best.

Publius will not allow his esteem for administration to trump his commitment to republican principles. Administration is instrumental for achieving higher political ends such as winning popular support for the new government. He admits, however, that Pope's heresy, like all heresies, is but a distortion of the truth: "We can safely pronounce that the true test of a good government is its aptitude and tendency to produce a good administration." If Publius is a reliable guide to the meaning of the Constitution, administration has an important role to play.

In view of Publius's serious attention to administration, it is somewhat remarkable that the modern administrative state is so frequently the object of attacks grounded rhetorically in our constitutional heritage. And yet who can deny that campaign oratory calling for a return to the ways of the founding fathers is often a thinly veiled attack on the administrative state? Such language should not be lightly dismissed. As Marvin Meyers has reminded us, "political talk has mattered in America."[9] It tells us much about our politics if an elected official can rally support by shouting "Who elected Paul Volcker?"[10]

The legitimacy problem is not simply the creation of the critics of the administrative state. In Public Administration literature we sometimes find an embarrassing impatience with a constitutional design that inhibits economy, efficiency, and effectiveness—the hallmarks of our calling. Dramatic calls for far-reaching constitutional reform are no strangers to the corpus of Public Administration literature. Fortunately for our profession, these calls are buried in academic publications where they are likely to escape the notice of elected officials who have always suspected that we are wayward sons and erring daughters of our founding fathers.[11]

The most direct link between the administrative state and constitutional illegitimacy, however, can be found at what is usually regarded as the beginning of American Public Administration: the work of Woodrow Wilson, Frank J. Goodnow, and the civil-service reformers of the late nineteenth century. For our purposes, Wilson's work is the most interesting. In the second section of his famous essay on administration, Wilson states his now-familiar instrumental view of administration.[12] The constitutional background of Wilson's understanding of administration can be found in his 1885 book *Congressional Government,* where he develops a rich polemic against separation of powers. What is remarkable, however, is that neither in the book nor in the essay does Wilson call for the constitutional amendment that was absolutely indispensable for the reforms he had in mind. In his earlier writings, Wilson had not been so bashful. In an article written in 1884 he issued a straightforward call for an American version of cabinet government, with specific language to amend the Constitution to bring about the desired change. Article 1, section 6, which reads in part, "and no Person holding any Office under the United States, shall be a Member of either House during his Continuance in Office," would be changed to read "and no person holding other than a Cabinet Office under the United States shall be a member of either House during his continuance in office." Thus the addition of four words ["other than a cabinet"] would introduce members of the president's cabinet into Congress and thereby destroy separation of powers.[13]

In chapter 5, I will develop more fully the explanations for Wilson's decision to omit the call for a constitutional amendment in *Congressional Government.* What is important for the present is to note that Wilson's instrumental view of administration in the second part of his 1887 essay was at odds with the Constitution of the United States—and Wilson knew it. Wilson, like Goodnow and many of the civil-service reformers, preferred separation of functions to separation of powers. The legislature embodied "the will of the state." Administration, which must be separated from the legislature, executes that will. This separation of functions is, of course, the familiar instrumental model of public administration; but it is not the constitutional theory of separation of powers. In constitutional theory the legislature does not embody the will of the state; it does not possess the totality of governmental power. By ratifying the Constitution, the people conferred governmental power on each of the three great branches in such a way that each is independent of the other. As Wilson read his times, this arrangement had led to the sorry state of affairs that he lamented so eloquently in *Congressional Government* and that he tried to correct in the 1887 essay.

The point of all this is that when Public Administration literature traces the birth of the administrative state to Wilson's essay, we find that it was conceived out of wedlock with the Constitution of the United States, and hence we should not wonder at subsequent attacks upon its legitimacy. Its presence has always been something of an embarrassment at patriotic reunions. How can a "real American" love OSHA? Administration, like political parties, congressional committees, and judicial review of acts of Congress, is not mentioned in the Constitution.[14] Yet parties, committees, and judicial review are seldom criticized on grounds of constitutional legitimacy. Only administration bears this burden. The reason for this different treatment lies, I believe, in the fact that the case for administration was grounded in a polemic against the constitutional principle of separation of powers—a point I shall develop more fully in chapter 6. Because of this polemic the administrative state has never been at ease in our constitutional tradition.

In tracing the legitimacy problem to Wilson, I do not propose to make him the posthumous recipient of unsolicited advice on how he might have accommodated his ideas on administration to American constitutional theory. Instead, I propose to follow Paul Van Riper's advice that we return to the founding of the Republic to see what congruence we might find between what the framers envisioned and what we know today as the administrative state.[15]


## FOUNDINGS

At the birth of societies, the rulers establish institutions; and afterwards, the institutions mould the rulers.

—Montesquieu


If it is of some importance to legitimate the administrative state, one might wonder why we must return to the *Constitution* to do so. The question is particularly germane if legitimacy means more than mere legality. If the administrative state can be squared with the principles of the Constitution, what "surplus value" over and above legality is thereby conferred? The answer to this question lies in the symbolic importance of the Constitution in American politics.

At a descriptive level, it is fairly obvious that the Constitution is of enormous public interest. As I write these sentences, many plans are afoot to mark its bicentennial in a rich variety of ways. Through our history, serious books on the Constitution abound: Kent, Story, Curtis, Thayer, Cooley, Beard, Corwin, Warren, Pritchett, Swisher, Crosskey, Bickel, Kurland, Tribe—the list goes on and on. Social scientists who have never read the Constitution can tell us all about Beard's interpretation of it. A recent, popular interpretation of the *Federalist* was promoted by the Book-of-the-Month Club.[16]

More important than the writings about the Constitution, however, is the habit of American statesmen to invoke its spirit in support of the policies of the day. As noted above, this invocation usually takes place in a context that is hostile to the ways of the administrative state. "Getting back to the spirit of the founding fathers" inevitably triggers the call to "get the government off our backs," which is an easily deciphered code calling for an indiscriminate reduction in governmental services and regulations. The assumption is that the framers of the Constitution would disapprove of the power of our contemporary federal government and that in allowing it to become so powerful, we have somehow betrayed them.

No doubt the framers would be amazed at what the government they created has become, but it is not clear that they would disapprove. The framers were unalterably committed to the preservation of individual rights as the purpose of government, but they did not see such rights as competitors with governmental power in some sort of zero-sum game. In *The Federalist* and in the secret debates in Philadelphia, one of the major arguments in favor of the new Constitution was that a strong government is needed to protect individual rights. This is precisely what was wrong with the Articles of Confederation—individual rights were not being protected.[17]

The framers of the Constitution might be somewhat sympathetic with those whose efforts to fashion new institutions of government are criticized on grounds of their legitimacy. The framers faced legitimating problems themselves. The 1787 Convention in Philadelphia was the creature of congressional approval of the recommendation from the Annapolis Convention of the previous year. There a handful of delegates had issued a call for a convention the following year "to devise such further provisions as shall appear to them necessary to render the constitution of the Federal Government adequate to the exigencies of the Union."[18] Congress approved this call but added an important qualification: the convention was to meet "for the sole and express purpose of revising the Articles of Confederation."[19]

During the debate over the ratification of the Constitution the Anti-Federalists scored some telling points against the proposed document by noting that the framers had exceeded their congressional mandate. Having been told to convene "for the sole and express purpose of revising the Articles," they proceeded to bring forth a new government. The Anti-Federalists had a good point; but the Federalists were ready with a reply that might well serve as the keynote for those Americans who support a vigorous federal government. They argued that it was more important to achieve the ends of the congressional mandate as stated at the Annapolis Convention ("render the Constitution of the Federal Government adequate to the exigencies of government and the preservation of the Union") than to scruple too nicely over the specified means ("revising the Articles"). Once it was clear that revision of the Articles could not meet the exigencies of government and preserve the union, the Federalists maintained that it was incumbent upon them to propose a new government.

In emphasizing the ends/means rationality of the framers' defense of a powerful government in support of individual rights, I do not suggest that they were so far removed from the Revolution as to have grown complacent about tyranny. Their fears of governmental abuse, however, are well known. It is this aspect of the framers' thought that is stressed almost to the exclusion of everything else they had to say when their "spirit" is invoked in contemporary political discourse. For this reason, the framers are presented inaccurately as implacable foes of the wide-ranging activities of modern government. If we are to legitimate the administrative state, we must at least "neutralize" the framers. I say *at least* neutralize designedly, because I think we can do better. I believe they can be enlisted in support of the modern administrative state. For the present, however, let us rest with neutralizing them so that opponents of the administrative state do not win cheap victories by exploiting the symbolic power of the Constitution. This neutralization is the first of two answers to the question I raised at the beginning of this section—namely, if legitimacy means more than legality, why return to the origins of the Constitution to legitimate the administrative state? We return to the origins of the Constitution to neutralize its framers in the public argument over the administrative state.

The second answer is that the Constitution is the symbol of the founding of the Republic and in politics, "foundings" are normative. Here I follow Hannah Arendt's treatment of "authority," which she sees as originally a Roman idea but one that is quite pertinent to American politics. Plato had no equivalent for the Latin word for authority, *auctoritas*. The Greeks saw public life in terms of either persuasion or coercion. Coercive regimes were not "political." Life in the polis demanded a public order based on persuasion and argument among equal citizens. The democratic execution of Socrates led Plato to despair of the politics of persuasion and to look for a new alternative to coercion. He found it in philosophy, for the few who would rule, and in myth for the many who would be ruled.[20]

Although the Romans reverently accepted the Greek sages as their teachers, their public order rested on a different set of principles. For the Romans, the founding of the city was the decisive political event. Their years were numbered from that event—*ab urbe condita* (from the founding of the city)—as ours are numbered from the birth of Jesus. Their great political myths—the stories of Aeneas and Romulus—were related to the founding of Rome and, in this respect, contrasted sharply with Plato's no-less-political myth of Er, which enlists cosmic order in support of virtue.[21] This emphasis on the unique character of the founding of Rome explains why the Romans, unlike the Greeks, never had a foreign policy of colonization. The Greeks frequently set out to establish new settlements in the belief that the polis was in their persons regardless of geography. Instead of founding new cities, the Romans expanded their rule by adding to the original foundation "until the whole of Italy and, eventually the whole of the Western world were united and administered by Rome as though the whole world were nothing but Roman hinterland."[22]

Underlying this emphasis on the founding of the city was the Roman idea of authority. Authority is a difficult concept for contemporary social scientists to grasp, because we have been taught to think in terms of function and behavior rather than nature and essence. When those in authority succeed in getting their subordinates to obey, we find it hard to see any meaningful distinction between authority and coercion. The distinction, however, was crucial for the Romans.

Theodore Mommsen, acknowledging the difficulty in getting a clear concept of Roman authority, described it as "more than advice and less than a command, an advice which one may not safely ignore."[23] Arendt suggests looking at the political language of the Romans to understand what they meant by authority as something that is powerful without being coercive. The word *auctoritas* is derived from the verb *augere*—to increase (whence the English word *augment*). Roman politics was looked upon as the "augmenting" of the great decisive act of founding the city.[24]

This reverence for the past is reflected in the use of the word *majores* (the greater ones) for those we call "ancestors." The great governing body of the Roman Republic was the senate (from *senior,* an elder). The well-known Roman regard for the father as head of the family *(paterfamilias)* had its political counterpart in veneration for the *patria* (fatherland; from *pater,* father). Ancestors, elders, and fathers were revered not just because they were old but because they were closer to the founding that gave meaning and purpose to public life.

Arendt notes that authority for the Romans was closely related to tradition and religion. *Traditio,* which means a handing down from generation to generation, explains in part the extraordinary—though at times quite dysfunctional—Roman tendency to preserve archaic forms of government. If tradition stresses the effect that ancestors have upon descendants, religion connotes action in the opposite direction. The noun *religio* is from the verb *religare,* which means to tie back—hence, to bind oneself to the past. Authority *augments* the founding by *tradition* and ties the citizen back to his past through *religion.*

As a telling summary of this linguistic examination, we should note that the Latin *principium* has the double meaning of both a beginning and a principle; it thereby captures the normative dimension of political foundings and brings us back to our own Constitution. The moral vitality of the Constitution as the great work of the founding period of the Republic is what makes it such a powerful symbol in our politics. This aspect of the Constitution—as the product of the normative event of founding—provides my second answer to the earlier question of why we should return to it to legitimate the administrative state. The legitimacy of the administrative state will be immeasurably strengthened if the founding fathers of the Republic are not only neutralized but enlisted in its support as well. The moral force of the founding period explains why it was so unfortunate for American Public Administration that Woodrow Wilson was unable or unwilling to ground his theory of administration in American constitutional principle and why it is so unwise for his intellectual progeny in the field to call for fundamental constitutional changes to accommodate administrative needs.[25]

The sanctity of the founding period for Americans will be quite clear to anyone who reflects on the path that tourists tread when they visit Philadelphia or the nation's capital. The salience of American civil religion is obvious. It is no accident that our heroic statues are larger than life. Like all peoples, we need our myths. Like the Romans, we have myths that are related to our founding; but unlike them, we have more than myth at our founding. We have written records that surrounded the event—notes from the participants at the Philadelphia Convention, summaries of the speeches at the ratifying conventions in the several states, and carefully edited texts of the pamphlets and newspapers that defended and attacked the proposed Constitution. Thus we can have it both ways: We can have our Constitution as the object of civil religion, and we can also have it as an object of close scrutiny and critical evaluation.

Throughout this book we shall emphasize the second aspect of the Constitution and the founding period. To legitimate the administrative state in constitutional terms, we must examine the Constitution rather than simply revere it. We shall examine it less as the product of the framers' will than as the centerpiece of the great public argument of 1787/88. Our task is to see how the administrative state can fit into American political orthodoxy—an orthodoxy that eludes capture in a set of officially approved propositions but emerges in the dynamism of the public argument itself. In emphasizing the public argument of 1787/88, careful attention must be given to the vanquished Anti-Federalists as important participants in the great debate. They lost the argument, but in so doing, they pointed to the glaring weaknesses in the Constitution—some of which are still with us today. In stressing the *argument* of the founding, rather than its outcome, we follow Arendt's observation on American politics that more fundamental than the written Constitution itself is the "principle of mutual promise and common deliberation" that made it possible.[26]

## THE ANTI-FEDERALISTS

> Upon the whole I doubt whether the opposition to the constitution will not ultimately be productive of more good than evil.
>                                                                                    —George Washington

Before addressing the substantive points of the founding argument, a preliminary comment is in order. Some of the sources cited in the discussion that follows may be somewhat unfamiliar. The text of the Constitution itself and *The Federalist* are, of course, well known; but the corpus of Anti-Federalist writings is far less familiar. Nevertheless their position is crucial for our purposes in examining the *argument* over the Constitution. Unfortunately, the *Federalist* and other writings in support of the Constitution are often read simply as authoritative expositions of the true meaning of the document. History has conferred the victors' laurels on these authors; but when they were writing, their purpose was more to persuade than to expound. To understand the arguments in support of the Constitution we must understand the arguments against it as well. Publius and the other writers who supported the Constitution shaped their arguments to meet the attacks of the Anti-Federalists.

We are fortunate that at last we have a critical and comprehensive edition of the Anti-Federalists' writings—Herbert J. Storing's seven-volume work *The Complete Anti-Federalist.* In his introductory essay, Storing argues that the Anti-Federalists should be counted among the founding fathers because of their contribution "to the dialogue of the American founding."[27] As Storing puts it, "the Constitution that came out of the deliberations of 1787 and 1788 was not the same Constitution that went in."[28] Under stern Anti-Federalist pressure, it was ratified on the understanding that a Bill of Rights would be added immediately. In addition to securing a Bill of Rights, the Anti-Federalists initiated the main lines of constitutional debate that dominated the early years of the Republic and, to a certain extent, are still with us today. The Anti-Federalists gave us the first warnings of where the polity was most vulnerable—a service no less patriotic, though far less celebrated, than the services of those who tell us where we excel.

In examining the founding argument for hints of what we call the administrative state, I will look to Publius and others who supported the Constitution to determine (1) what it was they wanted from the new Constitution and (2) what they thought they were providing. Conversely, the writings and speeches of the Anti-Federalists will tell us (1) what they feared from the new Constitution and (2) what they thought they were getting. The contrast between Federalists and Anti-Federalists, however, is not quite as neat as the previous sentences suggest. The Anti-Federalists were not *merely* opponents of the Constitution. Many of them saw considerable merit in the proposed Constitution but withheld their support in order to force a second convention that would amend it to meet certain—and in some cases very limited—objections. Thus some portions of the Anti-Federalist literature can correctly be read as *supporting* specific aspects of the Constitution—for example, federal regulation of commerce, equal representation of the states in the Senate, life tenure for federal judges, and so forth.

A final word on sources concerns the notes taken by participants at the Philadelphia Convention, especially James Madison's exhaustive notes. The speeches that were given in the convention are not, of course, part of the argument for or against the Constitution; rather, they are arguments over what the Constitution would be. These arguments are important for determining the intent of the framers for specific parts of the Constitution. For example, in discussing the executive powers of the Senate, it is important to know that at several points in the Philadelphia deliberations the Senate was to have *complete* power over treaties and the appointment of ambassadors and federal judges. This tells us that when the framers finally decided that the president was to share these executive powers with the Senate, they had in mind far more than a legislative check on the executive power of the president. The development of the Philadelphia document clearly indicates that the framers intended the Senate to be not only a second house of the legislature but an *executive institution* as well. Neither the text of the Constitution nor subsequent institutional history suggests the extent to which the framers looked to the Senate as part of the executive establishment. We learn this only from following the arguments over the development of what would eventually become the Constitution during the months from May to September of 1787.

The theme of founding-in-argument guides the development of the three parts of this book. Each of the parts deals with a "founding"—the first with the founding of the Republic in 1787/88; the second with the founding in the 1880s of Public Administration as a form of discrete, self-conscious governmental activity; and the third with the founding of the modern administrative state during the New Deal.

Each part has three chapters. The three chapters of Part 1 attempt to justify the modern administrative state in terms of the principles of government that motivated the framers of the Constitution.

Part 2 is entitled "Founding the Administrative State in Word, 1887–1900." In contrast, the title of Part 3 is "Founding the Administrative State in Deed: The New Deal." The "Founding in Word" refers to the theoretical writings of Wilson and Goodnow, which I maintain put Public Administration theory at odds with the founding principles of the Republic and thereby created a severe legitimacy problem for the administrative state. "Founding in Deed" refers to the writings of the New Dealers who developed their theories of administration while in the very act of creating administrative agencies and establishing new administrative practices. In contrasting the two foundings, I shall argue that the thoughtful practitioners of the New Deal period are more reliable guides along the path of reconciling the administrative state to the principles of the framers of the Constitution than are the elegant academicians Wilson and Goodnow. In the final chapter of Part 2, I examine the constitutional arguments that surrounded the establishment in 1887 of the first independent regulatory commission, the Interstate Commerce Commission. That chapter serves as a bridge between the founding in word of the 1880s and the founding in deed of the New Deal period.

The book concludes with a statement and defense of a constitutional theory of American Public Administration that is grounded in the principles of the founding of the Republic.

# PART 1

# FOUNDING THE REPUBLIC, 1787/88

And in every . . . nation, the most rational government will not find it a
superfluous advantage, to have the prejudices of the community on its side.
—*Federalist 49*

Following Publius's observation in this epigraph, Part 1 of this book attempts
to rally "the prejudices of the community" to the administrative state by
showing its basic compatibility with the plan of government designed by the
framers of the Constitution. Part 1 has three chapters. The first shows that the
combination of legislative, executive, and judicial powers in modern administrative agencies is not inconsistent with the framers' understanding of separation
of powers. The second section goes beyond a mere showing that the
administrative state is not inconsistent with the framers' intent. It examines
the Senate and finds that the higher reaches of the career civil service today
fulfill objectives the framers originally had in mind for the Senate. Thus the
argument escalates from a negative showing that the administrative state is not
inconsistent with the framers' intent to the positive affirmation that it fulfills
their constitutional design. The third section takes the argument further by
maintaining that the administrative state heals a defect in the Constitution—the
inadequate representation in the House of Representatives. Thus, I shall argue
that the administrative state is consistent with the Constitution, fulfills its
design, and heals a longstanding major defect.

13

# 2

# Separation of Powers

To what purpose separate the executive or the judiciary, from the legislative, if both the executive and the judiciary are so construed as to be at the absolute devotion of the legislative? Such a separation must be merely nominal and incapable of producing the ends for which it was established. It is one thing to be subordinate to the laws and another to be dependent on the legislative body. The first comports with, the last violates, the fundamental principles of good government; and whatever may be the forms of the Constitution, unites all power in the same hands.

*—Federalist 71*

One of the earliest criticisms of the governmental institution that is considered by many as the harbinger of the administrative state—the independent regulatory commission—was that it violates the principle of separation of powers.[1] This charge was quite common at the turn of the century. Friends of the administrative state might look upon this criticism as a badge of honor. The same attack was made against the Constitution itself. During the First Congress, James Madison opined that "perhaps there was no argument urged with more success, or more plausibly grounded against the Constitution . . . than that founded on the mingling of the Executive and Legislative branches of the Government in one body."[2] Reliance on the principle of separation of powers to attack the legitimacy of governmental institutions has become a staple of American politics. During the New Deal period, when regulatory agencies had been familiar for decades, James Landis, a staunch champion of administrative regulation, was deeply concerned over the attack on the blending of powers in these agencies. He considered this the strongest argument in the case against the regulatory economic order he favored.[3]

15

This longstanding, formalistic argument against administrative institutions must be met at the outset if we are to make any headway in legitimating the administrative state. As a practical matter, statutes, executive orders, judicial decisions, and administrative policies have tried to safeguard against abuses by agencies that exercise either two or all three types of governmental power. Without denigrating the importance of these practical accommodations, I shall address the formal argument against the mere existence of these powers in one agency, because this is where the framers of the Constitution are enlisted in the attack on the administrative state. This task involves two steps: (1) a brief examination of the text of the Constitution and (2) a fuller discussion of the framers' relaxed standards on separation of powers.

## THE CONSTITUTIONAL TEXT

> The Senate shall have the sole Power to try all Impeachments (art. 1, sec. 3).

> He shall have Power, by and with the Advice and Consent of the Senate, to make Treaties, provided two thirds of the Senators present concur; and he shall nominate, and by and with the Advice and Consent of the Senate, shall appoint Ambassadors, other public Ministers and Consuls, Judges of the Supreme Court, and all other Officers of the United States, whose Appointments are not herein otherwise provided for, and which shall be established by Law (art. 2, sec. 2).

Fortunately, we are in good company when we try to answer the objection that the combination of powers in administrative agencies violates the principle of separation of powers. Publius had to answer a similar attack against the Constitution itself: "One of the principal objections inculcated by the more respectable adversaries to the Constitution, is its supposed violation of the political maxim, that the legislative, executive, and judiciary departments ought to be separate and distinct."[4] Our problem in defending the blending of powers in administrative institutions is much easier than the problem Publius faced. We need only show that such blending is not contrary to the spirit or letter of the Constitution, whereas Publius had the more fundamental task of defending the blending in the Constitution itself. Our task is simply discharged by pointing to the Senate as a body that exercises powers that are (1) legislative (when it joins the House of Representatives in approving a bill); (2) executive (when it "advises and consents" to a treaty or to appointments of high-ranking federal officials); and (3) judicial (when it sits as a court to try impeachments).

The blending of powers in the Senate was a cause of considerable concern to the Anti-Federalists.[5] We have already noted James Madison's opinion that it gave them their strongest argument against the Constitution. History has taught us to look upon the Senate as almost exclusively a legislative body. As we shall see in the next chapter, this was not what the framers had in mind. The development of the executive agreement in foreign affairs and of the merit system in personnel management have considerably reduced the significance of the Senate's constitutional powers over treaties and appointments. Impeachments have been so infrequent that we hardly ever think of the Senate as a judicial body. The judicial character of the Senate is dramatically clear, however, in the provision in article 1 that the chief justice will preside over the Senate when it tries a presidential impeachment.[6] Because, fortunately, this has happened only once in our history, the awesome scene of a chief justice presiding over a Senate that can remove a president from office is more a majestic museum piece than an operating principle of government.

For the framers, however, this was not the case. Impeachment was discussed in remarkable detail at the Philadelphia Convention and during the debate over ratification. It is surprising to note that the impeachment power was a central consideration in the creation of the electoral college. Throughout the convention, the method of selecting the president was a matter of stormy controversy. At various times the Senate or the Congress as a whole were possible candidates for this responsibility.[7] Toward the end of the convention, a committee report came forward with what we know today as the electoral college. When Edmund Randolph and Charles Pinckney asked "for a particular explanation and discussion of the reasons for changing the mode of electing the Executive," Gouverneur Morris responded with an account that is worthy of the complexity of the college itself.[8]

Morris began by stating the committee's reasons for deciding that the Senate was the proper institution to try causes of presidential impeachment. This power could not be given to the Supreme Court because a president, after being removed from office, might still be tried in the federal courts for the offense that led to his removal. Since the Senate would try the impeachments, the House should bring them. Because, then, both houses of Congress would be involved in the removal of the president, neither should be involved in selecting him. Here the convention's reasoning was that a body that had chosen an officer would be likely to consider impeachment and conviction an adverse reflection on its earlier judgment. Hence, the committee recommended that a body of special electors (the electoral college as we have come to call it) should select the president. Only if this body failed to agree upon one person should the legislature—whose houses impeach and try presidents—be permitted to enter the process of selecting the president.

I mention this arcane point only to support my contention that the judicial power of the Senate was not a bizarre aberration but was an aspect of constitution making that was solidly integrated into the overall design of the document. The framers found it easier to achieve consensus on how to get rid of a president than on how to select one.

The salience of the impeachment power in the constitutional design provides *textual* evidence that the framers were quite willing to place all three powers of government in one institution when circumstances so required. Hence, any argument that administrative agencies act in a constitutionally suspect manner simply because they exercise two or even all three governmental powers can be refuted from the text of the Constitution itself. This is not to say that the principle of separation of powers can be treated in a cavalier manner. It is to say, however, that the mere presence of all three powers of government in one agency is not of itself constitutionally suspect. The responsible exercise of these powers is, of course, another matter; but this is true of an institution of such unquestioned legitimacy as the Senate, as well as of administrative agencies.

## THE FRAMERS ON SEPARATION OF POWERS

[Montesquieu's] meaning, as his own words impart, and still more conclusively as illustrated by the example in his eye, can amount to no more than this, that where the *whole* power of one department is exercised by the same hands which possess the *whole* power of another department, the fundamental principles of a free constitution are subverted.

*—Federalist 47*

The separation-of-powers attack on administrative agencies is usually based on an excessively rigid interpretation of this venerable doctrine. One careful student of the history of separation of powers has described the "pure position" as separation of functions, exercised by separate organs of government, with no overlap.[9] This is helpful as an ideal type, but it is far removed from the understanding of separation of powers that was common among the framers. Publius's position is instructive. He acknowledges the importance of the principle of separation of powers when he allows that "the accumulation of all powers, legislative, executive, and judiciary, in the same hands, . . . may justly be pronounced the very definition of tyranny."[10] After acknowledging "the celebrated Montesquieu" as "the oracle who is always consulted and cited on this subject," Publius maintains that Montesquieu "did not mean that these departments ought to have no *partial agency* in, or no *control* over, the acts of each other." He meant, "no more than this, that where the *whole* power of one department is exercised by the same hands which possess the *whole* power of another department, the fundamental principles of a free constitution are subverted."[11] This is not the place to evaluate Publius's reading of Montesquieu.[12] What is important for our purposes is that no less an authority than James Madison, writing as Publius in *The Federalist Papers*, subscribes to a remarkably relaxed view of separation of powers. Clearly no administrative agency ever has or ever could function as a "department" that exercises the *"whole* power" of another department. (By "department" Publius here means the three great constitutional branches of government—not the "executive departments" of article 2.) In effect, Publius has defined any likely violation of separation of powers out of existence for the entire government as well as for any administrative agency that we know today. Even Lincoln, during the darkest days of the Civil War, did not appropriate the "whole power" of either Congress or the courts.

In making this point, I do not suggest that Madison as Publius is the most reliable guide on the correct understanding of separation of powers. Nor do I suggest that his position would be approved by all the framers. Certainly he is not alone in his relaxed point of view, but other framers were a bit more moderate. Rufus King and James Wilson, for example, stress the independence of one department from another as the heart of the separation-of-powers doctrine.[13] This follows Publius's position without going to the extreme of saying that the principle is breached only when the *"whole* power" of one branch has been taken over by another. Hamilton, too, somewhat uncharacteristically, is less exuberant than his *Federalist* coauthor on this aspect of separation of powers. Toward the end of *The Federalist Papers* Hamilton seems to grow weary of the entire issue. In *Federalist 75* he dismisses lightly "the trite topic of the intermixture of powers" in order to move on to weightier matters. Earlier, in *Federalist 66,* he had given a subdued summary of Madison's position, which had appeared in *Federalist 47:* "The true meaning of this maxim [of separation of powers] has been discussed and ascertained in another place and has been shown to be entirely compatible with a partial intermixture of those departments for special purposes, preserving them in the main distinct and unconnected. This partial intermixture is even in some cases not only proper, but necessary to the mutual defense of the several members of the government against each other."

Madison would agree with Hamilton that a "partial intermixture" of the departments' powers is at times a good thing. Indeed, the main point of *Federalist 48* (written by Madison) is a positive defense of a blending of powers to preserve the principle of separation. It is not enough to rely on "parchment barriers" to keep the great branches independent of one another. The Constitution wisely preserves its intended balance by an elaborate series of "checks" which allow one branch to exercise in part the powers of another—for example, the president's legislative power of a conditioned veto over acts of Congress. Thus for Publius, a discreet blending of powers is the best way to preserve their sensible and effective separation.

It is not only in *The Federalist Papers* that one finds a relaxed standard of separation of powers. Throughout the Philadelphia Convention the principle was treated with profound respect tempered by pragmatic flexibility. James Madison's comments during the secret proceedings of the convention were quite consistent with his later public utterances as the polemical Publius.

For example, in the serious context of a debate on whether the executive should be reelected by the national legislature, Madison cited Montesquieu to link the principle of separation of powers to the prevention of tyranny. This debate took place on 17 July. At that time the convention delegates were still speaking in terms of the "national legislature" and "the Executive," rather than Congress and president. Just prior to Madison's remarks the convention had approved one motion calling for the election of the executive by the national legislature and a second motion that the executive could be reelected after a still-undetermined number of years. At this point, Madison's fellow Virginian Dr. James McClurg moved that the executive should serve during good behavior. McClurg's reason for this startling motion was that an executive who would be subject to reelection by a legislature after a fixed term would be "put into a situation that would keep him dependent forever on the Legislature."[14] It would be better to run the formidable risk of having a lifetime executive than to have an executive who was subject to the legislature.

Madison cautiously supported McClurg's notion. He did so for the reasons that McClurg had given: "The Executive could not be independent of the Legislature, if dependent on the pleasure of that branch for a reappointment."[15] It was in this context that Madison invoked Montesquieu and raised the specter of tyranny resulting from an egregious violation of separation of powers. The convention's decision (later reversed, of course) to have the legislature *initially* elect the executive brought forth no cries of tyranny from James Madison. It was *reelection* that alarmed him. Madison could easily envision such an executive becoming the mere tool of the legislature. This would meet the criterion for a violation of separation of powers that he would later announce in *Federalist 47*—"the *whole* power of one department is exercised by the same hands which possess the *whole* power of another department."

Madison as convention delegate, like Madison as Publius, took the principle of separation of powers seriously; but he saw a threat to its integrity only in the most extreme circumstances, such as an executive who would be subject to reelection by the legislature. For the most part, it was his relaxed view of separation of powers that guided his thinking during the convention. For example, one of his favorite projects throughout the convention was to get the judiciary involved in a "Council of Revision," which would share the executive's veto power over acts of the legislature. This proposal took many forms during the four months of the convention. One of the most remarkable aspects of the plan was that the judges' role would not be confined to constitutional questions. They could join the executive in rejecting legislative acts on grounds of policy.[16] Madison anticipated possible objections to the plan on the grounds "that the Judiciary ought to be separate and distinct from the other great Departments."[17] He was ready with a twofold reply. First he maintained that the objection "either had not weight, or it applied with equal weight to the Executive and to the Judiciary revision of the laws.''[18] Because there was widespread support in the convention for some sort of executive veto, Madison could not see any particular problem with having the judiciary share in that veto. To include the judiciary in the Council of Revision was simply to extend the mingling of powers that had already been approved in the executive veto.

Madison's second reason was more fundamental. He looked to England, "whence the maxim [of separation of powers] itself had been drawn.'' There he discovered that the "Executive had an absolute negative on the laws; and the supreme tribunal of Justice [the House of Lords] formed one of the other branches of the Legislature.''[19] Thus Madison turns to England, with its King-in-Parliament, for the model of what separation of powers should mean in practice. If Parliament, which combines the three great powers of government, is Madison's model of separation of powers, there is no reason to think he would find any problem with an administrative agency that combines the powers of rule making, investigation, and adjudication in a limited area specified by statute.

James Wilson was Madison's most prominent ally in the unsuccessful effort to bring the judiciary and the executive together in a Council of Revision over legislative enactments. The debate we have just described took place early in the convention—on 6 June. Madison and Wilson failed to convince their colleagues of the wisdom of their position. Six weeks later they were at it again. On 21 July, Wilson apologized for bringing up a topic that had already been discussed and rejected; "but he was so confirmed by reflection in the opinion of its utility that he thought it incumbent on him to make another effort.''[20] Madison answered the call by repeating the same two points that he had used earlier to answer separation-of-powers arguments against including the judiciary in a Council of Revision. This time, however, he developed more fully a point that he had only hinted at earlier. In his notes he reports himself as telling the convention that there was no particular danger in bringing the executive and judiciary together to check the legislature:

> It was much more to be apprehended that notwithstanding this co-operation of the two departments, the Legislature would still be an overmatch for them. Experience in all the States had evinced a powerful tendency in the Legislature to absorb all power into its vortex. This was the real source of danger to the American Constitutions; & suggested the necessity of giving every defensive authority to the other departments that was consistent with republican principles.[21]

This passage goes to the heart of Madison's thinking on separation of powers. He was interested, not in formal technicalities about the commingling of functions, but in the eminently practical task of preventing the tyranny that was likely to arise when the *"whole* power'' of one department fell prey to another department. In 1787 the legislature was the likely offender. To keep the legislature within its proper bounds, Madison would not scruple over bringing the executive and the judicial branches together to veto legislative enactments on grounds of policy. Such a blending of institutions did not violate the principle of separation of powers; on the contrary, it was the most apt means for preserving that principle.[22]

As a final testament to just how serious they were about allowing the judiciary to veto legislative enactments, Madison and Wilson once more tried their colleagues' patience. On 15 August, Madison moved and Wilson seconded a revised and more elaborate version of their now-familiar plan. Although we can be grateful that the convention rejected the cumbersome scheme, an examination of its language reveals its convoluted blending of powers and lays to rest any thoughts about Madison or Wilson as being purists in the matter of separation of powers.

> Every bill which shall have passed the two houses, shall, before it become a law, be severally presented to the President of the United States, and to the judges of the supreme court for the revision of each. If, upon such revision, they shall approve it, they shall respectively signify their approbation by signing it; but if, upon such revision, it shall appear improper to either, or both, to be passed into a law, it shall be returned, with the objections against it, to that house, in which it shall have originated, who shall enter the objections at large on their journal, and proceed to reconsider the bill: but if, after such reconsideration, two thirds of that house, when either the President, or a majority of the judges shall object, or three fourths, where both shall object, shall agree to pass it, it shall, together with the objections, be sent to the other house, by which it shall likewise be reconsidered; and, if approved by two thirds, or three fourths of the other house, as the case may be, it shall become law.[23]

As a congressman under the new Constitution, Madison persevered in his flexible approach to separation of powers. His comments during the lengthy debate in the First Congress on establishing the Treasury Department are particularly instructive. At issue was a section of the organic Treasury Act, which would make it the duty of the Treasury secretary "to digest and report plans for the improvement and management of the revenue and the support of the public credit."[24] Strenuous objections were brought against this proposal on constitutional grounds. Some felt that a statutory directive to the secretary to "digest and report plans" would preempt the prerogative of the House of Representatives to "originate" bills for raising revenue. Others thought it would undercut the president's constitutional duty to recommend to Congress "such Measures as he shall judge to be necessary and expedient."

Madison saw the issue quite differently. He ignored the constitutional issues and appealed instead to the fact that exactly the same words had been used for financial officers under the Articles of Confederation.[25] There was, of course, no formal separation of powers under the Articles. The executive departments—such as they were—were lineal descendants of committees under the old Congress.[26] Madison simply ignored the difference between the new and the old governments in this question of separation of powers. This is significant because it recalls his reference to Parliament as a model for resolving a separation-of-powers issue in the Philadelphia Convention. Although we know Madison could write about separation of powers with subtleties second to none, in practical decision making he was quite willing to analyze separation-of-powers problems with pointed references to institutions of government that have nothing like the separation of powers that exists under the Constitution.

Madison acknowledged that there was a "small probability" that the secretary of the Treasury might "have some degree of influence upon the deliberations of the Legislature"; but he was willing to run this risk to get the "well-formed and digested plans" he expected from the secretary. "Inconsistent, unproductive, and expensive schemes, will be more injurious to our constituents than the undue influence which the well-digested plans of a well-informed officer can have." Such was Madison's order of priorities in settling a practical separation-of-powers matter in the first Congress. "From a bad administration of the government, more detriment will arise than from any other source."[27] The benefit of having "the well-digested plans of a well-informed officer" justified the risk of "undue influence."

Throughout the Philadelphia Convention, Madison and Wilson were not alone in their flexible interpretation of the principle of separation of powers. To be sure, they had their critics. John Mercer, Elbridge Gerry, Luther Martin, and John Dickinson invoked the separation-of-powers principle to oppose a judicial veto over acts of the legislature.[28] For the most part, however, the principle was treated in a relaxed, pragmatic manner. A good illustration of this can be seen in the sorts of institutional arrangements the framers considered but did *not* adopt. We shall examine these considered-but-rejected arrangements to offset the idea that the framers thought they had pushed the outer limits of separation of powers in the familiar examples of the blending of powers that are always cited in the political-science textbooks: for example, the presidential veto and the Senate's role in treaties and appointments.

Two of these "might have been" provisions involving the blending of powers appeared in the Virginia Plan, submitted by Edmund Randolph at the very beginning of the convention. One we have already seen—a provision "that the Executive and a convenient number of the National Judiciary, ought to compose a Council of revision with authority to examine every act of the National Legislature before it shall operate."[29] The other involved conferring upon the national legislature the judicial power "to negative all laws passed by the several states, contravening in the opinion of the National Legislature the articles of the Union."[30] A negative by the National Legislature would then be reviewed by the Council of Revision before it would be final. Thus, under the Virginia Plan, all three branches of the national government would share the important power of judging the constitutionality (i.e., the conformity to the articles of union) of state legislation.

The report of the convention's Committee of Detail (submitted on 6 August) provided a draft for a proposed Constitution. A "might have been" provision that is interesting for our purposes is its conferral of judicial authority upon the Senate to settle "all disputes and controversies now subsisting, or that may hereafter subsist respecting jurisdiction or territory." The Senate was also empowered to make the final judicial determination of "controversies concerning lands claimed under different grants of two or more states."[31] Thus the Senate's role in adjudicating impeachments, which eventually became part of the Constitution, was but one of several judicial functions for which the Senate was considered the appropriate governmental body.

Throughout the course of the convention, there was considerable support for an executive council. The specific proposals were many and varied, but they always involved some form of the blending of powers. For example, on 18 August, Oliver Ellsworth proposed the establishment of an executive council to "be composed of the President of the Senate, the Chief Justice, and the ministers as they might be estab[lishe]d for the departments of foreign and domestic affairs, war, finance, and marine, who should advise but not conclude the President."[32] To appreciate the extent of the blending of powers in this proposal, we should recall that as of 18 August the office of vice-president of the United States had not yet been created. The president of the Senate would be a full-time senator who would preside over that body. Thus Ellsworth's executive council would bring together members from each of the three branches of government.

A proposal by George Mason on 7 September for a "privy Council of six members to the President" provides a particularly illuminating example of a relaxed understanding of separation of powers. After having announced his firm belief that the three branches of government "ought to be kept as separate as possible,"[33] Mason went on immediately to propose that the president's privy council be composed of six senators to be chosen by the Senate. Thus, in the very act of affirming his adherence to separation-of-powers orthodoxy, Mason called for a most remarkable form of blending those powers.

As a final example of a blending-of-powers proposal that was considered and rejected by the framers, we will examine the peculiar relationship that the framers saw between Congress and the Treasury Department. The text of the Constitution mentions executive departments without naming them. The creation of these departments and their official designation were left to Congress. There can be no doubt that the framers expected that one of these executive departments would be a Department of Treasury or Finance.

So confident were they of this that when the Committee on Style reported what it hoped would be the final version of the Constitution, section 8 of article 1 began as follows: "The Congress may by joint ballot appoint a treasurer." This was the first of Congress's enumerated powers. This provision had appeared in earlier drafts of the Constitution and was not deleted until 14 September, the third-to-last working day of the convention. Thus, until the very end of the convention, the framers were willing to vest the appointment of at least one executive officer in Congress alone.

Thus far we have examined some of the convention's proposals for the blending of powers that were seriously considered but eventually rejected. The purpose of our inquiry has been to show the free and easy manner with which the framers treated the principle of separation of powers. No one challenged the principle itself, but its application was quite relaxed in practice. Each of the proposals that we have considered was criticized on separation-of-powers grounds, but none of them was simply rejected out of hand for this reason. There was nothing shocking or unthinkable about the bold schemes of blending powers that they pondered. The arguments were prudential, not doctrinaire.

To supplement our investigation of constitutional "might have beens," let us consider a provision that found its way into the Constitution, which might appear to be a rigid application of the principle of separation of powers. I refer to the following provision from article 1, section 6: "No Senator or Representative shall, during the Time for which he was elected, be appointed to any civil Office under the Authority of the United States, which shall have been created, or the Emoluments whereof shall have been encreased during such time."

This provision would seem to be a strict application of the separation-of-powers doctrine, especially since it is followed by an absolute prohibition against having any officer of the United States serve as a member of either house of Congress.[34] When one examines the debates in the convention, however, it becomes clear that the prohibition against having members of Congress accept certain offices that were created during the term for which they had been elected has nothing to do with separation of powers. Earlier drafts of the provision were debated on 23 June and 14 August. In both cases the discussion centered on preventing a form of corruption that had flourished in England. Members of the legislature were to be prevented from using their position in order to create lucrative offices that they themselves could fill. The point at issue in the debate was how strict the Constitution could be in this matter without discouraging talented men from seeking a position in the legislature.

The relaxed, pragmatic approach to separation of powers that was evidenced during the Philadelphia Convention carried over into the early years of the new government. In 1790 President Washington wrote a short letter to the justices of the Supreme Court as they were about to begin their first tour of circuit riding. He assured them of his belief in the importance of the independence of the judiciary, but he did not scruple from politely inviting them to consider working some executive moonlighting into their busy schedules: "As you are about to commence your first circuit, and many things may occur in such an unexplored field, which it would be useful should be known, I think it proper to acquaint you, that it will be agreeable to me to receive such information and remarks on this subject as you shall from time to time judge expedient to communicate."[35]

The First Congress showed the same flexible attitude toward separation of powers by the way in which it structured the three original executive departments. The departments of War and of Foreign Affairs (later the Department of State) were formally designated as "executive departments" and were described in only the most general terms; but the Treasury was called simply a department, not an "executive" department, and was given a detailed statutory scheme. In showing their intense interest in the Treasury Department, the members of the First Congress were simply picking up where the Philadelphia Convention had left off. We have already seen that it was not until the very last days of the convention that the delegates finally decided to delete a clause that would have given Congress, as the first of its enumerated powers, the option of appointing a treasurer by joint ballot.

Under the Constitution, Congress, of course, could not make such an appointment, but it showed no hesitancy in stating in statutory language its serious interest in the details of managing the Treasury Department. In sharp contrast to the statutes creating the departments of Foreign Affairs and of War, the Treasury statute named the officers who were to be subordinate to the secretary of the Treasury (the comptroller, the treasurer, the auditor, and the register) and spelled out their duties in considerable detail.[36]

The uneven attention that Congress gave to Treasury vis-à-vis War and Foreign Affairs is a good indication of the flexible approach to separation of powers that characterized the early history of the Republic. Congress, because of its constitutional powers over the purse, had a great interest in managing the Treasury Department. Therefore it attempted to exert greater control over the way Treasury carried out its affairs than was the case with War and Foreign Affairs.

The investigative powers of Congress were handled in a similarly flexible manner. Congress' first occasion to investigate the executive branch came in the wake of Gen. Arthur St. Clair's disastrous defeat at the hands of an Indian confederation in the Northwest Territory in November 1791. When President Washington received Congress' inevitable message that it would investigate the affair, he realized that he was facing a crucial separation-of-powers issue that would be likely to establish an important precedent for his successors. He summoned his department heads and, after two days of discussion, decided to provide the House of Representatives with the documents it had requested; but he noted that he reserved the right to refuse to provide such papers as were likely to "injure the public." In this particular case, no records were withheld from Congress, so the test of Washington's Delphic formula on what could or could not be released would await another day. The separation-of-powers issue had arisen, but a practical accommodation was achieved.[37]

As the St. Clair investigation progressed, the reputations of Henry Knox (the secretary of War) and of Samuel Hodgdon (St. Clair's former quartermaster general) were called into question. To get to the bottom of the matter, the House of Representatives devised an investigatory mechanism that would be the despair of any separation-of-powers ideologue. The investigating committee permitted St. Clair, Knox, and Hodgdon to join the committee in interrogating the witnesses. Thus a committee composed of five congressmen, the secretary of war, a defeated general, and a cashiered quartermaster general sat down together to investigate a military disaster. Such was the practical meaning of separation of powers in 1792.[38]

Throughout this chapter, I have presented many examples from the founding period of words and deeds on separation of powers. With this relaxed teaching of the founding period in mind, we can see how wide of the mark are those formalistic attacks on the administrative state that are aimed at the mere existence of a combination of powers in administrative agencies. The problem is one, not of doctrine, but of prudence and accommodation. The doctrinal issue is triggered only when the *"whole* power," as Publius put it, of one branch of government is delivered to a competing branch. This has never happened with an administrative agency.

The powers of administrative agencies, unlike those of Congress, the president, and the courts, are always "partial," never *"whole."* They are partial because they are exercised over a narrowly defined scope of governmental activity—for example, TV licensing, railroad rates, food stamps, and so forth. Not only are these powers partial but—unlike those of Congress, the president, and the courts—they are formally subordinated in their entirety to one or another of the traditional constitutional branches. Thus, even egregious abuses by administrative agencies are far removed from "tyranny." There is, of course, a great difference between avoiding tyranny and providing good government. When the attack on the administrative state is launched from the high ground of separation of powers, the entire argument has an upward tilt toward high politics—like questions of tyranny. If administrative agencies were spared the sort of attack that questions their legitimacy, they might be as successful in providing good government as they are in avoiding tyranny.

# 3

# The Senate
# as Executive Establishment

And when I behold the Senate, . . . wielding in the one hand the strong
powers of the Executive, and with the other controuling and modifying at
pleasure, the movements of the legislature, I must confess that not only my
hopes of the beneficial effects of the government, are greatly diminished, but
that my apprehensions of some fatal catastrophe are highly awakened.

—James Monroe

The discussion in chapter 2 was intended to show that the blending of powers
in administrative agencies is not inconsistent with the principle of separation of
powers. The focus of the present chapter is the Senate. Here I shall escalate
my position from the negative statement that the Administrative State is not
inconsistent with the framers' intent to the positive affirmation that it fulfills
their design. I shall do this by examining the sort of institution the participants
in the founding debate had in mind when they discussed the merits and defects
of the proposed Senate. With allowance in mind for the havoc two hundred
years will wreak on anyone's intent, my point in this chapter is that the function
of the higher reaches of today's career civil service is, in broad outline, a
reasonable approximation to what the framers envisioned as the function of the
Senate in the proposed regime.

This chapter has two parts. The first maintains that the Senate was
intended to be part of an executive establishment and not simply a second
house of a national legislature. My argument is based on the spirit, not the
letter, of the Constitution; on what the framers meant, rather than on what
they stated in the final version of the Constitution. The Constitution is quite
explicit in vesting "all legislative powers herein granted" in a Congress, of

which the Senate is an integral part. No less clear is the vesting of "the executive power" in the president. The executive powers of the Senate are usually looked upon as "checks" on the president. This has proved to be a useful position for judicial resolution of questions about the separation of powers, as well as for offering a coherent explanation for the Constitution as a whole. It is therefore a *very* useful interpretation. Nevertheless, an examination of the founding debates suggests that this conventional interpretation, despite its usefulness, is somewhat inaccurate. Such an examination suggests instead that the framers envisioned the Senate as part of an executive establishment, rather than simply as a legislative body vested with certain executive powers in order to hold the president in check.

In the second part of this chapter, I examine certain salient characteristics the proposed Senate was expected to have, which, when combined with its participation in the executive establishment, suggest some striking similarities to the higher echelons of the civil service today.

## EXECUTIVE ESTABLISHMENT

The first point in establishing the executive character of the Senate is to note that it was not seen by anyone as *simply* a second house of the national legislature. This perception was universal; it was shared by friend and foe alike of the proposed Constitution. Publius is unequivocal on this point.[1] So are the Anti-Federalists. At times they list the legislative function of the Senate as but one of several powers they find objectionable.[2] At other times they use such terms as "veto" and "negative" to describe the Senate's legislative role. This language appears not only in the context of "money bills," which must originate in the House of Representatives, but in general discussions of the Senate's legislative powers as well.[3] Perhaps the clearest Anti-Federalist statement on the nature of the Senate's legislative power appears in the quotation from James Monroe cited as the epigraph of this chapter. He describes the Senate as "wielding in the one hand the strong powers of the Executive, and with the other controuling and modifying at pleasure, the movements of the legislature."[4] For Monroe, the House of Representatives is the *real* legislature; the Senate's role is to control and modify it.

This view of the Senate can be found in the language of the framers of the Constitution at Philadelphia. Roger Sherman, Gouverneur Morris, James Madison, and Rufus King are explicit in this matter.[5] The Senate is part of the legislative branch, but the nature of the Senate's legislative power is somewhat different from that of the House. Bicameralism did not mean simply that one house would check the other. As Gouverneur Morris put it, the Senate was to be "the checking branch" of the legislature.[6] The reason this function fell to the Senate was because of its executive character. Just as the president, the chief executive officer, had a conditional veto over both houses, so also his executive partner, the Senate, had a more extensive veto over the House of Representatives. In several early drafts of the Constitution the veto power of the Senate was unmistakably clear from the fact that the Senate could *neither amend nor alter* bills passed by the House "for raising or appropriating money, and for fixing the salaries of the officers of the United States."[7] Thus, on money bills, *including appropriations,* the Senate, like the president, could say either aye or nay, but nothing else.

Thus far I have tried to show that the Senate was intended to be something other than merely the second house of a national legislature. Was it also seen as part of an executive establishment? A strong indication that this is the case appears in the development of the text of the Constitution during the Philadelphia Convention. On 6 August the Committee of Detail reported a draft of the Constitution that referred to the Senate "when it shall be acting in a legislative capacity."[8] This clearly implied that legislation was but one of its functions.[9] The same draft included earlier agreements that the Senate should have *exclusive* power over treaties and the appointments of ambassadors and judges of the Supreme Court. When the Senate exercised these powers, the 6 August draft would have exempted it from a prohibition against adjourning "to any other place than that at which the two Houses are sitting."[10] Thus this draft would have allowed the Senate to meet in a place other than its ordinary legislative location to conduct such executive affairs as making treaties and appointing officers. The language of the final version of the Constitution is not explicit on this point, but it is open to this interpretation. The fourth paragraph of article 1, section 5, reads: "Neither House, during the Session of Congress, shall, without the Consent of the other, adjourn for more than three days, nor to any other Place than that in which the two Houses shall be sitting." The immobility of the two houses applies only when Congress is in session. It is possible, of course, for the Senate to be in session without Congress being in session, namely, when the Senate conducts its executive affairs. If such business were to be conducted in a place other than the chamber in which the Senate legislates, its executive character would be dramatically heightened. An early draft of the Constitution provided for this explicitly, and the final version at least implies the possibility.[11]

This textual argument is offered to support the point that the executive character of the Senate was not simply an afterthought; it was an integral part of the constitutional plan. Indeed, attempts to take from the Senate the exclusive power of appointing judges were defeated on 18 and 21 July.[12] The fact that earlier drafts of the Constitution gave the Senate even more executive power than the final version shows conclusively that these powers were no afterthought. It is not as though the Senate were given a share in the treaty and appointing powers simply to provide a legislative check on the president. It was the other way around. The president was eventually given a share in the

Senate's hitherto exclusive power over treaties and the appointments of ambassadors and judges of the Supreme Court.[13]

A profile of the Senate as an executive establishment emerges with striking clarity in the arguments of the Anti-Federalists. This is true even though the Anti-Federalists differ among themselves in what they find offensive about the Senate. One group fears a Senate-presidential cabal. For William Grayson, the senators are the president's "counsellors and partners in crime."[14] "To gain his favor, they will support him" and will unite with the president "to prevent a discovery of his misdeeds."[15] Cato complains that in trying an impeached President the senators "are to determine, as judges, the propriety of the advice they gave him, as senators." They will not "be an impartial judicature." Instead, they will serve as a screen to great public defaulters.[16] Luther Martin and James Monroe voiced similar concerns.[17]

A second group of Anti-Federalists feared that the executive powers of the Senate were so great that they would overwhelm the president.[18] Federal Farmer, for example, feared that "this sexennial senate of 26 members . . . will not, in practice, be found to be a body to advise, but to order and dictate in fact; and the president will be a mere *primus inter pares*."[19] Centinel sees the Senate as "the great efficient body in this plan of government," with the result that "the President, who would be a mere pageant of state, unless he coincides with the views of the Senate, would either become the head of the aristocratic junto in that body, or its minion."[20] The Anti-Federalist minority at the Pennsylvania Ratifying Convention voiced a similar concern: "The president general is dangerously connected with the senate; his coincidence with the views of the ruling junto in that body, is made essential to his weight and importance in the government, which will destroy all independency and purity in the executive department."[21]

A third group of Anti-Federalists criticized the Constitution for failing to provide an executive council to the president.[22] The Senate, they maintained, would be a poor substitute. At the Virginia Ratifying Convention, George Mason, after noting his fear of Senate-president conspiracies against the people, proposed a remedy: "a constitutional council, to aid the President in the discharge of his office." The Senate should have the power to impeach the president and his council. "Then we should have real responsibility. In the present form, the guilty try themselves. The President is tried by his counsellors."[23]

Mason's position on the issue of an executive council is important. As a delegate to the Philadelphia Convention, he had originally favored a plural executive. When this measure failed, he took as his backup position an executive council that would not only assist the president but would check him as well.[24] In wanting to put the check *within* the executive branch, Mason seems to have seen this as the best way to recoup some of his losses from having the plural executive rejected. The idea of a council within the executive branch to serve as a check on the president suggests interesting parallels with the contemporary bureaucracy, which is often criticized (and sometimes praised) for frustrating the president's will.[25] For the present, however, our main point is that Mason saw the Senate as a close executive partner of the president—"The Constitution has *married* the President and Senate," he tells us.[26] He objects to the relationship and proposes an executive council in its stead. A similar position is taken by the Anti-Federalist Richard Henry Lee in a letter to Governor Randolph and by Samuel Spencer at the North Carolina Ratifying Convention.[27]

From a variety of adherents to the Anti-Federalist persuasion, the image of the Senate as an executive establishment emerges clearly. The Federalists did not contest this point; they granted it. Their counterattack was aimed at Anti-Federalist positions that found the Senate's role in executive matters excessive, unwise, or inappropriate.[28] Thus there was no dispute in 1787/88 over the *fact* that the Senate was intended to serve as part of the executive. The dispute centered on the propriety of the arrangement.

A final indication of the executive character of the Senate can be seen in the evolution of the office of vice-president. He is a latecomer to the convention; no mention of the office is made until 4 September—less than two weeks before the four-months convention would adjourn. Today we tend to think of the vice-president's role as president of the Senate as rather strange, but it made good sense to the framers. An earlier draft of the Constitution had the Senate selecting the president. This arrangement was rejected as an excessive threat to the independence of the president. The senators would be all too likely to select one of their own number and then control the man they had selected. Since the president was not to be elected by the Senate, the framers logically concluded that the vice-president should not be elected in this way either. Since, however, they had given some thought to the Senate as a possible institution for selecting the president, it was only natural that they should look in this direction to find a successor for a deceased president. So natural was this that Gouverneur Morris could assure critics of the office of vice-president that if there were no such office, the president of the Senate would become a "temporary successor" to the presidency anyway. Roger Sherman agreed and supported the creation of the office of vice-president in order to avoid forcing one state to lose its full voting power when one of its senators would be elected president of the Senate. Thus, for the framers, the vice-president was primarily a senator. A special office was created for him so as to maintain the equal representation of the states in the Senate.[29]

## ATTRIBUTES OF THE SENATE

The founding argument highlights certain attributes of the Senate. Again, the argument was not so much over what these attributes were but over whether they were desirable. Let us look at the attributes that are important for our purposes.

## DURATION, EXPERTISE, AND STABILITY

These are actually three attributes, but Publius sees one as leading to the other and discusses them all in *Federalist 62*. The six-year term of office will give the Senators the firmness they need to resist "the impulse of sudden and violent passions" by which "factious leaders" might try to induce them to approve "intemperate and pernicious resolutions." The Senate must "possess great firmness and consequently ought to hold its authority by a tenure of consider-able duration." The six-year term will also give the senators time to develop the expertise they will need to master the intricacies of public life. *Federalist 64* discusses explicitly the need for time to develop the expertise in the complexities of foreign affairs that the Senate's treaty powers will require.[30]

"Expertise" may carry too technical a connotation to capture the peculiar excellence the framers looked for in senators. At the Philadelphia Convention they were more likely to speak of "wisdom." Thus Oliver Ellsworth said that "wisdom was one of the characteristics which it was in contemplation to give the second branch."[31] And Edmund Randolph, referring to the Senate, spoke of "the wisdom and stability of the Corps."[32] Madison looked to the Senate as "a body in the Govt sufficiently respectable for its wisdom and virtue."[33] He went on to assert: "One great end of the institution [the Senate] was, that being a firm, wise, and impartial body, it might not only give stability to the Gen. Govt. in its operating on individuals, but hold an even balance among different states."[34] Rufus King hoped the Senate would "give more wisdom, system, and stability to the Govt."[35] Thus, senators were to be wise, but their wisdom was linked to the stability of their position, to their duration in office.

When the Anti-Federalists looked at the six-year term, they tended to emphasize the indefinite reeligibility of the senators. This, they feared, would lead to a lifetime in office, which would lay the foundation for an eventual American aristocracy. The Anti-Federalists argued that because senators can be chosen again and again by their state legislatures, it is inevitable that they actually will be so chosen. For Centinel, this inevitability would come from "their extensive means of influence."[36] Brutus feared that "it will before long be considered as disgraceful not to be re-elected. It will therefore be considered as a matter of delicacy to the character of the senator not to return him again." Senators will, in effect, serve during good behavior. They will always be returned "except in cases of gross misconduct."[37]

Melancton Smith, Hamilton's great adversary at the New York Ratifying Convention, conceded the importance of stability in the Senate and agreed that a six-year term was not excessive. Reeligibility was the problem for Smith, and consequently, he proposed an amendment that would have enabled the state legislatures to recall any senator they had chosen and would have prohibited them from selecting any one man to serve for more than six years out of any twelve. This would head off the possibility of the Senate's becoming "a fixed and unchangeable body of men."[38]

The Federalists could not deny the possibility that some senators would probably serve for life. The text of the Constitution clearly allows for this. Instead, they spoke warmly of the lifelong tenure in the venerable senates of Sparta and Rome. This was not an embarrassment for the Federalists. At the convention, George Read supported a senatorial tenure during good behavior, while Gouverneur Morris explicitly favored a lifelong term. Hamilton thought the senators should "hold their places for life or at least during good behavior."[39]

Throughout American history enough senators have served for twenty or even thirty years that the good behavior or lifetime terms proposed by Read, Hamilton, and G. Morris have not proved altogether fanciful. Because, however, the Senate never achieved its potential as an executive institution, this senatorial longevity has done little for *executive* stability. The Twenty-second Amendment, which prohibits a third presidential term, is a further limitation on executive stability. Today the career civil service is the institution that is most likely to fulfill the vision that Read, Hamilton, and Morris had of achieving *executive* stability through a lifelong career. The link they forged between duration in office and senatorial independence goes back to the Virginia Plan, where it was provided "that the members of the second branch of the National Legislature ought . . . to hold their offices for a term sufficient to insure their independency."[40]

CONTINUING BODY

The Anti-Federalists feared that the Senate would become a continuing body. Section 3 of article 2 states that the president "may, on extraordinary Occasions, convene both Houses, *or either of them*" (emphasis added). The most obvious situation in which the president would want to convene one house but not the other would be when he wanted the advice and consent of the Senate on a treaty or an appointment. The Anti-Federalists maintained that the "extraordinary occasion" of section 3 would in practice become quite routine and that, as a result, the Senate would be in session permanently.[41] Thus, for George Mason, the Senate would be "a constant existing Body almost continually sitting."[42] For Luther Martin, it would be "in a great measure, a *permanent* body, *constantly residing* at the seat of government."[43] Cato maintained that the powers of the senators were so extensive "that it would be found necessary that they should be constantly sitting."[44]

The Anti-Federalists' comments were on target. Throughout the Philadelphia Convention the framers spoke frequently of the possibility of the

Senate's being constantly in session. Usually this point was made in a matter-of-fact way. Gouverneur Morris objected to the prohibition against having the Senate originate money bills because "they will sit constantly, will consist of a small number, and will be able to prepare such bills with due correctness."[45] George Mason did not like this prospect: "If the Senate can originate [money bills], *they will in the recess of the Legislative Sessions,* hatch their mischievous projects, for their own purposes, and have their money bills ready, cut and dried (to use a common phrase) for the meeting of the H. of Rep."[46] James Wilson thought that "the Senate will moreover in all probability be in constant session."[47] Edmund Randolph considered that the Senate "might possibly be always sitting, and aiding the Executive."[48] Nathaniel Gorham maintained that the senators should be paid more than the members of the House because it was likely that they would be obliged "in time of war perhaps to sit constantly."[49]

Thus there is considerable evidence that both friends and foes of the Constitution thought the Senate, like today's civil service, was likely to be a permanent body, constantly in session.

PERSONNEL MANAGEMENT

The Senate's role in appointments received considerable attention during the founding debate. As we have seen above, earlier drafts of the Constitution had given to the Senate the exclusive power over the appointments of ambassadors and Supreme Court judges. Thus the framers were quite serious about including the Senate in the appointing power. Indeed, so serious were they that it was not until the penultimate session of the convention (15 September) that the framers got around to giving Congress the power to "vest the Appointment of such inferior Officers, as they think proper, in the President alone, in the Courts of Law, or in the Heads of Departments." Had this clause not been added to section 2 of article 2, a literal reading of the Constitution would require senatorial approval for *every* federal appointment.[50]

Federal Farmer was one of the strongest critics of the Senate's role in appointments. He feared that the Senate would not approve legislation vesting the appointing power in department heads but would jealously guard this power for itself. He did not think the Senate itself would constantly be in session, but the demands of its personnel responsibilities would prompt it to select from its members a "council of appointment," which "must very probably sit all, or near all, the year."[51]

The Anti-Federalists tended to emphasize the extensive intervention of the Senate in what we might today call an aspect of personnel management. Hamilton took some trouble to deny this; such senatorial intervention would run counter to his cherished principle of unity within the executive.[52] In his eagerness to downplay the Senate's role in appointments, however, Hamilton proved a poor seer. He noted that the Senate's power to advise and consent referred only to *appointments*—not to nominations.[53] Thus, while the Senate can approve or reject, it cannot choose. Apparently, Hamilton would not have approved of what we have come to know as senatorial courtesy.

There was another matter touching the Senate's power over personnel matters in which history confounded Hamilton's crystal ball. This was the issue of removal from federal office. Aside from the provision for impeachment, the Constitution is silent on this topic. In *Federalist 77* Hamilton argued that the Senate would have to concur in a presidential decision to remove a federal officer. In making this argument, however, Hamilton compromised his belief in unity in the executive branch; but in this case it was a good bargain. Hamilton's commitment to stability in the public administration triumphed over his belief in unity. Presidents (especially after Washington) might come and go, but the Senate, with its staggered six-year terms, would provide stability. The passage is worth quoting in its entirety:

> It has been mentioned as one of the advantages to be expected from the co-operation of the Senate, in the business of appointments, that it would contribute to the stability of the administration. The consent of that body would be necessary to displace as well as to appoint. A change of the chief magistrate therefore would not occasion so violent or so general a revolution in the officers of the government, as might be expected if he were the sole disposer of offices. Where a man in any station had given satisfactory evidence of his fitness for it, a new president would be restrained from attempting a change, in favour of a person more agreeable to him, by the apprehension that the discountenance of the senate might frustrate the attempt, and bring some degree of discredit upon himself. Those who can best estimate the value of a steady administration will be most disposed to prize a provision, which connects the official existence of public men with the approbation or disapprobation of that body, which from the greater permanency of its own composition, will in all probability be less subject to inconstancy, than any other member of the government.

"That body" to which Hamilton refers is, of course, the Senate. Stability in high-ranking public servants is linked to the Senate, that most stable creature of the Constitution.

Hamilton's image of the civil servant whose tenure rests on "satisfactory evidence of his fitness" is instructive for our purposes. It fits neatly with the views of one of Hamilton's most formidable adversaries, Federal Farmer. The latter, as we have seen, objected to the Senate's role in appointments because he thought it unlikely that the senators would yield their appointing powers to department heads—as the Constitution permits but does not command. This the Federal Farmer found unfortunate because he envisioned the department heads as "well informed men in their respective branches of business," who "will, from experience, be best informed as to proper persons to fill inferior offices." Appointments of department heads "will not often occur." Federal Farmer thinks we can count on the department heads to make "impartial and judicious appointments of subordinate officers." In addition, Federal Farmer finds in the presence of these well-informed, experienced, stable, impartial, and judicious department heads a further, but decidedly un-Hamiltonian, advantage: "An executive too influential may be reduced within proper bounds, by placing many of the inferior appointments in the courts of law, and heads of departments."[54]

The idea of having subordinate executive officers check the president is strictly Anti-Federalist.[55] Hamilton would reject it out of hand. Despite this important difference, however, Hamilton and Federal Farmer agree on a rather lofty image of the civil service. This agreement is somewhat remarkable because the contexts of the discussions are (for Federal Farmer) how to get the senators out of appointments and (for Hamilton) how to get them into removals. Their agreement on the common end of a stable and competent civil service is all the more instructive because of their total disagreement over how to achieve it. A high-minded civil service is the goal of both the supporters and the opponents of Senate activism in personnel administration.

## "DUE SENSE OF NATIONAL CHARACTER"

In *Federalist 63,* Publius looks to the Senate to fill the need for "a due sense of national character." The expression occurs in the context of foreign affairs, but similar language in other parts of the *Federalist* and in speeches by both Madison and Hamilton at Philadelphia suggests a broader application of these intriguing words. In *Federalist 75,* Publius credits the Senate with "a nice and uniform sensibility to national character," and in number 65 he calls the senators "the representatives of the nation."[56] At the Philadelphia Convention, Hamilton had looked to the Senate, whose members in his plan would have served during good behavior for life, as embodying "a permanent will," a "weighty interest" in the government that would give them a reason to endure "the sacrifice of private affairs which an acceptance of public trust would require."[57] Also at the convention, Madison had looked to the Senate as an institution that would "protect the people against their rulers."[58] By *ruler,* the context makes clear, he meant the elected representatives in the House. On the same day, 26 June, he went on to hail the senators as "impartial umpires and Guardians of justice and general good."[59] As Publius, Madison echoed this theme in *Federalist 63,* where he looked to the Senate for that "cool and deliberate sense of the community" that will safeguard against the danger that the country "may possibly be betrayed by the representatives of the people."

There may be some significance in these references to the Senate as (1) providing a "due sense of national character"; (2) embodying a "permanent will"; and (3) enjoying some special insight into the "cool and deliberate sense of the community." Perhaps these characteristics prompted Publius to use the rather extraordinary image of the senators as "the representatives of the nation." This language is extraordinary not only because of the rather exalted position it suggests for the Senate—a position not easily squared with Publius's understanding of checks and balances[60]—but also because it implicitly denies a role for the senators as representatives of the states. Quite clearly, the Senate did not "represent" the people. All were agreed on that; but, interestingly, many Anti-Federalists joined Publius in denying that the Senate represented the states. Since the senators would vote *per capita*—that is, as individuals— they could not be said to represent their respective states.[61] One Senator might cancel the vote of his colleague who had been chosen by the legislature of the same state. The same legislature could not dismiss, impeach, or recall senators whose votes failed to reflect the state's interests. As A Farmer, a leading Pennsylvania Anti-Federalist, put it: "It is not the power of chusing to office merely that designates sovereignty, . . . but in the power of dismissing, impeaching, or the like, those to whom authority is delegated."[62] In an effort to make sure that the senators did represent their states, Anti-Federalist George Livingston introduced an amendment before the New York Ratifying Convention, which provided in part: "It shall be in the power of the legislatures of the several states to recall their senators, or either of them, and to elect others in their stead, to serve for the remainder of the time for which such senator or senators, so recalled, were appointed."[63]

This amendment was eloquently defended by Melancton Smith precisely on the grounds that it would ensure that the Senate would be an institution that would represent the states.

If, as all agree, the Senate does not represent the people and if, as the Anti-Federalists maintain, it fails to represent the states as well, then what does the Senate represent? Perhaps Hamilton's expression "representatives of the nation" is meaningful. This central role of the Senate in the regime is captured nicely in a comment during the First Congress by Senator William Maclay of Pennsylvania, for whom the Senate is "the great check, the regulator, and the corrector, or, if I may so speak, the balance of this government."[64]

In reviewing our examination of the Senate in the founding debate, what emerges is an institution

1. in which legislative, executive, and judicial powers are combined;[65]
2. which functions as part of an executive establishment, working (or conspiring) with the president and checking him as well;
3. whose members will serve for a long period and possibly for life or during good behavior;
4. whose members are expected to have a wisdom and expertise not found in the House of Representatives;

5. whose members will have the institutional support to resist popular whims of the moment;
6. which could be constantly in session;
7. which may conduct its affairs in a place other than the legislative chamber;
8. which exercises some supervisory power over federal personnel matters; and
9. which expresses a permanent will and national character.

I do not suggest that all the participants in the debate anticipated any one of the above characteristics or that any one of the participants saw all of them. What I do contend is that an institution with these characteristics can be found in the great normative act of founding the Republic.

Today's Senate, of course, resembles hardly at all the institution envisioned in the debate of 1787/88. The adoption of the Seventeenth Amendment (the direct election of senators), a wise and long-overdue recognition of the democratic spirit of the United States, formalized the role of the Senate as being almost exclusively a second legislative chamber—a role that had characterized the Senate long before the amendment was adopted in 1916. Executive agreements in foreign affairs and a merit system in personnel administration have considerably reduced the Senate's executive powers under the Constitution as well. Today's Senate is not an executive council in any sense; its judicial powers are hardly ever exercised; it is not notably more effective at resisting popular whim than is the House; it is not constantly in session; relatively few of its members serve for more than twenty years; its wisdom and expertise may not be greater than that of the House; and so on and so forth. In a word, today's Senate is not the sort of institution the Federalists wanted and the Anti-Federalists feared.

The closest approximation to such an institution today is the career civil service, especially in its higher reaches. I resist the temptation to point to the Senior Executive Service (SES) because I do not want to burden my argument with all the problems that face that unhappy institution. The pre-SES writings on some sort of senior civil service seem closer on paper than the SES does in fact to the sort of institution that is revealed in the founding argument.[66] This, however, is not the place to call for specific institutional reforms. My argument has been aimed at legitimacy, not at reform. Neither a Senate nor a bureaucracy that resists popular whim is a likely candidate for plaudits today. We tend to call such institutions unresponsive. I am not addressing the issue of how to make bureaucracy more responsive—nor even whether it should be. What I do suggest is that there are aspects of the administrative state that roughly fulfill the vision of the framers. Today's Administrative State is fair game for criticism, but not on grounds of constitutional legitimacy.

# 4

# Representation
## as a Constitutional Defect

To make representation real and actual, the number of Representatives ought
to be adequate; they ought to mix with the people, think as they think, feel as
they feel, ought to be perfectly amenable to them, and thoroughly acquainted
with their interest and condition.

—George Mason

The preceding chapter argued that the senior levels of the career civil service
fulfill some of the functions the framers expected from the Senate. Its emphasis
was on how an important element of the administrative state conforms to the
intent of the framers. The present chapter makes a bolder claim: that the
administrative state heals a defect in the Constitution. The defect is the
inadequate number of representatives the Constitution allots to the first branch
of the national legislature. Here the Anti-Federalists had a powerful argument,
and they knew it. The Federalists knew it too; they put up only token
resistance. The defect is healed through the mass participation in government
that the administrative state brings in its train. The preceding chapter focused
on the higher ranks of the civil service. This chapter has a broader focus that
includes the "street level bureaucrat."[1]

There are two major sections in this chapter: (1) the number of
representatives and (2) the character of representatives.

## THE NUMBER OF REPRESENTATIVES

But as the state governments will always possess a better representation of
the feelings and interests of the people at large, it is obvious that those

powers can be deposited with much greater safety with the state than with the general government.

—John Lansing

The Constitution provides that when the First Congress met there would be sixty-five members in the House of Representatives, apportioned as follows: New Hampshire, 3; Massachusetts, 8; Rhode Island, 1; Connecticut, 5; New York, 6; New Jersey, 4; Pennsylvania, 8; Delaware, 1; Maryland, 6; Virginia, 10; North Carolina, 5; South Carolina, 5; and Georgia, 3. The text of the Constitution makes it clear that this distribution was to be merely provisional. "Within three Years after the first Meeting of the Congress," there was to be an "actual Enumeration" that would redistribute representatives (and liability for direct taxes) in accordance with the standards of apportionment mentioned in article 1, section 2. These standards were based primarily on population.[2] The process of reapportioning representatives was to be taken up every decade after the constitutionally mandated decennial census had been taken. The ultimate size of the House was not fixed in the Constitution. The only provision was that "the Number of Representatives shall not exceed one for every thirty Thousand, but each State shall have at Least one Representative."

The Anti-Federalists attacked this arrangement. They maintained that there were too few members in the House to provide adequate representation and that the provision that there can never be more than one representative for every thirty thousand persons ensured the perpetuation of the problem. Their argument was solidly grounded in a theory of representation that was held by nearly all Anti-Federalists who addressed the issue and, at times, by some Federalists as well.[3] The theory held that a representative assembly should be a microcosm of the society as a whole. With so few representing so many under the proposed Constitution, it was likely that very few men "of the middling sort" would ever be elected. This basic theme is captured in George Mason's epigraph for this chapter; representatives "ought to mix with the people, think as they think, feel as they feel."[4]

The theme is played throughout the Anti-Federalist literature with only minor variations. To grasp the argument of this chapter, it is necessary to examine in detail the variety of ways in which different Anti-Federalists made what was essentially the same point: representatives should be close to and resemble the people they represent, but the small number of representatives in the proposed Constitution will make this impossible. Excerpts from Anti-Federalist authors will convey the various ways in which this point was made. For example, Centinel links inadequate numbers of representatives with safeguards against corruption: "The number of the representatives (being only one for every 30,000 inhabitants) appears to be too few, either to communicate the requisite information, of the wants, local circumstances and sentiments of so extensive an empire, or to prevent corruption and undue influence, in the exercise of such great powers.''[5] Federal Farmer connects the representation issue with the Constitution's failure to provide for jury trials in civil cases:

> The essential parts of a free and good government are a full and equal representation of the people in the legislature, and the jury trial of the vicinage in the administration of justice—a full and equal representation, is that which possesses the same interests, feelings, opinions, and views the people themselves would were they all assembled—a fair representation, therefore, should be so regulated, that every order of men in the community, according to the common course of elections, can have a share in it—in order to allow professional men, merchants, traders, farmers, mechanics, etc. to bring a just proportion of their best informed men respectively into the legislature, the representation must be considerably numerous.[6]

Brutus finds it impossible to have adequate representation in a nation as large as the proposed United States and gives this as one of his reasons for opposing the Constitution:

> If the people are to give their assent to the laws, by persons chosen and appointed by them, the manner of the choice and the number chosen, must be such, as to possess, be disposed, and consequently qualified to declare the sentiments of the people; for if they do not know, or are not disposed to speak the sentiments of the people, the people do not govern, but the sovereignty is in a few. Now, in a large extended country, it is impossible to have a representation, possessing the sentiments, and of integrity, to declare the minds of the people, without having it so numerous and unwieldy, as to be subject in great measure to the inconveniency of a democratic government.[7]

Samuel Chase fears that the House of Representatives will be dominated by the rich:

> I object because the representatives will not be the representatives of the people at large but really of a few rich men in each state. A representative should be the image of those he represents. He should know their sentiments and their wants and desires—he should possess their feelings—he should be governed by their interests with which his own should be inseparably connected.[8]

Anti-Federalist literature abounds with similar attacks on representation in the Constitution.[9] As we have just seen, the argument may be paired with fear of corruption, opposition to an extended republic, and so on; but the common thread in the Anti-Federalist attack is the need for the representation to reflect (to *re-present*) the society as a whole. ''The representation ought to be fair, equal, and sufficiently numerous, to possess the same interests, feelings, opinions, and views, which the people themselves would possess, were they all assembled.''[10]

The Federalists' reply to this argument was weak, confused, and disorganized. The reason for this was that many Federalists were quite sympathetic with their opponents on this issue. This was true even of Madison, whose view of representation as "filtering" and "refining" public opinion was the most serious principled reply to the Anti-Federalists' microcosm theory.[11] Despite Madison's theoretical differences with the Anti-Federalists' position on representation, as a practical matter he agreed with them that the number of representatives in the proposed House was too small; there were limits to filtering and refining.[12] At the Philadelphia Convention, Madison had argued on several occasions that the number of representatives ought to be substantially increased.[13] Interestingly, Hamilton agreed with him. As Madison relates in his notes:

> Col: Hamilton . . . avowed himself a friend to a vigorous Government, but would declare at the same time, that he held it essential that the popular branch of it should be on a broad foundation. He was seriously of opinion that the House of Representatives was on so narrow a scale as to be really dangerous, and to warrant a jealousy in the people for their liberties. He remarked that the connection between the President and Senate would tend to perpetuate him, by corrupt influence. It was the more necessary on this account that a numerous representation in the other branch of the Legislature should be established.[14]

Since both Hamilton and Madison were displeased with the size of the House (Madison wanted the number of representatives doubled), it is no wonder that as Publius they approached the defense of the actual number of representatives with little zest.[15] Madison's discussion of representation in the *Federalist* is brilliant and justly famous;[16] but on the sixty-five-member House, he is disappointing.

Concern over the size of the House was widespread at the Philadelphia Convention. James Wilson explicitly defended the microcosm theory of the legislature.[17] So, of course, did George Mason, who, as an Anti-Federalist after the convention, mercilessly hammered away at the representation issue. Having been one of the most active delegates at the convention, he knew the weak spots of the Constitution better than any other Anti-Federalist.[18] The most dramatic moment in the convention's discussion of representation came on the very last day, 17 September. The final version presented to the delegates provided that there could not be more than one representative for every forty thousand persons. With a motion on the floor to approve the entire document, Nathaniel Gorham of Massachusetts said that "if it was not too late," he would like to see the number forty thousand reduced to thirty thousand "for the purpose of lessening objections to the Constitution."[19] The reduction would not affect the sixty-five members approved for the First Congress, but it would give Congress greater discretion to *increase* the size of the House in the future. One can imagine the anger of the weary delegates when, literally at the last moment, Gorham raised this intractable issue which, by his own admission, "had produced so much discussion."[20]

Whatever restlessness the delegates might have felt was summarily quashed when General Washington, the president of the convention, rose and, for the first time during the four months of the convention, expressed his opinion on a substantive matter on the floor. Madison reports Washington as stating that "the smallness of the proportion of Representatives . . . had always appeared to himself [Washington] among the exceptionable parts of the plan and late as the present moment was for admitting amendments, he thought this of so much consequence that it would give him much satisfaction to see it adopted."[21]

The restless delegates gave the general the satisfaction he sought. Madison notes: "No opposition was made to the proposition of Mr. Gorham and it was agreed to unanimously."[22]

The consensus that settled around the inadequate representation in the House of Representatives has a normative bearing on today's administrative state. No one would seriously contend that today's House of Representatives is in any sense a microcosm of American society. Its elite character is obvious. It has developed in a manner consistent with the worst fears of the Anti-Federalists.

The House appears in a better light if one follows Madison's filtering and refining view of representation. A charitable observer of American politics might find a certain human excellence in the men and women who sit in the House today. Even if this point is conceded, however, today's House, with its 435 members representing over two hundred million people, does not meet an important precondition of Madison's filtering theory. In *Federalist 58*, Madison argues convincingly against a legislature that is too large. Without deciding how large is too large, he warns against adding members to the legislature; but he cautions that his warning should be observed only *"after securing a sufficient number for the purpose of safety, of local information, and of diffusive sympathy with the whole society."* The italics are Madison's; this is his generous concession to the Anti-Federalist microcosm argument. It is a concession, but not a surrender. Information and sympathy on the part of the representatives is not the same thing as thinking as the people think and feeling as they feel. Throughout the debate on representation, Madison tended to stress the *knowledge* the representatives should have of the people's circumstances; the Anti-Federalists tended to stress the representatives' feelings and character. Madison's reference to "sympathy" in *Federalist 58* is not as common in his writings on representation as are his references to knowledge and information.[23]

Given a ratio of 435 to more than 200 million, it is quite doubtful that today's representatives could meet the Madisonian criterion of information *and* sympathy. Indeed, it is doubtful that they could meet the criterion of information alone. It is absolutely certain that they cannot meet the Anti-Federalist standard of feeling and character.

If one takes the founding argument as normative, it seems fair to conclude that the House of Representatives presents a serious defect in the Constitution, a defect that has been with us from the very beginning. There is a certain illegitimacy about the House of Representatives; not in a technical, legal sense, of course, because the House exists in a way that the text of the Constitution clearly permits. The illegitimacy is at a deeper level. The formal constitutional provision for apportionment belies the principles of representation that dominated the founding debate. The House of Representatives is at odds with what the founding generation thought representation should be. This defect is serious and perennial.

It is no answer to call for a larger House of Representatives. Publius argued convincingly against that approach: "The countenance of the government may become more democratic, but the soul that animates it will be more oligarchic."[24] Any freshman congressman would surely agree. In calling for a larger House of Representatives in 1788, the Anti-Federalists knew there was an outer limit. A mob was not what they had in mind. As Melancton Smith noted, "Ten is too small and a thousand too large."[25] The Anti-Federalists had no intention of destroying the deliberative character of the legislature. In all likelihood, they would have been appalled at a legislature with 435 members.

If the House is too small and yet cannot be increased, the solution to the representative problem may lie elsewhere. During the past two decades, considerable professional attention in the field of Public Administration has been given to the question of representative bureaucracy.[26] The literature is rich and varied. Sometimes it raises questions of equity: the distribution of jobs in the career public service should bear some resemblance to the make-up of society as a whole—an interesting reprise on the Anti-Federalist microcosm theme. Sometimes it stresses control: for example, a truly representative public service is the most effective safeguard against a runaway bureaucracy. Again, the echo of the Anti-Federalists is heard: it is important to have in *goverment* (if not in the legislature) people who think as we think, feel as we feel. Sometimes the literature makes the bold claim that under certain circumstances the bureaucracy can *govern* more effectively than Congress because it represents important interests and attitudes that are nearly always excluded from Congress.[27]

If one combines the literature on representative bureaucracy with the literature that stresses the discretionary power of the modern administrative state,[28] what begins to emerge is the image of a *governing* (because of discretion) institution whose personnel distribution comes much closer to the microcosm the Anti-Federalists had in mind than the House of Representatives ever could. This is not to say that the bureaucracy *is* a microcosm, but only that it comes much closer than does the House of Representatives. Although the bureaucracy is not and perhaps should not be a microcosm of American society in any exact sense, it may be the sort of microcosm the Anti-Federalists had in mind. The Anti-Federalists were not doctrinaire; they were more interested in making the rather easy point that the House of Representatives is *not* a microcosm than in explaining the fine points of what they meant by thinking as the people think, feeling as they feel. There was no need for them to develop the point. The Federalists' attack was not coming from that flank. A careful review of the Anti-Federalist literature, however, suggests a rather clearly middle-class idea of microcosm. Though they feared "the better sort" as a fledgling aristocracy, it was "the middling sort" they favored.[29] Little is said about the poor.

Thus, even if today's bureaucracy can be justly faulted for not being "truly" a microcosm, it may well meet the more relaxed middle-class standards of the Anti-Federalists. With its merit system, it aspires at least in principle to achieve the filtering and refining effect of representation that Madison envisioned without sacrificing the "diffusive sympathy" with society as a whole that was also part of Madison's view. With its affirmative-action policies, it is driven—again at least in principle—to seek out those qualified persons who have been excluded from serving in a governing institution in which they (and, by implication, people like them) will have a voice, not just a job, in the public service. The House of Representatives simply cannot do this. For this reason, I would suggest that the Administrative State, with its huge career public service, heals a defect in the Constitution of the United States.[30]

A massive public service may well be looked upon as one result of combining Madison's argument for an "extended republic" with the universal desire in 1787 for effective government.[31] When these two goals are parlayed, it is not surprising that the result is what we know today as "big government." This is not to say that it had to work out this way. There is no logical *necessity* that finds big government nestling in the bosom of the founding principles—as a public-choice theorist would be quick to point out.[32] It is only to say that it is not terribly surprising to discover that as a matter of fact, it did work out this way. Given the political climate of the 1980s, to say even this is to say quite enough.[33]

## THE CHARACTER OF REPRESENTATIVES

> The idea that naturally suggests itself to our minds, when we speak of representatives is, that they resemble those they represent; they should be a true picture of the people; possess the knowledge of their circumstances and their wants; sympathize in all their distresses, and be disposed to seek their true interests.
>
> —Melancton Smith

The previous section stressed the Anti-Federalist attack on the inadequate *number* of representatives in the first branch of the national legislature.

Needless to say, the Anti-Federalists were not concerned about numbers for their own sake. Numbers were important because of their link to the character of the representatives. The Anti-Federalists did not believe that by simply providing *more* representatives, they would ensure better representatives. Their quantitative argument was negative. *Absent* a sufficient number of representatives, it would be arithmetically impossible to elect men who were "close to the people," who "think as they think and feel as they feel." The ten congressmen from Virginia simply could not be "close" to the seven hundred thousand Virginians they represented. Regardless of how decent such representatives might be as individuals, the number of their constituents foreclosed the possibility of their meeting an essential criterion of good representation in Anti-Federalist theory.

Thus the emphasis on numbers of representatives in the founding debate was instrumental to the deeper question of the character of the representatives and the character of representation itself. If one follows the lead of the "representative bureaucracy" literature and allows that nonelected officials can be "representatives," the administrative state, with its massive public service, surely responds to the numerical concerns of the Anti-Federalists.[34] But what about the question of character? Is the administrative state helpful in providing the quality of representation that the founding generation might have considered acceptable? To answer this question, we shall examine the contemporary public service in the light of two issues at the founding period: (1) the problem of antirepublican institutions and (2) the jury as a representative institution.

## ANTIREPUBLICAN INSTITUTIONS

> He could never agree to give up all the rights of the people to a single Magistrate. If more than one had been fixed on, greater powers might have been entrusted to the Executive. He hoped this attempt to give such powers would have its weight hereafter as an argument for increasing the number of the Executive.
>
> —George Mason, as reported in Madison's Convention Notes

Although many Anti-Federalists attacked the republican character of the Constitution as a whole, there were two specific provisions that drew particular criticism for their alleged violation of republican principles. The first was the explicit constitutional provisions for one person to head the executive branch, or "the single executive" issue as it was usually called. The second was the possibility of a standing army.

On the issue of a single executive, as on so many other issues, George Mason was the most articulate spokesman for the Anti-Federalists. During the Philadelphia Convention, before there were Federalists and Anti-Federalists,

Mason raised a fundamental challenge to the possibility of reconciling a single executive with republican principles. Mason's position was truly *fundamental* because, unlike other framers, he was not content with saying that the single executive must be reconciled with republicanism. He questioned whether it could be so reconciled. He acknowledged the appeal of secrecy, dispatch, and energy as the hallmarks of executive power: but he found these qualities too closely akin to monarchy. He wondered if "perhaps a little reflection may incline us to doubt whether these advantages are not greater in theory than in practice, or lead us to inquire whether there is not some pervading principle in republican government which sets at nought and tramples upon this boasted superiority."[35]

Not surprisingly, Mason proceeded to discover a suitable pervading principle. It is "the love, the affection, the attachment of the citizens to their laws, to their freedom, and to their country."[36] In a well-ordered republic, it is the civic virtue of the people, not a vigorous executive, that will ensure strong and effective government.[37]

Mason's argument struck a responsive chord at the convention. When the topic of a single executive had first been raised, Madison tells us that "a considerable pause ensued."[38] He goes on to report: "DOCr FRANKLIN observed that it was a point of great importance and wished that the gentlemen would deliver their sentiments on it before the question was put."[39] It was a rare day in Philadelphia when the articulate statesmen at Independence Hall had to be coaxed to speak. John Rutledge of South Carolina finally broke the silence and "animadverted on the shyness of gentlemen."[40] He, Roger Sherman, and James Wilson supported the single executive with uneven enthusiasm, but Edmund Randolph denounced it as "the foetus of monarchy."[41] Randolph was joined by Charles Pinckney, a self-proclaimed friend of a vigorous executive, who nevertheless feared that we might end up with a monarchy "of the worst kind, to wit an elective one."[42]

Although Mason's direct attack on executive power in a republic touched the sentiments of the framers, his views did not prevail. His appeal to civic virtue in the people was unrealistic. Was it not the excesses of democracy that had brought the delegates to Philadelphia in the first place? Despite his failure to convince the convention, however, Mason raised a standard to which critics of executive power could repair.

The modern administrative state, with its vast number of public employees, holds out the possibility of giving us the best of both worlds—Mason's world of reliance on civic virtue in ordinary citizens and the framers' prudence in hedging their bets on virtue with a powerful unitary executive. The administrative state necessarily engages millions of very ordinary people in the systematic execution of public law. As mediators of the will of the single executive, they may well serve as a corrective against the likely excesses of a single executive prone to carry out his constitutional powers in a haughty or arrogant manner that offends republican principle.

This possibility puts the "problem of bureaucracy" in a different light. The problem is not one of simply reducing the number of bureaucrats and making sure that the president controls those who survive—as the Heritage Foundation would have it.[43] Rather, the problem is one of concern for the level of public spiritedness and civic virtue within the bureaucracy. I am not prepared to offer any assessment on the present state of civic virtue in the bureaucracy, but I can point to the work of a distinguished political scientist who did not shrink from saying, some thirty years ago, that we should rejoice that we have "a bureaucracy indoctrinated with the fundamental ideas of constitutionalism" and that bureaucrats' "working attitudes towards the rule of law, civil liberties and due process" are likely to compare quite favorably with the attitudes of elected officials.[44]

Pursuant to the Anti-Federalist attention to the character of those who represent us, we might be well advised to ponder the public spiritedness of today's bureaucrats, instead of simply fulminating about how to curtail and control them.

A second antirepublican institution that drew Anti-Federalist criticism was the danger of a standing army under the proposed Constitution. Here it is the Federalist reply that is instructive for our purposes. The supporters of the Constitution pointed to the explicit provision for the maintenance of the state militia as an appropriate safeguard against any threat from a national standing army. Upon examination of the text of the Constitution, however, this reply was not altogether reassuring. Article 1, section 8, provides: "The Congress shall have Power . . . To Provide for calling forth the Militia to execute the Laws of the Union, suppress Insurrections and repel Invasions; To provide for organizing, arming, and disciplining, the Militia, and for governing such Part of them as may be employed in the Service of the United States, reserving to the States respectively, the Appointment of the Officers, and the Authority of training the Militia according to the discipline prescribed by Congress."

Although the Anti-Federalists acknowledged that the state militias would indeed survive under the Constitution, they were not at all pleased with the degree of federal control over this last bastion of state security. The new government would organize, arm, and discipline the militia, as well as call it into federal service for such broadly defined purposes as executing the laws of the Union, suppressing insurrections, and repelling invasions.

All able-bodied men might in principle be included in a state's militia; nevertheless, the Anti-Federalists speculated that within the ranks of the militia, "select corps may be formed, composed of the young and ardent, who may be rendered subservient to the views of arbitrary power."[45] That is, the Anti-Federalists feared that the effective members of the militia might be nationalist sympathizers whose military skills would too readily be turned against the states in support of national objectives.

Publius derides this fear. He readily concedes that, of course, the effective members of the militia will be a "select corps." How could it be otherwise? A well-regulated militia requires considerable military skill in its members. It would be senseless "to oblige the great body of yeomanry and of the other classes of the citizens to be under arms for the purpose of going through military exercises and evolutions as often as might be necessary" for the relatively few militia men who would be likely to be called to military service.[46] A select corps is precisely what is needed.

Although this corps is "select" vis-à-vis the male citizenry as a whole, it is nevertheless in itself a mass institution with thousands of participants throughout the several states. Publius relies on the mass character of the "select corps" to answer the Anti-Federalist argument that sees potential enemies of liberty in such a corps. He complains: "Where in the name of common sense are our fears to end if we may not trust our sons, our brothers, our neighbors, our fellow-citizens? What shadow of danger can there be from men who are daily mingling with the rest of their countrymen; and who participate with them in the same feelings, sentiments, habits, and interests?"[47]

Publius maintains that such men—our sons, our brothers, our neighbors, our fellow citizens—pose no threat to our liberties. Their presence in a select corps of military personnel is the best safeguard we have against the danger of a standing army.[48]

To apply Publius's reasoning to the modern administrative state, we might well argue that we have little to fear from today's massive bureaucracy. Though millions of persons compose the bureaucracy, they are a "select corps" vis-à-vis the citizenry at large. They are our sons and daughters, our brothers and sisters. They think as we think and feel as we feel. They need not be an embodiment of arbitrary power; they can be a safeguard against it. They will fulfill this high civic potential only if they interiorize the values that Norton Long mentioned three decades ago: "rule of law, civil liberties and due process."[49] Hence, we find ourselves once again returning to the Anti-Federalists' concern over the character of their representatives. Perhaps we should attend less to the size and scope of the bureaucracy and more to the education and training of its personnel. All public servants take an oath to uphold the Constitution. Does the government provide the opportunity for career personnel to learn what their oath might mean in practice, to become the sort of persons who cherish constitutional norms and principles?

## THE JURY AS A REPRESENTATIVE INSTITUTION

The essential parts of a free and good government are a full and equal representation of the people in the legislature, and the jury trial of the vicinage in the administration of justice.

—Federal Farmer

The quotation above from the Federal Farmer will be familiar to the careful reader. We saw it earlier in this chapter when we discussed the Anti-Federalists' insistence upon adequate numbers of representatives. It surely is no surprise that the Federal Farmer should include "a full and equal representation of the people in the legislature" as one of his two "essential parts of a free and good government." It may be surprising, however, to find "the jury trial of the vicinage in the administration of justice" as the second essential part.

Today we have lost sight of the political significance of the jury. We do not think of the jury as an attribute of good government. This was not true in the eighteenth century. John Adams saw in the jury a powerful instrument for curbing an overbearing executive. It was through the jury that people shared in the execution of the laws. Adams found this venerable institution critical "in establishing the equipoise of the English Constitution in that it introduced into the 'executive branch of the constitution . . . a mixture of popular power,' and as a consequence 'the subject is guarded in the execution of the laws.' "[50]

The jury in republican America enabled the people to be present at the end of the political process, when their laws were applied, just as they had been present through their representatives at the beginning, when their laws were enacted. Executive power was thus controlled at both ends of the political process.

The Federal Farmer extols not just the jury trial, but the "jury trial of the vicinage." One reason for Federal Farmer's being an Anti-Federalist was because the Constitution failed to provide a jury trial "of the vicinage" and therefore failed one of the two tests of good government. Article 3 of the Constitution guarantees the right of trial by jury in criminal cases and specifies that "such Trial shall be held in the State where the said Crimes shall have been committed." For Anti-Federalists like the Federal Farmer, it was not enough to have the trial in one's state; it should be in one's "vicinage" as well. This consideration flows from the Anti-Federalist principle that government should be close to the people and underscores the connection between jury trials and good government.[51]

In the administrative state, citizens usually find laws applied to themselves concretely by "street level bureaucrats"—for example, by caseworkers, policemen, meat inspectors, customs officers, draft-board members, immigration officials, and others. In the overwhelming majority of these cases, the political process comes to an end in the hands of a career civil servant, just as the restricted scope of government activity in the eighteenth century often ended with a jury. This is another reason why it is important to have ordinary citizens in the bureaucracy. It is fitting that for the most part the political process should terminate in the hands of people who think as we think, feel as we feel; just as it was no less important two centuries ago. To be certain that we have ordinary citizens in the bureaucracy, it is imperative that there be *many* bureaucrats. Thus the Anti-Federalist theme that links the number and character of representatives finds an echo in the mass public employment of the modern administrative state.

The analogy to the eighteenth-century jury can be pressed further in thinking about the administrative state. Jurors then and now—but perhaps more then than now—are significant political actors.[52] They take their turn at ordering the polity, albeit in a modest fashion. In so doing, they fulfill the classical notion of a citizen as one who both rules and is ruled.[53] The same is true of today's administrators, especially those whose positions include the exercise of some discretionary power. They rule and are ruled. Some of these civil servants are in a position not only to fulfil the ideals of citizenship in their own lives but also to enable persons who are not governmental employees to do the same. The means for doing this is a certain form of public instruction— not instruction in the bookish sense of the schools but in the daily interaction between the citizen and the bureaucracy.

To explain my point, let me borrow a page from Tocqueville.[54] The context concerns his enthusiastic description of American juries in the 1830s. He candidly acknowledges his skepticism on whether "the jury is useful to those who have lawsuits," but he has no doubt that it is "highly beneficial" to the jurors themselves. This is because the jury is "one of the most efficacious means for the education of the people which society can employ." It is "a gratuitous public school, ever open, in which every juror learns his rights." Jury service teaches the citizen "not to recoil before the responsibility of his own actions and impresses him with that manly confidence without which no political virtue can exist." Acting as a juror "invests each citizen with a kind of magistracy; it makes them all feel the duties which they are bound to discharge towards society and the part which they take in its government." The jurors must "turn their attention to other affairs than their own," and this effort at disinterested judgment "rubs off that private selfishness which is the rust of society."

Tocqueville's encomium of the jury may strike us as being a bit quaint. For many citizens today, jury service is something that clever people avoid. Few indeed would consider it a school for civic virtue. If, however, we were to look for a contemporary institutional surrogate for Tocqueville's jury, we might find a useful parallel in one of the hallmarks of the administrative state—the administrative hearing. Could such hearings do today what Tocqueville saw the American juries doing in the 1830s? Recall that Tocqueville was not convinced that the jury excelled in rendering justice; its excellence lay in the role it forced upon the jurors themselves. It turned a private man into a public-spirited citizen. Perhaps the administrative hearing might provide a somewhat similar function. Open hearings may not always ensure the best decision-making process, let alone the best decision; but like Tocqueville's jury, they may be a remarkably powerful instrument for turning consumers of government services into citizens in the classical mold.

The effectiveness of Tocqueville's jury in playing its high-minded role was due to the crucial leadership of the judge. "His influence over them [the jurors] is almost unlimited." They "look up to him with confidence and listen to him with respect. . . . It is the judge who sums up the various arguments which have wearied their memory and who guides them through the devious course of the proceedings." He "appears as a disinterested arbiter between the conflicting passions of the parties."

Tocqueville's image of the judge might serve as a useful (albeit inexact) model for the administrator who presides over formal or informal hearings. Like the judge, the administrator has an expertise that is not merely technical. A good judge must be a good teacher in his relationship with the jury. He must explain the esoteric principles of the law in a way that is both intelligible to the layman and relevant to the case at hand, and he must do all this without sacrificing technical correctness. The skills of the administrator who listens to the public in some sort of open forum, however informal, are not altogether unlike those of the judge.

Nevertheless, the parallels are not exact. Jurors are disinterested parties, whereas participants in administrative hearings are just the opposite. The differences between the two types of institutions govern the type of leadership that is appropriate for each. The task of the administrator is to invite the participant, whose primary concern is quite properly his or her own interest, to the higher ground of public interest. Many, perhaps most, will refuse the invitation because many, and perhaps most, are incapable of the rigorous demands of classical citizenship. Nevertheless, the invitation should be offered, cautiously, prudently, kindly. Some will accept and, in so doing, will experience the more demanding, but ultimately more rewarding, meaning of citizenship.[55]

The administrative state offers millions of its employees the opportunity to fulfill the aspirations of citizenship—to rule and be ruled. Of these millions, thousands have the opportunity to instruct millions of nongovernmental employees in the ways of citizenship. Thus the administrative state has the capacity to increase and multiply public spiritedness and thereby infuse the regime with active citizens. This could bring government close to the people and thereby heal a defect in the Constitution that has been with us from the beginning. If this does not happen at present, one reason may be because we have such a negative attitude toward the administrative state, and this attitude may be grounded in a distorted interpretation of our constitutional heritage. In Part 1 of this book, I have attempted to correct this distortion by suggesting a constitutional place for administrative institutions as the first step toward releasing the energies of high civic purpose latent in the Public Administration.

# PART 2

## FOUNDING THE ADMINISTRATIVE STATE IN WORD, 1887–1900

"Come, now," I said, "let's make a city in speech from the beginning."
—Socrates

Part 2 of this book examines the period that saw the development of the classical theory of American Public Administration. This was the time of the founding of the administrative state in word; the New Deal period, the subject of Part 3, brought the founding of the administrative state in deed.

In making a distinction between foundings in word and in deed, I am, of course, following Plato's lead in the contrast he draws between his utopian *Republic* and his more plausible *Laws*.[1] In the *Republic,* Socrates, Glaucon, and Adeimantus struggle over founding a city in speech. In the *Laws,* the Athenian Stranger, the Cretan Kleinias, and the Spartan Megillus discuss the practical details of founding an actual regime as they make their pilgrimage from Knossus to the cave sanctuary of Zeus. The distinction between the two Platonic dialogues is one of emphasis; a rather strong emphasis but emphasis none the less. It is not as though the *Republic* were purely speculative and the *Laws* a how-to-govern manual. The same is true of the differences between Parts 2 and 3 of this book. Both parts examine ideas and action, but Part 2 emphasizes the former, and Part 3 the latter.

The emphasis on ideas in the period from 1887 to 1900 gives the founding in word something of a utopian character that contrasts with the pragmatic style of the New Dealers, who were busy running real governmental institutions as they thought and wrote about the new order of American politics they were creating.

The Platonic imagery can be sustained beyond the theory/practice disjunction. In the utopian *Republic,* Socrates' interlocutors are young men without experience in affairs of state. They are bold in expressing their extreme ideas. In the *Laws,* the Athenian Stranger, who is probably Socrates himself,[2] talks with two old men who have a certain worldly caution that contrasts sharply with the brilliance of the youthful circle in the *Republic.* In the *Laws,* the old men are on a religious pilgrimage, and as a result, they show considerable deference to established views and conventional pieties. The young men of the *Republic,* however, have no such reverence. Socrates encourages their reckless statements by his harsh treatment of Cephalus, the only old man in the *Republic* other than Socrates himself.[3] Cephalus is a man of conventional opinion who leaves the Socratic circle in the first book to perform an act of civic piety.[4] These contrasts between experience and inexperience and between acceptance and rejection of conventional norms help to pinpoint the difference between founding the administrative state in word and founding it in deed.

The leading theoreticians of the founding in word were Woodrow Wilson and Frank Goodnow; both were academics. Their writings, freed from the shackles of governing responsibilities, are more elegant, cogent, and logical than anything the busy New Dealers would produce. At the same time, they are less worried than their New Deal progeny would be with conforming their ideas to the constitutional structures of the day and, more importantly, to the principles that undergird those structures. Indeed, the main point in Part 2 is to show that the constitutional theory of the leading administrative theoreticians— Wilson and Goodnow—was fundamentally at odds with the principles of the founding of the Republic. I do not mean they simply updated the founding principles to meet new exigencies; I mean they consciously and flatly rejected the work of the framers. We shall examine this rejection in some detail. If it is true that foundings are normative in politics, we shall see why a Public Administration founded in principles antithetical to the founding of the Republic has been cursed from its birth with the bar sinister of illegitimacy.

Our examination has three parts. First, we shall consider the constitutional theory of Woodrow Wilson, whose famous 1887 essay "The Study of Administration" is usually credited with establishing Public Administration as a field of self-conscious governmental activity in the United States.[5] Then we shall study Frank Goodnow's elegant and influential book *Politics and Administration* (1900), wherein the classical theory of American Public Administration is framed in a sustained polemic against separation of powers.[6] Finally, as a foil to the theoreticians, we shall examine the constitutional arguments that surrounded the establishment in 1887 of the first independent regulatory commission, the Interstate Commerce Commission, and the statements of its first chairman, the renowned constitutional scholar Judge Thomas M. Cooley. There we shall find arguments less sophisticated than those of Wilson and

Goodnow but much closer to the thought of the framers of the Constitution. The examination of the constitutional arguments of the men involved in the practical task of creating a new institution of government will serve as a bridge to the chapter on the New Deal where men and women involved in the enormous task of founding the administrative state in deed replace the cool theoreticians who would found it in speech.

# 5

# Woodrow Wilson
# as Constitutionalist

Sensible shareholders, I have heard a shrewd attorney say, can work *any*
deed of settlement; and so the men of Massachusetts could, I believe, work
*any* constitution.

—Walter Bagehot

Throughout his long and distinguished career, Woodrow Wilson had much to
say about constitutions in general and the Constitution of the United States in
particular. The scope of our inquiry is limited to the years just before and after
his 1887 essay. We are interested in Wilson's constitutional thought at the time
when he was doing his most creative work in administrative theory. This work
can be found in his book *Congressional Government,* in his elaborate notes for
an extended series of lectures on administration at Johns Hopkins University,
and in the famous 1887 essay (hereafter this essay will be referred to as the
"centennial essay," because the American Society for Public Administration
has declared 1987 the centennial of American Public Administration in honor of
Wilson's essay).[1] Because Wilson is often looked upon as the most prominent
and most thoughtful of the founders of Public Administration in the United
States, it is important for our purposes to understand his constitutional views
at the time when he was doing his most serious thinking about administration.[2]

The first section of our inquiry explores Wilson's extremely broad
understanding of *constitution* in an attempt to explain why his vigorous attack
on separation of powers in *Congressional Government* stopped short of a call for
amendments to the Constitution of the United States. The next section
examines the ambitious view of administration implicit in Wilson's remark that
"it is getting harder to *run* a Constitution than to frame one" (Wilson's

emphasis). Particular attention is given to Wilson's argument that administration is a more fundamental sort of political activity than is constitution making. The third section looks to Wilson's conservative views on democracy to explain his distinction between politics and administration. Administration will rescue democracy from its own excesses and thereby preserve the "constitution" in the broad sense of the dynamic fundamental order of the state. A final section links Wilson's democratic conservatism to the need the framers of the Constitution saw to curb "the excesses of democracy." This link salvages a certain compatibility between the administrative state and the constitutional heritage, despite Wilson's trenchant rejection of the fundamental organizing principle of the Constitution, separation of powers.

## WILSON AND CONSTITUTIONAL CHANGE

But constitutions are not mere legal documents: They are the skeleton frame of a living organism.

—Woodrow Wilson

Throughout his life, Wilson was an enthusiastic constitutionalist. As a dreamy boy of seventeen he drafted a constitution for an imaginary Royal United Kingdom Yacht Club, with himself as commodore. During his student days at Davidson, Princeton, Virginia, and Johns Hopkins, he took an active role in writing constitutions for debating and literary societies, a practice he continued as a young professor at Wesleyan University. He even referred to his marriage as a compact. As president of the United States, he did not shrink from drawing up a constitution for all mankind.

One of Wilson's biographers traces this enthusiasm for constitution making to the tradition of covenant theology that Wilson learned from his father, a leading southern Presbyterian minister.[3] Whatever the explanation, the fact is unmistakably clear that Wilson had a profound and abiding interest in constitutions and constitutionalism. The word *constitution* and its derivatives pervade his writings.

Considering Wilson's interest in constitutionalism and the fact that he had practiced law briefly before commencing his graduate studies in political science, it is surprising to note Wilson's failure to ground the centennial essay in American constitutional law. To be sure, the essay is replete with references—forty-seven by actual count—to constitutionalism in general and to American constitutions in particular, but only one of these references deals with specific provisions in the federal Constitution.

To understand the constitutional background of the essay, one must turn to Wilson's *Congressional Government,* which was published in 1885. Although the book addresses broader issues than those in the essay, questions of public administration play an important part in its overall argument. Specifically, Wilson scores the constitutional principle of separation of powers for its unsettling effect on Public Administration. Separation of powers has led to congressional hegemony. Congress, in turn, has parceled out its governing authority among its disparate standing committees. Congressional government has thus collapsed into committee government. This has created an absence of unified direction over the public administration. In its place, key committees dominate individual executive departments, which are accountable in theory, but not in fact, to the president.[4] With the British cabinet system clearly in mind, Wilson deplores the "unnatural divorcement of legislation and administration."[5] Curiously, however, he does not call for the specific constitutional amendments that would be necessary to realize the reforms he envisions in *Congressional Government.*

To pin Wilson down to specific proposals for constitutional amendments that would remedy the evils of separation of powers, we must go back to his article "Committee or Cabinet Government," which appeared in *Overland Monthly* in 1884.[6] There Wilson allows that to move from committee government to cabinet government, "one or two alterations in the Constitution" would be necessary.[7]

The initial amendment Wilson calls for would change section 6 of article 1 in such a way as to permit members of the cabinet to hold seats in Congress. Section 6 provides: ". . . and no Person holding any Office under the United States, shall be a Member of either House during his Continuance in Office." Wilson would amend this prohibition to read: ". . . and no Person holding any other than a Cabinet Office under the United States shall be a member of either House during his Continuance in Office." Wilson maintains that "the addition of four words [other than a cabinet] will have removed the chief constitutional obstacle to the erection of cabinet government in this country." Under Wilson's proposed change, the president would be "authorized and directed to choose for his cabinet the leaders of the ruling majority in Congress." The cabinet, "on condition of acknowledging its tenure of office dependent on the favor of the House," would take over "those privileges of initiative in legislation and leadership in debate which are now given . . . to the Standing Committees."[8]

Wilson went on to propose that the terms of both the president and the members of the House of Representatives be lengthened. He does not specify just how long the terms should be nor whether the terms of the president and the representatives should be coextensive. The reason for lengthening the term of the president is to safeguard against a president's making irresponsible cabinet appointments to win political support for an upcoming election. What Wilson seems to have in mind is a nonpartisan president who serves as head of state and appoints his ministers from the leadership of the majority party in Congress. In principle, such an officer could serve for life, but prudence may have restrained Wilson from drawing this conclusion. Perhaps this is why he calls for lengthening the president's term without saying just how long it should be.

Wilson would also lengthen the two-year term of congressional representatives, because "no executive cabinet which was dependent on the will of a body subject to biennial change . . . could have that sense of security without which there can be neither steadiness of policy nor strength of statesmanship."[9] He is silent on how the new president would be elected. If the president is to be a nonpartisan head of state, the electoral college would seem a likely candidate for further constitutional revision. The nonpartisan character of the presidency is crucial to Wilson's scheme. Otherwise, what would happen if the president belonged to a party other than the party that controlled Congress? Wilson says the president would be "authorized and directed to choose for his cabinet the leaders of the ruling majority in Congress." Who would do the authorizing and directing? Congress, by statute? Such a statute would almost certainly be an unconstitutional infringement of the president's appointing powers. Rather than calling for a constitutional amendment directing the president to appoint his cabinet from the congressional leadership, Wilson hopes to achieve the same result by lengthening the president's term without changing the mode of election. Somewhat ironically, in his effort to undo the work of the framers of the Constitution, Wilson follows their method of designing offices in such a way as to enlist the self-interest of the officeholder in pursuit of the goals Wilson has in mind.[10] The framers used this technique to maintain the separation of powers, whereas Wilson uses it to bring the executive and the legislature together.

Wilson ignores the possibility that the two houses of Congress may be controlled by different parties. Should this happen, from which House would the nonpartisan president pick his cabinet? He also fails to mention in which house of Congress the cabinet members would sit. He probably has the House of Representatives in mind. If senators were selected on any basis other than equal representation for each state, there would be a violation of one of the two provisions in the Constitution that cannot be amended.[11] Further, he ignores the fact that the word *cabinet,* which he would insert in the first of his proposed amendments, has no constitutional meaning. The Constitution speaks of executive departments but not of a cabinet. Finally, there is the provision in section 2 of article 2 that empowers the president "to require the Opinion, in writing, of the principal Officer in each of the executive Departments, upon any Subject relating to the Duties of their respective Offices." Unless this provision were removed from the Constitution, the president could undermine the unity of the cabinet that Wilson envisions by habitually asking each member of the cabinet to express his opinion on matters relating to his own department. Indeed, one might intepret this clause of the Constitution as an implicit rejection by the framers—or at best a vestigial remain—of the executive council that was discussed and found wanting in 1787.

Wilson's proposed amendments are so riddled with difficulties that it is no wonder he dropped them. In *Congressional Government,* which appeared in 1885, the year following "Committee or Cabinet Government," Wilson eschews specific amendments and tells his readers he is merely "pointing out facts . . . diagnosing, not prescribing remedies."[12] And yet, despite this disclaimer, Wilson does not give up. *Congressional Government* presents an unrelenting attack on separation of powers that unmistakably favors the cabinet alternative, even though he stops short of calling for the amendments he had discussed in earlier writings.[13]

It seems plausible to assume that Wilson dropped his specific constitutional amendments because he realized how inadequate they were for the task at hand. To introduce cabinet government into the United States would require a massive rewriting of the Constitution that simply was not practical. Yet his enthusiasm for cabinet government is undiminished in *Congressional Government.* The interesting question arises as to why Wilson did not simply abandon his crusade for cabinet government once he realized the almost insurmountable constitutional obstacles in the way of his cherished reform. Or conversely, why did he not meet these constitutional problems directly and call for drastic revisions of the Constitution, regardless of how impractical such a call might be? Why did he choose the seemingly untenable middle ground of calling for reforms that clearly implied constitutional changes without mentioning the changes that would be necessary to effect the reform? To answer these questions, we must look more closely at Wilson's understanding of the word *constitution.*

A good place to look is in Wilson's 1893 book *Division and Reunion, 1829-1889,* where the author examines several constitutional issues in an American context.[14] It is Wilson's discussion of the constitutional argument for secession that is most illuminating. He maintains that the legal theory behind secession "would hardly have been questioned in the early years of the government, whatever resistance might then have been offered to its practical execution. It was for long found difficult to deny that a State could withdraw from the federal arrangement, as she might have declined to enter it. But constitutions are not mere legal documents: they are the skeleton frame of a living organism; and in this case the course of events had nationalized the government once deemed confederate."[15]

Wilson's image of a constitution as "the skeleton frame of a living organism" is crucial for our purposes. He supports his comment that "the course of events had nationalized the government once deemed confederate," by pointing to the difference between the new states of the West and the original thirteen colonies. Those who settled the new states had "no corporate individuality such as had been possessed by the people of each of the colonies." Their states were "arbitrary geographical units rather than natural political units."[16] Further, these new states had been settled to a considerable extent by immigrants from abroad, who sought "the West" in general rather than a particular state. Although the West was "divided into states by reason of a form of government," it was really a homogeneous region "into which the whole national force had been projected, stretched out and energized."[17]

Having traced the development of the West, Wilson then makes this telling comment: "These are not lawyer's facts: they are historian's facts. There had been nothing but a dim realization of them until the war came and awoke the national spirit into full consciousness. They have no bearing upon the legal intent of the Constitution as a document, to be interpreted by the intent of its framers; but they have everything to do with the Constitution as a vehicle of life."[18]

The distinction between historian's facts and lawyer's facts, the awakening of national spirit into full consciousness, the Constitution as a vehicle of life—these are the images and sentiments that explain Wilson's understanding of constitution and integrate his constitutional thinking into his organic theory of politics.[19]

The passages cited above are not isolated examples. Wilson develops the same argument in his treatment of the Webster-Hayne debate. He dismisses Hayne's argument for nullification as "bad logic and bad statesmanship." A state cannot disregard the laws of the Union without seceding. He sees nullification as a "poor, half-way inference," a stalking horse for the more fundamental issue of secession. On this more fundamental issue, Wilson maintains, Hayne had the better argument in terms of the original understanding of the Constitution; but that was all he had. "Webster's position was the one toward which the greater part of the nation was steadily advancing. . . . Conditions had changed in the North and were to change in the immediate future with great and unprecedented speed. . . . The North was now beginning to insist upon a national government." Wilson maintains that Webster had no trouble disposing of the argument for nullification, but "he was unable to dislodge from its historical position" the state-sovereignty premise of nullification. The case for state sovereignty was "to be overwhelmed only by the power that makes and modifies constitutions—by the force of national sentiment."[20]

Wilson's approach to constitutionalism was much more philosophical and historical than legal. Constitutions express the dynamic fundamental order of the state, and the state, for Wilson, is "the historical form of the organic life of a particular people."[21] The case law that dominates the lawyer's approach to constitutional questions holds little interest for Wilson. His five-volume *History of the American People* devotes more time to John Marshall's diplomatic career and the dramatic scenes in which he administered the oath of office to Jefferson and Jackson than it devotes to analyzing his leading constitutional opinions. *Marbury* v. *Madison* and *Gibbons* v. *Ogden* are not even mentioned.[22] The examinations from courses in constitutional law taught by Wilson feature questions such as: "Expound the nature of constitutional law by means of the distinction between 'the state' and 'the government.' "[23]

These are more than straws in the wind. They are solid indicators of what Wilson meant by *constitution* during the years surrounding the centennial essay.[24] This broad understanding of constitution explains why Wilson ignored the practical constitutional difficulties that stood in the way of realizing the reforms he proposed in *Congressional Government*. He preferred to trust in the historical process that would eventually bring the "living nation" to see the wisdom of his position.[25]

## CONSTITUTIONS AND ADMINISTRATION

The functions of government are . . . independent of legislation, and even of constitutions, because [they are] as old as government and inherent in its very nature.

—Woodrow Wilson

From 1888 to 1897 Wilson delivered a series of annual lectures on administration at Johns Hopkins University. His notes for the 1891 lectures provide a detailed statement on "the constitutional state." Here his interpretation of *constitution* is narrower than the interpretations we have just examined—and less representative of his overall position. Nevertheless, the lecture notes are valuable for our purposes because they reveal what *constitution* meant to Wilson when his attention was directed specifically and formally to Public Administration. In this context his understanding of constitution was neatly tailored to fit his polemic against separation of powers.

In his notes, Wilson distinguishes between the constitution of a state before and after "the modern time," which he calls "the regime of liberalism."[26] The older constitutions were concerned "only with make-up and method." Modern constitutions add "an authoritative body of limitations or a grant of power from without." The modern constitutional state is "a self-conscious, adult, self-regulated (democratic) State," with the following characteristics:

1. A law-making body representative of the State, not of the Government: set to direct and control the Government. With this body, however, the Head of the State shares the law-making power.
2. An administration subject to the laws; but not necessarily energized and commissioned by the laws in respect of all its acts.
3. A judiciary equipped with a wide range of independent powers and secured, by an independent tenure, against corrupt or other improper influences.
4. A more or less careful and complete formulation of the rights of individual liberty, i.e. the rights of the individual against the Government. A pledge taken by the Community of the Government.[27]

Not surprisingly, the English Constitution meets all four criteria but that of the United States does not. Hence, the United States falls short of being a "constitutional state." Constitutionalism is the third stage in the development of the life of a state. It is preceded by the "Weal State," which is characterized by unfettered discretion, and by the "Law State," which is intended "to build bulwarks about popular rights,—to effect a 'balance' between opposing forces,—to establish a system of checks."[28] Wilson finds the United States to be still a law state.

If we compare the four criteria of a "constitutional state" with the United States, we discover that it is the second criterion that is wanting. England had "brought the ministers directly under parliamentary control" and thereby had met the requirement of "an administration subject to the laws." It should be carefully noted, however, that the very criterion of constitutionalism that subjects administration to law also states unequivocally that administration is "not necessarily energized and commissioned by the laws in respect to all its acts." Here we find the basis for Wilson's insistence that administration has a life of its own, independent of legislative enactments. This is the foundation of Wilson's "high-profile" administration, discussed below. Administration enjoys a "high profile" in Wilson's thought because it is the most fundamental sort of governmental activity.

For the present it will suffice to observe that in consigning the United States to the limbo of a "Law State," Wilson repeats in a lecture on administration the thesis of *Congressional Government,* namely, that American administration is not subject to the laws, but to the whims of congressional committees. This suggests a continuity in his thought that illuminates the relationship between constitutions and administration in the centennial essay. If we look upon the essay as a midway point between *Congressional Government* and the early Hopkins lectures, an argument can be made that in this essay, Wilson is groping toward a high-profile model of Public Administration that becomes quite explicit in 1891.

In the first section of the centennial essay, Wilson says little about politics. Constitutions and administration are what interest him. When the word *politics* appears, it is used in the high-toned sense of constitution making. The message of section 1 is that administration has begun to replace politics because the era of constitution making is over. The old-style politics, in which "monarchy rode tilt against democracy" in the "high warfare of principle," has ended. "It is getting to be harder to *run* a constitution than to frame one," because we are basically content with our constitution but we have neglected the science of administration.

In the first section of the essay the task of administration is nothing less than to run a constitution. The connection between administration and constitution is immediate and direct. There is no mention of a legislature that intervenes between constitution and administration. The high politics of constitution making has yielded to high-profile administration.

In the second section of the essay, Wilson states the familiar instrumental relation of administration to politics. Here politics includes the legislature's conventional tasks of resolving conflicts and formulating policies. Even in its instrumental aspect, however, administration is open to a high-profile interpretation. The subordination of administration to politics rests on a sliding scale of what one considers to be the business side of governmental affairs. There is good reason to think Wilson would push administration high up on the scale and confine politics to a small spot at the very top.[29]

The text of *Congressional Government* supports this surmise. In chapter 5, "The Executive," Wilson states the politics/administration dichotomy in its instrumental aspect; calls for "the drawing of a sharp line of distinction between those offices which are political and those which are *non*-political"; allows that it is "extremely hard to determine where the line should be drawn"; and ends up by giving serious consideration to drawing the line in such a way as to make cabinet members part of the permanent civil service.[30] Indeed, Wilson is not entirely sure where the president belongs. His veto power "constitutes him a part of the legislature." Otherwise, however, "the President might, not inconveniently, be a permanent officer; the first official of a carefully-graded and impartially regulated civil service system. . . . He is part of the official rather than of the political machinery of the government."[31]

Wilson departs sharply from the framers of the Constitution when he maintains that the veto power makes the president part of the legislature. The veto power *is* legislative power, but the framers did not give it to the president to make him part of the legislature. They gave it to him to ensure his independence from the legislature. This is what was meant by a constitutional "check." Wilson ignores all this in his rush to elevate administrative power. In finding in the veto power the only reason for making the president an unlikely candidate for a merit system, Wilson implies that "administration" encompasses all other powers of the president. Quite logically, he seriously ponders placing the heads of executive departments under a merit system, because they have no veto power and are therefore purely administrative officers.[32]

Other indicators of high-profile administration in the centennial essay are the two great tasks that Wilson sets for the study of administration. Wilson tells us there is "one point at which administrative studies trench on constitutional ground." In examining the distribution of authority and the ways of fixing officials' responsibilities, the study of administration reaches "a central constitutional question." Wilson hopes that some day, administrative study will render "constitutional study an invaluable service." To enlighten constitutions is the first great task of administrative studies. The second task is no less grand. It is to solve the problem of making "public opinion efficient without suffering it to be meddlesome." "Administrative study," not constitutional law, is to "find the best means for giving public criticism this control and for shutting it out from all other interference."[33]

The high profile of administration suggested in the centennial essay becomes unmistakably clear in the lectures at Johns Hopkins, delivered early in 1891. This can be seen under three headings.

## ADMINISTRATION PRECEDING CONSTITUTIONS

In the centennial essay, Wilson described administration as "the most obvious part of government," but in the 1891 lectures it is promoted to the most basic governmental activity. In describing the "weal state," the first of Wilson's three stages of state evolution, he tells us: "All functions were legitimate for the State whose object was the promotion of the interests of the State and of its members; but no new or certain means of determining the common good was provided: all was left to the discretion of an unchecked Administration."[34]

Thus, in the beginning, all was administration. In a sense, "the functions of government are . . . independent of legislation, and even of constitutions, because [they are] as old as government and inherent in its very nature."[35] Wilson suggests a historical development that contradicts American opinion. For Americans, constitution making is the primordial political act, and Public Administration is its legal, logical, and historical derivative. This may help to explain why Americans are not reconciled to a modern administrative state.[36]

## LAW AND ADMINISTRATION

In the centennial essay, Wilson saw Public Administration as "detailed and systematic execution of public law," but by 1891 it has become "indirectly a constant *source* of public law."[37] Law relies upon the experience of the state, and since administration is "the State's experiencing organ . . . it becomes a source of law."[38] Here Wilson still insists that administration is subject to law, but it is not simply the creature of law. Its scope, which involves "all the necessary and characteristic functions of the State,"[39] is too broad to be captured by law. Administration is seen as "serving the State, not the law-making body in the State, and possessing a life not resident in statutes. The administrative organs of the Community thus become organically whole, vigorous and full of purpose."[40]

## ADMINISTRATIVE AND EXECUTIVE POWER.

In the centennial essay, Wilson hopes that constitutional theory, once it is in tutelage to the study of administration, may discover that "Montesquieu did not . . . say the last word."[41] In discussing separation of powers in 1891, Wilson's wish is fulfilled. The traditional classification of legislative, executive, and judicial power creates confusion. This is particularly true of the word *executive*, because it "implies that the administrative organs of the government are simply the agents of the law-making organ, that they simply execute its will."[42] Actually, "the administrative power is considerably wider and much more inclusive" than executive power. It includes, in addition to "the duty of executing positive law, . . . those duties of provident protection and wise co-operation and assistance which, though nowadays generally explicitly enjoined by enactment, would be,—as they have always been,—part of the State's normal and essential function, whether enjoined or not."[43] Thus, administration has a life of its own, independent of statutory enactment. To grasp the significance of this independence, we must examine Wilson's broad political thought at the time of the centennial essay and of the lectures at Johns Hopkins.[44]

## WILSON AS CONSERVATIVE DEMOCRAT

The effect of liberty to individuals is that they may do what they please: we ought to see what it will please them to do before we risque congratulations which may soon be turned into complaints.

—Edmund Burke

The progressive president of the United States who fought a war to make the world safe for democracy was indeed always a democrat, but he was not always a progressive. Arthur S. Link, Wilson's definitive biographer, maintains that Wilson was a conservative until 1902.[45] Regardless of when Wilson changed from conservative to progressive, there can be no doubt that at the time of the centennial essay, Wilson's commitment to democracy, though clear and serious, was tempered by considerable reserve on the proper role of the people in regulating public affairs. An examination of Wilson's conservatism reveals the normative content of his broad understanding of *constitution* and integrates into Wilson's general political thought the "high-profile" administration that is implicit in the politics/administration dichotomy.[46] We shall briefly consider three aspects of Wilson's conservatism: (1) the organic nature of the state, (2) popular sovereignty, and (3) the "English race."

### ORGANIC NATURE OF THE STATE

The origins of Wilson's organic view of politics can be traced to the early influence on him of the English conservatives Walter Bagehot and Edmund Burke. Perhaps the spirit of Wilson's enthusiasm for Burke's conservatism is best captured in a quotation from Burke that Wilson commends as "the best maxim of statesmanship among a free people": "It was my aim," said Burke, "to give the people the substance of what I knew they desired, and what I thought was right whether they desired it or not."[47]

The implication of Wilson's accolade for this remark as "the best maxim of statesmanship" is that the will of the state is not discovered on majoritarian grounds. Wilson develops this point quite clearly in an 1891 lecture on democracy in which he insists that the will of the majority is not the same as the general will. His example is taken from the Catholic challenge to the Revolution of 1688—a challenge the Whigs turned aside so effectively that the Tories eventually abandoned any thought of a Catholic restoration. Wilson goes on to observe:

> It is certain that in the same kingdom of Britain those who were either Catholics themselves or sympathizers with the plans for a Catholic restoration were considerably in the majority,—and were influential people, at that! What does it mean? It means that the will of majorities is not the same as the general will: that a nation is an organic thing, and that its will dwells with those who do the practical thinking and organize the best concert of action: those who hit upon opinions fit to be made prevalent, and have the capacity to make them so.[48]

## POPULAR SOVEREIGNTY

Closely related to the antimajoritarian aspect of Wilson's thought is his fierce polemic against "popular sovereignty." Few other topics trigger Wilson's wrath as this one does. Popular sovereignty is usually denounced as "dogma" that stands for nothing less than the proposition "that anything that the people willed was right."[49]

At the heart of Wilson's attack on popular sovereignty is his belief that the term confuses the source of authority with authority itself; "the springs of political action are hopelessly confused with governing power"; voting is mistakenly considered to be a governing act instead of an act in which the people consent to be governed.[50] All this had the pernicious effect of misleading the people into thinking that they, the governed, are actually the governors.[51] This, for Wilson, is impossible. "There must be rule, under whatever polity and there must be rulers; command and obedience, authority and submission to authority."[52] The doctrine of popular sovereignty muddles the clear distinction between the powers and processes of governing, on the one hand, and the relations of the people to those powers and processes, on the other:

> Those relations are relations of assent and obedience,—and the degree of assent and obedience mark the limits,—the sphere—of Sovereignty. Sovereignty is the daily operative power of making and giving efficacy to laws. It is the substantive, living, governing power. It is daily in command of affairs. It lives; it plans; it originates, it executes. It is the organic origination by the State of its law and policy. The Sovereign Power is the highest originative organ of the State. That free populations themselves elect the sovereign body

by the selection of its members, does not make those populations that sovereign body. That that sovereign, originative body must prudently regard the state of opinion among those populations, does not make them any less sovereign than kings have been who reigned by hereditary right and yet found it needful to please their subjects.[53]

As an object lesson in the evils of popular sovereignty, Wilson points to the unhappy fate of the Bank of the United States at the hands of Andrew Jackson. Henry Clay, Jackson's rival, urged Congress to renew the bank's charter in 1832, four years before the old charter was to expire. Congress did so, and quite predictably, Jackson, an implacable foe of the bank, vetoed the bank bill. Congress failed to override the veto, and Clay, Jackson's presidential challenger, turned the election of 1832 into a referendum on the bank. Jackson won and, according to Wilson, interpreted the election "to mean that he had a commission from the people to destroy the Bank."[54] In criticizing Clay's strategy, Wilson says it was "madness to stake the existence of a great bank on the popular vote."[55] It was "folly" on Clay's part to suppose "the respect for a great and useful moneyed corporation would be as universal or as powerful a motive among the voters as appreciation of General Jackson, the man of the people."[56]

We shall return to the theme of popular sovereignty in chapter 6, where we shall see that Wilson's views were utterly at odds with those of the framers of the Constitution. For the present, his position on popular sovereignty is presented to establish his conservative credentials.

## THE "ENGLISH RACE"

Another important aspect of Wilson's conservatism appears in his reliance on the character of "the English race" to curb the excesses of democracy. The framers of the Constitution relied upon separation of powers, but as we have seen, Wilson found this institutional arrangement unsatisfactory. A conservative legal historian, Sir Henry Maine, criticized Wilson's attack on separation of powers precisely on the grounds that Wilson would remove the barrier against "democratic impatience" so wisely erected by the framers.[57] Wilson, of course, was sympathetic to the problem Maine raised, but his response was Darwinian rather than Newtonian. That is, he eschewed mechanical devices such as separation of powers and checks and balances and relied instead on the political evolution of the people themselves. He countered that Maine had "utterly failed . . . to distinguish the democracy, or rather the popular government, of the English race, which is bred by slow circumstance and founded upon habit, from the democracy of other peoples, which is bred by discontent and founded upon revolution. He has missed that most obvious teaching of events, that successful democracy differs from unsuccessful in being a product of history, a product of forces not suddenly become operative, but slowly working upon whole peoples for generations together."[58]

In other words, Wilson would rely on a benevolent historical process to safeguard the "English race" from democratic excesses. These are Wilson's glad tidings. A happy outcome of the organic state is that we can count on the English race to learn restraint from its own history. For Americans, though part of that English race, there is one serious problem—the changing patterns of immigration. Lecturing at Hartford in 1889, Wilson fretted over "changes which threaten loss of organic wholeness and soundness in carrying on an efficient and honest government."[59] He worried about the

> character of the nation which is being most deeply affected and modified by the enormous immigration which year after year pours into the country from Europe: our own temperate blood, schooled to self-possession and to the measured conduct of self-government is receiving a constant infusion and yearly experiencing a partial corruption of foreign blood: our own equable habits have been crossed with the feverish habits of the restless old world. We are unquestionably facing an ever-increasing difficulty of self-command with ever-deteriorating materials, possibly with degenerating fibre. We have so far succeeded in remaining
>
> > "A nation yet, the rulers and the ruled—
> > Some sense of duty, something of a faith,
> > Some reverence for the laws ourselves have made,
> > Some patient force to change them when we will,
> > Some civic manhood firm against the crowd."[60]

This heady language must be read against the spirit of Wilson's times. His talk of race, blood, and stock, though embarrassingly prominent in his thought, cannot be freighted with the sinister overtones that our own century has taught us. Nevertheless, the point is blatantly clear. Wilson's organicism is seriously threatened by the arrival of new groups of people. Popular sovereignty in the hands of such parvenus could undermine organic wholeness.[61]

My conclusion from examining Wilson's democratic conservatism is that his famous dichotomy between politics and administration can be best understood as an expression of this conservatism. The dichotomy introduced a primitive zero-sum game. Whatever goes into the administrative category is removed from politics and therefore from the people. By expanding the content of administration—superficially in *Congressional Government* but clearly and systematically in the Hopkins lectures—Wilson linked high-profile administration with democratic conservatism. That is, he had a principled basis for checking the dangers to democracy—popular sovereignty, the spoilsmen, and the new immigrants—without simply destroying democracy.

It is Wilson's understanding of constitution that undergirds the enterprise. He is not interested in case law or constitutional fine points. Indeed, he is rather unenthusiastic about written constitutions because they thwart the natural development of the organic state—as in the case of the American

Constitution's separation of powers. He would flatly reject William Gladstone's assessment that "the American Constitution is the most wonderful work ever struck off at a given time by the brain and purposes of man."[62] Much closer to Wilson's position is Walter Bagehot's observation: "Sensible shareholders, I have heard a shrewd attorney say, can work *any* deed of settlement; and so the men of Massachusetts could, I believe, work *any* constitution." For Wilson, *constitution* meant the expression of the dynamic fundamental order of the state which was inextricably bound to a people's character. He feared that the headlong rush toward democracy would upset the gradual growth that was the genius of the "English race." The dichotomy between politics and administration would rescue government from the vortex of popular sentiment and grant the nation's leaders sanctuary from meddlesome public opinion. Then "the old vitality in our national character" will assert itself and "impress and mould those who come to us from abroad."[63]

## WILSON AND THE FRAMERS

How shall such service be made to his [the administrator's] commonest interest by contributing abundantly to his sustenance, to his dearest interest by furthering his ambition, and to his highest interest by advancing his honor and establishing his character?

—Woodrow Wilson

The fact that the centennial of Wilson's essay falls in the same year as the bicentennial of the Constitution is a coincidence, but a very fitting one. It is fitting for two very different reasons. First, Wilson presents himself as a critic of the work of 1787. His dissatisfaction with separation of powers challenges one of the crucial principles of the Constitution. If Wilson is the father of American Public Administration, it is no wonder that his daughters and sons have had such difficulty legitimating their activities in the courts created by the Constitution that Wilson attacked. Administrative agencies with powers of rule making, enforcement, and adjudication dwell uneasily in a regime of separation of powers. As we saw in chapter 2, there are alternatives to addressing this problem short of making a frontal assault on the principle of separation of powers itself. The fact that Wilson neglected these alternatives helps to explain why Public Administration is tarred with the brush of constitutional illegitimacy. By examining Wilson's rejection of the framers, we enhance our understanding of where Public Administration theory went wrong.

Second, despite his rejection of separation of powers, Wilson is at one with the framers when his democratic conservatism leads him to join them in the intellectual struggle to find the proper role for the people in a regime based on popular consent. The tension between popular government and the administrative state is a commonplace in today's field of Public Administration, but is it simply the contemporary manifestation of a more fundamental political issue that was addressed explicitly in 1787 as well as 1887?[64] Looked at from this point of view, Public Administration is more readily integrated into our political heritage. It is the bulwark against what the framers called "the excesses of democracy."[65] Wilson shared with the framers the fear of these excesses, but he found wanting their reliance on separation of powers. He would amend their means but not their ends. Wilson hoped that enlightened administration would replace separation of powers in the noble task of saving democracy from its own excesses.

The link between Wilson and the framers can best be seen in the penultimate paragraph of the centennial essay, where he raises the question of how the administrator can be made "to serve, not his superior alone but the community also."[66] For his answer, Wilson, like Publius, looks to the self-interest of the officeholder. He urges the public to see to it that it is always in the interest of the administrator to have this broad view of the needs of the community rather than those of his superior alone. Instead of merely preaching to the administrator that it is his moral duty to develop this generous sense of public spirit, Wilson wants the American people to see to it that it is in the administrator's interest to do so. He states his position (somewhat awkwardly) as follows: "How shall such service be made to his [the administrator's] commonest interest by contributing abundantly to his sustenance, to his dearest interest by furthering his ambition, and to his highest interest by advancing his honor and establishing his character?"[67]

Wilson's clumsy syntax must not mask the serious point he makes. The grand ascent from sustenance to ambition to honor presents a lofty image of the public service that appropriately reflects the weighty tasks Wilson assigns to administration. Sustenance touches the interest of all, but ambition and honor direct attention to the few who govern. Wilson's concern for administrators' ambition and honor belies the narrowly instrumental view of administration so often attributed to him. Administration, for Wilson, is the new statesmanship.

To conclude our discussion of Wilson, let us note that, despite his rejection of separation of powers, he had much in common with the framers of the Constitution. His alert sense of the need for a government that "could respond positively to the problems of a complex industrial society" recalled Publius's effort to fashion a government "adequate to the exigencies of the union."[68] Wilson's reliance on administration to initiate this positive response tracks Publius's reliance on administration to win popular support for the new government proposed in the Constitution.[69] Wilson's high-profile administration is quite consistent with the expansive definition of administration that Publius offers in the first paragraph of *Federalist 72*.[70] Both Wilson and Publius see administration as fundamental governmental activity. Wilson's careful attention to the interests of administrators recalls not only the famous paean to interest in *Federalist 51* but also the less-well-known passages in *Federalist 77*, where Publius explicitly addresses the connection between sound government and the interests of high-ranking administrative personnel.

Both Wilson and Publius feared the excesses of democracy, and both looked to men of "the better sort" to curb these excesses. Publius would do this through a filtered form of representation, whereas Wilson relied on a trained civil service which "substitutes for the average man or 'the man of the people,' the man of the schools; that is, the instructed and fitted man."[71]

The similarities between Wilson and the framers must not distract us from the main point of our inquiry—the constitutional foundations of Public Administration. From this perspective, Wilson's rejection of separation of powers decisively overrides his link to the framers. If Wilson's theory of Public Administration were reduced to practice, the first hurdle it would meet would be separation of powers, which is not just a theory but a stubborn fact of American government. Despite the richness of Wilson's understanding of administration, as a practical matter his views were doomed at the outset because he wrote with a parliamentary form of government in mind.[72] Parliamentary administration, which rests on the foundation of legislative supremacy, cannot achieve legitimacy in a regime founded on three separate and equal branches of government. This proposition will be brought into clear focus in the examination of the writings of Wilson's fellow academician and civil-service reformer Frank Goodnow.

# 6

# Frank J. Goodnow and the Framers

Once the Federalists perceived "the great principle of the primary right of power in the people," they could scarcely restrain their enthusiasm in following out its implications. One insight seemed to lead to another, until the Federalists were tumbling over each other in their efforts to introduce the people into the federal government, which they had "hitherto been shut out of." "The people of the United States are now in the possession and exercise of their original rights," said [James] Wilson, "and while this doctrine is known and operates, we shall have a cure for every disease."

—Gordon S. Wood

The origins of Public Administration theory in the United States are usually traced to the civil-service reform movement of the final third of the nineteenth century. Like the framers of the Constitution, the reformers were practical men bent on practical results; but also like the framers, they took principles of government seriously. After their immediate goal had been achieved in the Pendleton Act of 1883, certain reformers began to look for ways to ground their merit-system triumph in a broad theory of Public Administration. Chief among these theoreticians were Woodrow Wilson and Frank Goodnow.

As we have just seen, Wilson's position on constitutional issues and Public Administration must be pieced together from a wide range of his writings and lectures. Not so with Goodnow. His influential book *Politics and Administration* presents an elegant theory of Public Administration that addresses constitutional issues in a cogent and systematic manner.[1] Because of the clarity of Goodnow's position, it is easier to contrast his constitutional theory with that of the framers of the Constitution than was the case with Wilson. For this reason, the constitutional theory of the framers will be presented in juxtaposition to Goodnow's work so as to highlight the profound differences between the principles of the founding of the Republic and those of the founding of the administrative state.

## THE CONSTITUTIONAL THEORY OF THE FRAMERS

> The Anti-Federalists were . . . the conservatives believing that the framers of the Constitution had fallen awkwardly and dangerously between the two stools of simple, responsible government and genuine balanced government.
> —Herbert J. Storing

A thorough discussion of the theory of the United States Constitution is far beyond the scope of this book. Indeed, it is probably beyond the scope of any book for the very good reason that no single theory is equal to the task of explaining the Constitution of the United States. Many, perhaps most, of the framers of the Constitution were men who gave serious attention to the principles of government and the political science of their day. The records of the 1787 convention amply support this judgment. This is not to say, however, that the convention was a seminar and that the Constitution was the product of applied research. There could be no theory of the Constitution during the convention because no one knew what the final result would be. Certain principles guided the framers' debate: for example, popular government, individual rights, federalism, separation of powers, republican institutions, bicameralism, and efficient administration. It was only after the document had been completed that the men of "the Federalist Persuasion" could look back on what they had done and try to present a coherent argument in support of their handiwork. The contributions of Madison, Hamilton, and Jay in *The Federalist Papers* are, of course, the best-known efforts of this genre. Important statements were also made by James Wilson, Charles Pinckney, John Dickinson, James Iredell, and a host of pseudonymous pamphleteers.[2]

The postconvention effort to discover a theory in the Constitution was only the beginning of a long and rich tradition. This effort continues to the present day through the scholarship of historians, lawyers, and political scientists. In explaining the theoretical foundation of the Constitution that is pertinent to Public Administration, I shall rely chiefly on *The Federalist Papers*, the postconvention activities of James Wilson of Pennsylvania, and the recent scholarship of Gordon Wood and Herbert Storing.[3]

For our purposes the central issue is the framers' innovation in constructing a regime that was democratic in principle but was not endowed with a supreme legislature. During the ratification debate of 1787/88, many Anti-Federalist critics of the Constitution found this to be no innovation at all, but simply an impossibility. As Herbert Storing observes: "The Anti-Federalists were . . . the conservatives, believing that the framers of the Constitution had fallen awkwardly and dangerously between the two stools of simple, responsible government and genuine balanced government."[4]

The Anti-Federalists maintained that there were only two ways to design a government that could legitimately be considered popular. What Storing calls "simple, responsible government" was republican in spirit and featured a unicameral legislature that was directly responsible to the people. The "genuine balanced government," which came out of the Whig tradition, attempted to balance the various orders in society—King, Lords, and Commons in the British experience—in the legislature.[5] What both systems had in common was the principle of legislative supremacy. With this principle as a starting point, the Anti-Federalists had considerable difficulty grasping the theoretical foundation of the new Constitution.[6]

Nowhere is this clearer than in the interminable debate over sovereignty which the Anti-Federalists linked to their belief in legislative supremacy. Sovereignty is supreme and undivided power, and the legislature, as Blackstone had insisted, is its accustomed place.[7] Since the proposed Constitution created a legislature whose acts would be the supreme law of the land, the Anti-Federalists argued that the new government would be sovereign and therefore its nature would be national and consolidated rather than federal. Hence, the rights of the states, and perhaps even their very existence, were in jeopardy.

The Federalists' reply in defense of the Constitution rested on an appeal to sovereignty in the people, with a consequent denial of legislative supremacy. The object of the people's choice was not a supreme legislature that embodied their will but a constitutional order, an arrangement of offices, a "system" that would provide efficient government and protect individual rights.

James Wilson was perhaps the most articulate spokesman of this Federalist theme during the debate over ratification. Speaking in support of the Constitution at the Pennsylvania Ratifying Convention, Wilson argued that the sovereignty of the states would not be destroyed by the new Constitution for the excellent reason that the states had never been sovereign. The people had always been sovereign. At one time they chose to delegate some powers to their state governments and others to Congress under the Articles of Confederation. Now they wished to rearrange this distribution of powers. Wilson put it thus:

> When the principle is once settled that the people are the source of authority, the consequence is that they may take from the subordinate governments powers with which they have hitherto trusted them, and place those powers in the general government, if it is thought that there they will be productive of more good. They can distribute one portion of power to the more contracted circle called State governments: they can also furnish another portion to the

government of the United States. Who will undertake to say as a state officer that the people may not give to the general government what powers and for what purposes they please? how comes it, Sir, that these State governments dictate to their superiors?—to the majesty of the people?[8]

Throughout the process of shifting these powers from one level of government to another, it is the people alone who possess that power "from which there is no appeal and which is therefore called absolute, supreme, and uncontrollable."[9] Although the principle of popular sovereignty was invoked most frequently in debates over federalism, the application of the principle to the structure of the federal government itself is what is of interest to students of Public Administration. On the issue of federalism, popular sovereignty nullifies state sovereignty; the states are not supreme because the people are. On the issue of separation of powers within the federal government, the legislature is not supreme because the people are. The object of the choice of the sovereign people is not a group of legislators who will carry out their will. What the people have chosen is a constitutional order which balances the powers they have delegated to three equal branches. In describing "the Federalist Persuasion," Gordon Wood has noted that because "the Federalists were equating representation with the mere flow of authority, every officer would be in some way a representative of the people."[10]

Every *officer* a *representative?* Here is interesting language for students of Public Administration. It is pregnant with a legitimating argument for the nonelected official to participate in rule.

Herbert Storing makes the same point from a different angle. Because it exists as *part* of a constitutional order that the people have chosen, "the legislature is a body of constitutional *officers,* not a microcosm of the sovereign people." Members of Congress, "like *other officers* of government, derive their authority from the Constitution, not from their election." Elections are "merely a method of choosing, not a method of authorizing."[11]

Although Storing speaks of *officers* and Wood of *representatives,* they are at one in leveling the differences between elected and nonelected government personnel. For Storing, elected officials are officers; for Wood the nonelected officials are representatives. What both men imply is the *irrelevance of election* to ground a superior claim to speak for the people. This is an important consideration in any effort to legitimate the administrative state. It provides the beginnings of a principled response to the congressman who would raise doubts about the legitimacy of monetary policy by asking, "Who elected Paul Volcker?"

The tendency of the language used by Storing and Wood to level the difference between elected and nonelected officials is not a recent innovation of their own. Frank Goodnow used similar language, and more importantly, so did such significant figures of the founding period as Publius, James Wilson, John

Adams, Thomas Jefferson, Alexander Hamilton, Elbridge Gerry, Hugh Williamson, and the participants in the Pennsylvania Ratifying Convention of 1787. In England, Edmund Burke spoke of both elected and nonelected officials as "representatives."[12]

Although there are important differences between Storing and Wood, they are at one in interpreting the Federalist argument as pointing to ratification as the decisive act of the sovereign. Wood notes that the Federalists "were equating representation with the mere flow of authority," whereas Storing describes the Federalist theory of election as "merely a method of choosing, not a method of authorizing." The emphasis is different, but the main point is the same. It is the act of ratification that initiates the "flow of authority" for Wood and that is "authorizing" for Storing.[13] The authoritative act is the people's ratification of the distribution of various offices in the proposed Constitution. The fact that some offices are filled by election and others by appointment says nothing about the connection between the people and the occupant of a particular office. The senators and representatives of article 1; the president, the department heads, and the inferior officers of article 2; and the judges of article 3 are all the objects of a popular choice that determined how each officeholder would be selected—some by popular election, some by indirect election, some by appointment. They are all *equally* the object of constitutional choice, though they are most emphatically unequal in the scope and nature of their constitutional duties. The "inferior officers" of article 2 are indeed inferior to the president and to the heads of the executive departments. Their offices, however, *ultimately* depend upon the same authoritative source that has created the office of the president. The difference is not one of more or less constitutional legitimacy but, rather, of explicit and implicit constitutional authorization.

When Wood maintains that the Federalists "were equating representation with the mere flow of authority," he is distinguishing the innovative Federalist position on representation from the traditional understanding that through representation in a legislature the entire society was *re-presented*—that is, presented a second time on a smaller scale. Storing speaks to the same point when he maintains that for the Federalists "the legislature is . . . not a microcosm of the sovereign people." It was the microcosm view of representation in a legislature that grounded the case for legislative supremacy. That is why Wood refers to the *Federalist* interpretation of representation as "a *mere* flow of authority."[14] It is "mere" because it is a purely juridical act that lacks the rich sociological flavor of the legislature as microcosm. If the legislature is a microcosm of society as a whole, then, of course, it should be supreme. There is no principle of popular government that would allow an executive or judiciary that is *not* part of the microcosm to "check" a microcosm of society itself. If the legislature is supreme, the executive and judiciary are inferior to it. This the Federalists denied. The three branches are equal. The only way to justify their position was to consider the Constitution as a whole, with its separate and balanced powers, as the object of sovereign popular choice.

In putting forward this theory, the Federalists were departing from the traditional idea of a mixed regime. Publius notes this departure explicitly in *Federalist 14.* The theory of a mixed regime was based on the British experience, where the various orders in society—King, Lords, and Commons—came together in Parliament. This was balanced government, but the balance was struck *in the legislature,* in Parliament, which was sovereign.

In republican America, where there were no "orders" in society, the mixed-regime theory continued to flourish because of a belief in a "natural aristocracy" that would have to be represented and balanced in the legislature. John Adams, of course, is the most famous advocate of this position. In his celebrated *Defense of the Constitutions of Government of the United States of America* he presented an elaborate justification of the need for a balanced legislature in a republican society. His adversaries were Turgot in France, and Franklin and Paine in America. All three of these men had argued that under a republican government there was no need for a bicameral legislature because there was only one order of society—the people themselves. To speak of an "upper" and a "lower" house was inconsistent with the genius of republicanism. Where there was only one order in society, there should be a unicameral legislature.

Adams's rejoinder to this argument was that every society had an inevitable tendency toward aristocracy. If the aristocrats are not recognized as a class by law, they will find other ways to assert themselves. They will quickly dominate a unicameral legislature in such a way as to deny the common people an effective voice; and this while paying homage to the principles of republicanism. For Adams, the path of wisdom was to maintain bicameralism as a way of constitutionally confining the natural aristocrats in a legislative chamber of their own which would be part of the legislature as a whole. This would preserve one house for the people and thereby assure a balanced constitution.[15]

The argument between the unicameral republicans and the advocates of the balanced constitution as an American version of the mixed regime became inextricably entwined in the argument over the ratification of the Constitution. Many Anti-Federalists attacked the Constitution as an expression of Adams's version of the mixed regime. Indeed, Adams himself supported the Constitution because of its similarities to his own position. This similarity, however, was only on the surface. President, Senate, and House in the Constitution were by no means the same as King, Lords, and Commons in Parliament.[16] Nor were they the same as the aristocrats and the common people of the American version of the mixed regime. The Federalists' theory of the Constitution challenged both the unicameral republicans and the advocates of a mixed regime on the issue of legislative supremacy. The unicameral republicans saw the legislature as the supreme institution of government because it was chosen by the one social order in a republic, the people. They hailed Pennsylvania's unicameral legislature as comporting with sound republican doctrine. The advocates of the mixed regime saw Parliament (or the bicameral state legislatures in America) as supreme because the various social orders had a voice in Parliament. The constitutional balance was struck in Parliament itself. There and only there was *all* of society represented, and hence Parliament was supreme.

In preferring constitutional supremacy over legislative supremacy, the Federalists by-passed the unicameral/mixed-regime argument and broke new ground. Instead of balancing social orders in a legislature, they would balance *interests* in the Constitution itself. Congress, the legislative branch, was not where the balance would be struck; it was itself part of the balance.

Herbert Storing captures the spirit of the Federalist argument when he describes their handiwork as "a balance of constitutional orders or powers . . . requiring only the impulse of popular consent to breathe life into it." This breath of popular consent is the taproot of the democratic character of the regime. It allows James Wilson to say of the government created by the Constitution: "In its principles, Sir, it is purely democratical."[17]

Throughout the Philadelphia Convention, the proponents of a strong central government consistently maintained that it was "indispensable that the new Constitution should be ratified in the most unexceptionable form, and by the supreme authority of the people themselves."[18] From Edmund Randolph's submission of the Virginia Plan at the convention's beginning to the polished language of the final product, popular ratification was defended time and again as a principle of the highest order.[19] This principle was solidly integrated into the overall strategy of the nationally minded delegates. For example, when James Madison attacked the New Jersey Plan, he noted its provision that "all Acts of the U. States in Congress . . . shall be the supreme law of the respective States."[20] He argued that this provision was incompatible with the New Jersey Plan's reliance on the several state *legislatures* for formal approval. Ratification by the state legislatures would be in accord with the Articles of Confederation, but no act of a legislature can bind a future legislature to agree that acts of Congress will be superior to its own acts. The "supreme law" clause of the New Jersey Plan showed that its supporters correctly understood the need for a considerably stronger federal government, but they erred in thinking they could reach this goal simply by amending the Articles of Confederation. What was needed was a new form of government, and this would require action from the people as a whole.[21]

An interesting exchange between Oliver Ellsworth and Edmund Randolph shows how crucial the principle of popular ratification was for the delegates of a nationalist persuasion. On 20 June the convention took up a revised version of the Virginia Plan, which Randolph had originally submitted on 29 May. The first resolution of the revised plan proposed "that a national government ought to be established consisting of a Supreme Legislative, Judiciary, and Executive."[22] Ellsworth objected to the word *national*. He felt that if this word were dropped, the plan could still "go forth as an amendment to the articles of Confederation."[23] The state legislatures, he thought, could still ratify it. This, for Ellsworth, would be a welcome alternative to submitting the plan to the people in a ratifying convention. Madison reports that Ellsworth acknowledged his dislike for these popular conventions because "they were better fitted to pull down than build up Constitutions."[24]

It fell to Randolph to reply to Ellsworth. Although Randolph would eventually become an Anti-Federalist, he was at this point in the convention a strong nationalist. He said he had no objection to deleting the word *national*, but he added the significant caveat "that apprised the gentlemen who wished for [the change] that he did not admit it for the reasons assigned; particularly that of getting rid of a reference to the people for ratification."[25] Thus Randolph drew a sharp distinction between an essential and a nonessential matter as far as the nationalist cause was concerned. The word *national* was expendable; popular ratification was not. Randolph and his fellow nationalists had a clearheaded understanding of what they were about. The creation of a new form of government requires the consent of the governed. The new government will govern, not the states, but the people as individuals. Therefore the people themselves must ratify the Constitution.

In *Federalist 78*, Publius justifies his remarkable defense of judicial review of acts of Congress on the grounds that the Constitution, if approved, will be the immediate object of popular choice and therefore superior to any enactments by elected legislators. He goes on to argue that not only would the Constitution be superior to a statute, but it would in a sense be superior to the people themselves. For even if the people should approve of a congressional action contrary to the Constitution—for example, an ex post facto law—the judiciary should nevertheless void the statute. Such a statute should be looked upon as the product of a "momentary inclination" or "ill humors" and should be resisted by the judiciary until "the people have by solemn and authoritative act, annulled or changed the established form."[26] The Constitution is to be preferred to an unconstitutional but popularly acclaimed statute because the people as authors of "a solemn and authoritative act" are to be preferred to those same people when they are under the influence of a momentary inclination. This is a republican remedy for a republican disease.

If we apply the framers' position on popular ratification to Public Administration, we can begin to see administrative activities in a new light. For example, all would agree that an employee of the Department of Transportation should obey the will of Congress as manifested in public law. He or she should do this, however, not simply because members of Congress are elected by the people but also because the Constitution—that supreme object of a popular choice that is direct, immediate, and abiding—vests the commerce power in Congress. At a behavioral level, it would ordinarily make no difference how the employee looks upon Congress; what is important is that he obey. However, a complex view that sees in a particular Congress both the result of an election and a temporary trustee of abiding constitutional powers gives administrative action a richer perspective. This perspective could have important behavioral consequences in those interesting situations in which a president, also an elected official, signals to an executive department an enforcement policy that seems to be at odds with what Congress has mandated by law. In such a situation, an administrator with a principled belief in his duty to carry out the will of elected officials will receive no guidance from his principles. To break the deadlock he must choose between competing elected superiors on some grounds other than the fact that they are elected. If these grounds are related to the constitutional principles of his oath of office, he could justify preferring one elected official to another on a democratic principle that is deeper than mere election. This principle is, of course, the framers' principle that grounds the constitutional order in a popular choice of a most fundamental nature. When such difficult choices are called for, the administrator is in effect deciding how best to run a constitution. We shall return to this theme briefly at the end of this chapter and in some detail in the Conclusion of this book. For the present, let us use our reflection on Public Administration as the transition to the work of Frank J. Goodnow.

## FRANK J. GOODNOW

> Political functions group themselves naturally under two heads, which are equally applicable to the mental operations and the actions of self-conscious personalities. That is, the action of the state as a political entity consists either in operations necessary to the expression of its will, or in operations necessary to the execution of that will.
>
> —Frank J. Goodnow

Frank Goodnow's most significant departure from the constitutional theory of the framers centered on the issue of popular sovereignty. On this point, Goodnow joined Woodrow Wilson and the other civil-service reformers, but his thinly veiled Hegelianism led to important variations on this common theme.

For Wilson, the term "popular sovereignty" suggested the excesses of Jacksonian democracy and found nothing but withering scorn in his writings. He rejected the term as a product of muddled thinking that confused the source of authority with authority itself. As Wilson put it, "the springs of practical action are hopelessly confused with governing Power." This misleads the people into thinking that they, the governed, are actually the governors. It confuses the act by which the people consent to be governed with the actual activity of governing.[27]

For the framers, it was the doctrine of sovereignty remaining in the people that enabled them to explain how there could be three equal branches of government without one being superior to the others. Sovereignty, as all admitted, was supreme and indivisible. For the Federalists, this supreme and indivisible power remained with the people. Each of the constitutional branches had specific powers that were carefully limited and therefore by definition were less than sovereign.

Although there are important differences between Woodrow Wilson and Frank Goodnow, the two men depart from the framers together when they locate sovereignty within an institution of government and not with the people themselves once a government has been formed. Although Wilson and Goodnow depart from the framers in holding this position, they faithfully restate the earlier teaching of Blackstone, who identified Parliament as the sovereign power.[28] It was from this pulpit of sovereign power in Parliament that the Anglophile civil-service reformers preached their famous instrumental view of administration.

An instrumental view of administration fits neatly into a model of government that rests on legislative supremacy. The people elect their representatives, who, acting in their sovereign capacity, pass laws which are duly carried out by the Public Administration. The Hegelian foundations of Goodnow's political philosophy led him to express this process in terms of the two basic governmental operations that constitute "the action of the state as a political entity": (1) the expression of the will of the state and (2) the execution of the will of the state.[29]

Goodnow usually avoids a simple identification of the legislature with the body that expresses the will of the state. He prefers to speak of the function of expressing that will, regardless of the institution that happens to express it in particular circumstances. When he speaks of the United States, however, where the legislature and the executive are separated, the supremacy of the legislature is unmistakably clear.[30] Thus Frank Goodnow joins Woodrow Wilson in supporting legislative supremacy which neatly accommodates an instrumental Public Administration. Paradoxically, their instrumentalism was intended to strengthen the Public Administration and to free it from politics in its daily operation though not in its overall objectives. What is crucial for our purposes, however, is to note the compatibility between an instrumental view of administration and a regime of legislative supremacy. This compatibility explains why both Woodrow Wilson and Frank Goodnow favored profound changes in American government that would alter or circumvent the constitutional principle of separation of powers. Wilson, as we saw above, once favored a constitutional amendment that would permit members of the cabinet to hold seats in Congress.[31] Goodnow, despairing of a constitutional amendment, looked to renewed and strengthened political parties to bring together the legislative and executive powers that the Constitution kept apart.

Goodnow's position is particularly interesting because he brings the executive and legislative powers together in order to separate administrative functions from both of them. When Goodnow designated the two great operations of government as the expression of the will of the state and the execution of that will, he did not identify execution with "executive power" in the constitutional sense of that term. Constitutional executive power is but one of three ways in which the will of the state is executed. Goodnow puts it thus:

> If we analyze the organization of any concrete government, we shall find that there are three kinds of authorities which are engaged in the execution of the state will. These are, in the first place, the authorities which apply the law in concrete cases where controversies arise owing to the failure of private individuals or public authorities to observe the rights of others. Such authorities are known as judicial authorities. They are, in the second place, the authorities which have the general supervision of the excecution of the state will, and which are commonly referred to as executive authorities. They are, finally, the authorities which are attending to the scientific, technical, and, so to speak, commercial activities of the government, and which are in all countries, where such activities have attained prominence, known as administrative authorities.[32]

This threefold way of executing the will of the state is crucial for understanding Goodnow's book. A careless reading of Goodnow might lead one to equate execution of the will of the state with constitutional executive power and to equate both of these with Public Administration. This would be a serious error and would tend to distract the reader from the profound disparity between the origins of Public Administration theory and the Constitution of the United States. When Goodnow calls for vigorous parties to unite legislative and executive power, he means the constitutional executive—the president and the state governors whose independence from their respective legislatures he deplores.[33] When he designates the "administrative authorities" as different institutions charged with the execution of the will of the state, he does so to keep administrators independent of the legislature. This is because the administrative authorities "are attending to the scientific, technical, and, so to speak, commercial activities of the government." Throughout his book Goodnow offers the independence of the "judicial authorities" as the proper model for the "administrative authorities."[34] For example, he notes that individual rights may be "as easily violated by a corrupt and partial administration of a tax law as by a corrupt and partial judicial decision."[35] This model contrasts sharply with the "executive authorities" who are linked to the legislature through vigorous parties so as to remedy, by informal means, the constitutional defect that formally separates them.

The reasoning behind Goodnow's plan is quite clear. The "executive authorities" are generalists who are charged with "the general supervision of the execution of the state will." The administrative and judicial authorities also execute the state will, but they rely on technical expertise to do so. The generalist who executes the state's will must be closely linked with the legislature that expresses that will. Otherwise, there will be a "lack of harmony between the law and its execution."[36] This will lead to "political paralysis."[37] Hence, Goodnow, unlike Woodrow Wilson, has no hesitation in exempting high-ranking executive officers from the reach of civil-service reform.[38]

Judicial and administrative authorities are subordinate to the legislature because execution is ultimately subordinate to expression. Subordination, however, is not enough. Judicial and administrative authorities must also be separated from the legislature to ensure that their technical execution is consistent with the expression of the will of the state. There is no inherent contradiction between being ultimately subordinate and institutionally separate, as the British courts have shown.[39] If judges and administrators are influenced by politics, there is a danger that their powers will be "discharged not so much with reference to the execution of an already expressed state will as with reference to influencing the future expression of the state will, *i.e.* in the interest of a political party or social class."[40] Thus Goodnow argues that the executive authorities must be joined to the legislative authorities for the same reason that the administrative authorities must be kept separate from both of them—to ensure that the expressed will of the state is carried into execution. The separate-but-subordinate character of administration, true to its judicial model, brings with it a degree of independence. The rationale of this independence is to safeguard the integrity of the execution of the will of the state by ensuring its conformity to the *previous* expression of that will. This can be done by staffing the judiciary and the Public Administration with nonpolitical experts who will not be tempted to execute the already expressed will of the state with an eye to influencing its future expression. In this way, administration will rescue popular government from its own excesses.[41]

On the surface, Goodnow made his peace with the Constitution by issuing his call for the reform of the party system. All would be well if disciplined parties would unite the constitutional executives (the president and the governors) with their respective legislatures and together would discipline themselves to leave the courts and the administrative agencies alone. The obvious problem Goodnow faced—and never resolved—was what to do when the executive was controlled by one party and one or both houses of the legislature by another. The fact that each house of a given legislature is elected by a different constituency and that the executive is elected by a third constituency doomed Goodnow's call for partisan reform. The kind of disciplined parties Goodnow wanted was severely disadvantaged by the formal constitutional provisions that envisioned something other than the parliamentary system he had in mind. This problem plagued Goodnow throughout his career. In testifying before a congressional committee on a national budget some two decades later, Goodnow's otherwise informed presentation faltered badly when he was questioned about how the executive/legislative harmony that he advocated would be achieved when these separate institutions were controlled by different parties.[42]

At the most fundamental level, Goodnow's problem was the same as Woodrow Wilson's; he was at heart a parliamentarian trying to reform a separation-of-powers regime. The parliamentary character of Goodnow's position was abundantly clear in his unflagging demand that the expression of the will of the state must be superior to the execution of that will. This is hierarchical language; its conceptual tidiness satisfies the need for some person or institution to be in charge. Although Goodnow maintained that expression and execution were functions, not institutions, he often ignored this caveat when discussing practical problems. The supremacy of the expression of the will of the state over its execution meant, as a practical matter, legislative supremacy. An independent executive was an embarrassing nuisance for a man like Goodnow, whose most serious political thinking was grounded in a Hegelian will of the state. His monistic view of politics demanded Parliament, and his theory of Public Administration yielded to this demand.

## A REFLECTION

> The world of administration is a *pluralistic* rather than a *monistic* world and reposes in great measure on the loyalty and competence of individual bureaucrats, qualitites that thrive best in conditions making for independence of judgment and pride in a job well done.
>
> —Edward S. Corwin

In my discussion of both Woodrow Wilson and Frank Goodnow, I have attempted to locate the origins of the illegitimacy of administrative institutions in certain contrasts between the theory of the Constitution and the original theory of American Public Administration. The latter rests on a rejection of the former. In highlighting these contrasts, I am not suggesting that Wilson and Goodnow were simply out of touch with American political thought. The men of "the Federalist Persuasion" who successfully argued for the ratification of the Constitution are not the sole architects of our constitutional heritage. Goodnow's inclusion of judicial authority as part of executive power finds explicit support in John Locke. John Adams would agree with Woodrow Wilson that the veto power of the president makes him part of the legislature. Leading Anti-Federalists championed the principle of legislative supremacy no less than did

Wilson and Goodnow. Indeed, as we saw above, when Wilson gets away from the issue of separation of powers, his views track the principles of *The Federalist Papers*.

It is not enough, however, for a theory of Public Administration to be well integrated into the broad sweep of American political thought if at the same time it is fundamentally at odds with that aspect of American thought that forms the principled basis of the Constitution. This is because the Constitution is not only a set of principles; it is positive law as well. When American Public Administration moves from theory to practice,[43] it is necessarily and appropriately caught in the perennial cross fire involving a Congress, a president, and courts—all fiercely independent of one another. American Public Administration can never be purely instrumental because there is no way of telling whose instrument it will be. A struggle for control of the Public Administration is part of the wholesome politics of a regime of separation of powers.

If we are to make any progress in legitimating the administrative state, we would do well to swim with the constitutional tide rather than against it.[44] A good starting point might be the constitutional principle of sovereignty in the people, which teaches us to think of the Public Administration as the instrument of the Constitution itself, rather than simply of the officers who are elected according to constitutional prescription. This suggests that administrators should become active participants rather than feckless pawns in the constitutional struggle for control of the Public Administration. Rather than wait to be captured now by Congress, now by presidents, now by the courts, statesmanlike administrators might consider delivering their agencies for a time to a constitutional master of their own choosing. Which master the administrators would favor and for how long would depend on the administrators' judgment of which branch of government needs to be strengthened to maintain the correct constitutional balance and to achieve the appointed ends stated so elegantly in the Constitution's Preamble. An administrative theory resting on such principles would have the advantage of preserving a certain professional autonomy within the framework of the Constitution and would thereby capture the professionalism that was at the heart of the reforms Wilson and Goodnow had in mind. Without some sort of principled autonomy, professionalism in Public Administration can never be taken seriously. A purely instrumental profession is no profession at all.

# 7

# Thomas M. Cooley
# and the Interstate
# Commerce Commission

It is sometimes our boast that in this country we have given to our possessions a protection that is found nowhere else; for the Government itself, even in the greatest emergencies, cannot impair the obligation of contracts, or take from the most humble citizen his property. But as the benefit of this protection is reaped by those who have possessions, the Constitution itself may come to be regarded by considerable classes as an instrument whose office is to protect the rich in the advantages they have secured over the poor, and one that should be hated for that reason.

—Thomas M. Cooley

Eighteen eighty-seven was an important year in American Public Administration. It brought not only the publication of Woodrow Wilson's essay but also the creation of the Interstate Commerce Commission (ICC), the first of the independent regulatory commissions. In this chapter we shall examine the constitutional origins of the ICC and the arguments that arose both at the founding and during the early years of this new federal institution. Our inquiry has three major divisions. The first looks to the constitutional background of railroad commissions in the period prior to 1887. The second analyzes the arguments that surrounded the passage of the Interstate Commerce Act (ICA), in which provision was made for the new commission. The third studies the early years of the commission under its first and greatest chairman, the famous constitutional scholar Judge Thomas M. Cooley.

Throughout this chapter we shall observe the constitutional arguments of the busy men who took the first steps toward building the administrative state. Some of their arguments recall issues that were raised at the founding of the

Republic, and others anticipate issues that would emerge clearly during the New Deal period. This chapter serves as a transition between founding the administrative state in word and founding it in deed.

## THE CONSTITUTIONAL BACKGROUND

> Every statesman long in public life has had occasion thus for a time to disobey the popular will; and his statesmanship is shown by his skill in judging what is the passing breeze of opinion, and what the fixed and certain current. To the former he may trim his sail for the time, but the latter is his master.
> —Thomas M. Cooley

On 4 July 1828, Charles Carroll, the last surviving signer of the Declaration of Independence, laid the first rail of the Baltimore and Ohio Railroad. Thus, as nineteenth-century historian A. T. Hadley noted, "One man's life formed the connecting link between the political revolution of the last century and the industrial revolution of the present."[1]

During the 1830s and 1840s, railroads were in an experimental stage; their primary function was to supplement water transportation in the seaboard states. During the next two decades there was a rapid expansion of railroads into the interior of the United States. The development of the south and central West, the discovery of gold in California, the general prosperity of the 1850s, and the transportation demands of the Civil War were among the causes for a jump in the number of miles of railroad line from some nine thousand in 1850 to about fifty-three thousand in 1870. During this period the railroad expansion was free from governmental restraint. Indeed, federal, state, and local governments generously subsidized the new industry through the purchase of securities, grants of public land, and direct grants of public funds.

This harmonious relationship changed around 1870, when it became clear that the railroads had overexpanded with speculative gain, rather than the needs of the public, in mind. Farmers were especially outraged at what they saw as the exorbitant rates imposed upon them by the railroads. Their cause was espoused by the farmers' granges of the midwestern states and soon led to the Granger movement's effective campaign for *state* regulation of railroads.

The full force of the Granger movement eventually waned, but the state regulations remained in place thanks, in no small part, to an important ruling of the Supreme Court in 1877.[2] Because of the interstate nature of the railroad industry, many of these state regulations proved cumbersome and impractical. Sentiment began to increase for federal regulation of railroads. In 1886 the Supreme Court of the United States declared that state regulation of railroads was unconstitutional because of the burden that such regulations placed on interstate commerce.[3] This decision made it imperative that Congress undertake the regulation of the railroads, since the states could no longer do so.[4]

During the period preceding 1887, the states relied on several types of commissions to regulate the railroads. The oldest type was found in Connecticut, New Hampshire, and Vermont. Their powers were limited to inspecting railroad accounts and roadbeds and reporting to the legislature. A second type, found in Massachusetts and New York, was empowered to hear complaints from shippers but had no power to enforce whatever decisions they might reach. A third type, found in California, Alabama, and Iowa, had fuller regulatory powers that included the power to set rates and fares.[5]

A variety of constitutional questions arose concerning these state commissions. The most important arguments centered on section 10 of article 1, where the states are forbidden to pass any "Law impairing the Obligation of Contracts." This provision, under the creative jurisprudence of Chief Justice John Marshall, enjoyed an illustrious history during the first third of the nineteenth century. Prior to the ratification of the Fourteenth Amendment in 1868, there was no due process clause in the federal constitution to restrain the states. The prohibition in the Fifth Amendment against the government's depriving any person of life, liberty, or property without due process of law applied only to the federal government. Chief Justice Marshall, however, found in the obligation-of-contracts clause, which *did* apply to the states, an apt tool for limiting what he considered excessive state intervention in economic affairs. He did this in two ways: (1) by an expansive reading of the word *contract* and (2) by holding that the states, in granting charters, were themselves parties to a contract. This meant that state efforts to regulate corporations had to proceed in such a way as not to impair any contractual obligations the state might have incurred in granting corporate charters.

This was the constitutional doctrine announced in the famous *Dartmouth College* case in 1819.[6] Its practical effect, of course, was to limit severely the regulatory capacity of the states. This was part of Marshall's grand strategy of nation building: the federal government would be enhanced as the states were weakened.[7]

By mid century, however, Marshall's version of the contracts clause had suffered a bad case of "goal displacement." Although recruited to build a nation at the expense of the states, it actually fought in the ranks of laissez-faire economics. The contracts clause was a reliable weapon in the arsenal of those opposed to state regulation of railroads. They argued that to regulate a franchise was tantamount to altering it and therefore violated the federal constitutional prohibition against the states' impairment of contractual obligations.[8] This argument reached rate fixing by state commissions, because the new rates would make it difficult or impossible for railroads to pay the interest on their bonds and would therefore impair the railroads' contractual obligations to their creditors.[9]

The states took a variety of approaches to parry the contracts clause argument. Wisconsin, for example, argued that since it had the sovereign power to repeal charters, it also had the lesser power to set rates for chartered corporations.[10] The most creative suggestion appeared in an article in the *American Law Review* of 1866. The author urged state legislatures to repeal railroad charters with statutes that would include a provision rendering the repeal void if a railroad would meet certain requirements. Thus regulation would be embedded in statutes authorizing the conditional repeal of corporate charters.[11]

After the ratification of the Fourteenth Amendment in 1868, the due process clause of that amendment began to replace the contracts clause as the centerpiece of constitutional argument over state regulation of railroads. As far as commissions were concerned, a number of challenges were raised against them on the grounds that they represented allegedly unconstitutional delegations of legislative authority. These challenges were usually settled in favor of the states.[12] The arguments were somewhat obscured, however, by analogies that were drawn between trustees and legislatures—obscured at least to the eye of twentieth-century readers. Instead of approaching questions of delegation in terms of public law, the argument at times was diverted into the similarities of the principles that govern both a legislature's power to delegate and the power of a broker or a trustee to delegate.[13] The analogy tended to weaken a legislature's capacity to delegate. This issue arose in discussions of the constitutional law both of the states and of the federal government.

Federalism presented another constitutional problem for state regulation of a railroad operating outside its state of incorporation. This discussion trailed off into awkward analogies from international law for a corporation operating beyond the boundaries of the nation in which it had been chartered.[14] International analogies were not terribly impressive when invoked to solve problems that arose from the nationalizing effects of railroad technology.

The police power of the states presented still another problem. This traditional constitutional power supported state efforts to regulate railroads insofar as public health, safety, or welfare were involved. Not surprisingly, railroad lawyers pressed for narrow definitions of these terms and succeeded in persuading some state courts to draw a crabbed distinction between the convenience of passengers and their health, safety, and welfare. Convenience was not a constitutionally permissible object of the police power.[15]

In 1884, just three years prior to the enactment of the ICA, an important judicial precedent was created on the constitutionality of the formal structure of the commission as a regulatory instrument. In *Louisville & Nashville Railroad Co. v. Railroad Commission of Tennessee*,[16] a federal circuit court found several constitutional flaws in the regulatory scheme that Tennessee had devised for railroads operating within its borders. One of these flaws was the statutory provision that the members of the commission should be elected by the people every two years. Although the court did not draw an explicit distinction between politics and administration, it clearly abhorred the prospect that "railroad property, on the successful, judicious, and just management of which the future growth and prosperity of the state so essentially depend, would become the prey of spoilsmen."[17] This objection was part of an argument that the regulatory scheme violated both the due process and the equal protection clauses of the Fourteenth Amendment. The judge saw no need to state precisely where one constitutional constraint ended and the other began. The elective character of the commission was woven into the fabric of an argument that found an entire regulatory scheme unconstitutional.

At another point in the argument, the *Louisville & Nashville* court attacked the statutory provision that the commission could only make recommendations to the railroad companies on what would be a "just and reasonable" compensation for their services. If the companies disregarded this advice, the commission could bring a suit in which a jury would decide what was just and reasonable. The court held that it was unconstitutional for a jury to make such a decision because of the unpredictability of juries in such matters. One jury might find an annual return of 10 percent just and reasonable, while another might not allow any more than 2 or 3 percent.

*Louisville & Nashville* was an important case, because on the eve of the debate over the establishment of the ICC, we find a federal court marrying constitutional principles to principles of administration. The jury and the elected commission were both found objectionable, because it was most unlikely that they would treat various railroad companies in an even-handed manner. Further, the presumed lack of railroad expertise among jurors and elected commissioners presaged an unconstitutional attack on corporate property. Thus the administrative values of uniformity, expertise, and liberation from electoral politics were linked to the constitutional principles of equal protection and due process. *Louisville & Nashville* did not have the precedential force of a Supreme Court decision, but it was mentioned frequently during the congressional debate over the ICA. It provided a constitutional check on the populist argument in Congress that the creation of the ICC would be a step toward taking government away from the people.

The constitutional arguments over state regulation of railroads came to an abrupt end in 1886, when the Supreme Court, in *Wabash, St. Louis, & Pacific Railway Co.* v. *Illinois,* found such regulation a violation of the commerce clause.[18] Congress had been discussing federal regulation for years, but the Supreme Court forced its hand in *Wabash.*[19] After 1886, there would be either federal regulation or no regulation at all.

## THE INTERSTATE COMMERCE ACT

It is a great public calamity when people in a free country are brought to believe that the tendency of public institutions is to make the strong stronger and weak weaker. Other things, they think, have a sufficient tendency in that direction without any aid from Government, or the institutions Government may control.

—Thomas M. Cooley

One of the most controversial aspects of the ICA was its provision for a railroad commission, the ICC. The House approved a regulatory scheme that would have been administered through the courts. It was the Senate, encouraged by strong support from the railroad industry, that insisted upon a commission.[20] There was a wide variety of constitutional issues that enveloped the commission, but conspicious by its absence was the issue that would later become a leading constitutional question associated with the ICC and the subsequent regulatory agencies created in its image. This was the issue of the independent status of the commission.

The ICC is an *independent* regulatory commission because it is independent of the president. It is not housed in an executive department. The same is true of the Federal Trade Commission, the Federal Communications Commission, the Securities and Exchange Commission, and so forth. The independence of these agencies has presented a series of troublesome constitutional issues for nearly a century. As we shall see in chapter 9, President Franklin Roosevelt launched an unsuccessful attack on the independence of these agencies in his herculean effort to reorganize the government in 1937.

There was little discussion of commission independence in 1887 for the excellent reason that under the ICA, the commission was not independent. It was located in Interior as "a permanently established bureau of an appropriate department," as one supporter of the ICC put it during the congressional debate.[21] Two years after creating the commission, Congress conferred independent status upon it "without a single hearing or a word of recorded debate."[22] It was removed from the Interior Department and given exclusive authority over its own budget, personnel, and internal management.[23] It is not clear why Congress did this, but the best surmise notes that Congress acted just two days before Benjamin Harrison, a Republican railroad lawyer, was to become president. Democrats in Congress, and many Republicans as well, may have feared for the effectiveness of the new commission if it were under the control of President Harrison. If this was the case, the independent regulatory commission "arose from a desire by Congress to insulate the agency from Presidential influence."[24] Regardless of the constitutional or political reasons that Congress may have had for creating an *independent* regulatory agency in 1889, the issue was simply ignored in 1887.

The commission itself, however, was not ignored. Like any political parvenu, it was labeled with such unflattering epithets as "un-American" and "a despotic, irresponsible junta."[25] At a more serious level, the commission was criticized for being remote from the people. If approved, it would be far away in Washington, unlike the courts, which were close to the people and familiar to them.[26] This line of argument recalls the Anti-Federalist attack on the Constitution, with its strange new powers exercised in a far-off "federal city."[27] The commission in the Senate bill was contrasted unfavorably with the courts of common law, which would enforce regulations in the House version.

In repairing to the standard of the common law against legal innovation, the opponents of the commission once again showed themselves the spiritual heirs of the Anti-Federalists, who had strenuously objected to the Constitution's failure to provide for common-law juries in civil cases.[28]

So forceful was the defense of the common law against the intruding commission that the final version of the ICA smiled in both directions and proceeded to create the commission without disturbing the traditional right to bring a suit at common law. This compromise invited forum shopping by aggrieved shippers for two decades until the Supreme Court in 1907 voided the clause permitting actions at common law.[29] In a remarkable opinion, Justice Edward D. White held, in effect, that Congress could not have meant what it said when it permitted common-law actions to survive. He argued that one of the main purposes of the act was to achieve a uniform standard of rates which would be administered by the ICC. Under a literal reading of the statute, a shipper could bring an action at common law to challenge the reasonableness of a rate that had been approved by the commission. If the shipper were to prevail, there would be two rates in effect—the commission's rate and whatever lower rate might satisfy a judge or jury. As more cases came to court, it would be unlikely that any two judges or juries would arrive at precisely the same understanding of what a reasonable rate might be.[30] Thus the availability of a suit at common law would undermine the policy of the Interstate Commerce Act, which was supposed to achieve uniform standards for rates. Therefore, Justice White concluded, the statutory provision for a common-law suit had to be set aside because it would lead to "the absolute destruction of the act" and the remedies it had created through the commission.[31]

Justice White went on to become chief justice of the Supreme Court from 1910 until his death in 1921. In a memorial eulogy, his successor, Chief Justice William Howard Taft, made an extended reference to this case and described White's opinion as "statesmanlike."[32] The word was well chosen. Twenty years after the passage of the ICA, Justice White, departing from the judicial pattern of hostility toward the ICC, deftly removed from the act a political compromise that inhibited the effective regulation of the railroad industry. White could have merely noted the inconsistency and waited for Congress to change the law. That would have been the more proper course; but rather than blowing on the dying embers of an old political controversy, he wisely quenched the coals and helped to establish the important doctrine of administrative law that directs litigants to administrative agencies before they go to court.[33]

The most spirited argument about the commission concerned its formal structure and its relation to more familiar institutions of government. Some critics, for example, looked upon the commission as a court and proceeded to show what a strange court it was. It conducts investigations without an interested party—that is, without a "case or controversy" before it. It exercises judicial power even though its members hold office for a fixed number of years rather than during good behavior. It exercises the power of both a grand and a petit jury on the same issue. Complaints before it need not be dismissed upon a finding of the absence of damages to the plaintiff. It violates the Seventh Amendment's guarantee of a jury trial in common-law suits where more than twenty dollars are involved.[34]

These attacks came from critics with a firm opinion that the ICC was a court. This *idée fixe* made it easy for them to pillory the commission for not looking like a real court. Complaints about the ICC conducting an investigation without an interested party simply ignored the policy-making character of the commission, which was no less important than its adjudicative function.[35]

While critics of the commission found it wanting as a court, its more thoughtful critics recognized the complex nature of the institution they were creating. This was apparent both during the congressional debates and during the exhaustive hearings of the Senate Committee on Interstate Commerce—or the Cullom Committee, as it was called after its chairman, Senator Shelby Cullom of Illinois.[36] Perhaps the most startling suggestion on what the commission ought to be came from Yale Professor A. T. Hadley. Although he favored the establishment of a commission, he did not think it should have judicial power or the power to fix rates. Instead, it should have "the mere purpose of securing publicity."[37] This would be power enough, because with high-minded men appointed to the commission, each side would see "the commission as in a certain sense the representative of the more enlightened opinion of the other side."[38] The commission would represent the "interests of the public as against the Railroads," but it would "also represent the intelligible and intelligent interest of the railroads as against the public."[39] It would stand, therefore, "between the actual manager of the roads on the one hand, and the legislature, representing merely local interests, on the other."[40] Thus the commission would "stand between the two to see that justice is done to both."[41] Clearly, Hadley had a bold new institution in mind; like a colossus, it would stand astride the railroads and the legislature, representing the one to the other.[42]

Two experienced railroad men, Charles Francis Adams and Albert Fink, joined Hadley in calling for a commission without coercive power. Fink hoped that the commissioners would be men so well versed in railroad management that their sound judgment would suffice to win the compliance of the industry. The commission should act as "a mediator and counsellor between the railroads and the public."[43] He strongly opposed conferring judicial power on the commission, because it would be impossible for Congress to write statutes with sufficient specificity to permit meaningful judicial interpretations. Anticipating a very modern problem, Fink argued that if statutes couched in broad, general terms were presented to a commission with judicial powers, the commission would in effect be "law-maker, judges, and sheriffs"—a situation that was "not to be tolerated in a free country."[44] Thus Fink enlisted the constitutional principle of separation of powers to support his recommendation to withhold judicial power from the commission.

Like Fink, Charles Francis Adams opposed giving judicial power to the commission; but his argument rested on the prestigious record of the Massachusetts Railroad Commission, of which he had been a prominent member. Adams saw no need for judicial power in the proposed ICC. His experience as a Massachusetts commissioner had convinced him "that in dealing with the railroad companies all that was necessary to bring about the results we desired was an intelligent appeal to reason and to public opinion."[45]

A sharp rejoinder to Adams came from Simon Sterne of New York's Board of Trade and Transportation. Like Adams, Sterne supported the commission; but, unlike Adams, Sterne would give it judicial power with life tenure for its members.[46] In a nineteenth-century gloss on Publius's defense of the extended republic, Sterne maintained that reliance on public opinion was prudent at the state level but not at the national level. Sterne's position is quite interesting if one keeps in mind Publius's 1787 argument that it is only the extended republic that can preserve both liberty and popular government. In the extended republic, there will be enough diversity of interests to prevent any stable coalition from forming a permanent majority to oppress the minority. One hundred years later, when statesman were about to put their hand to building the administrative state, Publius's argument takes a fascinating turn. Sterne concedes that Adams's reliance on public opinion is perfectly sound as long as one considers state government; and the smaller the state, the more persuasive is Adams's argument. In every state—and especially in every small state—there is a *concentrated* public opinion which enlightened commissioners can lead so as to focus on particular wrongdoings by the railroads and thus eventually to compel obedience under threat of legislative action.

At the national level, there is no such concentration of public opinion. What little pressure of public opinion there is, "when spread over the whole United States, is an extremely attenuated thing," which produces little effect on delinquent railroad corporations. Thus, Adams's successful reliance on public opinion in Massachusetts is irrelevant to national politics. A century after Publius argued that only the extended republic could preserve liberty, Sterne argues that it is only the small republic that can rely on public opinion. In the extended republic Publius created, effective regulation demands coercion.

Not everyone agreed with Sterne's assessment of the inadequacy of public opinion at the national level. One enthusiastic supporter of the commission, Congressman Charles B. Baker of New York, tried to add a clause that would enable the commission to arbitrate labor disputes between the railroads and their employees. To the question as to how the commission's labor awards would be enforced, Baker stated: "My reply is, the highest court of the land. It is always in session, and its decrees are more binding than any statute—public sentiment.''[47]

Earlier, Baker had spoken of the commission, though unelected, as being a representative institution—''representing at once public sentiment and the law.''[48] He seemed to see the commission as an institution that would settle great labor disputes by appealing to its own peculiar constituency, national public sentiment, for its effectiveness. This is a rather robust view of Public Administration, but it helps to illustrate the confusion surrounding the precise nature of the institutions that the proponents of the first regulatory commission had in mind.[49]

In examining the debate over the establishment of the ICC, certain themes emerge that recall the ratification debate of 1787 and anticipate the constitutional debate over the New Deal.

The clearest example of a theme anticipating the New Deal is the tendency of proponents of a commission with strong enforcement powers to view the relationship between the public and the railroad industry as fundamentally harmonious.[50] As we shall see below, Thomas Cooley, the first chairman of the ICC, initiated his regulatory responsibilities with this idea in mind. The early New Dealers began in the same spirit. In the first few months of the New Deal, President Roosevelt's supporters spoke of a great "business commonwealth" that was afoot and applauded the intimate connection between business and government that characterized the National Industrial Recovery Act of 1933.[51]

Eventually, both Cooley and the New Dealers would change their minds and adopt a confrontational stance vis-à-vis the industries they encountered. For our purposes, however, it is interesting to note that both the ICC and the National Recovery Administration (NRA) raised serious questions in regard to separation of powers that proponents of these agencies tended to brush aside.[52] Their attitude was sensible, if one accepts their premise of a basic harmony in society. The case for separation of powers is at its best when addressing those who see conflict as more fundamental than harmony in human affairs. A presumption of harmony provides solid underpinnings for an administrative state. Woodrow Wilson's essay on administration proceeded on the assumption that the great political issues had been solved and that the real problem of his day was one of administration. We know what Wilson thought of separation of powers.

The debate over the ICC not only anticipated constitutional issues of the New Deal period; it also brought to mind some aspects of the ratification debate of 1787. Recall that the Federalists saw the representation scheme in the Constitution as a filtering process whereby "the better sort" would be likely to achieve high office. Publius assigned considerable importance to filling such offices with men who were knowledgeable and wise. He seemed to prize intellectual qualities more than he prized qualities of the heart, whereas the Anti-Federalists tended toward the opposite position.

The late-ninteeenth-century version of this argument can be found in the remarkable frequency with which the members of the proposed commission were referred to as "representatives."[53] Just as the framers of the Constitution blurred the distinction between representatives and officers, so also the framers of the ICC blurred the distinction between representatives and commissioners. To fulfill a representative function, one need not be elected. Like the framers of the Constitution, the framers of the ICC hoped that men of considerable intelligence would occupy the high office they had created. The emphasis on intellect pervades legislative testimony in support of the commission. This is true both of those who supported a commission with vigorous enforcement powers and of those who favored a commission with no enforcement powers at all. Questions of moral character were by no means ignored, but it was intellect that was stressed without surcease.

The emphasis on intellect fit in nicely with the harmonious view of society. The "railroad problem" was not intractable; it could be solved if only a group of intelligent men, safely insulated from partisan passions, could get together and talk it over.[54]

In stressing intellect and harmony, the proponents of the commission at once affirmed and departed from important ideas of the founding period. We have already noted the similarity to Publius's emphasis on things of the mind; but there is an important difference between Publius and the proponents of the commission on this point. Publius looked for the wide-ranging intelligence that marked the best among eighteenth-century gentlemen—the statesmanlike intelligence that orders the polity. The proponents of the commission held a narrower view of intelligence; it was a view that collapsed rather easily into knowledge about railroads and experience as railroad managers. There was little doubt that at least some of the commissioners would come directly from the railroad industry. This is clear from the stringent conflict-of-interest provision in the act, which required commissioners to divest themselves of any railroad company's stocks or bonds they might own and to sever any connections they might have with such companies.[55] The friends of the commission were serious reformers. There would be no corruption in the new institution they were creating; but there would be considerable railroad experience that could serve as a surrogate for the architectonic intelligence that was the ideal of the founding period.[56]

The stress on harmony in society bore some resemblance to the position of the Anti-Federalists, but, again, with an important difference. It would not be correct to say that the Anti-Federalists thought that, *as a matter of fact,* harmony was more fundamental in human affairs than conflict. They did believe, however, that if republican institutions were to survive, there *ought* to be such harmony. This was an important element in their "small republic" argument. It is only in small republics that there is likely to be enough homogeneity to support republican institutions. There was a good chance to achieve and preserve such harmony in each of the thirteen states; but there was no chance to do so in the new Constitution that would bring all the states under one government. Such a government would never be a republic, and therefore, as good republicans, they were Anti-Federalists as well.

The proponents of the commission went beyond the Anti-Federalists and affirmed, as a matter of fact, a nationwide harmony sufficient to support a commission that could reconcile whatever differences existed among railroad companies themselves and between the railroad industry and the public. Their belief in national harmony, however, did not go beyond the railroad and the public; nor should it have done so. They were founding a railroad commission, not a nation. Unlike their opponents and unlike the Anti-Federalists, they did not consider the likely impact of their actions on republican institutions. If pressed on this point, they probably would have agreed with Woodrow Wilson that these great issues had been settled definitively and that it was now time to get on with the serious, but less fundamental, business of administration.

## THOMAS M. COOLEY

> The chief concern of every political society is the establishment of rights and of adequate securities for their protection.
>
> —Thomas M. Cooley

The ICC enjoyed the good fortune of having as its first chairman the most prominent constitutional scholar of the day, Judge Thomas M. Cooley. Cooley had served on the Supreme Court of Michigan from 1865 to 1885. His national reputation was due, however, to his famous book *A Treatise on the Constitutional Limitations Which Rest upon the Legislative Power of the States of the American Union.*[57] The book was known familiarly (and mercifully) simply as Cooley's *Limitations.* As its full title indicates, the treatise dealt primarily with state constitutional law, although each of the six editions gave considerable attention to the Constitution of the United States as well. The short title, *Limitations,* captures the book's reputation. Until the 1960s, Cooley was widely regarded as a champion of a restrictive interpretation of governmental power over private enterprise. He has been correctly identified as one of the architects of the constitutional doctrine of "substantive due process," which wreaked such havoc on efforts at progressive social reform. One historian notes that the first edition of Cooley's *Limitations,* which appeared in 1868, supplied laissez-faire capitalism with a legal ideology "almost as a direct counter to the appearance a year earlier of Karl Marx' *Das Kapital.*"[58] Another maintains that Cooley "regarded the judges as the spokesmen for the principle of the unfettered rights of property and as protectors of the *status quo* against the threat of popular power."[59]

Parts of Cooley's writings invite this interpretation. In the first edition of *Limitations,* he planted the tiny acorn whence sprang the mighty oak of substantive due process: "Due process of law in each particular case means, such an exertion of the powers of government as the settled maxims of law sanction, and under such safeguard for the protection of individual rights as those maxims prescribe for the class of cases to which the one in question belongs."[60] This famous sentence in legal history was based, in turn, on a New York case, *Wynehamer* v. *People,* which Cooley dutifully cites.[61] To change the metaphor above, it might be more accurate to say the New York Court planted the acorn and Cooley watered the sprout. In any event, this sentence, perhaps more than anything else that Cooley ever wrote, linked him inextricably with conservative crusades against governmental intervention in economic affairs.

The significance of Cooley's statement was that "due process" was not merely procedural. It bore a substantive content that included "the settled maxims of the law" and "the protection of individual rights." In the years ahead, the briefs of corporation lawyers and the opinions of sympathetic judges would embellish Cooley's statement to include within due process the right to "freedom of contract" which proved such a stumbling block to progressive reform.[62]

A fair reading of Cooley's statement would note the historical content of his reference to "the settled maxims of the law." What Cooley seemed to have in mind was that tradition would instruct judges on how to read the due process clause and in so doing would limit judicial discretion. This, of course, is itself a conservative position, but it is a very different brand of conservatism from the laissez-faire jurisprudence that found in the due process clause a judicial carte blanche to overturn legislative enactments through judicial innovation. It is the difference between the conservatism of Edmund Burke and that of Herbert Spencer.

There was quite a difference between the Thomas Cooley of the lawyers' briefs and the real Thomas Cooley—as historian Alan Jones has shown so convincingly.[63] During his four and one-half years as chairman of the ICC, Cooley was an administrative activist. Just as Alexander Hamilton as the first secretary of the Treasury found extensive "implied powers" in the Constitution, Cooley found implied powers for the commission in the broad statutory language of the ICA. Chief among these powers was the inference he drew that from an explicit provision to find rates unreasonable, the ICC had the implicit power to set reasonable rates.[64] He boldly discovered the discretionary power to investigate a railroad strike, despite the ICA's silence on such labor issues. Openly and covertly he lobbied Congress for legislation that would increase the ICC's jurisdiction to include intrastate as well as interstate railway traffic.[65]

In all these efforts his position ran contrary to the dominant opinion in the railroad industry. He confided to his diary that his colleagues on the commission were too timid in confronting the railroads. "It was our duty," he wrote, "to strengthen the law by vigorous action under it: we ought to make ourselves more felt by the railroads; be the master of the situation; be the authority in railroad matters and by asserting authority take leadership."[66]

His vigorous view of governmental power went beyond railroads. In 1889, during his third year as chairman of the commission, this erstwhile champion of limitations on government advised a North Dakota constitutional convention against writing excessive restraints on government into the fundamental law of the state. A restrictive constitution, Cooley warned, would tie the hands of the people against the machinations of corporations. In language reminiscent of *The Federalist Papers,* Cooley made his case for broad constitutional grants of power by reminding the North Dakotans "that times change, that men change, that new things are invented, new devices, new schemes, new plans, new uses of corporate power."[67]

The living Thomas Cooley was a different man from the bloodless legal authority who was cited in the courts. It would be tempting to attribute Cooley's change to his new role as the chairman of a regulatory commission. In his diary, Cooley had recorded his fear that "our office was about to be rendered ridiculous."[68] To attribute so dramatic a change to Cooley's linking his own interest with the interest of the office he held would be to attribute to *Federalist 51* a prescience that might surprise even Publius.

Undoubtedly, Cooley took pride in the work of the commission, but his aggressive advocacy of the use of governmental power to regulate railroads in the public interest can be explained on other grounds as well. Throughout his career on the bench, Cooley had been a careful student of the history of the common law. In cases involving corporations, he was quite alert to the historic role of corporations as instruments of state policy as well as of their more modern character as business organizations for private interests.[69] He had also been a consistent critic of Chief Justice Marshall's opinion in the *Dartmouth College* case for sixteen years before his appointment to the ICC.[70] It was in *Dartmouth College* that Marshall had interpreted the obligation-of-contracts clause to include charters granted by a state and had thereby seriously weakened the states' regulatory capacity. Cooley did not mince his words in attacking the great chief justice. The second edition of Cooley's *Limitations* (1871) contained this censure of *Dartmouth College:* "It is under the protection of the decision in the Dartmouth College Case that the most enormous and threatening powers in our country have been created; some of the great and wealthy corporations having greater influence in the country and upon the legislation of the country than the states to which they owed their corporate existence."[71]

With his strong sense of the original purpose of corporations and with his hostility toward the effects of *Dartmouth College,* Cooley had a principled basis for his aggressive posture vis-à-vis the railroad industry. *Dartmouth College,* of course, involved state regulatory power and therefore was technically irrelevant to the federal power that Cooley exercised as chairman of the ICC. More important than the technical point of law, however, was Cooley's attitude toward powerful corporations. The ill effects of *Dartmouth College* would never permit Cooley to be an apologist for laissez faire.

As a justice of the Michigan Supreme Court, Cooley had stressed the public character of business associations which, arguably, might have been considered as instruments of private enterprise.[72] His most interesting judicial posture toward railroad corporations surfaced in *People* v. *Salem*,[73] a case involving a tax that had been levied to benefit a railroad. Cooley found unconstitutional the statute that had authorized the tax. His argument was that by its nature a tax "must be imposed for a public and not for a private purpose" and that railroads are a form of private property. This line of reasoning flew in the face of an impressive string of precedents holding that a railroad was a public highway. Cooley distinguished these precedents with the rather startling statement that the same railroad might be treated as public for regulatory purposes and private for other purposes, such as benefiting from a tax. "An object may be public in one sense and for one purpose, when in a general sense and for other purposes, it would be idle and misleading to apply the same term."[74]

Cooley's willingness to work both sides of the public/private distinction to the disadvantage of the railroads perhaps should have alerted the industry to the threat he would present to its interests. However, Cooley's record contained enough evidence of his sympathy toward propertied interests to allay excessive fears. He was no Jacobin. His efforts seemed directed toward urging moderation upon the wealthy and toward saving the institution of private property from its own excesses. In a speech in which he extolled the common law for its capacity to adapt to changing circumstances, he could also remark that "the lawyer is and should be conservative" and that the wise will "keep an eye to the old landmarks."[75]

Cooley was able to keep this balance throughout his career. This was one important reason why his appointment to the ICC was enthusiastically supported by railroadmen and the public alike.[76]

In 1886, during the congressional debate over the ICA, Cooley submitted a written response when Senator Cullom's committee solicited his views on federal regulation of railroads. In his statement, Cooley supported the commission he would eventually head but did so in an oracular fashion that masked just what role he thought the new institution would play. He thought the railroad interest should be treated "as constituting in a certain sense a section by itself of the political community and then combining in its management the State representing the popular will and general interests, with some definite, recognized authority on the part of those immediately concerned, much as State and local authority are now combined for the government of municipalities."[77] He assured the committee that "something of the sort would neither be unphilosophical nor out of accord with the general spirit of our institutions."[78] It is not entirely clear just what Cooley had in mind by treating "the railroad interest as constituting in a certain sense a section by itself of the political community" in a way that would not be "out of accord with the general spirit of our institutions." Since he did not appear in person before the Cullom Committee, he was not questioned on his views. Whatever he meant, his vision of the proposed commission included representatives both from the state and from the railroad industry. This sounds like a blueprint for a "captured agency"; but the ICC under Cooley was nothing of the sort, although later it became the paradigmatic case of such an agency.[79]

The key to Cooley's later success as chairman of the commission may lie in the analogy he drew between the fusion of public and private power in the proposed commission and the fusion of state and local power in government. The analogy is purely public and hierarchical. The states are the constitutional masters of local governments, and both, of course, share purely public power. If Cooley approached his regulatory duties with such an analogy in mind, it is no surprise that he championed government dominating industry rather than simply serving industry's interests.[80] Such a viewpoint would be quite consistent with Cooley's longstanding views on corporations as instruments of the state—at least when the state chooses to treat them as instruments. This is one way of rendering intelligible Cooley's bland assurance to the Cullom Committee that the opaque institution he favored was not "out of accord with the spirit of our institutions."

Cooley's view on corporations offers one explanation for his aggressive administration of the ICC that is linked to his previous writings and behavior. A second and supplementary explanation can be found in his position on the Jacksonian doctrine of "equal rights."

Cooley was a native New Yorker who went west to Michigan as a young man of nineteen in 1843. His early political and literary writings, which included poems with a strong egalitarian flavor, mark him as a latter-day Jacksonian. During the 1840s he was active in the Young American movement, which stressed the "equal rights" tradition of "the Jacksonian Persuasion."[81] The theme of equal rights pervades Cooley's writings. Unlike the framers of the Constitution, Cooley did not hold a theory of natural rights. Indeed, he explicitly rejected this theory in his treatise on torts and adhered instead to the view that rights were created by law through history.[82] The epigraph at the beginning of this section captures the essence of Cooley's position: "The chief concern of every political society is the establishment of rights and of adequate securities for their protection."[83] If he departed from the dominant view of the framers in holding that rights are created by society, he was at one with them in affirming the protection of rights as the great task of government.

Cooley's emphasis on rights would become grist for the mill of the laissez-faire constitutionalists who read his *Limitations*. There was, however, an important qualification in Cooley's position on rights that his laissez-faire readers ignored. This was his emphasis on *equal* rights. When Cooley opposed governmental intervention in the economy, his opposition was based on a Jacksonian fear of special legislation that would favor the privileged and the wealthy. In particular he was afraid of governmental intervention in support of monopolies. If one finds laissez-faire doctrine in Cooley's writings, it is laissez faire in support of equality and against privilege. It is a Jacksonian version of laissez faire that is always suspicious of governmental action as a form of "partial legislation" intended to make the strong stronger.[84] This suspicion was what made Cooley, long before he joined the ICC, an implacable foe of the grants and subsidies that state governments were lavishing on the railroads.[85]

The laissez-faire constitutionalists did not do violence to Cooley's writings. As an author, he *was* critical of government intervention, and he *did* vigorously support the right to private property, along with other rights. What they chose to ignore was the complexity of his position insofar as his advocacy of government restraint was instrumental for the defense of equal rights. The flavor of this complexity can be found in an article Cooley wrote in reaction to the Supreme Court's important 1877 decision in *Munn* v. *Illinois*.[86] In this case, the Court upheld rather broad regulatory powers for the states. Cooley criticized Chief Justice Morrison R. Waite's loose language in allowing state regulation over businesses "affected with a public interest." He found this standard too flexible to ensure proper protection for private property. This, however, was not the only problem with Waite's loose standard. Cooley found lurking in state regulatory power over business "affected with a public interest" an invitation to monopoly and class legislation.

This twofold concern goes to the heart of Cooley's jurisprudence and, along with his views on corporations as state instruments, helps to explain the broad support for his appointment as first chairman of the ICC. It also helps to explain the conciliatory style that characterized the commission's posture toward the railroads during its first year, as well as the adversarial stance during the rest of Cooley's tenure. When he found the railroads intransigent, he could respond in kind. His responses included expansive interpretations of ICC statutory powers, unembarrassed reliance on administrative discretion, and forthright appeals to Congress for still more power. Nor did he shrink from using his office as a "bully pulpit" to attack the morality of railroad managers. In an address to a group of general managers of railroads in 1888, he acknowledged that his remarks might sound more like those of a clergyman than of a railroad commissioner. He then unleashed a tirade against sharp business practices and ordered the managers to "stand before the community in some other light than as lawbreakers."[87]

Unfortunately, Cooley's health was not equal to the regimen he had imposed upon himself. He suffered pneumonia in 1888 and an epileptic seizure in the following year. His health continued to deteriorate until his resignation in September 1891.

Henry Carter Adams, the famous economist who headed the statistics bureau of the ICC, considered Cooley's ill health a "national calamity."[88] He drew a persuasive analogy between Cooley's activist interpretation of the commission's power and Chief Justice Marshall's interpretation of the Constitution. I am inclined to agree with Adams that the brevity of Cooley's tenure at the ICC—just four and one-half years—was a "national calamity"; but I would reach this conclusion for reasons somewhat different from those of Adams. Adams made his comment in 1898—the year following two Supreme Court opinions that virtually unraveled the regulatory scheme Cooley had put in place. One decision overturned an important ICC ruling on the famous "short haul" clause of the ICA, and the other rejected the ICC's contention that it had implied statutory power to set railroad rates.[89] These decisions were indeed calamitous for the ICC's early efforts, and one might well surmise that if Cooley had served as chairman for a decade or so, his presence might have prompted a more favorable response from the Court.

Be that as it may, I look upon Cooley's untimely resignation as "a national calamity" from today's perspective, rather than from the perspective of whatever immediate effect it might have had on such museum pieces as the short-haul clause and the fixing of railroad rates. To indulge the weakness for speculating on history's "might have beens," I see Cooley's resignation as a calamity because he might have given the administrative state the kind of constitutional respectability it has never had.

There are several reasons for this speculation. First, and most importantly, there is the man himself. He was the foremost constitutional authority of his day, with twenty years' experience as a highly respected justice of a prestigious state supreme court. He had a principled basis for introducing regulation of industry in a manner that was compatible with constitutional traditions, the intellectual force to think through the implications of these principles, and the prudence to apply them in a sensible manner.

Second, there is the consideration that Cooley's reputation might have softened judicial hostility toward the ICC and the subsequent regulatory agencies that were made in its image. Throughout his career, Cooley had been an advocate of judicial restraint—a simple corollary of his early Jacksonian beliefs that was integrated into his traditional understanding of separation of powers.[90] The leading nineteenth-century advocate of judicial restraint, James Bradley Thayer, has explicitly acknowledged that he follows Cooley in this matter.[91] Cooley's position on the judiciary was skillfully integrated into an elegant, if somewhat conventional, treatment of separation of powers. With Cooley at the helm of the ship of the administrative state, conscientious judges might have been a bit more willing to let her "sail on." Judges whose commitment to laissez faire followed Cooley much further than Cooley had ever led might have broadened their discipleship to include the master's teaching on judicial restraint as well.[92]

Third, there is the effect Cooley might have had on the Supreme Court's doctrine that due process means judicial process. This doctrine surfaced in the famous *Minnesota Rate* case, which was decided during Cooley's tenure at the ICC. The case involved a severe regulatory scheme in Minnesota that fixed intrastate railroad rates in such a way as to preclude review by the state courts. The Supreme Court of the United States found this exclusion unconstitutional. In an opinion that had the dubious distinction of being at once sweeping and garbled, Justice Samuel Blatchford interpreted the due process clause to require judicial review of governmental activity that was as legislative in nature as rate making seemed to be. Hence, the summary description of the holding as "due process means judicial process."

Although the case directly involved state governments, the implications for the ICC were ominous, since the due process clause of the Fifth Amendment limited the federal government. It would be but a small step for the Court to apply the same due process ruling against the ICC. Cooley feared that the integrity of the administrative process would be severely compromised if the commission's fact finding were subject to judicial review. In the Annual Report of the ICC for 1890, he vigorously attacked the judicial practice of taking original testimony upon appeal from ICC decisions. He declared this practice "fatal to effective regulation."[93]

Cooley's fears were well founded. In 1897 the Supreme Court exercised review over the ICC's fact finding with a boldness it might not have displayed had Cooley still been chairman.[94] The reason for this conjecture is that Cooley was in a particularly strong position to defend the commission against judicial encroachment through the due process clause. In the very first edition of his *Limitations*—some twenty years before the *Minnesota Rate* case, he had developed his position on due process without linking it necessarily to the courts.[95] As a justice of the Michigan Supreme Court, he had been quite explicit in insisting that the demands of due process could be met in governmental institutions other than courts; this included administrative agencies.[96] Thus Cooley was both in the battle and above it. He could defend his commission's independence from the courts without being vulnerable to the criticism of simply protecting his turf. He was, of course, protecting his turf when he argued in 1890 that courts should not review the commission's fact finding; but he was doing so on the basis of a constitutional principle he had articulated both in his judicial opinions and in his authoritative treatise long before he came to the ICC.

The question of whether due process requires judicial process has taken many forms over the past century; it is still with us today.[97] Congressional efforts to exclude the judiciary from the administrative process have proved ineffective against courts that were determined to intervene.[98] I am inclined to believe that in a regime of separation of powers, a definitive solution to the problem is beyond the wit of man. It would involve nothing less than a definitive solution to the proper role of the judiciary in United States government. It takes nothing from Cooley to say he could not have solved this problem. What he might have done, however, is to have illuminated the problem in a way that would have headed off the crushing defeat the ICC and its progeny suffered at the hands of the Court in 1897.

The fourth and final reason for thinking that Cooley might have won constitutional respectability for the administrative state is the responsible manner in which the ICC carried out its administrative tasks under his leadership. We have seen that Cooley was a vigorous administrator. I have stressed this aspect of his work to correct the false image of Cooley as simply a laissez-faire apologist. To present a balanced picture of Cooley as an administrator, we should note that where constitutional principles were involved, Cooley had an admirable sense of administrative restraint.

For example, in the Annual Report of the ICC for 1890, he criticized the judicial tendency to equate due process with judicial process but then proceeded to urge Congress to draw up a set of statutory procedures that would safeguard the ICC from some of the administrative excesses the Supreme Court had noted in the Minnesota regulatory scheme.[99] Cooley's strategy was to preserve the independence of the agency from the courts by petitioning Congress to legislate procedures that would reduce the likelihood of administrative abuse and thereby make the ICC a less likely target of close judicial scrutiny.[100] In this, Cooley was decades ahead of his time. The specific proposals he mentioned anticipate some of the happier aspects of the Administrative Procedure Act of 1946.[101] Unfortunately, Congress ignored Cooley's recommendation, and even more unfortunately, within a year, Cooley had resigned from the commission. Had Cooley importuned Congress on these matters for a decade or so, we might have had a regularized administrative procedure by the turn of the century.

Another example of administrative restraint on Cooley's part was his scrupulous deference to the Seventh Amendment's requirement that a jury trial be made available in suits at common law "where the value in controversy shall exceed twenty dollars." In the ICC's first annual report, Cooley noted that the commission had been pressed to award damages to complainants who provided evidence to support grievances against a carrier under the commission's jurisdiction. The report noted that in the absence of an explicit statutory authorization to make such awards, the commission would not do so.[102] The report then opined that even if Congress should grant such an authorization, it would be difficult to square it with the jury-trial requirement of the Seventh Amendment. Congress ignored the commission's scruples and in 1889 conferred explicit authority upon the ICC to make reparations awards which would be enforced through the courts. Under Cooley's leadership, the commission refused to use this new power. In its Annual Report for 1891, Cooley's last year with the commission, the ICC explained its refusal to consider reparation awards on the grounds that such a question "seemed so peculiarly suitable for jury trial, [that] it was deemed proper to leave it for determination in the courts."[103]

Thus, the ICC under Cooley's leadership provides the extraordinary example of a vigorous administrative agency explaining to Congress its failure to use certain explicit statutory powers on the grounds that the exercise of such powers might be in violation of the Constitution. Had Cooley's health allowed him to remain on the commission, perhaps the example of a self-imposed constitutional restraint on administrative power—a decision made independently of the courts and of Congress—would not seem so extraordinary today. The commission's self-denying action carried the clear implication that it was ultimately responsible to the Constitution, rather than to the will of elected officials.

At the time of his unfortunate resignation, Thomas Cooley, the constitutionalist turned regulator, seemed to be leading the ICC toward providing a wholesome example of administrative statesmanship for a constitutional republic in an industrial age.

# PART 3

## FOUNDING THE ADMINISTRATIVE STATE IN DEED: THE NEW DEAL

> On this solemn anniversary I ask that the American people rejoice in the wisdom of their Constitution. . . . I ask that they give their fealty to the Constitution *itself* and not to its misinterpreters. I ask that they exalt the glorious simplicity of its purposes rather than a century of complicated legalism.
>
> —Franklin D. Roosevelt, Constitution Day, 20 September 1937

In Part 2 we found in the early writings of Woodrow Wilson both a reaffirmation and a rejection of the views of the framers of the Constitution. Like the framers, Wilson was partial to high-toned government by the better sort; but unlike them, he had no confidence in separation of powers. In the face of a rising immigrant population, Wilson restated the social values of the framers, even as he was rejecting their constitutional principles. Because Wilson was an academic writer free from the burden of carrying out his own ideas in practice, he could afford to be cavalier about the actual framework of government.

Not so the men and women of the New Deal, whose thoughts we examine in Part 3. Many of them were academics; but regardless of their backgrounds, all of them felt the hot breath of events as they put their ideas into practice. Because these ideas would become incarnate in a regime of separation of powers, few New Dealers were inclined to question openly the fundamental structure of the polity.[1] They were not timid; they questioned everything else. Their ideas were often bold and sometimes radical. They eagerly embraced the democratic spirit of the times with a zest that surely would have appalled the patrician framers of 1787. Thus, like Woodrow Wilson, the New Dealers at once reaffirmed and rejected the views of the framers. They rejected the social

111

values of the framers but reaffirmed their constitutional principles. Wilson had done just the opposite.

The New Dealers made the better choice. It was a choice Publius would have grudgingly approved. He knew times would change and values with them. The need to anticipate and accommodate drastic, unforeseen changes is thematic in *The Federalist*.[2] Publius defended his constitution on the grounds that it would be flexible enough to permit this accommodation without permanently endangering individual rights. This was because Publius knew the structure of his constitution was rooted in man's unchanging nature.[3] The New Dealers, perhaps more from necessity than from conviction, worked within Publius's structure to bring about changes that were intended to safeguard the purposes of the Constitution in an industrial age.

In choosing to fill old structures with new values, the New Dealers provided a wholesome example for their administrative progeny. It is not the task of administration to challenge constitutional principles.[4] This is best done, in word, by philosophers and, in deed, by revolutionaries. It is emphatically, however, the administrator's task to understand changing values and abiding principles and the difference between them. Alertness in these matters enables administrators to join judges and elected officials in making real their oath to uphold the Constitution of the United States.

Part 3 follows the New Dealers as they go about their task of founding a modern administrative state within the framework of an eighteenth-century Constitution. Not all New Dealers, of course, were committed to an administrative state. For those who were, however, the primary task was to establish the centralized government that is the precondition of an administrative state. To do this they advanced simultaneously on two fronts: (1) to make the federal government supreme over the nation's economy and (2) to make the executive branch of the federal government supreme over Congress and the courts. On the first front, they swept the field; on the second, they settled for a negotiated peace. The effort to achieve executive supremacy through delegation from Congress was defeated by the Supreme Court's 1935 decision in the *Schechter* case.[5] The effort to reach the same end through reorganization of the government was defeated by Congress when it rejected the recommendations of the Report of the Brownlow Committee in 1937.[6] These setbacks were only partial, however. The courts applied the *Schechter* principle gingerly,[7] and in 1939 the Congress gave the president many of the reorganization powers it had denied him in rejecting the Brownlow Report. The most important limiting principles on executive power came from within the ranks of the New Dealers themselves. In the spirit of the framers' unswerving commitment to individual rights and the Anti-Federalists' suspicion of executive power, thoughtful New Dealers in the late 1930s and the early 1940s developed principles to curb the excesses of the administrative state they had created. These principles were announced in 1941 in the *Report of the Attorney General's Committee on Administrative Procedure*.[8]

Our examination of the constitutional principles in this third founding will center around three great arguments: (1) the national-supremacy argument; (2) the executive-supremacy argument; and (3) the individual-rights argument. The three chapters that follow examine these three arguments.

# 8

# National Supremacy

Let the end be legitimate, let it be within the scope of the Constitution, and all means which are appropriate, which are plainly adapted to that end, which are not prohibited, but consist with the letter and spirit of the Constitution, are constitutional.

—Chief Justice John Marshall, in *McCulloch* v. *Maryland* (1819)

The story of President Roosevelt's titanic struggle with the Supreme Court over New Deal legislation has been told often and well.[1] By narrowly interpreting the constitutional power of Congress to regulate commerce among the states, the Court severely limited the scope of federal intervention in economic affairs. Conversely, by a broad interpretation of the due process clause of the Fourteenth Amendment, the Court restricted the power of the states to regulate their own economies. The result of these two lines of constitutional interpretation was the creation of an economic "no man's land" that was free from regulation by both state and federal governments.

Aspects of the nation's economy that involved manufacturing, mining, and agriculture could not be reached by the federal government because the courts had sharply distinguished these activities from "commerce," which alone could be reached. Wages and working conditions in many of those activities were off-limits to the state governments as well, because these were contractual matters included by the Court in the "liberty" that the Fourteenth Amendment protected from state interference through its due process clause.

Thus, by judicial interpretation, a laissez-faire economic theory had been read into the Constitution of the United States that effectively blocked state and federal efforts to address the economic problems of the Great Depression.

115

Roosevelt eventually triumphed over the Court by parlaying his outstanding reelection triumph in 1936 and his heady threat to "pack" the Court with judges of a more friendly persuasion. Helpful too were the retirement of some conservative justices and a change of heart by others who remained. By the late 1930s the Supreme Court had overruled or disregarded many of the precedents that had once stood in the way of New Deal reform. Both the commerce clause and the due process clause had been tamed, and the Constitution had been reinterpreted to clear the way for the regulatory/administrative state that the New Dealers envisioned.

FDR's struggle with the Court is one of the most interesting stories in United States history. At times, however, the moral drawn from the story is not always helpful for legitimating the administrative state that was the upshot of Roosevelt's triumph. For example, a standard American-history textbook during the 1950s told students that one of the lessons of Roosevelt's victory was "the inability of any department, including the Supreme Court, to resist indefinitely the popular will."[2] There is much to be said for this observation, but it creates the impression that the constitutional triumph of the New Deal can be explained exclusively in terms of considerable political power being brought to bear over a sufficiently long period of time to effect the desired changes. At times this "persevering majority" argument is linked to a hint of cowardice on the part of certain justices—notably Justice Owen J. Roberts, who dramatically changed his interpretation of fundamental constitutional principles at the very time when President Roosevelt was asking Congress for the power to increase the number of judges on the Supreme Court from nine to fifteen. Roberts's change of heart has been cleverly described as "the switch in time that saved nine."[3] Today, historians tend to treat Roberts more kindly, because there is considerable evidence that he had advised his judicial brethren of his "switch" prior to the announcement of FDR's court-packing plan. One historian absolves Roberts of the charge of caving in to presidential pressure only to surmise that it was FDR's decisive electoral victory in 1936 that turned Roberts around. Thus the aphorism about switches in time is replaced with Mr. Dooley's famous line from the turn of the century: "No matter whether th' constitution follows th' flag or not, th' supreme coort follows th' iliction returns."[4]

There is more to the constitutional triumph of the New Deal than popular will, presidential threats, decisive elections, and astute (or cowardly) judges. There are also questions of constitutional principles, which inform and give meaning to the interesting men and events that dazzle the political realist. If the administrative state is to be legitimated in terms of constitutional priniciple, we must go beyond the positivist position that as a matter of fact, the Supreme Court has upheld its founding in the New Deal period. We must look at the efforts of the New Dealers themselves to justify the new order they were founding as something that was compatible with the constitutional order that the framers had established in 1787.

To do this we shall examine the way in which the New Dealers would weave the "intent of the framers" into the fabric of their constitutional arguments in support of New Deal proposals. There was much "law office history" in these endeavors.[5] These men were advocates, not historians. They spoke their constitutional lines as actors in a great constitutional drama. Our inquiry is aimed at evaluating them, not as historians, but as statesmen. We are not grading term papers for schoolboys. We are examining the writings of the founders of our modern administrative state to see if they made a serious and plausible effort to square their innovations with the founding principles of the regime.

We shall examine their efforts under three headings: (1) the commerce clause; (2) the general welfare clause; and (3) the necessary and proper clause.

## THE COMMERCE CLAUSE

The Congress shall have Power . . . To regulate Commerce with foreign Nations, and among the several States, and with the Indian Tribes.
—Article 1, section 8

The most notable attempt by a New Dealer to return to the framers for guidance on the meaning of the commerce clause appeared in an article in the *Harvard Law Review* in 1934.[6] The author was Robert L. Stern, a recent graduate of Harvard Law School, who began his government career in the Interior Department and later joined the Solicitor General's staff at Justice. Stern's article was extremely influential. It was cited repeatedly in government briefs supporting New Deal legislation.[7]

The article was significant not only for its content but in its title and structure as well. Its title was "That Commerce Which Concerns More States Than One." These words were taken from Chief Justice Marshall's interpretation of the meaning of "commerce among the several states" in *Gibbons* v. *Ogden* (1824), the first major case in which the Supreme Court had construed the commerce clause.[8] By using Marshall's language, Stern was reminding his readers that neither the Constitution itself nor its most celebrated expositor, John Marshall, had used the popular term "interstate commerce." That was a later gloss both on the Constitution and on Marshall's authoritative interpretation. For New Dealers the gloss was unfortunate, because it invited a narrow interpretation of the commerce clause, such as "the movement of commodities or persons or information across state lines."[9] If this was all that the federal government could reach through its regulatory powers, the New Deal would be a modest endeavor indeed.

To this day we speak of the "Interstate Commerce Clause"; so we must conclude that Stern's effort to purify our language was unsuccessful. He even failed to get his fellow New Dealers to change their ways. Roosevelt himself continued to refer to "the Interstate Commerce Clause" in the very act of excoriating the Supreme Court for its narrow interpretation of the meaning of "commerce among the several states."[10]

The structure of Stern's article is also of interest. Its two major sections are entitled "I. The Constitution" and "II. The Court." The implication of this structure was bold and clear: The Constitution says one thing about commerce; the Court has said something else. This distinction led Stern back to the framers and to the text of the Constitution, where he found a meaning of "commerce among the several states" that was congenial to the exigencies of a modern administrative state. Stern beat a path that would become quite familiar to New Deal lawyers and speech writers. As the courts become more hostile, the framers became more important to New Deal strategists. They saw in the framers ancient and venerable allies who would stand in judgment on the erring courts of the 1930s.

Stern begins his analysis of the constitutional language with the flat assertion that "the Constitutional Convention was called because the Articles of Confederation had not given the Federal Government any power to regulate commerce."[11] He supports his point by highlighting the emphasis on commerce in the resolution of the Virginia General Assembly, which called for the Annapolis Convention of 1786. This convention led to the Philadelphia Convention, which opened on 25 May 1787. Not surprisingly, Stern stresses the broad language of the Virginia Plan, which was presented at the beginning of the Constitutional Convention and was approved by nine of the ten states present on 31 May. The sixth resolution of that plan included the provision "that the National Legislature ought to be impowered to enjoy the legislative Rights vested in Congress by the Confederation & moreover to legislate in all cases to which the separate States are incompetent, or in which the harmony of the United States may be interrupted by the exercise of individual Legislation."[12]

The reference to the incompetence of the states was particularly important for Stern's argument. The New Deal rested on the assumption that the states were incompetent to handle the economic crisis of the 1930s. Few state governments challenged this assumption. The States' rights case was made by private interests hostile to New Deal regulatory schemes. It was not uncommon for state attorneys general to file amicus curiae briefs in support of New Deal programs that were being attacked for invading the sphere of state activity. The New Dealers would have no trouble demonstrating the incompetence of state economic regulation during the 1930s.[13] Hence the importance of the sixth resolution of the Virginia Plan. It showed that at the very outset of the convention the overwhelming majority of the framers were willing to vest in the proposed national legislature a power "to legislate in all cases to which the separate states are incompetent." Such language would have included much more than commerce.

Stern recounts the reaction that set in at the convention with the presentation of Patterson's New Jersey Plan, which would have narrowed Congress's power so that it could "pass Acts for the regulation of trade and commerce as well with foreign nations as with each other." James Wilson contrasted the two plans by saying that under the Virginia Plan "the National Legislature is to make laws in all cases at which the several states are incompetent"; whereas under the New Jersey Plan "in place of this Congress are to have additional power in a few cases only." Stern is pleased to report that on June the nineteenth the New Jersey Plan was rejected and "the Virginia Plan re-approved by a vote of seven states to three, one being divided."[14]

On 17 July the sixth resolution of the amended Virginia Plan was again under discussion as part of the report of the Committee of the Whole House. After rejecting an amendment proposed by Roger Sherman that would have narrowed the scope of congressional power, the convention approved expansive language urged by Gunning Bedford, Jr., of Delaware. By a vote of eight states to two the convention adopted Bedford's proposal permitting Congress "to legislate in all cases for the general interests of the Union and also in those to which the States are separately incompetent, or in which the harmony of the United States may be interrupted by the exercise of individual Legislation."

This resolution, along with many others, was referred to the Committee of Detail, whose task was to draft a constitution out of the various resolutions the committee had approved. The committee made its report on 6 August. It had changed the indefinite language of the sixth resolution into an enumeration of powers that closely resembled what would eventually become section 8 of article 1 of the Constitution. Among those enumerated powers the committee included: "To regulate commerce with foreign nations and among the several states."

Stern finds great significance in the fact that the convention "accepted *without discussion* the enumeration of powers made by a committee which had been directed to prepare a constitution based upon the general propositions that the federal government was to 'legislate in all cases for the general interests of the Union . . . and in those to which the states are separably incompetent.' "[15] Stern argues that the convention's acquiescence in the committee's change from indefinite to enumerated powers is "susceptible of only one explanation—that the Convention believed that the enumeration conformed to the standard previously approved, and that the powers enumerated comprehended those matters as to which the states were incompetent and in which national legislation was essential."[16]

Since the commerce clause was the only enumerated power that would enable Congress to regulate trade or business, Stern concludes that the convention must have seen in the commerce clause all the power over trade or business that the national government would need to solve problems that the states separately would be unable to meet. Since "centralized commercial regulation was universally recognized as the primary reason for preparing a new constitution, the Convention would not have been likely to have meant the commerce clause to have a narrow or restrictive meaning.''[17]

Stern goes on to analyze speeches made at the convention after the commerce clause had been adopted and finds further support for his broad interpretation.[18] He draws a similar conclusion both from an argument based on internal consistency in the text of the Constitution itself and from the definition of the words *commerce* and *among* in eighteenth-century dictionaries.[19]

Stern's work is not without flaws. He probably sees too much importance in the convention's silence on the shift from indefinite to enumerated powers in the 6 August report of the Committee on Detail. His inferences are persuasive but not convincing. At times he pays too little attention to the context in which the convention discussed the broad language of the sixth resolution of the Virginia Plan.[20] At other times he ignores the significance of variations in the text he cites.[21] These, however, are matters that invite judgment on Stern's capacity as a historian—a judgment that is beyond our purposes. What is sufficient for our purposes is that Robert Stern, a New Deal activist who played an important role in important New Deal cases,[22] took the trouble to present a serious, informed, and plausible interpretation of the commerce clause that would support the sort of centralized economic power the new administrative state would demand.

## THE GENERAL WELFARE CLAUSE

The Congress shall have Power To lay and collect Taxes, Duties, Imposts and Excises, to pay the Debts and Provide for the common Defence and general Welfare of the United States.

—Article 1, section 8

The term "general welfare" appears twice in the Constitution; once in the Preamble and once in section 8 of article 1, where the powers of Congress are enumerated. In the Preamble the promotion of the general welfare is listed as one of the six purposes for which the Constitution was ordained and established. Because the Preamble is technically not part of the Constitution and therefore is not legally enforceable, most of the controversy surrounding the term "general welfare" has centered on article 1, where Congress is declared to have the power "To lay and collect Taxes, Duties, Imposts and Excises, to pay the Debts and Provide for the common Defence and general Welfare of the United States."

Controversies concerning the meaning of the general welfare clause were not long in coming. During the last days of the Constitutional Convention, a committee of five was appointed "to revise the stile of and arrange the articles which had been agreed to by the house."[23] Some of the convention's staunchest nationalists were included on the five-man committee, composed of Alexander Hamilton, Gouverneur Morris, James Madison, Rufus King, and William Johnson.

According to Madison's notes, the draft reported by the Committee of Style had a semicolon between the word "Excises" and the clause beginning "to pay."[24] This punctuation invited the interpretation that Congress had a power to lay and collect taxes, duties, imposts, and excises and an *independent* power to pay the debts and to provide for the common defense and general welfare of the United States. Such an interpretation was not in accord with the previous decisions of the convention. It would seem to render superfluous the subsequent enumeration of powers in the remainder of article 1, section 8: for example, the power to borrow money, to regulate commerce, to declare war, and so forth. If Congress can provide for the general welfare, what need is there for any other specific power? Before the final version of the Constitution was engrossed, the error was caught by Roger Sherman. A comma assumed its rightful place, dislodging the upstart semicolon.

This grammatical legerdemain was not soon forgotten. For several years thereafter, Gouverneur Morris, the principal draftsman of the Committee of Style, was accused of trying to trick the convention into approving a document that was more suited to his nationalist vision than the framers really intended.[25] As late as 1830—more than forty years after the convention—an aged James Madison was still attacking spurious texts of the Constitution that had smuggled in the nationalistic semicolon.

President Franklin Roosevelt took some liberties with the general welfare clause during the height of his struggle with the Supreme Court. In a radio address on 9 March 1937 the president explained to the American people why he thought it imperative to increase the number of justices on the Supreme Court. He solemnly proclaimed that we have "reached the point as a Nation where we must take action to save the Constitution from the Court and the Court from itself." FDR enlisted the services of the general welfare clause in his attack on the Court. First he assured his listeners that the Constitution is "an easy document to understand" as long as one remembers the broad purposes for which it was drawn up to enable the new nation "to meet each and every problem which then had a national character and which could not be met by merely local action." He added: "But the framers went further. Having in mind that in succeeding generations many other problems then undreamed of would become national problems, they gave to the Congress the ample broad powers 'to levy taxes * * * and provide for the common defense and general welfare of the United States.'"[26]

In a radio address the listener, of course, would have no way of knowing about the hiatus in the quoted text. It may have been inadvertence on the president's part that led him to substitute "levy" for "lay and collect"; but it was not inadvertence that prompted him to mislead the listener into thinking the Constitution gave Congress an unqualified power to provide for the general welfare. This was clearly the meaning of Roosevelt's edited text. Such tampering with the Constitution was secular blasphemy in the serious setting of a nationwide address on a constitutional issue of the highest order. It was particularly offensive in the one officer in the Republic whose oath of office is spelled out in the Constitution itself, an oath in which he pledges that he will "to the best of my Ability, preserve, protect, and defend the Constitution of the United States."[27]

Roosevelt's distortion of the text of the Constitution was both unwise and unnecessary. Much of his radio address faithfully reflected the broad goals of the framers. He had a strong case to make against the Court without fudging the evidence. There is an elegant irony, however, in FDR's choice of the general welfare clause as the object of his fudging. In distorting the meaning of that particular clause, he follows the example of no less a founding father than Gouverneur Morris.

Fortunately, not all New Dealers followed FDR's bad example in their treatment of the general welfare clause. A particularly good example was set by attorneys from the Justice and Agriculture departments in the government's brief in *U.S.* v. *Butler* (1936), an important case in which the Supreme Court declared unconstitutional the centerpiece of New Deal agricultural policy, the Agricultural Adjustment Act of 1933.[28]

This case is famous on several counts. For one, it featured Justice Roberts's celebrated statement of "mechanical jurisprudence," which has provided generations of legal realists with no end of merriment. For Justice Roberts, the Court's task is simply "to lay the article of the Constitution which is invoked beside the statute which is challenged and to decide whether the latter squares with the former."[29]

*Butler* is also famous for the extremely bitter dissent of Justice Harlan Fiske Stone, in which Justices Louis D. Brandeis and Benjamin N. Cardozo joined. Roosevelt and his supporters used this dissent to great advantage in their effort to pack the Court. Some of Stone's language was interpreted as a virtual invitation for reprisals against an irresponsible Supreme Court. Particularly memorable were his references to his judicial brethrens' "tortured construction of the Constitution" and his menacing reminder to them that "courts are not the only agency of government that must be assumed to have capacity to govern."[30]

As a matter of constitutional law, *Butler* is famous for its interpretation that followed closely the argument in the government's brief. The case involved federal payments to farmers who had agreed to reduce production as part of a government plan to stabilize agricultural prices. The funds for paying the farmers came from a federal tax on processors of agricultural commodities.

Butler, a receiver for a bankrupt cotton mill, refused to pay the tax on the grounds that it was not really a tax at all, but simply a step in a regulatory scheme intended to control agricultural production. Because agriculture, like mining and manufacturing, was not part of commerce, Butler maintained that it could not be regulated by the federal government.

The government's strategy in the case was to rely on the general welfare clause. Counsel for the government argued that the United States was simply taxing and spending to provide for the general welfare of the nation by maintaining price stability in agricultural commodities. The commerce clause was irrelevant.[31]

To make this argument the government had to blaze a trail, because, remarkably, prior to *Butler,* there had never been an authoritative Supreme Court decision that bore directly upon the meaning of the general welfare clause. A crucial issue in the case, then, was what does general welfare mean. To answer this question, the government's lawyers returned to the writings of the framers of the Constitution, where they found a narrow interpretation associated with James Madison and a broad interpretation attributed to Alexander Hamilton.

The brief maintained that both Madison and Hamilton had interpreted the general welfare clause as a limitation on the powers of Congress to tax and to spend. Neither of them believed that Congress had an independent power to provide for the general welfare as one of several enumerated powers. Thus the government brief rejected the position suggested in both the questionable punctuation attributed to Gouverneur Morris and in Roosevelt's radio editing of the general welfare clause. Although Madison and Hamilton agreed that the general welfare clause stated one of the purposes for which Congress could tax and spend, they disagreed on what "general welfare" means. Madison maintained that the term included only those powers enumerated in section 8: naturalization, bankruptcies, coining money, establishing post offices, maintaining armies, and so forth. Hamilton saw it differently. In the famous *Report on Manufactures,* which he submitted as secretary of the Treasury, Hamilton argued that the term could not be restricted to the enumerated powers because the new government would then be unable to tax and spend to meet the "numerous exigencies incident to the affairs of a nation."[32] An expansive term such as "general welfare" was needed to cover unforeseen events "which are susceptible neither of specification nor of definition."[33] Hamilton conceded, however, that the generality of the language allowed one important qualification. The welfare involved had to be general. The purpose for which an appropriation is made must "be general and not local: its operation extending, in fact, or by possibility, throughout the Union, and not being confined to a particular spot."[34]

Not surprisingly, the government's lawyers favored Hamilton. They attacked Madison's position as rendering the general welfare clause meaningless if it stood for only the sum of enumerated powers. In this cause they enlisted the authority of Justice Joseph Story's celebrated commentaries on the Constitution.[35] Story rejected the Madisonian interpretation because "it robs the [general welfare] clause of all efficacy and meaning." According to Story, one should be extremely cautious in assuming that a part of the Constitution is without meaning. This is even more true when the words have a meaning that is "natural and appropriate to the language" in its context; as is the case if one reads general welfare as one of the purposes for which Congress can tax and spend. Story maintains that if Madison were correct, the framers would have said "to provide for the common defense and general welfare in the manner following *viz.*"[36] They then would have listed the specific powers that constituted the general welfare.

Not content with so distinguished a jurist as Story, the government's attorneys next turned to Chief Justice Marshall for support. Whereas Story's *Commentaries* had spoken directly to the issue of the general welfare clause, Marshall's help was oblique but politically significant in the milieu of New Deal controversy. New Dealers had frequently been attacked for their "loose construction" of the Constitution and had been urged to return to the high ground of "strict construction" associated with the Jeffersonian origins of the Democratic party. The government's brief defended the broad interpretation of general welfare by citing the following passage from Marshall's opinion in *Gibbons* v. *Ogden*[37] and, in so doing, tamed the self-righteousness of the strict constructionists:

> This instrument contains an enumeration of powers expressly granted by the people to their government. It has been said, that these powers ought to be construed strictly. But why ought they to be so construed? Is there one sentence in the constitution which gives countenance to this rule? * * * What do gentlemen mean, by a strict construction? If they contend only against that enlarged construction, which would extend their *natural* and *obvious* import, we might question the application of the term, but should not controvert the principle. If they contend for that narrow construction which, in support of some theory not to be found in the constitution, would deny to the government those powers which the words of the grant, *as usually understood,* import, and which are consistent with the general views and objects of the instrument—for that narrow connection, which would cripple the government, and render it unequal to the objects for which it is declared to be instituted, and to which the powers given, *as fairly understood,* render it competent—then we cannot perceive the propriety of this strict construction, nor adopt it as the rule by which the constitution is to be expounded [italics supplied].[38]

Having exposed strict construction to the full force of Marshall's derision, the government's lawyers next turned to the Articles of Confederation. There they found unmistakable evidence of the term "general welfare" being used in the broad sense Madison had rejected. They argued that if the term had a broad meaning under the Articles of Confederation, "which was meant to create only a loose association of independent states," then surely it would not have a narrow meaning under the authentic government created by the Constitution.[39]

This was a rather weak argument. The authors of the Articles of Confederation might well have been far less concerned about a broad delegation to tax and spend for the general welfare than the framers of the Constitution precisely because the confederation was "only a loose association of independent states." Under the Articles, the states retained the power to recall wayward delegates who might be inclined to join forces with peers inclined to abuse the general welfare language. There would be no such safeguard under the Constitution. Many Anti-Federalists faulted the Constitution on this score. They were particularly critical of the fact that senators would vote per capita (as individuals) and not as instructed delegates from the state legislatures who would be subject to immediate recall. It was precisely because the states were giving up so much under the new Constitution that the general welfare clause appeared so menacing.

Although the government's attorneys in *Butler* took the intent of the framers quite seriously, there is one aspect of their argument that recalls the disingenuousness of Gouverneur Morris and of FDR. In stating Madison's position, the government's brief cited two sources. One was a veto message that *President* Madison had sent to Congress shortly before he left office in 1817—thirty years after the Constitutional Convention. The second source was a letter written in 1830—forty-three years after the convention. Madison's position is basically the same in both these documents and is reported accurately in the *Butler* brief. What is missing in the brief, however, is any reference to *Federalist 41,* where Madison makes his first public statement on the general welfare clause, a statement that is remarkably consistent with what he had to say in 1817 and in 1830.[40]

The government's brief is not misleading; it simply is incomplete. It states Madison's position accurately, but it fails to note that the position was the one he held even before the Constitution was ratified. This was Madison's nationalist period, long before the controversies during his presidency over the scope of congressional power. The references in the brief are to relatively obscure sources: Richardson's *Messages and Papers of the Presidents* and Gaillard Hunt's nine-volume edition of *The Writings of James Madison.* These sources would be known to legal historians in the 1930s, but *The Federalist* would be known to everyone.

Why did the government's lawyers ignore *Federalist 41?* Perhaps they did not know about it; but this, I doubt. References to *The Federalist Papers* abound in briefs drawn up by New Deal lawyers,[41] whereas references to Madison's writings other than his convention notes are extraordinary.[42] My guess is that the oversight was deliberate. In pitting Hamilton against Madison, they wanted to mask the fact that the prestigious *Federalist Papers* were against them. As Publius, Hamilton was ominously and uncharacteristically silent on the general welfare clause. The only place in *The Federalist* where he discusses the general welfare directly is in number 23, and there he refers to the phrase as it is used in the Articles of Confederation.[43] Thus, Hamilton as Publius was of no help to the New Dealers on the general welfare clause. As the author of the rejected *Report on Manufactures*—where he was helpful—he would be no match for Madison as the preeminently successful Publius. So the New Dealers decided to ignore Madison as Publius and to present him, instead, first as a politically interested outgoing president and then as a tired old man some forty-three years after the drafting of the Constitution that he was interpreting.

If my surmise is correct, the New Deal lawyers were shrewd but not dishonest. They were advocates, and therefore their situation was quite different from both that of Gouverneur Morris, who was accused of abusing his position as the convention's faithful scribe, and that of President Franklin Roosevelt, who changed the meaning of the Constitution as he was purporting to explain it to the people who looked to him to preserve, protect, and defend it. Indeed, if the New Deal lawyers were as shrewd as my interpretation suggests, it is an indication that they were quite serious about the importance of the framers, and as skillful advocates, they did not want the weight of *The Federalist Papers* opposing them. They left to their adversaries the task of finishing the accurate but incomplete picture they had drawn for the justices of the Supreme Court. They told no lies: what they said was the truth but not the whole truth.[44]

The result of the *Butler* case was as strange as the history of the general welfare clause. Somewhat surprisingly, the conservative court accepted the Hamiltonian view of the meaning of general welfare. On this point, the Court was unanimous. The six-man majority (Roberts, George Sutherland, James C. McReynolds, Willis Van Devanter, Pierce Butler, and Charles Evans Hughes) and three dissenters (Stone, Brandeis, and Cardozo) agreed that the general welfare clause permitted Congress to tax and spend for the general welfare. The Court split, however, on the issue of whether Congress could regulate agriculture through its general welfare powers. The majority said it could not, and so the government lost its case.

The majority based its decision on the Tenth Amendment: "The powers not delegated to the United States by the Constitution, nor prohibited by it to the States, are reserved to the States respectively, or to the people." Justice Roberts maintained that the regulation of agriculture was not a power that had been delegated to the United States, and therefore it remained with the states.

Although there were precedents of recent vintage to support Roberts's broad interpretation of the Tenth Amendment and his exclusion of agriculture from commerce, these precedents should have been irrelevant once the Court had conceded that Congress has the power to tax and spend for the general welfare. To invoke the Tenth Amendment against a power that admittedly had been delegated to Congress was a marked departure from well-established constitutional principles. Chief Justice Marshall, following Hamilton, had held in *McCulloch* v. *Maryland* (1819) that the federal government, "though limited in its powers, is supreme within its sphere of action."[45] This has been a cardinal principle of constitutional law. The federal government is "limited in its powers": that is, there are some spheres of human affairs in which it may not act. Once, however, it is established that the federal government may act in a particular sphere, it is "supreme within its sphere of action." In such spheres the Tenth Amendment cannot be invoked, because it applies only to those powers that are *not* delegated to the United States. It is only the powers that are not delegated that are reserved. Conversely, if a power has been delegated to the United States, it cannot be reserved to the states. The *Butler* majority agreed that the power to tax and spend for the general welfare had been delegated to the federal government. The Agriculture Adjustment Act involved taxing and spending for the general welfare, and therefore it should have been sheltered from the Tenth Amendment. The *Butler* majority was troubled by the fact that the general welfare clause would allow Congress to reach an activity such as agriculture, which it could not reach through the commerce clause. This, of course, ignored the precise point of the Hamiltonian position that Congress has the power to tax and spend for the general welfare because the enumerated powers (such as commerce) are too specific.

In invoking the Tenth Amendment, the *Butler* majority was trying to head off the logical conclusion of its ruling that Congress has the power to tax and spend for the general welfare. The same section of article 1 that gives this power to Congress concludes with a further grant to Congress of the power "To make all Laws which shall be necessary and proper for carrying into Execution the foregoing Powers." One of these "foregoing Powers" is the power to tax and spend for the general welfare. Therefore, Congress has the power to pass any law that is necessary and proper for taxing and spending for the general welfare. As we shall see in the next section, "necessary and proper" has traditionally been interpreted very broadly. By putting the broad interpretations of these two clauses together, it became clear that the national supremacy required by the administrative state would be readily at hand.

The conservatives on the *Butler* court saw this only too well. Their recourse to the Tenth Amendment was a futile flight from the logic of their concession that Congress can tax and spend for the general welfare. Their opinion would have been stronger had they chosen the Madisonian interpretation of the general welfare. They realized, however, that it was too late to follow Madison. For a century and one-half, Americans had been Hamiltonians in practice as they enthusiastically supported the federal government's spending for the general welfare in health, science, social welfare, agriculture, and education.[46]

Like the general welfare clause it interpreted, the *Butler* case is filled with irony. This decision, so reactionary in the short term, soon became one of the cornerstones of the regulatory administrative state. A year later, in 1937, a Supreme Court that had made "its switch in time" used *Butler* to justify a decision upholding challenged sections of the Social Security Act of 1935.[47] *Butler's* Tenth Amendment aberration was soon ignored, but its Hamiltonian interpretation of general welfare waxed mighty in founding the administrative state.[48]

## THE NECESSARY AND PROPER CLAUSE

The Congress shall have Power . . . To make all Laws which shall be necessary and proper for carrying into Execution the foregoing Powers, and all other Powers vested by this Constitution in the Government of the United States, or in any Department or Officer thereof.

—Article 1, section 8

In our examination of the commerce and general welfare clauses, we found the New Dealers examining directly the writings of the framers of the Constitution. Their general welfare arguments took them back to the framers because there were no controlling judicial precedents to guide them. The commerce arguments of the New Dealers did the same, but for a contrary reason—an embarrassing abundance of judicial precedents that were hostile to New Deal objectives.[49]

The necessary and proper clause presented a different situation. Here the New Dealers could cite judicial precedent comfortably, thanks to John Marshall's broad interpretation of "necessary and proper" in *McCulloch* v. *Maryland* (1819).[50] Since *McCulloch,* the courts had followed Marshall's lead in allowing remarkable latitude to the federal government to pass laws necessary and proper to exercise the powers enumerated in article 1, section 8—for example, commerce, naturalization, coining money, and so forth.

It was because the necessary and proper clause had been interpreted so generously that the New Dealers were so anxious to expand the boundaries of the commerce and general welfare clauses. Expansion in these areas produced a double benefit: (1) the federal government could reach the activities freshly drawn within the expanded sphere of general welfare or commerce, and (2) it could pass laws that were necessary and proper for carrying into effect the powers gained over the newly acquired activities. As we saw in the preceding section, the importance of *Butler* lay in its acceptance of the Hamiltonian interpretation of general welfare. Each activity that is swept under the general welfare clause brings in its train endless possibilities for federal regulation through the courts' generous reading of the necessary and proper clause. The upshot of marrying such indefinite terms as "general welfare" and "necessary and proper" was a solid constitutional foundation for the administrative state.

Because the judicial climate was favorable to the New Dealers' version of "necessary and proper," there was no need to return to the framers. To do so could only cause trouble. In the spirit of "if it ain't broke, don't fix it," the New Dealers were content to ignore the framers on the necessary and proper clause. *McCulloch* was their Genesis: in the beginning was John Marshall.

Constitutional latitudinarianism might well number Marshall among the framers. He was a delegate to Virginia's ratifying convention, and therefore he participated formally in the creation of the new government. Although he did not become chief justice until 1801, he is without peer in his influence on the development of the federal judiciary and might be considered a founder in that sense. Important as Marshall is in the history of American constitutional law— and no one is more important—on the necessary and proper clause he is Hamilton's disciple. Of the definitive ruling in *McCulloch,* it can truly be said that the voice was the voice of Marshall, but the hands were the hands of Hamilton.[51]

*McCulloch* v. *Maryland* examined the question of whether the state of Maryland could tax a branch bank of the United States which had been established in Baltimore. Before the question of the constitutionality of the Maryland tax could be addressed, the Supreme Court first had to address the question of whether Congress has the power to charter such a corporation as the Bank of the United States.

The question was not a new one; it had been debated vigorously during President Washington's administration. When the question first arose as to whether Congress had the constitutional power to charter a bank, Washington asked for the opinions of his attorney general, Edmund Randolph; his secretary of state, Thomas Jefferson; and his Treasury secretary, Alexander Hamilton. James Madison, then a member of Congress, had vigorously argued against the constitutionality of such power and had even gone to the trouble of preparing a veto message for the president. Randolph and Jefferson agreed with Madison; Hamilton did not.

The debate was one of the most important in American constitutional history. Indeed, it may be *the* most important. Clinton Rossiter considers Hamilton's opinion in support of the constitutionality of the bank the most brilliant statement ever written on the United States Constitution.[52] The debate on the bank can easily generate superlatives. The fact that congressmen and administrative officers were the leading figures in this debate lends support to FDR's remark, on the one hundred and fiftieth anniversary of the Philadelphia Convention, that the Constitution was intended to be a practical instrument of government and not simply a text awaiting judicial interpretation.

The salient role of administrative officers in this debate is of some importance in an effort to legitimate administrative institutions. No less important is the fact that the substance of the debate was over the creation of an administrative institution: a government corporation. These considerations supplement nicely the fact that the first significant constitutional debate in the First Congress concerned an issue of personnel administration—the removal powers of the president.[53] Together these events help to consolidate the place of Public Administration in the American constitutional tradition.

Jefferson's attack on the constitutionality of the bank rested on a literal interpretation of the word *necessary.* The Constitution permits only those laws that are necessary to enable Congress to exercise its enumerated powers. It is not necessary for Congress to have a bank in order to exercise its power to borrow, to regulate the value of money, and so on. Therefore the bank is unconstitutional.

Hamilton's task centered on showing that the word *necessary* was not confined to the rigid interpretation Jefferson gave it. The word can also mean "needful, requisite, incidental, useful, or conducive to."[54] He found it "a common mode of expression to say, that it is *necessary* for a government or a person to do this or that thing, when nothing more is intended or understood, than that the interests of the government or person require, or will be promoted, by the doing of this or that thing."[55]

Hamilton's linguistic argument would have been strengthened had he pointed out that section 10 of article 1 prohibits any state from taxing exports or imports without congressional approval, and then makes an exception for "what may be absolutely necessary for executing its inspection laws." Thus article 1 draws an explicit distinction between absolute necessity (section 10) and necessity that is less severe (the necessary and proper clause of section 8). This point eventually found its way into the arsenal of the friends of the bank and was used to advantage by Marshall in *McCulloch.*[56]

Hamilton can be forgiven for overlooking a narrow textual argument in support of his position. His sights were trained on higher ground. He saw the bank controversy as a great opportunity to advance his nationalist interpretation of the Constitution. To do this, he identified as the central issue the question of how much power is delegated to Congress in the Constitution. Anticipating Justice Stone's criticism of the *Butler* Court, Hamilton scolded Jefferson and Randolph for citing the Tenth Amendment's provision that "powers not delegated to the United States by the Constitution . . . are reserved to the States respectively, or to the people." The point at issue, he insisted, is what powers have been delegated.

To answer this question, Hamilton called for reliance on "fair reasoning and construction upon the particular provisions of the constitution—taking as guides the general principles and general ends of government." The guides that Hamilton selected are quite significant—"the general principles and general ends of government." Not the principles and ends of this particular government, the federal republic created by the Constitution; but the general principles and ends of any government—of government as such. It is these general principles of government that will tell us what powers have really been delegated to the federal government. His method is deductive. It is based "on the nature of political society."[57]

Applying this method, Hamilton notes three kinds of powers. The first two are well known: implied and expressed. Everyone would acknowledge "that the former are as effectually delegated as the latter."[58] Hamilton then proceeds boldly to maintain that "there is another class of powers, which may be properly denominated *resulting* powers. It will not be doubted that if the United States should make a conquest of any of the territories of its neighbors, they would possess sovereign jurisdiction over the conquered territory. This would rather be a result from the whole mass of the powers of the government and from the nature of political society, than a consequence of either of the powers specially enumerated."[59]

The reference to "resulting powers" clearly suggested that the Constitution had created a government like other governments—a national, consolidated government. Having dropped the mask, Hamilton quickly retrieved it: "But be this as it may, it furnishes a striking illustration of the general doctrine contended for."[60] He then picks up a more conventional line of argument: "To return—It is conceded, that implied powers are to be considered as delegated equally with express ones." He then proceeds with the more cautious argument that the power to charter a bank is a power implied in the expressed powers of Congress to collect taxes, to borrow money, to regulate trade, to raise and maintain fleets and armies, and manage the property of the United States.[61] The exercise of the implied power to charter a bank is necessary and proper (i.e., "needful, requisite, incidental, useful or conducive to") the execution of the expressed powers and is therefore constitutional.

The implied-powers argument was a prudent measure for winning the approval of President Washington. Hamilton was wise to place his primary reliance upon it. His brief and bold sketch of resulting powers, however, was enough to share with Washington and posterity his grand vision of the great commercial empire he cherished.[62] Let Jefferson play Adeimantus in his City of the Sows; Hamilton, like Glaucon, would build a feverish city.[63]

Madison's argument against the bank is quite instructive—especially in view of Hamilton's position on resulting powers. The following paragraph is taken from a lengthy report of Madison's congressional speech on the bank on 2 February 1791:

> He [Madison] here adverted to a distinction, which he said had not been sufficiently kept in view, between a power necessary and proper for the Government or Union, and a power necessary and proper for executing the

enumerated powers. In the latter case, the powers included in the enumerated powers were not expressed, but to be drawn from the nature of each. In
the former, the powers composing the government were expressly enumerated. This constituted the peculiar nature of the Government; no power,
therefore, not enumerated could be inferred from the general nature of
Government. Had the power of making treaties, for example, been omitted,
however necessary it might have been, the defect could only have been
lamented, or supplied by an amendment of the Constitution.[64]

Madison's position is directly opposed to Hamilton's resulting-powers
argument. The necessary and proper clause refers only to powers that are
actually enumerated. It cannot be used to justify laws that are necessary and
proper for political functions that are derived from "the general nature of
government." Thus Madison flatly rejects Hamilton's guidelines. The nature
of government teaches us nothing about the meaning of the Constitution. The
enumerated powers have "constituted the peculiar nature of the Government"—that is, the government of the United States, the only government
that is at issue in the bank controversy. Lest anyone miss the full force of his
point, Madison uses the example of the power to make treaties. If any powers
can be derived from the nature of government, treaty making would seem to be
among them. He who says "government" says "treaty"; but not so for the
United States. If the framers had forgotten to provide for a power to make
treaties, the United States could not make them. Madison's argument is
inductive and positivistic. One learns what powers the government has by
reading them, not by reflecting on the nature of government.[65]

This dispute between the coauthors of *The Federalist Papers* must have
been bittersweet to the erstwhile Anti-Federalists—bitter because it was too
late to undo the Constitution they opposed; sweet because they could say "we
told you so." The Anti-Federalists had argued that the new government was a
hopeless compromise between a consolidated nation, on the one hand, and a
treaty among sovereign states, on the other. The compromise is hopeless
because there is no middle ground between these positions. The Constitution
was denounced as a "spurious brat," a "13 horned monster," and a
"heterogeneous phantom."[66] A cardinal point of Federalist doctrine in the
debate over ratification was the defense of such a middle ground. Patrick
Henry, the most colorful of the Anti-Federalist orators, noted that the
"favoured bantling" would have no name had not James Wilson, "in the
fertility of his genius, suggested the happy epithet of a *Federal Republic.*"[67]

The split between Madison and Hamilton over the bank threatened to
vindicate the Anti-Federalists in a way that not even the genius of James Wilson
could reverse. Hamilton saw the Constitution as the blueprint of a consolidated
national government, while Madison denied that the Constitution permitted the
exercise of any power—*no matter how necessary*—that was simply deduced
from the nature of government. Mount Vernon must have seemed very

pleasant to President Washington in February 1791 as he pondered these weighty matters in far-off Philadelphia.

It was not only James Wilson's theory of a federal republic that came under attack in 1791. His popular-sovereignty theory took heavy losses as well. This was because it so happened that a government corporation was the concrete issue that triggered the high politics of constitutional debate. A well-established legal principle of the time held that the power to form corporations was an attribute of sovereignty. Attorney General Randolph maintained that an implied power to charter a corporation would carry the further implication that the federal government was sovereign. Hamilton's reply was that the federal government *is* sovereign, but only "in relation to the objects intrusted to the management of its care."[68]

This line of reasoning led Hamilton to the conclusion that the federal government is sovereign as to some matters and the states are sovereign as to others. This invocation of sovereignty meant that as long as the federal government stayed within its proper sphere, it could not be challenged by the states.

It was unfortunate, but perhaps inevitable, that the debate over the bank reopened the Anti-Federalists' issue of sovereignty. In so doing, it undercut James Wilson's brilliant argument that only the people are sovereign and *that they would remain so* even after establishing the new government. The beauty of Wilson's theory was that he saved the traditional principle that sovereign power is indivisible and integrated it into the new federal republic—a philosophical tour de force. Hamilton's position on limited sovereignty was a contradiction in terms, however effective it might have been in answering Randolph. It was a clever answer, but one that exacted a high price because it compromised the fundamental theory of the Constitution.

For Hamilton, the specific areas in which the federal government is sovereign provided the criterion for resolving questions of constitutionality. Fortunately for the long-term interests of sound constitutional theory, Hamilton was able to state this criterion without making any mention of sovereignty: "This criterion is the *end* to which the measure related as a *mean*. If the end be clearly comprehended within any of the specified powers, and if the measure have an obvious relation to that end, and is not forbidden by any particular provision of the constitution—it may safely be deemed to come within the compass of national authority."[69]

In Marshall's skillful hands, nearly three decades later, Hamilton's language was revised into the sonorous prose of one of the most important sentences in American constitutional history: "Let the end be legitimate, let it be within the scope of the constitution, and all means which are appropriate, which are plainly adapted to that end, which are not prohibited, but consist with the letter and spirit of the constitution, are constitutional."[70]

It is fortunate that in these often-quoted words the undergirdings of sovereignty have disappeared without a trace. The constitutional case for the administrative state needs both the expansive reading of the necessary and proper clause and the theory that sovereignty remains in the people.

Marshall's adaptation of Hamilton's opinion on the bank was a favorite quote in briefs for New Deal programs. An elaborate chain of reasoning that rested on the necessary and proper clause was central to New Deal strategy. Even though commerce might not include manufacturing, the New Dealers argued that Congress could nevertheless regulate labor relations in the steel industry. This was because disorderly labor relations lead to strikes, and strikes disrupt production, and reduced production has an adverse impact on commerce, which Congress is explicitly authorized to regulate.[71]

The necessary and proper clause required a less-elaborate line of reasoning when enumerated powers other than commerce were involved. The New Dealers won an important victory from the conservative Court in the *Gold Clause* cases because of the clear relationship between the New Dealers' gold policy and Congress's explicit power to regulate the value of money.[72] Another victory came when the Court upheld the government-operated enterprises under the Tennessee Valley Authority because of the explicit federal power over military affairs. The latter case prompted FDR to savor "that perfectly lovely thought that the Government is making fertilizer based, constitutionally, on the national defense."[73] Hamilton would have approved.

# 9

# Executive Supremacy:
# The Brownlow Report

But it would be an alarming doctrine that Congress cannot impose upon any
executive officer any duty they may think proper, which is not repugnant to
any rights secured and protected by the Constitution; and in such cases, the
duty and responsibility grow out of and are subject to the control of the law,
and not to the direction of the President.

*—Kendall* v. *U.S. ex rel. Stokes*

The New Dealers eventually had their way in the interpretation of the
commerce, general welfare, and necessary and proper clauses. Their triumph
ensured the federal government's constitutional capacity to order the nation's
economy as the nation's needs would demand. This capacity brought about a
limited form of national supremacy—limited because that capacity would not
always be exercised. Vast powers would remain with private, state, and local
institutions; but they would remain there because the federal government
chose not to act, not because it could not act. This limited national supremacy
was the first of the two pillars on which the New Dealers would raise the
administrative state. The second was the supremacy of the executive branch
within the national government. The most important New Deal statement in
support of executive supremacy was the "Brownlow Report." Its formal title
suggests its purpose: "Report of the President's Committee on Administrative Management."[1]

Relying on fashionable principles of scientific management, the Brownlow
Report condemned the federal government's absence of planning, its archaic
personnel system, and its chaotic financial management. In addition, the report
issued a clarion call for exclusive presidential control of governmental re-

organization. Rowland Egger, a distinguished political scientist, maintained that the Brownlow Report "was the first comprehensive reconsideration of the Presidency and the President's control of the executive branch since 1787, and is probably the most important constitutional document of our time."[2]

If one allows that constitutional documents can issue from institutions other than courts, Egger is surely correct. Congress at first rejected most of the Brownlow proposals. They were casualties of the Court-packing fight. Opponents of the New Deal successfully linked the two issues in the public mind and pinned the "dictator bill" label on the legislative effort to enact the Brownlow recommendations into law.

Eventually, however, and quite incrementally, Congress gave the president much of what the Brownlow Committee had called for.[3] No less important than its legislative offspring was the impact that the Brownlow Report had on popular and academic thought about the presidency. The Brownlow Report prepared us to accept President Truman's description of his office—"the buck stops here." Before Brownlow, we might have thought the genius of American government lay in the fact that the buck stops nowhere. We might have said that it floats freely among such competing institutions as the Senate, the House, the courts, the presidency, the bureaucracy, the states, our allies, our enemies, and a host of private organizations blessed with either fat coffers or righteous fervor or both. As disciples of Brownlow, we came to believe that the buck *should* stop with the president until Richard Nixon put the buck in his pocket. Then we knew something had gone wrong.[4]

President Roosevelt was aware of the constitutional significance of the Brownlow Committee. Luther Gulick, who joined Louis Brownlow and Charles Merriam to constitute the committee, tells of a committee meeting with the president just after Roosevelt's landslide reelection in 1936. Riding the crest of overwhelming popular support, Roosevelt was ready to institutionalize his political advantage. According to Gulick's notes, at the 14 November meeting, the president said "that since the election he had received a great many suggestions that he move for a constitutional convention for the United States and observed that there was no way of keeping such an affair from getting out of hand what with Coughlin and other crackpots about. 'But,' he said, 'there is more than one way of killing a cat, just as in this job I assigned you.' "[5]

Thus, according to one member of the committee, the president saw the committee as doing the work of a constitutional convention. This is a remarkable statement. So remarkable is it that Brownlow prudently omitted it from the lengthy discussion of this meeting in his autobiography, *Passion for Anonymity*.[6] Historian Barry Karl reports that the Gulick memorandum appeared in a manuscript version of the Brownlow autobiography but was omitted from the printed text.[7]

The constitutional significance of the committee's work did not escape Brownlow. Witness his description of an important meeting of the president, the committee, and key congressional leaders just prior to the release of the report:

> Here, that Sunday afternoon in the White House [10 January 1937], for the first time in the history of the great American Republic, a President of the United States, deeming himself in fact as well as in name the head of the executive branch of the government, had come to close grips with the leaders of the legislative branch, who from the beginning of the government had considered themselves responsible for the control, confinement, bridling, and ultimate determination of the organization of all branches of the government.[8]

The scholarly judgment of Rowland Egger, the startling comments attributed to FDR, the prudent omission of these comments by Brownlow, and Brownlow's own sense of history-in-the-making—all conspire with the later development of the presidency to suggest that the Brownlow Report was indeed a constitutional statement of considerable significance. In this chapter, I analyze the constitutional principles in the document.[9] My remarks fall under five headings: (1) the managerial presidency; (2) the president and Congress; (3) fundamental principles; (4) government personnel; and (5) the rhetoric of the Brownlow Committee.[10]

## THE MANAGERIAL PRESIDENCY

> The constitutional principle of the separation of powers . . . places in the President, and in the President alone, the whole executive power of the Government of the United States.
>
> —Brownlow Report

The formal designation of the Brownlow Committee as the President's Committee on Administrative Management made clear to all a change in administrative thought that had been recognized by the initiated for several decades.[11] No longer would it suffice to think of efficiency in government in terms of cost cutting alone. A positive state demanded the effective delivery of promised services. This change was captured in the committee's definition of the term "administrative management": "organization for performance of the duties imposed upon the President in exercising the executive power vested in him by the Constitution of the United States."[12]

Applying the principles of scientific management, the committee drew a sharp distinction between policy and administration. This distinction found its institutional embodiment in Congress, where policy was made, and in the executive branch, where it was carried out. Thus, the budget would serve as "the means of control of the general policy of the Government by the Legislative Branch and of the details of administration by the Executive."[13]

This tidy arrangement, whereby policy was assigned to Congress and administration to the executive, was central to the committee's strategy. By describing virtually every governmental activity as some kind of "administrative management"—personnel management, fiscal management, planning management, or administrative reorganization—the committee asserted the president's power over the government as a whole.

The committee's broad understanding of administration sprung from vigorous Federalist roots. In *Federalist 72*, Publius offered two definitions of administration. "In its largest sense," the word "comprehends all the operations of the body politic, whether legislative, executive, or judiciary"; but a more modest meaning of administration restricts the term to "executive details." These "details," however, are rather impressive in their scope: "the actual conduct of foreign negotiations, the preparatory plans of finance, the application and disbursement of the public monies, in conformity to the general appropriations of the legislature, the arrangement of the army and navy, the direction of operations of war; these and other matters of a like nature constitute what seems to be most popularly understood by the administration of government."

Publius would have approved the Brownlow Committee's broad understanding of administration. His own definition of even the modest version of administration was broad enough to support the "Administrative Republic" he had in mind.[14] What would have puzzled him, however, is the committee's distinction between politics and administration. Publius assigned to administration a political task of the highest order; it was through sound administration that the loyalties of the people would gradually be transferred from the states to the federal government.[15] For the authors of the Brownlow Report, the sharp distinction between politics and administration provided rhetorical cover for the far-reaching changes they envisioned for the United States.

Perhaps the most startling statement of the Brownlow Committee was its contention that government reorganization was an administrative matter and therefore should be under the exclusive control of the executive.[16] In his message to Congress urging support of the Brownlow Committee's recommendations, President Roosevelt commented favorably on the proposition that "reorganization should be a continuing duty and authority of the Chief Executive on the basis of standards set by Congress."[17]

As the text of the document unfolds, it becomes quite clear that the "standards set by Congress" will be quite narrow indeed. For example, the committee calls for the addition of a Department of Social Welfare and a Department of Public Works to be added to the ten executive departments then in existence. Congress's task is simply to create the new departments and name them. Having discharged these responsibilities, Congress is then to "authorize the President to determine the appropriate assignment to the 12 executive departments of all operating administrative agencies and fix upon the

Executive continuing responsibility and power for the maintenance of the effective division of duties among the departments.''[18]

Lest anyone miss the point of the division of labor the committee has in mind, the report recommends that the ''two new departments be set up *by law* to cover these two fields [public welfare and public works], and that there be assigned to these departments *by the president* not only the appropriate new activities in these fields but also the old activities closely related thereto.''[19] Thus Congress will establish the departments and then graciously step aside while the president, in accordance with the principles of scientific management, assigns them their activities.

The conceptual support for this breath-taking view of a managerial presidency was rooted in the committee's constitutional theory of executive power. The principle of separation of powers, the committee announced, ''places in the President, and in the President alone, the whole executive power of the Government of the United States.''[20] President Roosevelt gave his own version of the same point in his message to Congress when he stated that ''the Presidency was established as a single strong Chief Executive Office in which was vested the entire executive power of the National Government.''[21] Roosevelt is more modest than the committee; he substitutes ''Presidency'' for the committee's ''President.'' He agrees with the committee in insisting that executive power is associated exclusively with the president.

It would be hard to find such a doctrine in the framers of the Constitution. Hamilton's most exuberant defense of executive power appears in his first essay as Pacificus. This essay is remarkable for the *extent* of executive power it envisions, that is, the types of things the president can do on his own. Nowhere, however, in this essay does Hamilton claim exclusive executive power for the president. This doctrine found its origins, not in the framers of the Constitution, but in the presidency of Andrew Jackson. Its fulfillment comes in the presidency of Richard Nixon. At the heart of the doctrine is a fundamental error that transforms the president from chief executive officer into sole executive officer.[22]

It is textually demonstrable from the Constitution itself that the whole executive power is not vested in the president. The Senate's executive role in treaties and appointments is spelled out in terms in article 2. Both houses of Congress share executive functions in their constitutional powers to declare war, to make rules for the armed forces, to create offices, to prescribe the discipline for the state militias, to grant letters of marque and reprisal, and to vest the appointing power of inferior officers in the heads of the executive departments or in the courts of law.

The explicit constitutional recognition of heads of executive departments negates the notion of the president as sole possessor of executive power. FDR described the presidency as the ''Chief Executive Office,'' but in so doing he undercut his committee's position that the Constitution "places in the President and in the President *alone,* the *whole* executive power of the Government of the United states."[23] If the president is the government's *chief* executive officer, he cannot be at the same time its *sole* executive officer. *Chief,* as a hierarchical term, necessarily implies that subordinates possess to a lesser degree the power that is the chief's in the fullest, but not exclusive, sense.

A dramatic illustration of a presidential claim similar to the committee's position was provided in *Kendall* v. *U.S. ex rel. Stokes,* a Supreme Court case from the Jacksonian era.[24] William B. Stokes, a contractor with the Post Office Department, claimed that that agency owed him a substantial sum of money. Congress agreed and then passed a law directing the solicitor of the Treasury to investigate the matter and to determine a suitable sum "according to the principles of equity."[25] Congress further directed the postmaster general to award the sum fixed by the solicitor. This figure came to $161,563.89. President Jackson's postmaster general, Amos Kendall, was suspicious of Stokes. He found the award excessive and certified the release of only $122,102.46. Stokes appealed to President Jackson for the remaining funds, which came to nearly $40,000. Jackson shared Kendall's suspicion of Stokes and offered him no help. Instead he suggested that Stokes take his troubles back to Congress. There was nothing more that Congress could do, since it had already passed an act on Stokes's behalf, which the postmaster had defied. Stokes's only recourse was to sue, and so he did. The circuit court for the District of Columbia issued a writ of mandamus directing the postmaster general to obey the act of Congress and to give Stokes the full sum as determined by the solicitor of the Treasury. The postmaster general appealed to the Supreme Court of the United States.

Kendall's argument was that Congress could not fix a statutory responsibility upon a subordinate of the president. To do this, he maintained, would undercut the president's control over the executive branch of government. The Constitution places upon the president the duty to "take Care that the Laws be faithfully executed." If Congress can designate a presidential subordinate as the officer responsible for executing a law, the unity of the executive branch would be undermined, and the president would not be able to ensure the faithful execution of the laws.

The Supreme Court was unanimous in rejecting this argument. The decision of the Court was 6 to 3 against the postmaster general, but the three dissenters based this position on a technical question about the jurisdiction of the lower court in issuing a writ of mandamus. All the justices agreed that Congress could impose statutory responsibilities upon presidential subordinates. In delivering the opinion of the Court, Justice Smith Thompson noted that although the executive power is directly vested in the president, "it by no means follows that every officer in every branch of that department is under the exclusive direction of the President."[26] Thompson granted that there are "certain political duties imposed upon many officers in the executive department, the discharge of which is under the direction of the President."[27] He followed this concession with the most important sentence in the opinion on the relationship between the president and his subordinates: "But it would be an alarming doctrine that Congress cannot impose upon any executive officer any duty they may think proper, which is not repugnant to any rights secured and protected by the Constitution; and in such cases, the duty and responsibility grow out of and are subject to the control of the law, and not to the direction of the President."[28] The *Kendall* Court made it abundantly clear that as a matter of constitutional law it is incorrect to maintain that the executive officers are "all the President's men." They are preeminently officers of the law. The Brownlow Committee's position on the president as the sole executive officer is irreconcilable with *Kendall*.[29]

The underpinnings of the committee's position on presidential power can be found in its democratic view of the office of the president. We shall examine this point in some detail below. Here it will suffice to note that the managerial view of the presidency, with its strict control of subordinates, was justified on the grounds that it is "of the essence of democratic government that these offices be selected by the Administration in office." In the name of democracy the issue of executive control was linked to the committee's call for the abolition of multimember administrative boards in favor of single-headed agencies that would transmit presidential directives efficiently throughout the entire executive establishment.[30]

The committee's call for single-headed agencies to promote executive efficiency was faithful to Publius's fondness for "unity, vigor, and dispatch" in the executive branch of government. Less faithful to Publius, however, was the committee's support for giving the president a free hand in picking his high-ranking subordinates. In *Federalist 77,* Publius maintained that the president would need the consent of the Senate to *remove* officers as well as to appoint them. The Constitution is silent on the matter of a removal power; its directives concern only how to get people into office, but not how to get them out. Thus Publius's musings on removal from office were purely speculative. As a matter of fact, events did not support his musings. The First Congress vested the removal power in the president alone.[31] Nevertheless, Publius's opinion is important for our purposes because it gives a good indication of how he saw the relationship between the president and high-ranking executive officers. The first paragraph of *Federalist 77* is worth quoting in full:

It has been mentioned as one of the advantages to be expected from the co-operation of the senate, in the business of appointments, that it would contribute to the stability of the administration. The consent of that body would be necessary to displace as well as to appoint. A change of the chief magistrate therefore would not occasion so violent or so general a revolution in the officers of the government, as might be expected if he were the sole disposer of offices. Where a man in any station had given satisfactory evidence of his fitness for it, a new president would be restrained from attempting a change, in favour of a person more agreeable to him, by the apprehension that the discountenance of the senate might frustrate the attempt, and bring some degree of discredit upon himself. Those who can best estimate the value of a steady administration will be most disposed to prize a provision, which connects the official existence of public men with the approbation or disapprobation of that body, which from the greater permanency of its own composition will in all probability be less subject to inconstancy, than any other member of the government.

Nothing in this passage indicates that Publius would quarrel with the Brownlow Committee's insistence that the president be able to control his subordinates. He would have some reservations, however, about the freedom the committee would give the president in picking his subordinates—or his "team," as we are wont to say today. Publius wants a stable administration and turns to the Senate, that most stable of constitutional bodies, to protect high-ranking officials from the postelection ravages of an incoming president. He seems to call for something akin to a merit system at the very top of the executive establishment and is pleased to report that the "official existence of public men" will be linked to a senatorial check, instead of being simply at the whim of a newly chosen president.[32]

So serious is Publius on this matter of administrative stability that in *Federalist 72* he defends the reeligibility of the president on the grounds that a frequent turnover of presidents "could not fail to occasion a disgraceful and ruinous mutability in the administration of the government." Thus an important constitutional principle, the indefinite reeligibility (until passage of the Twenty-second Amendment) of the president, was justified by Publius on administrative grounds.[33] If Publius would applaud the Brownlow Committee's endorsement of presidential control of the executive branch of government, he would surely reject its effort to distinguish politics from administration. The stable administration Publius prized—even to the extent of protecting it from presidential whim—was part of his general strategy of winning popular support of the new government through sound administration. For Publius, stable administration was high politics.[34]

The final point on the committee's advocacy of a managerial presidency concerns the call for the heads of the twelve proposed executive departments to work together collectively as an executive council, or "council of state," to advise the president.[35] The committee follows the framers' plan in looking upon the heads of the executive departments as assistants to the president,[36] but the recommendation that they render their assistance collectively is somewhat problematic. At the Constitutional Convention in 1787, the issue of an executive council was hotly debated. A vestigial remain of that debate appears in section 2 of article 2, where we find that the president "may require the Opinion, in writing, of the principal Officer in each of the executive Departments, upon any Subject relating to the Duties of their respective Offices." The fact that the president may *require* written opinions only on subjects pertinent to each officer's specific responsibilities suggests a decisive rejection of the idea of an executive council.[37] Presidents, of course, are free to discuss anything they please with their department heads as a group—as presidents have done with their cabinets since the earliest days of the Republic. This practice is not what the Brownlow Committee had in mind. The committee was not interested in reinforcing the status quo. The "council of state" that it envisioned was more formal and ambitious than the American cabinet, which is neither a cabinet in a parliamentary sense nor an executive council in any sense.

What is interesting about the Brownlow Committee's recommendation is that the executive council was a favorite idea of the Anti-Federalists and especially of those Anti-Federalists who thought the president had too much power.[38] During the convention, George Mason was the most forceful advocate of an executive council.[39] The failure of the convention to accommodate his wishes in this matter was one of the major reasons he gave for refusing to sign the Constitution that he had labored on so diligently for nearly four months.[40] It is ironic that the Brownlow Committee would call for an executive council as a means of strengthening the president's power, while Mason had favored a similar institution for the opposite reason.[41]

## THE PRESIDENT AND CONGRESS

The President is a political leader—leader of a party, leader of the Congress, leader of a people.

—Brownlow Report

The Brownlow Committee had a ready answer to the anticipated objection that its recommendations would distort the constitutional balance by giving excessive powers to the president. The answer was that it was only by centralizing executive power that the president could be truly accountable to Congress. Thus, whatever fears might have been aroused at the thought of a managerial presidency would be quickly allayed by the assurance that these powers would have the happy result of "restoring to the Congress effective legislative control over the Executive."[42]

The strategy of the committee was to justify exclusive presidential control over the executive branch as merely a means of making the president accountable to Congress. This argument pervades the committee's report.

President Roosevelt agreed that the reforms called for in the report would be helpful "for making the Executive more strictly acountable to the Congress."[43] The point of the argument was that it was only by centralizing executive power in the hands of the president that Congress could actually hold him accountable.

The committee had little to say about just what Congress might do if it should find that its centralized executive had not acted responsibly. And for good reason: short of impeachment, there is little that Congress could do. It could reduce or eliminate appropriations for programs favored by the president, but such actions are simply part of the ordinary operation of the principle of separation of powers. They are appropriate actions between equals who are trying to influence each other's behavior. They are not relevant to the issue of enforcing responsibility. The language of responsibility and accountability suggests superior and subordinate—not separate and equal institutions. One who is accountable to another can be removed from office or at least have his decision reversed by the superior upon appeal. This is why the argument of executive accountability is a ruse. In constitutional theory, the president is accountable to Congress only in the sense that both houses of Congress, acting in concert, can remove him from office;[44] but the Brownlow Committee is not concerned with impeachable offenses.[45]

Lest there be any doubt that the committee's concern for executive accountability to Congress is disingenuous, consider the way it interprets the president's duty to recommend to Congress "such Measures as he shall judge necessary and expedient" (art. 2, sec. 3). From this clause and the clause that empowers the president to require written opinions from the heads of executive departments on matters under their jurisdiction, the committee concludes that "it is the duty of the executive departments to supply the Congress with information and advice concerning the laws which they administer."[46] To carry out this duty to provide Congress with the information that it needs to legislate, the committee calls for an elaborate clearance system within the executive branch, so that Congress will not be confused by differences that might happen to exist among departments. The Bureau of the Budget should provide the clearance before bills are submitted to Congress. Thus, from the president's constitutional duty to recommend legislation, the committee deduces a further duty to keep from Congress any information and proposals that the executive does not want Congress to have. This is executive accountability to Congress—Brownlow style.

Interestingly, the committee's meaningless appeal to presidential responsibility is not without precedent. Andrew Jackson, whose views on the presidency are closely akin to those of the Brownlow Committee, described himself as "the responsible head of the Executive Department." The context involved a fierce fight with the Senate over the scope of the president's power. The term "responsible head" appeared in a formal protest that Jackson sent to the Senate because of its resolution censuring him for exercising powers that the Senate maintained did not belong to the president.

To be sure, Jackson did not say he was responsible to Congress; for Jackson that would be unthinkable. He just said he was responsible. Daniel Webster, Jackson's arch foe in the Senate, attacked this free-floating responsibility. He argued that Jackson could not mean that he was legally responsible, because "legal responsibility signifies liability to punishment for misconduct or maladministration."[47] Webster then asked what Jackson meant by responsibility and went on to answer his own question: "Sir, it is merely responsibility to public opinion. It is a liability to be blamed, it is the chance of becoming unpopular, the danger of losing a re-election. Nothing else is meant in the world. It is the hazard of failing in any attempt or enterprise of ambition. This is all the responsibility to which the doctrines of the Protest hold the President subject."[48]

Webster's analysis might well apply to what the Brownlow Committee really meant by presidential responsibility. Responsibility to Congress was a distortion of constitutional theory that was intended to sugar-coat the pill that the committee wanted Congress to swallow. Responsibility to public opinion, which for men of Webster's Whiggish persuasion was no responsibility at all, was the sort of responsibility that the committee had in mind. This is quite consistent with the democratic and almost plebiscitary tone of the report.

The text of the committee's report betrays the disingenuousness of the frequent calls for presidential responsibility to Congress. This is clear at the very beginning of the document. In its introduction, the committee states forthrightly that "the President is a political leader—leader of a party, leader of the Congress, leader of a people."[49] A president who leads Congress is the sort of president the committee had in mind. Unfortunately, a president as "leader" was one of the great fears of the framers of the Constitution. One of the reasons for the intricate system of presidential selection through the electoral college was to safeguard against the choice of a "leader." In *The Federalist Papers, leadership* is used pejoratively; it is closely associated with *favorite* or *demagogue*.[50] As Robert Eden has noted, the only time Publius uses *leader* favorably is when he discusses the Revolution. This is a clear indication of the antinomian character of the word.[51] A leader is a blessing in times of Revolution when legally constituted offices are often irrelevant; but a duly authorized constitutional order has no need for "leaders." Officers, representatives, and statesmen are quite enough. The Brownlow Committee's description of the president as a leader in a threefold sense was an important departure from the language of the framers. It captured the frustration that FDR, like Theodore Roosevelt and Woodrow Wilson before him, must have felt from the constitutional constraints of the office that the framers had designed.

The most telling expression of the committee's real position on the relationship between the president and Congress appeared in a section of the report entitled (significantly) "Accountability of the Executive to the Congress." The first paragraph of this section reads: "Under the American system the Executive power is balanced and made safe by freedom of speech, by elections, by the protection of civil rights under an independent judiciary, by the making of laws which determine policies including especially appropriations and tax measures, by an independent elective Congress, and by the establishment of Executive accountability."[52]

For the Brownlow Committee "the Executive Power is balanced and made safe . . . by an independent elective Congress." Strange language this. At the founding of the Republic, the framers were careful to provide for a method of selecting the president that would assure his independence from Congress. They feared that the "legislative vortex" would swallow up the other two branches. Legislative power was divided between two houses of Congress to weaken the legislature and to offset the natural advantage that it enjoyed. The founders of the administrative state substitute an executive vortex for the legislative vortex of the framers. They look to Congress and the courts to balance and limit the executive, which now plays the lead role in the constitutional drama. Instead of dividing executive power in order to weaken it, as the framers had done to legislative power, the Brownlow Committee argues vigorously for its unification under the managerial control of the president.

If one ignores the committee's misleading language on executive accountability to Congress, one finds in the Brownlow Report both an adherence to and a departure from the thought of the framers. The committee follows the framers in maintaining the principle of three separate, equal, and independent branches of government. Also, like the framers, the committee recognizes that one of the three is likely to overwhelm the other two and therefore needs to be balanced and limited by them. Unlike the framers, however, the committee makes no effort to tilt the system against what they see as the dominant branch. Their failure to do this puts the Brownlow Committee at odds with the framers on a fundamental point of constitutional design and goes a long way toward explaining in the formal terms of constitutionalism the profound changes in American political attitudes and behavior over the century and one-half that separates 1787 from 1937.

## FUNDAMENTAL PRINCIPLES

The whole basis of reorganization must not be superficial appearance but the integrity of the social services underneath, which are the end of government.

—Brownlow Report

The Brownlow Report has been taken seriously for the past half-century because it is one of the few statements in Public Administration literature that attempts to ground the teachings of scientific management in constitutional theory and fundamental principles of American government. In this section we shall examine how the report both affirmed and departed from the fundamental principles of 1787. The most striking similarity is the committee's thematic argument that effective government is instrumental for higher ends. Here the report follows the argument of *The Federalist Papers*.

At the founding of the Republic, there was a solid consensus that the primary purpose of government is the protection of individual rights.[53] One of the major disputes between Federalists and Anti-Federalists was over the best means to achieve that end. The Anti-Federalists tended to see in the Constitution a government so powerful that it would threaten individual rights. Publius met this argument head-on by contending boldly that only a strong government could protect rights effectively. Publius would use power in defense of individual rights.

The Brownlow Committee joins Publius in defending powerful government as instrumental for higher ends.[54] It departs from him and from the founding generation, however, in its articulation of those higher ends. In the Brownlow Report, democracy replaces individual rights. The Brownlow Report was written at a time when democracy was subject to severe doubts at home and severe attacks abroad. In his message to Congress, President Roosevelt noted that just as "our forefathers" struggled against tyranny and "against government by birth, wealth, or class," Americans of 1937 must struggle against confusion, ineffectiveness, waste, and inefficiency. "This battle, too, must be won, unless it is to be said that in our generation national self-government broke down and was frittered away in bad management."[55] Will it be said, the President asked, that "democracy was a great dream, but it could not do the job?"[56]

It is not surprising that the Brownlow Report should have grounded its case in an appeal to democracy that would sound quite strange to the framers of the Constitution. The Brownlow Committee was faithfully reciting appropriate norms for an American society that had become far more democratic than the sort of society envisioned by the men of the late eighteenth century. What is surprising, however, is the absence of a serious discussion of the protection of individual rights as government's primary purpose. Twentieth-century Americans would reject the idea that their commitment to democracy had weakened their commitment to individual rights, despite the warning of their forefathers that they could not have it both ways. Twentieth-century Americans would be inclined to say they can have democracy in addition to, not instead of, individual rights. If the Brownlow Committee's virtual silence on rights can be interpreted as indifference to what the framers saw as the primary purpose of government, the committee's report and the administrative state that it envisioned would represent a serious departure from the founding principles of the Republic.

In defense of the Brownlow Committee, one might note that *The Federalist* has little to say explicitly about individual rights, because the matter was not in dispute. Like the Brownlow Report, *The Federalist* was a political document, intended to persuade people to take a certain action. There was no need to discuss what everyone took for granted. The fact that Publius does not have much to say about individual rights does not mean he was indifferent to them. It means only that the opponents of the Constitution needed no instruction in this matter.[57]

Can the same argument be made in defense of the Brownlow Committee? I do not think so—for four reasons. First, there is, as we have seen, the pattern in the document of incessantly reminding the reader of the contribution the committee's proposal would make to democratic government. The most important readers of this document were the congressmen and senators who were being asked to enact its provisions into law. If members of Congress did not need to be reminded of the importance of individual rights, why should they be reminded of the importance of democracy? Fair-minded congressmen might legitimately worry about the threat that the managerial presidency was presenting to democratic government; but surely they would worry no less about the threat to individual rights. If the committee were concerned about *both* democracy and individual rights, why was it so eloquent on the former and virtually silent on the latter?

Second, the only explicit mention of individual rights in the entire report appears in a list of "aims and activities" undertaken by the government. Individual rights and liberties are but one of several such aims and activities—along with "the frame of our national and community life, our economic system, . . . a democracy that has survived for a century and one-half."[58]

In fairness to the Brownlow Committee, I should note that this list appears in the very first paragraph of the report. Thus, even though the expression "individual rights" appears only once in the entire report, it appears in a prominent place. Further, I should note that the preamble of the Constitution itself lists securing the "Blessings of Liberty to ourselves and our Posterity" as but one of six purposes for which the Constitution was ordained and established. Nevertheless, I would support my position that the committee is indifferent to rights by contrasting the subsequent development of the democracy theme with the subsequent disregard for individual rights. It is democracy that supports the idea of the president as "leader of the people," which in turn supports the committee's effort to centralize executive power in his hands. Individual rights are marginal to the committee's grand strategy.

The marginality of individual rights is underscored by my third and strongest argument—the explicit mention of the purpose of government as something other than the protection of individual rights. In discussing governmental reorganization, the committee emphasizes its managerial focus when it insists that the "whole basis of reorganization must not be superficial appearance but the integrity of the social services underneath, *which are the end of government.*"[59] One would like to think that this was a slip of the pen. In the American constitutional tradition, social services are not the end of government. As it stands, the sentence is a textbook example of the triumph of administrative means over liberal ends.

At the beginning of the report, the committee gave a fuller statement of the purpose of American government in self-conscious language that was surely no slip of the pen. Our goal as a nation is nothing less than "the constant raising of the level of the happiness and dignity of human life, the steady sharing of the gains of our Nation, whether material or spiritual, among those who make the Nation what it is."[60]

Surely, it is significant that the same paragraph that provides this high language of the positive state does not shrink from proclaiming that "our American Government rests on the truth that the general interest is superior to and has priority over any special or private interest." Thomas Jefferson thought that government rested on a different set of truths.[61]

The Brownlow Report is vulnerable in its treatment of individual rights. This is probably because many of the successful attacks against the New Deal and its programs were packaged in terms of rights. Indeed, among New Dealers, the expression "private rights" tended to be used as a code for business interests and is often used pejoratively. An approach to American government that ignores individual rights signals a serious departure from the intent of the framers. The Brownlow Committee's treatment of individual rights demanded a corrective which was not long in coming. The Attorney General's Report of 1941 provided the corrective. It offered what the Brownlow Committee failed to provide—a serious discussion of individual rights *within the framework of the administrative state.* Just as the Anti-Federalists corrected the excesses and defects of the Federalists, the Attorney General's Report would do the same for the Brownlow Report. In both cases, the act of founding was in the public argument.

## GOVERNMENT PERSONNEL

Though prestige and recognition are and should be marked incentives to those in the public service, there must also be an adequate salary as a foundation and tangible mark of public respect.

—Brownlow Report

To students of public personnel administration, the Brownlow Report is best known for advocating the separation of personnel management from protection of the merit system.[62] This principle was eventually enacted into public law in the Civil Service Reform Act of 1978. In making the case for a single-headed executive to replace the Civil Service Commission, the Brownlow Committee used such vintage Hamiltonian expressions as "unity, energy, and responsibility" in support of vigorous personnel administration.

There were further Hamiltonian overtones in the committee's suggested method of selecting the "Civil Service Administrator," the single-head executive of the proposed Civil Service Administration. The Civil Service Board, the body charged with defending the merit system, would appoint a special examining board which would administer a nonpartisan, competitive examination. The president would appoint the administrator with the advice and consent of the Senate from the three candidates with the highest scores on the examination. As a result of this elaborate procedure, "careful attention would be given to the professional and technical qualifications required by the office and the merit principle would be extended to the very top of the Civil Service Administration."[63]

Although the administrator would serve at the president's pleasure, a newly elected president might be inclined to keep an established administrator in place because the president would not have an entirely free hand in selecting a replacement.[64] As we saw above, Publius, in *Federalist 77*, looked for ways to reduce the likelihood that an incoming president would remove a competent and experienced administrator from high office on political grounds. In the same spirit, the Brownlow Committee tried to protect its proposed civil-service administrator without undermining the president's ultimate control over personnel administration.

In addition to structural reforms in the personnel field, the Brownlow Committee had some interesting observations on the character and motivation of men and women in the public service. The most famous phrase in the entire report is the "passion for anonymity" that was to characterize the six executive assistants to the president the committee recommended. The expression is said to have greatly amused FDR and was used by Louis Brownlow as the title of his amiable autobiography.[65]

It should be noted that these executives could be taken from and returned to the ordinary agencies of government. There is nothing in the text of the Brownlow Report that would preclude the selection of career personnel as executive assistants to the president. Luther Gulick told the president that this could happen, and the president approved.[66] Keeping all this in mind, we find the "passion for anonymity" appearing in a remarkable context. It refers to persons who could be chosen from the ranks of either political appointees or the career service and, after serving for an unspecified time in a position "directly accessible to the President," could return to the positions whence they came. Although they should be the sort of men who "would not attempt to exercise power on their own account," they should be politically reliable enough to enjoy the president's "personal confidence."[67]

This complex composite of high-ranking public servants is thematic throughout the Brownlow Report. Following Publius, the committee sees a legitimate place for ambition for high office among administrators, and this ambition includes career personnel. The reason given for making the position of assistant director of the Bureau of the Budget a career appointment is precisely to encourage such ambition. In discussing salary levels for high-ranking career personnel, the committee mixes monetary rewards with such considerations as prestige, recognition, and honor. At one point the committee notes that although "prestige and recognition are and should be marked incentives of those in public service," an adequate salary is also necessary "as a foundation and tangible mark of public respect."[68] Elsewhere, increases in salary are suggested as a sort of compensation to career personnel "who have no opportunities to enjoy the honor and prestige of Cabinet and sub-Cabinet posts."[69]

These are two different arguments for increasing the salaries of high-ranking career personnel. What they have in common, however, is the link they forge between increased salaries and the sorts of motives that drive political figures—honor, prestige, and recognition.[70] In the one case, an adequate salary would provide a certain "public respect" to accompany the desire for recognition that appropriately motivates career personnel. In the other, salary compensates for the honor the career person seeks but cannot have. In both cases, the Brownlow Report discusses salary in a manner that diverges sharply from the justification of the bonus system in the Civil Service Reform Act of 1978. There the analogies were not statesmanlike but commercial. Public administrators were to be rewarded for the same reason and in the same manner as good shoe clerks: bonuses for outstanding performance. Although the Brownlow Committee relies on the *structure* of the private sector as a model of government—the Congress as board of directors and the president as chief executive officer—it wisely abandons this model when it discusses the character of those who make their careers in government. On this latter point it follows the lead of both Publius and Woodrow Wilson, who understood the intimate connection between good Public Administration and the love of honor.[71]

Despite its formal commitment to the dichotomy between politics and administration, the Brownlow Committee entrusted to career personnel tasks that would require consummate political skills.[72] To lead career personnel to the high ground of administrative statesmanship, more than effective training programs would be needed. The fundamental need was for a certain type of person—an ambitious man or woman who could be reached by appeals to honor, recognition, and prestige.

## THE RHETORIC OF BROWNLOW

[The independent regulatory commissions] constitute a haphazard deposit of
irresponsible agencies and unco-ordinated powers. They do violence to the
basic theory of the American Constitution that there should be three major
branches of the Government and only three.

—Brownlow Report

The Brownlow Report is a well-written document. Like the authors of the
Declaration of Independence and *The Federalist Papers,* the Brownlow Committee feels obliged to relate the cause that it defends to goals that transcend
national interests and will "serve mankind."[73] This is especially true "in these
troubled years of world history."[74] Whereas the Declaration of Independence
and *The Federalist Papers* are content with a rather perfunctory reference to
world events, the Brownlow Committee returns to this theme with impressive
regularity. The report is particularly effective in linking administrative management to the principles of democratic government and in presenting these united
forces against the threatening rise of Fascist governments in Europe. This
must have been a persuasive position for a nation that would soon become "the
arsenal of democracy." Patriotic rhetoric gets out of hand, however, when,
after referring to the dangerous condition of world affairs, the committee
charged that "only a treasonable design could oppose careful attention to the
best and soundest practices of government available for the American Nation in
the conduct of its heaviest responsibilities."[75] Treason is the only crime
defined in the Constitution of the United States. It "shall consist only in levying
War against them [the United States], or in adhering to their Enemies, giving
them Aid and Comfort." The committee's loose talk of treason was a flagrant
departure from the letter and spirit of the Constitution. It suggested that
opponents of the administrative state, including, presumably, a majority of the
justices of the Supreme Court, were traitors. Such language was inappropriate,
if not ominous, in the context of the high politics of the president's simultane-
ous effort to pack the Court.

There was a second rhetorical blunder in the report, and that was its
unfortunate reference to the independent regulatory commissions as "a
headless 'fourth branch' of government, a haphazard deposit of irresponsible
agencies and unco-ordinated powers."[76] President Roosevelt repeated the
expression "fourth branch" in his message to Congress, and the term has
become something of a household word in journalistic and academic literature.[77]

The Brownlow Committee included only the independent regulatory
commissions in its broadside against the "headless fourth branch." This
restriction was soon forgotten, however, with the result that all administrative
agencies were tarred with the "fourth branch" brush. So common has the

expression become that it has taken on something of a neutral, purely descriptive connotation. It is as though the expression simply described the way things are. If it is important to legitimate the administrative state in terms of constitutional principle, the "fourth branch" image must go. It cannot shed its pejorative overtones. From a constitutional point of view, "fourth branch" can mean only illegitimacy. This is precisely the meaning that the Brownlow Committee intended to convey, for immediately after denouncing the independent commissions, the committee adds: "They do violence to the basic theory of the American Constitution that there should be three branches of the Government and only three."

It was both unfortunate and ironic that the Brownlow Report, the great charter of the administrative state, should pin the "fourth branch" label on administrative agencies.[78] With Frederick Douglass, these agencies could justly complain, "We have been wounded in the house of our friends." The committee had no intention of undercutting the legitimacy of the activities of the independent regulatory commissions. Their independence was the committee's target. The committee was eager to assert presidential control over all the nonadjudicative functions of the regulatory commissions. The committee would bring the commissions under the president, the head of the second branch. History has lost sight of this limited objective, which was never achieved; but the offensive "fourth branch" language has survived and flourished as an unsettling monument to the law of unintended consequences.

The rhetoric of the Brownlow Committee provides an unhappy contrast with the rhetoric of the framers of the Constitution. As we saw above, James Wilson hit upon the felicitous term "federal republic" to describe the innovative government created at the Constitutional Convention.[79] The Anti-Federalists, we recall, maintained that the new government was a senseless compromise between a consolidated nation and a mere treaty, on the one hand, and a republic and a mixed regime, on the other. They called it "spurious brat" and "13 horned monster."[80] Patrick Henry, a leading Anti-Federalist and no mean rhetorician himself, had a grudging admiration for the "fertile genius" of James Wilson in devising so clever a term as "federal republic" to describe the "favoured bantling" that Henry opposed.[81] Unfortunately, such fertile genius was missing at the founding of the administrative state. The rhetoric of the Brownlow Committee unwittingly christened its offspring with a name redolent of illegitimacy. It is a name friends of the administrative state will do well to avoid.

# 10

# Individual Rights:
# The Attorney General's Report

It is also plain that persons dealing with the Government have an interest—
one might say a right—to prompt knowledge of the official understanding of
the law, of the way in which it will be enforced, of the path by which it is
intended to achieve the congressional purpose.
—Attorney General's Report on Administrative Procedure

The purpose of the Attorney General's Report on Administrative Procedure
(hereafter referred to as AGR) is stated in its lengthy, formal title: "Report of
the Committee on Administrative Procedure, Appointed by the Attorney
General, at the Request of the President, to Investigate the Need for
Procedural Reform in Various Administrative Tribunals and to Suggest Im-
provements Therein."[1] The immediate origin of the report was Attorney
General Homer Cummings's letter of 14 December 1938 to President
Roosevelt, suggesting the creation of such a committee. In his letter the
attorney general stressed the need for "proper safeguards for the protection
of substantive rights and adequate, but not extravagant, judicial review."[2] The
president, in his reply of 16 February 1939, authorized the attorney general to
establish a committee to investigate the reform of administrative procedure,
but interestingly, he omitted any reference to rights or judicial review. Instead,
the president stressed the likelihood that administrative reform would make
the Justice Department more effective "in endeavoring to uphold actions of
administrative agencies of the Government, when the validity of their decisions
is challenged in the courts."[3] Thus the correspondence initiating the AGR
presaged its two dominant themes—protection of rights and effective administration. Not surprisingly, the tension between these goals was never entirely

resolved in the report; but just as the report originated in a concern over rights, so its final version clearly leaned in that direction as well.

The members of the committee were appointed by Attorney General Frank Murphy, Cummings's successor. The report was finally presented to Murphy's successor, Robert H. Jackson, on 22 January 1941. Two days later, Attorney General Jackson submitted the report to the Senate.

The AGR was at the center of a long struggle over administrative reform that began in the spring of 1933 when the American Bar Association appointed a Special Committee on Administrative Law and ended—at least for a while— with the passage of the Administrative Procedure Act in 1946. World War II accounted for the struggle dragging on into the mid 1940s. The best and most serious arguments over administrative reform were developed in the crucial period from 1939 to 1941. While the Attorney General's Committee was conducting its exhaustive research on administrative practices, congressional critics of the New Deal, overriding the strenuous objections of Chairman Emanual Celler of the House Judiciary Committee, seized the initiative by passing the Walter-Logan Act in 1940.[4] This act was vetoed by President Roosevelt with an unusually stern message to Congress. One of the reasons that FDR gave for vetoing Walter-Logan—one of his milder reasons—was that he was awaiting the AGR, which was released a month after the president's veto. The AGR itself was accompanied by a strong minority report, which had a profound impact on the legislation that finally emerged from Congress (after the hiatus of World War II) as the Administrative Procedure Act of 1946 (APA). Thus, during the 1939–41 period, there were five important documents on administrative procedure: (1) the Walter-Logan Act, accompanied by supporting statements from Senator Marvel M. Logan and Congressman Francis E. Walter; (2) Congressman Celler's minority report from the Judiciary Committee on the Walter-Logan bill; (3) President Roosevelt's veto message on the Walter-Logan Act; (4) the AGR; and (5) the minority report of the AGR.

The centerpiece of these documents was the AGR. It was anticipated throughout the debate over Walter-Logan and was, of course, the target of its own minority report. Together with its minority report, it adumbrated the APA. These documents are mentioned at the outset to introduce the "cast of characters" in the discussion that follows.

The precise points to cover in comparing the AGR with the founding period present something of a problem. There are any number of topics which are mentioned both in 1787 and 1941. Secrecy in government is a good example. The AGR frequently insists upon openness in administration, both in its formal and in its informal procedures.[5] There is to be no "secret law."[6] This aspect of the AGR recalls the Anti-Federalist attack on secrecy in the Constitution. The secrecy of the Philadelphia Convention itself was a favorite target of such Anti-Federalist stalwarts as Luther Martin, Cato, and Centinel.[7] A pamphleteer who signed himself as a Friend to the Rights of the People saw a connection between the constitutional provision for secret sessions in each house of Congress (art. 1, sec. 5) and the power of the senators and representatives to fix their own salaries (art. 1, sec. 6). They will fix their salaries in secret, he concluded.[8] The provision in article 1, section 5, that Congress must publish a record of its proceedings only "from time to time" was too vague for Patrick Henry and had the bad luck of falling within range of his oratorical fire.[9]

It is tempting to develop the parallels between 1787 and 1941 that the secrecy issue presents; but to yield to that temptation would take us too far afield. Instead, I shall examine only those parallels between the two periods that bear directly on major themes (as opposed to points made in passing) in the AGR. The major themes are: (1) the adjudication of individual rights; (2) uniformity in administrative procedure; (3) the scope of review of administrative action by the courts; and (4) the rule-making power of administrative agencies.

## INDIVIDUAL RIGHTS AND ADJUDICATION

It is this action, the establishment of a society for Public Administration, that we are ratifying and approving today. These officials and these citizens are no hirelings of a despotic power, taking orders from above. . . . They do not wish to diminish either civil liberties or individual responsibilities in society. On the contrary, they cherish these eternal values and intend to discover and develop schemes and methods of administration deliberately adapted to the perpetuation of these precious elements in American heritage.

—Charles A. Beard, on the occasion of the establishment of the American Society for Public Administration in December 1939.

Questions on adjudication within the administrative process and judicial review of such adjudication provide the substance of four of the AGR's nine chapters. The central issue in these chapters is the protection of rights. This heavy emphasis on rights provides a welcome corrective to the critical disregard of this topic in the Brownlow Report and leads the New Deal argument back to the founding period.

In looking for parallels between the respective public arguments of the founding and New Deal periods, one is inclined to see in the Brownlow Report a reincarnation of *The Federalist Papers* and in the AGR a born-again Anti-Federalist rejoinder. Unfortunately, the parallel is not that neat. In its cavalier treatment of rights, the Brownlow Committee departs both from the Federalists and from the Anti-Federalists and, indeed, from the American political tradition as a whole. It is Federalist in its admiration of vigorous and effective government, but not in its understanding of the ends of such government. The

AGR departs from the Anti-Federalists in its unflagging defense of the new administrative order. Unlike Anti-Federalist literature, the AGR does not offer a principled argument against a proposed innovation. Instead, it offers a principled argument in support of a recently established innovation. Its concern with rights, procedures, and public participation recalls sound Anti-Federalist sentiment, but its purpose is to rescue the new administrative state from its likely defects. Many Anti-Federalists may well have had similar intentions vis-à-vis the Constitution. Certainly many of them are on record, not as opposing the Constitution outright, but as insisting upon certain amendments as preconditions of their approval. Nevertheless, one must not put too fine a point on exact parallels between 1787 and the New Deal. The fact that the Bill of Rights emerged from the ratification debate and the Administrative Procedure Act (APA) from the 1939–41 debate over administrative reform certainly is worthy of comment. APA is akin to a Bill of Rights in the administrative state. The more important point, however, is that the AGR, with its emphasis on rights, procedures, and participation, helped to integrate the public argument over the administrative state into the perennial American public argument.

On the subject of rights, the AGR and the Walter-Logan Act were at one in insisting on their protection within the administrative process. Where these two documents differed sharply, however, was on the problem of how rights could be protected without jeopardizing the integrity of the administrative process. In the Walter-Logan Act the integrity of the Public Administration was not a serious issue. This act would surely have gone a long way toward protecting rights, but it would have dismantled the New Deal administrative apparatus in the process. For example, under Walter-Logan, any individual or corporation "substantially interested in the effects of any administrative rule" could file a petition with the United States Court of Appeals for the District of Columbia to have that court "hear and determine whether any such rule is in conflict with the Constitution of the United States or the statute under which [it was] issued."[10] This litigation would take place *before* the rule went into effect, and while the litigation was in progress, the rule could not be enforced.[11] This could impose serious delays in the execution of agency policy. Further, as Attorney General Jackson noted, there was nothing in the Walter-Logan Act "to prevent a succession of litigations by different individuals about the same rule."[12] Thus, litigation could delay enforcement indefinitely. Finally, the Walter-Logan Act provided that even if the rule were upheld by the Court of Appeals *before* it went into effect, it could be challenged anew in another court *after* it had gone into effect. The upshot of the Walter-Logan Act was that it would have "put new and advantageous weapons in the hands of those whose animus is strong enough and whose purse is long enough to wage unrestricted warfare on the administration of the laws."[13]

In contrast to Walter-Logan, the AGR made a self-conscious effort to safeguard the integrity of the administrative process along with its protection of individual rights. The best example of this twofold effort is the committee's careful attention to the use of "informal methods of adjudication," the title of the third chapter of the AGR. Grounding its position in a solid empirical base that established the salience of informal adjudication, the AGR concludes that even where formal procedures are available, "informal procedures constitute the vast bulk of administrative adjudication and are truly the lifeblood of the administrative process."[14] The "informal process-as-lifeblood" metaphor is an expression that Kenneth C. Davis, a member of the committee's staff, has never tired of calling to the attention of students of administrative law.[15] It is a crucial element in the overall argument of the AGR, because the expression is used both in a descriptive and in a prescriptive sense. Informal adjudication *is* the primary way in which rights are protected in the administrative state, and this is the way it ought to be.

The discussion of informal procedure in the AGR precedes the treatment of formal procedure and judicial review, which come into play only in those relatively few cases when the informal procedure fails to solve a problem satisfactorily. By stressing the *exceptional* nature of formal procedure and judicial review, the AGR invited Congress and an informed public to look to the activities of the agencies themselves, not just to judicial utterances about these agencies, for the realistic protection of individiual rights.

The AGR puts considerable emphasis on the need for agencies to police themselves and to adopt voluntarily the sorts of administrative procedures that will guarantee both fair play and mission effectiveness. This approach contrasts sharply with the Walter-Logan Act and to a lesser extent with the AGR minority report, which places much more faith in the capacity of courts to discipline the agencies. The AGR's willingness to make a moral appeal to the agencies' sense of decency and fairness explains its frequent references to the character of significant actors within the administrative process.[16] This concern with the character of administrators was quite common among New Dealers who favored administrative reform and helped keep the argument over reform in line with the public argument of the founding period.[17]

Both the Federalists and the Anti-Federalists had much to say about character and civic virtue. A main theme in Anti-Federalist thought was that it was only the small homogeneous republic that could promote civic virtue; this was one reason—and a very important reason at that—why the proposed Constitution was dangerous. The Federalists had a variety of responses to this position. Most of them ignored it, some denied it, and a few misunderstood it. The most serious response came, of course, in the famous argument in *The Federalist*, where self-interest is called upon to do the work of virtue.[18] Although this is a major line of argument in *The Federalist Papers*, Publius is careful not to press the logic of his position. There are many references in *The*

*Federalist Papers* to the need for civic virtue and good character, even though these references are not solidly integrated into the overall argument, which decisively favors interest over virtue.[19]

The 1939–41 debate on character lacked the depth of its illustrious predecessor of 1787/88. The sponsors of the Walter-Logan Act supported their call for vigorous judicial intervention in the administrative process with inflammatory references to career civil servants as persons "attempting to control all the processes of government for their selfish ends." Career civil servants were described as "employees who tend in some cases to become contemptuous of both the Congress and the courts."[20] They are "disregardful of the rights of the governed."[21] This mistrust of the civil service was quite consistent with Walter-Logan's intention to subject the Public Administration to rigid judicial control.[22] This position was just the opposite of the AGR's reliance on the character of civil servants to buttress its commitment to informal administrative procedure as the first and most important bulwark in support of individual rights.

The main difference between the character arguments of 1787 and 1941 was not the presence of name-calling in the latter. The Anti-Federalists were not reticent in such matters, especially when it came to describing the likely denizens of the proposed "federal city," which would some day become the nation's capital.[23]

What was missing in 1941 was serious attention to what was meant by good character and, more importantly, how it is produced and sustained. The New Dealers frequently sounded a high-minded call for "reasoned decision making" and a sense of fair play on the part of administrators.[24] The contexts suggest that what they meant was the sort of attitude that one might expect from men who were steeped in the tradition of American constitutional law. To get such decisions from such men would be no small accomplishment in a very imperfect world. It certainly would satisfy Montesquieu, who once wrote: "At the birth of societies, the rulers of republics establish institutions; and afterwards the institutions mould the rulers."

It is not surprising that at the founding of the Republic, the question of virtue and the proposed constitution could be examined in a more clear-headed fashion than it could be some one hundred and fifty years later. By the later period the people had learned to equate the Constitution with virtue itself, without looking too closely at the self-interest that undergirds constitutional principle. One might doubt whether interest could do the work of virtue, but there was little doubt in administrative reform circles that constitutional principles were virtue's surrogate. It was too late in the day to wonder with Mercy Warren, the superb chronicler of Anti-Federalist sentiment, whether the Constitution, with its exaltation of self-interest, had led to the situation in which most of the inhabitants of the United States were "too proud for monarchy, yet too poor for nobility, and it is to be feared, too selfish and avaricious for a virtuous republic."[25]

The AGR presented its own case for reform without attacking the Walter-Logan Act directly. The official attack on Walter-Logan came in FDR's veto message, which was supplemented by an extensive academic literature harshly critical of the vetoed act.[26] The intemperate tone of FDR's veto message, which at times amounted to an indictment of the legal profession, made the more deliberate academic articles welcome additions to the cause of administrative reform from within the New Deal camp.

One of the most serious defects in FDR's veto message was his defense of the administrative process against judicial usurpation on the grounds of the large quantity of decisions to be made in modern government. "The judicial process requires to be supplemented by the administrative tribunal wherever there is a necessity for deciding issues on a quantity production basis."[27] This line of reasoning suggests that administrative adjudication is simply a necessary evil that, unfortunately, must be called upon to do what judges could do much better if they had the time. It ignores the excellence of administrative agencies and their superiority to courts in rendering certain types of decisions regardless of their quantity. Such decisions are best made initially by administrative agencies, even if individual rights are concerned.

The academic literature was helpful in turning the New Deal case for administrative reform away from the shoals of a view of administration that rested on nothing more than a grudging concession to the inevitable. The academic authors understood that such a shallow position would only play into the hands of Walter-Logan's supporters, who wanted judges to substitute their own judgments for those of administrators and wanted the Supreme Court to prescribe uniform rules of practice and procedure for quasi-judicial proceedings in administrative agencies.[28]

A common tactic in challenging the Walter-Logan effort to protect rights by denigrating the administrative process was to meet the rights argument head-on with the assertion that the judicial process protects only the rights of the few who are rich, whereas administrative tribunals defend everyone's rights. Charles Grove Haines presented a particularly persuasive version of this argument in his 1939 presidential address to the American Political Science Association. There he questioned the motives of lawyers whose commitment to rights does not go beyond "the presentation of the rights of clients that have ample funds to engage in the slow and tortuous process of expensive litigation."[29] This was a useful line of argument for New Deal purposes because it linked the Brownlow Report's concern for democracy to a populist notion of rights.

And yet at a deeper level the argument is wanting. What it ignores is that in the administrative state the government often relieves the individual of the burden of initiating litigation. The citizen's initiative begins and ends with a complaint to an administrative investigator who sets in motion the process that could eventually lead to having the ICC or the NLRB represent the public's interest in court. Such a procedure is a remarkably effective way of vindicating the rights of a middle-class or indigent plaintiff and all who are similarly situated.

What is missing, however, is the individual's active role in the lawsuit, which, prior to the days of the administrative state, was a practical way of enabling a citizen to act like a citizen—to take his or her turn at ordering public affairs. Tocqueville grows lyric in describing the possibilities for civic activism he sees in the civil lawsuit.[30]

The administrative state tends to push the possibility for such citizen involvement rather high up on the economic scale. To the extent that administrative agencies bring the possibilities of initiating a lawsuit within the economic range of the poor and the middle class, such agencies democratize the defense of rights at the price of civic activism. Some might say this is a small price to pay, because, absent the administrative state, such persons would not be very active anyway. By protecting individual rights on a mass scale—and despite the paradox, that's what the administrative state does—the administrative state would seem to be a faithful servant of the original covenant by which we do the bidding of Hobbes and Locke and enter civil society to secure the protection of our individual rights. All of us do this; not just the rich. So far, so good for the administrative state and the founding prinicple of initiating governments to protect rights. The only problem is that in the common-law tradition, protection is what the *subject* expects from his king.[31] It is not what the citizen expects from a republic. Citizenship means activism—taking one's turn at ruling and being ruled.[32] The administrative state can protect rights en masse, but can it nourish citizens en masse?[33]

## UNIFORMITY IN ADMINISTRATIVE PROCEDURE

> In Suits at common law, where the value in controversy shall exceed twenty dollars, the right of trial by jury shall be preserved, and no fact tried by a jury, shall be otherwise re-examined in any Court of the United States, than according to the rules of the common law.
>
> —Seventh Amendment

A major point of contention between the AGR and the Walter-Logan Act was the need for a uniform administrative procedure. The AGR, which was based on exhaustive study and observation of actual administrative practice, stressed the diversity of administrative agencies and opposed any statutory effort to order a uniform procedure across the administrative board. Instead, the AGR recommended the creation of an Office of Federal Administrative Procedure, which would examine the agencies on an ongoing basis and make recommendations for coordinating administrative procedures wherever practical. The director of the office would also make such legislative recommendations to Congress as he "may deem appropriate."[34]

The Walter-Logan Act favored a rather rigid procedure, with exceptions for certain named agencies—for example, the Internal Revenue Service, Customs, the comptroller of the currency, and the military and naval establishments. Critics of Walter-Logan found the distinction between included and excluded agencies arbitrary. One critic suggested that the only common element among the agencies tied to Walter-Logan's rigid procedure was that they were frequent targets of the foes of the New Deal.[35]

The minority report of the AGR favored a uniformity that was less rigid than Walter-Logan's. Eschewing any effort to place all the agencies in a "rigid mold," the minority thought that uniformity could be achieved on such fundamental matters as whether there should be notice in adjudication, whether a litigant should see the evidence and know the witnesses against him, and whether consideration of cases should be confined to the record. If such matters were mandated by statute for all agencies, each agency would then develop its own particular additional procedures. Significantly, however, the minority tempered its enthusiasm for uniformity by permitting the president "to suspend the operation of any provisions as to any type of function or proceeding of any agency whenever he finds it impracticable or unworkable."[36]

The majority of the attorney general's committee rejected the idea of having a code of administrative procedure with a provision for presidential exceptions. Citing the complexity and diversity of the administrative process, the majority wondered how the president could make "findings" about which agencies should be exempt from the code and under what circumstances. This was precisely what had eluded the committee after two years of exhaustive study. How could the president be expected to make serious findings on practicability on an ad hoc basis?

The debate over uniformity in the administrative state recalls the argument at the time of the founding over the failure of the unamended Constitution to provide for jury trials in civil cases. The second section of article 3 provides: "The Trial of all Crimes, except in Cases of Impeachment, shall be by Jury; and such Trial shall be held in the State where the said Crimes shall have been committed; but when not committed within any State, the Trial shall be at such Place or Places as the Congress may by Law have directed."

Thus the Constitution guarantees a trial by jury in criminal cases but is silent on juries in civil suits. This silence alarmed the Anti-Federalists and gave them one of their main arguments against the Constitution.[37] So strong was their argument that the Federalists eventually agreed to the adoption of the Seventh Amendment, which provides for jury trials "in Suits at common law, where the value in controversy shall exceed twenty dollars."

The main line of the Anti-Federalists' argument was the straightforward assertion that the new Constitution would deprive Americans of a cherished fundamental right. Occasionally, this point was embellished with references to the history of Sweden, Rome, Sparta, and Carthage to show that liberty is doomed where jury trials are either unknown or abandoned.[38] James Wilson of

Pennsylvania took the lead in fashioning the Federalist reply to this charge. Events forced leadership in this matter upon him because the Pennsylvania Ratifying Convention—one of the earliest of such conventions—had almost come to blows over it.[39] Wilson defended the absence of jury trials in civil cases on the same grounds that the AGR was to defend the absence of uniformity in administrative procedure: the legal practices in the several states were simply too diverse to warrant a constitutional mandate for juries in civil cases. In New York, there were juries in civil cases at common law, but not in probate, admiralty, or chancery. In New Jersey there were no courts of admiralty or probate. Such actions were heard in courts of common law, where juries were the rule. Thus an admiralty case that would be decided without a jury in New York would come before a jury in a common-law proceeding in New Jersey. Given this diversity, the Federalists argued, how could the Constitution guarantee juries in civil cases without committing Congress to selecting a procedure that would inevitably seem to favor one state's practice over another's?[40]

The AGR continually refers to the diversity of administrative practices to ward off the movement for uniform administrative procedures.[41] The most succinct statement of this concern can be found in a letter from Attorney General Jackson, over whose name the AGR was issued, to President Roosevelt, recommending a veto of Walter-Logan: "This bill abandons all account of underlying diversities and imposes the same procedures upon agencies as different in structure and function as the Veterans Administration, The Bureau of Reclamation, the Pure Food and Drug Administration, and the Office of Education. It is as if we should average the sizes of all men's feet and then buy shoes of only that size for the Army."[42]

The Federalists of 1787 and the New Dealers of 1941, having agreed on the folly of uniform procedures for things that were substantively diverse, concluded by recommending that whatever uniformity might be needed in the future was best left to Congress.[43] On this point neither the Federalists nor the AGR prevailed. The Seventh Amendment was an explicit rejection of the position of James Wilson and the Federalists. The APA imposed far more uniformity than the AGR had had in mind. Despite these failures, however, the founders of new political arrangements in 1787 and 1941 were at one in trying to resist the imposition of procedural rigidities on their new institutions of government.[44]

## SCOPE OF REVIEW

In all the other Cases before mentioned, the supreme Court shall have appellate Jurisdiction, both as to Law and Fact, with such Exceptions, and under such Regulations as the Congress shall make.

—Article 3, section 2

Another issue in administrative reform that recalled the founding debate was the question of the "scope of review." The expression refers to the scope or extent of a court's review of administrative action. For example, one statute might direct the courts to uphold an agency's decision if it is supported by "substantial evidence." Another statute might say the agency's action should be overturned only if it can be shown to be "arbitrary and capricious." The arbitrary and capricious standard gives the court a *narrower* scope of review than the substantial evidence standard. That is, it is easier for an agency to pass judicial scrutiny if it only needs to show that it has not acted in an arbitrary and capricious manner. If the court's scope of review is confined to that narrow issue, the agency will win its case if it can satisfy the court that its action was not arbitrary and capricious. The agency does not have to show that its action was supported by *substantial* evidence. *Any* evidence—a "mere scintilla" some critics were wont to say—will suffice.[45]

Scope of review is an extremely difficult question in administrative law. If the court applies a stringent test—for example, the preponderance of evidence—there is a danger that the court will end up substituting its own judgment for that of the expert judgment of the agency. This is a particularly serious problem in questions involving complex scientific and technical matters in which judges have no particular competence.[46] On the other hand, if the scope of review is quite relaxed (arbitrary and capricious), there rises the specter of government by arrogant technocrats.

In its simplest form, the question of scope of review is reduced to the distinction between questions of law (in which courts would exercise an extensive review) and questions of fact (in which they would tend to defer to administrative expertise). The problem with the law/fact distinction is that experts seldom agree on where the line should be drawn in all but the simplest cases. Consider the following example. The National Labor Relations Act gives the National Labor Relations Board (NLRB) jurisdiction over certain types of relationships between employers and employees. The NLRB decides that it has jurisdiction over a dispute between a newspaper publisher and the "newsboys" who distribute the paper on the streets. The agency bases its decision on the "fact" that the newsboys are employees. The publisher says they are not. Has the agency decided a question of law or of fact?[47]

The AGR gave considerable attention to the scope of review in a discussion that even today would serve as a splendid introduction to this important topic. The marginal value of the law/fact distinction was recognized with the shrewd observation that "the knife of policy alone effects an artificial cleavage at the point where the court chooses to draw the line."[48] Emphasizing diversity in administration, the AGR thought it unwise to impose anything resembling a fixed formula for the scope of review. Instead, it favored letting the courts define their own role on a case-by-case basis, as they had been doing in the years immediately preceding the AGR. Only if Congress became dissatisfied with the relationship between courts and agencies in a specific area should the scope of review be regulated by legislation.[49] The AGR's friendly outlook on the courts is somewhat remarkable in view of FDR's titanic struggle with the judiciary in 1937. The AGR is a New Deal document, but it is the product of the late New Deal; a time when the Supreme Court of the United States had become "the Roosevelt Court." The irenic tone of the AGR vis-à-vis the judiciary is somewhat amusing when one recalls that the attorney general, over whose name the report was issued, was Robert H. Jackson. In the same year in which the AGR appeared, Jackson's book *The Struggle for Judicial Supremacy* was published.[50] It is an unrelenting and bitter attack on the Supreme Court that had so frustrated FDR and the New Dealers. The AGR's willingness to trust the courts had a very different court in mind from Jackson's target in *The Struggle for Judicial Supremacy.*

The AGR's reluctance to call for statutory mandates on the scope of review contrasted sharply with the Walter-Logan Act, which would have imposed upon the courts a standard of review that would have led to "independent judicial determination of the facts."[51] This fit the pattern of principled division between the AGR and the Walter-Logan Act—with the AGR trying to curb administrative agencies without destroying the integrity of the administrative process. The Walter-Logan Act did not fret over making administrative agencies the wards of the courts.

The dispute over the scope of review could trace its ancestry to the founding period. Article 3, section 2, establishes the jurisdiction of the federal judiciary. The first paragraph of this section lists a long string of cases and controversies to which "the judicial Power shall extend"—for example, "all Cases, in Law and Equity, arising under this Constitution, the Laws of the United States, and Treaties made, or which shall be made, under their Authority; . . ." The second paragraph reads: "In all Cases affecting Ambassadors, other public Ministers and Consuls, and those in which a State shall be Party, the supreme Court shall have original Jurisdiction. In all the other Cases before mentioned, the supreme Court shall have appellate Jurisdiction, both as to Law and Fact, with such Exceptions, and under such Regulations as the Congress shall make."

The Anti-Federalists attacked the provision in this section that gives the Supreme Court appellate jurisdiction over questions of fact as well as questions of law. Even in the eighteenth century there was some difficulty about the differences between questions of law and questions of fact.[52] The distinction was clear enough for the Anti-Federalists, however, to know that they did not approve of an appellate court's having jurisdiction over a question of fact. This meant that a distant court in an (as yet) unnamed "federal city" could overturn any findings of fact made by a jury in criminal cases—and in civil cases as well if Congress should ever be pleased to allow juries in such cases. Such a prospect is startling enough to contemporary opinion, but it was absolutely appalling to eighteenth-century Americans. This is because the jury was looked upon as a central political institution. It was prized less for its capacity to decide correctly than for its function as a limit on governmental power. It was a bulwark of civil liberties.

The appellate provision in the Constitution was the eighteenth-century version of the "scope of review." So broad was the scope of the Supreme Court's review that it threatened the integrity and independence of the jury. This was similar to the fears of the AGR a century and one-half later. An excessive scope of judicial review of agency actions threatened to undermine the Public Administration by enabling judges to substitute their judgment for the expert judgment of the administrator. In the case of the eighteenth-century jury, the expertise was not technical but political. The "twelve good men and true" were expected to monitor their government by making decisions that were at least in some sense *final*. This finality is what article 3 threatened.

The Anti-Federalists had a good issue, and they knew it. The Federal Farmer argued that the logic of allowing an appeal on questions of fact was to replace common law with European civil law, because the finality of jury decisions on factual matters was an essential element in common-law jurisprudence.[53] Luther Martin said that the appeal on questions both of law and of fact would render the jury useless—"a *needless expence*." For if "the general government is not satisfied with the verdict of the jury, its officer may remove the prosecution to the supreme court, and *there* the *verdict of the jury is to be of no effect*, but the *judges of this court* are to *decide upon the fact* as well as the law."[54]

An army of Anti-Federalists joined the chorus.[55] The Federalist response was weak and unconvincing. Not even the "fertile genius" of James Wilson was equal to the task.[56] Wilson's efforts in Pennsylvania were embarrassed by Judge Thomas McKean, a fellow Pennsylvania Federalist, whose imprudent remarks were interpreted (perhaps correctly) as an attack on the jury system itself.[57] Even the indomitable Publius seemed to have met his match. The best he could do was to suggest rather lamely that the Supreme Court might make use of a second jury in hearing questions of fact on appeal.[58] His argument then trailed off into querulous comments about the difficulty of separating questions of law from questions of fact. It was an embarrassing issue for the friends of the Constitution. Surely they were relieved when the Seventh Amendment removed the issue from the public argument with the words "and no fact tried by a jury, shall be otherwise re-examined in any Court of the United States, than according to the rules of the common law."

The APA's solution to the scope-of-review debate of 1941 was not as neat and decisive as the Seventh Amendment. It achieved a brief truce in a battle that has its origins in the founding of the Republic.

## RULE MAKING

The promulgation of general regulations by the executive, acting under statutory authority, has been a normal feature of Federal administration ever since the Government was established.

—Attorney General's Report

Administrative rule making is the topic of the AGR's seventh chapter. The report consciously anchors the practice of such rule making in the American tradition by opening its discussion of it with a reference to an act of the First Congress providing "that traders with the Indians should be licensed and bonded to observe 'such rules, regulations and restrictions' as might apply, including 'such rules and regulations as the President shall prescribe.' "[59] From this tiny acorn grew the mighty oak of administrative rule making pursuant to statute.

Consistent with its opposition to uniform administrative procedure imposed by statute, the AGR examines a remarkable range of rule-making methods but recommends none of them for legislative enactment. The proposed bill that accompanied the AGR treats rule making in a sketchy fashion that belies the sophisticated discussion in the report itself.[60] The minority report is more detailed and anticipates some of the provisions of what will eventually become the famous "notice and comment" section of the APA.[61]

The aspect of the AGR's discussion of rule making that is most likely to recall the founding debate is the emphasis on public participation in the governing process. In our discussion of representation in chapter 4, we saw how the Anti-Federalists wanted a government that was close to the people. They wanted their representatives to be men who "think as [we] think and feel as [we] feel."[62] These representatives were to be sufficiently numerous as to be readily accessible to the people who had elected them, and this was why the Constitution—with its mere sixty-five representatives—was suspect.

Many prominent New Dealers shared twentieth-century versions of this attitude. Frances Perkins, FDR's secretary of labor, took a particular interest in this question. She accepted the New Deal orthodoxy that democratic government could be preserved only through the sorts of vigorous and expansive programs that FDR was advocating; but she was also aware of the need for popular participation in these programs. Getting people to participate in New Deal programs "is the modern substitute for the old town meeting and the old talk around the stove."[63] A good illustration of Perkins's concern to make government intelligible to ordinary citizens is her concern, prior to the creation of the *Federal Register,* for an official publication that would advise the public about governmental programs that were under way. At a meeting of the National Emergency Council (NEC) in January 1934, she described what she had in mind: "You know the type of thing in the European Countries called the

*Official Gazette* where they have been operating many years under councils and boards.''[64]

A few months later, Perkins had some second thoughts about the overtones of an *Official Gazette:* ''But an official gazette is associated in most minds with orders which have the binding effect of law issued by a government which has police powers over its people.''[65]

Clearly, Frances Perkins was struggling with the problem that bedeviled all New Dealers—how to arrange a government powerful enough to meet twentieth-century needs without becoming arbitrary, secretive, and oppressive.[66]

The AGR addressed Perkins's global problem in the narrower context of rule making and called for close cooperation between regulatory agencies and regulated industries. Surprisingly, the problem of the "captured agency" was virtually ignored, although the problem was not unknown during the New Deal period. The AGR emphasized the benefits of participation, rather than the dangers of capture.[67] Regulated parties will have different interests, and these differences "should be reflected in . . . procedures, which should be adapted to giving adequate opportunities to all persons affected to present their views.''[68] To present these views, there is seldom need for hearings in any technical sense—and hardly ever for adversary hearings with cross-examination of witnesses.[69] Informal consultation and conferences are the AGR's preferred methods for rule making: "If the interested parties are sufficiently known and are not too numerous or too hostile to discuss the problems presented, conferences have evident advantages over hearings in the development of knowledge and understanding.''[70] There is no way to determine in advance just when conferences rather than hearings should be used to make rules, and this is why the AGR makes no recommendation for legislation on this subject. The use of conferences must be "left to administrative devising, in the light of a conscious policy of encouraging the participation of those regulated in the process of making the regulations.''[71]

Looking back at the AGR after four decades, the contemporary reader is appalled at the report's nonchalance in regard to the danger that private interests might capture governmental agencies. One might paint on the AGR the happy face of Anti-Federalist sentiment for a government that is close to the people; but such paint wears thin over the years.

Fortunately, public participation is not the AGR's only reason for favoring conferences with regulated parties. They are also looked upon as particularly apt means for administrators to learn more about the industries they regulate.[72] This line of argument gives a Federalist orientation to the AGR. As we saw in chapter 4, the Federalist view of representation rested on a "filtering" principle. Through representation, public opinion would be refined, and the more capable men would rise to the top. Unlike the Anti-Federalists, the Federalists did not expect those who governed to be a microcosm of the people as a whole. They were to be better than the people as a whole. Representative government for Publius was not a necessary evil, created by the practical impossibility of bringing all the people together to deliberate public affairs. It was a positive good. It improved upon the people as a whole, but it did so in a manner that was consistent with the principles of popular government.

The AGR follows the Anti-Federalist line that the legislature should be "as far as possible a crossection of the community."[73] It is in administrative agencies that one should look for specialized expertise. As we saw in chapter 6, the Federalist idea of representation was not limited to elected officials. All officers are representatives of the people, because the distribution of office outlined in the Constitution was the object of popular approval in 1787.[74]

Needless to say, the AGR did not address the question of representation in the eighteenth century. It followed the conventional twentieth-century opinion that only elected officials are representatives and that administrative officers are something else. If, however, we impose a Federalist view of representation on the AGR, its expert administrators begin to emerge as the sort of person Publius hoped might govern the Republic through the filtering process of representation.

The expert administrator is not a know-it-all. He is wise enough to know what he does not know. Hence, he enters the conference to *learn* from those whom he will regulate. The regulated parties will provide him with "the facts within their knowledge"; they will "permit administrative agencies to inform themselves."[75] When conferences prove inadequate and adversary hearings become necessary, the hearing will serve "to enlighten the administrative agency and to protect private interests against uninformed or unwise action."[76]

Throughout the discussion of rule making, the AGR gives serious attention to making sure that expert administrators are really experts. The patent concern in this lawyerly document for genuine administrative expertise belies an endemic hostility between the legal and administrative cultures. The emphasis on knowledge strikes a familiar Federalist chord. As we saw in chapter 4, Publius was more concerned that representatives should *know* the people's needs than that they should feel as the people feel.

What is missing in the AGR is Publius's broad understanding of representation. In the AGR, administrators are never representatives. The AGR is a product of its times. Publius's view of representation had long since been forgotten—or perhaps more precisely rejected—by the American people. The argument of the AGR would have been immeasurably strengthened—at least conceptually, if not politically—had it been grounded in a Federalist theory of representation that would include administrators.

There are some indications that the AGR was groping toward such a position. We have already noted its strange silence on the danger of industry participation leading to a captured agency. We have also noted the AGR's strong emphasis on the character of administrators. If these two points are linked, we might conclude that the AGR did not worry about agencies being captured, because the sort of men and women whom it envisioned in such agencies would not allow themselves to be captured. The same conclusion might explain why the AGR is quite chary of regulating administrative behavior by law; the report prefers to rely on the good sense and good character of the administrators, along with the periodic studies and recommendations of the proposed Office of Federal Administrative Procedure.[77]

The reliance on good character gives the AGR a certain flavor of naïveté that is quite at odds with *The Federalist Papers*. As noted above, Publius recognizes the importance of good character; but he recognizes its limitations as well. There is every reason to think that Publius's "filtered representative" would be a good citizen. His entire argument on representation rests on the assumption that there are some excellent citizens in our midst. Indeed, he even goes so far as to say that members of the learned professions (presumably lawyers) are likely to be the best sort of representatives.[78] Publius's reputation for hard-headed realism came from his recognition of the need for constitutional arrangements that will supplement the bruised reed of civic virtue and supply "by opposite and rival interests the defect of better motives."[79] It is the part of statesmanship to temper the aggressive passions of even the best of men. That is, good citizens in public office, as well as those who are not so good, must be controlled by constitutional means. Hence Publius's elaborate discussion of and profound reliance on separation of powers, which will be preserved by letting ambition counteract ambition and by letting the interest of the man coincide with the constitutional rights of the office.

The AGR's call for good character in administrators sounds shallow and preachy because, unlike Publius, the AGR fails to integrate the administrator into the constitutional system and to give him both appropriate constitutional incentives to excel and effective constitutional protections against competing constitutional actors.

# 11

# Conclusion

[The responsible administrator] must be fully familiar with the difficulties and obstacles in the way of administrative achievement; he must realize how to strive for efficiency without losing sight of other and more important objectives. Above all, he must know the inherent limitations which the American Constitution imposes upon administrative work. Such knowledge and experience will make it possible for him to guide the development of American governmental services without getting them embroiled in insoluble conflicts with the American tradition and Constitution as a whole.

—Carl J. Friedrich

In the first part of this book, I argued that the administrative state is capable, in principle, of being integrated into the sort of polity that the framers envisioned. That argument had three steps: (1) the combination of powers in administrative agencies does not violate Publius's relaxed standard of separation of powers, (2) the higher reaches of the career civil service fulfill the constitutional design of the framers by performing a balancing function originally assigned to the Senate, and (3) the career civil service en masse heals the defect of inadequate representation in the Constitution.

In Part 2, I showed that the academic founders of Public Administration (Wilson and Goodnow, the "founders in speech") consciously departed from the framers of the Constitution. Their unhappy legacy is a theory of Public Administration that is at odds with the primary legitimating symbol of American politics, the Constitution of the United States. I somewhat softened this harsh judgment on the end of the last century by finding in the origins of the Interstate Commerce Commission an approach to Public Administration that was more attuned to the founding norms of the Republic.

In Part 3, I showed that the New Dealers, the "founders in deed" of the administrative state, made a serious effort to square their administrative innovations with the founding principles of the Republic. Despite notable lapses, especially in the Brownlow Report, the practical thoughts and actions of the New Dealers offer more reliable guidance on aligning the administrative state with constitutional principles than did the elegant academic works of Wilson and Goodnow.

With this summary in mind, we are ready to bring this book to a close. I will do this in three steps: (1) an analysis of the book's argument, (2) a statement of a theory of American Public Administration grounded in the constitutional considerations we have examined, and (3) a closing reflection on the oath of office as a pledge to uphold the Constitution of the United States.

## ANALYZING THE ARGUMENT

> The citizens of the state should always be educated to suit the constitution of their state. The type of character appropriate to a constitution is the power which continues to sustain it, as it is also the force which originally creates it.
>
> —Aristotle, *Politics*

This book began with a statement of its purpose: "to legitimate the administrative state in terms of constitutional principles." I envisioned two groups of readers: "public administrators themselves and interested Americans who are the beneficiaries, victims, citizens, and authors of the administrative state." In looking back over the book's development, it will be helpful to separate these two groups.

### PUBLIC ADMINISTRATORS

> That to the height of this great argument I may assert eternal Providence,
> And justify the ways of God to men.
>
> —John Milton, *Paradise Lost*

In addressing my argument to the Public Administration community, I was preaching to the choir. It was the heroic task of the poet "to justify the ways of God to men." My prosaic charge was merely to justify the ways of the Constitution to those who make it work—to those who "run a constitution."

Although the predispositions of the Public Administration community simplified this task, there were several difficult choices to be made on how to go about it. Chief among these was the decision to emphasize the constitutional tradition rather than the text of the Constitution.[1] A particularly inviting textual argument beckoned from section 1 of article 3, which states explicitly that the existence of federal courts other than the Supreme Court is a matter for congressional discretion: "The judicial Power of the United States, shall be vested in one supreme Court, and in such inferior Courts as the Congress may from time to time ordain and establish." The wording of article 2, however, suggests that although the framers left to Congress the decision as to which executive departments would be created, they clearly intended that it should create some executive departments: "he [the President] may require the Opinion, in writing, of the principal Officer in each of the executive Departments, upon any Subject relating to the Duties of their respective Offices."

Thus the text of the Constitution demands that Congress create executive departments, but explicitly refrains from demanding that Congress create federal courts inferior to the Supreme Court. This suggests that the executive departments were at least as important as the inferior federal courts for the government the framers had in mind and that they should therefore enjoy no less legitimacy than these courts. The text of the Constitution itself lays to rest the erroneous, though common, observation that the framers made no explicit provision for administrative institutions. Although the Constitution does not use the word *administration,* article 2 explicitly assumes that Congress will create executive departments. What the framers made no explicit provision for was a federal judicial *system.* They explicitly provided for one Supreme Court, which would be supreme over state courts exercising federal jurisdiction. The possibility of this sort of arrangement accounts for the provision in article 6 that the "Judges in every State shall be bound" by the Constitution, laws, and treaties of the new government. These judges could be state judges exercising federal jurisdiction. They could also be federal judges exercising their authority *in* a particular state, if Congress should agree to create such courts for such judges.[2] In a word, the framers said that there *will* be executive departments and that there *may* be federal courts other than the Supreme Court.

Interesting as this line of inquiry might be, I chose to abandon it in favor of emphasizing the constitutional heritage and its relation to modern Public Administration. This seemed the wiser course to follow in view of the normative argument I had in mind. I found compelling the image of the Constitution as the conclusion of the great public argument of one hundred and fifty years of colonial experience and the premise of the great public argument of the next two centuries.[3] This put the Constitution at the center of American political experience and defined that experience in terms of civilized public argument. It was to this high ground that I wanted to bring the administrative state so that it could claim its rightful place in the public argument alongside such established worthies as judicial activism, presidential leadership, the war powers, and civil liberties.

If I have succeeded in introducing the Public Administration to the constitutional heritage, I have no way of knowing what will become of the relationship—a casual acquaintance or a serious and abiding friendship. I simply arranged an introduction; I did not play the matchmaker. Nevertheless, I can hope that the relationship will be warm and enduring. We will know that this is the case if the schools of Public Administration and government management training centers eventually incorporate constitutional themes into their curricula. These institutions already stress the importance of the organizational skills that are needed to succeed in public management; but these skills are inadequate if presented as nothing more than "skills"—with the full value-free flavor of that word. Organizational skills tend to sink to the level of the shrewd operator and the artful dodger; but they could ascend to the higher plane of administrative statesmanship, if they are grounded in constitutional principle. Sound managerial practice is a constitutional imperative as well as a technique of organizational survival.

## THE INTERESTED PUBLIC

> Our discussion will be adequate, if it has as much clearness as the subject matter admits of, for precision is not to be sought for alike in all discussions, any more than in all the products of the crafts.
>
> —Aristotle, *Nicomachean Ethics*

My second task in writing this book was more difficult than the first. It was to convince an interested public of the compatibility of the administrative state with constitutional principle. The task was made more difficult by my announced purpose of enlisting this compatibility in the cause of supporting a claim to legitimacy that goes beyond mere legal correctness. It is not enough to show that the Supreme Court has, as a matter of fact, regularly turned aside constitutional challenges to the creation of administrative agencies. The writ of the argument runs beyond judicial fiat. In the Preface, I described legitimacy in terms "at least of confidence and respect and at times of warmth and affection."

In this section, I shall address a special word to those readers who believe I have failed to achieve my stated goal. I shall adopt a somewhat "chatty" style in doing this because my purpose is more rhetorical than substantive.

Unfortunately, the splendid word *rhetoric* has fallen on hard times; it calls for a word of explanation. By *rhetoric*, I mean the art of persuasive speech and writing, not flamboyance, deception, or gimmickry. *Rhetoric*'s fall from grace is a misfortune in a free society. That the word today almost always connotes sham and hypocrisy points to serious defects in our public argument. The alternative to persuasion is force.

When I say that my position is more rhetorical than substantive, I mean that I will not attempt to strengthen the substance of the argument that I have already presented in the hope of capturing a wavering reader at the eleventh hour. Instead of strengthening my argument, my strategy is to persuade such a reader to reconsider the criterion that he or she has used in judging the argument. Thus my efforts are rhetorical in the sense that they are intended to persuade unconvinced readers to reflect seriously on their threshold of acceptable argument. What would it take to win them over? I adopt this posture in the spirit of Aristotle's prudent counsel on how to think about politics:

> We must be content, then, in speaking of such subjects and with such premises to indicate the truth roughly and in outline, and in speaking about things which are only for the most part true and with premises of the same kind to reach conclusions that are no better. In the same spirit, therefore, should each type of statement be *received;* for it is the mark of an educated man to look for precision in each class of things just so far as the nature of the subject admits.[4]

The field of public law provides a helpful example of what I mean by changing one's criterion of acceptable argument. In constitutional and administrative law, courts frequently change the criteria by which they judge governmental action under different sets of circumstances. For example, if an economic regulation is challenged on constitutional grounds, the government (state or federal) usually needs to show only that the regulation in question is "reasonable." This is usually an easy test for the government to pass. There is no need to show that the regulation is the best possible choice under the circumstances. It will suffice for the government to show that it has not acted in an arbitrary manner, that there is a plausible connection between the regulation in question and its stated goal. If, however, a "fundamental right" (e.g., speech, press, or religion) is involved, it is not enough for the government to show that it has acted reasonably. These rights enjoy greater constitutional protection; hence the government must pass a more stringent test to justify its activities in these areas. For example, the courts, before they will approve governmental intrusion into these specially protected areas, are likely to require the government to show that a "compelling state interest" was involved and that "no alternative means" that would have been "less restrictive" of liberty could have been used to protect this compelling interest. When the courts impose a test of this nature, they are said to be exercising "strict judicial scrutiny," as opposed to the more relaxed judicial scrutiny of "mere reasonableness." That is, they change the criterion of acceptable governmental action.

In administrative law, the courts often use varying standards in adjudicating appeals from agency decisions. The agencies must always give evidence to support their decisions, but the quality of this evidence may vary from case to case, depending on the statutory provisions that govern judicial review of a particular agency's action. At one time, for instance, decisions of the National Labor Relations Board were likely to be upheld if they were supported by "evidence"—any evidence, "a mere scintilla" of evidence, as critical lawyers were wont to say. Under the Administrative Procedure Act, the agencies need more than a mere scintilla of evidence to prevail in court. They are held to the higher standard of producing evidence that "on consideration of the whole record" is "reliable, probative, and substantial." Sometimes, agencies must meet the more demanding test of "preponderance of evidence"—that is, the "weight" of the evidence must favor the agency.

In criminal law, of course, there is the most stringent standard of all: the state must prove its case "beyond a reasonable doubt."

Judicial practice suggests that the courts have taken Aristotle's admonition to heart. They look for greater certitude in some matters than in others. They impose a very high threshold against the government when it is about to put someone in jail or limit someone's freedom of speech, press, or religion. They impose a lower threshold of proof when called upon to review a governmental finding of an unfair labor practice.

To apply this public-law analogy to the argument of this book, consider my chances of successfully convincing a reader that I have made an acceptable *tu quoque* (you also) argument for the legitimacy of the administrative state. The demands of a *tu quoque* argument are not rigorous; they would be satisfied if I could show that the administrative state is *no less* a departure from the intent of the framers of the Constitution than, say, an "imperial" presidency or an "activist" judiciary. In response to attacks on the constitutional legitimacy of the administrative state, I could say to the contemporary presidency and the courts—"you also" or "and so are you." As a matter of fact, I believe there is evidence to support such a *tu quoque* argument, especially an argument aimed at the "imperial presidency." However, I would not be satisfied with such an argument. I am not interested in dragging the courts and the presidency down to the level of an illegitimate bureaucracy. The aftermath of such an argument might take some political heat off the administrative state, but it would do so only by tarring other institutions with the brush of illegitimacy. The upshot of such reasoning would weaken public confidence in the legitimacy of the existing order and provide a strong incentive to ignore any talk about the intent of the framers. This, in my judgment, would cut us loose from the moorings of our public morality. To mix the metaphor, the fruit of that tree is cynicism.

Although I reject the *tu quoque* argument as inadequate, it joins the public-law analogy in providing a good example of what I am trying to persuade the reader to do—reflect on the criterion by which he or she judges my argument.

Having given examples of what I mean by shifting the criterion for judging an argument, I shall now give two reaons why the argument in this book warrants a criterion less severe than the customary criteria in social-science literature. The reasons are grounded in (1) the novelty of the argument and (2) the fact that the founding of the Republic was itself an act of public argument.

## Novelty of the Argument

> What he was, he was:
> What he is fated to become
> Depends on us.
>
> Remembering his death,
> How we choose to live
> Will decide its meaning
> —W. H. Auden, "Elegy for JFK"

In a recent book entitled simply *Tradition,* sociologist Edward Shils advances the remarkable claim that his is the first book ever written about tradition. He notes that there are many books about specific traditions in religion, literature, art, and law but that there is no book "which tries to see the common ground and elements of tradition and which analyzes what difference tradition makes in human life."[5] He correctly points out that social scientists look to irrational fears, desires for power, pecuniary interests, and group solidarity to understand or explain events; but they seldom summon tradition to this task. When tradition is considered, it is usually consigned to the residual category of "historical factors."[6] This Shils finds unfortunate, because "human beings need the help of their ancestors"—both "their own biological ancestors . . . and the ancestors of their societies and their institutions."[7]

Although I agree with Shils's concern over the neglect of tradition, I cite his work primarily to establish the point that social scientists are somewhat ill-at-ease with tradition. We are not quite sure what to do with the past. One reason for our uncertainty is, as Shils points out, our awareness that "there are two pasts." There is the noumenal past, which is "the sequence of occurred events." There is also "the perceived past," which is a "much more plastic thing, more capable of being retrospectively reformed by human beings living in the present."[8] This is the past that "is recorded in memory and in writing."[9]

It is the "perceived past" that bothers us as social scientists. Poets handle it much better than we do. In his elegy for John F. Kennedy, W. H. Auden could say that how Americans choose to live will decide the meaning of the president's death. Thus, "the future of the past depends on us."[10] Social scientists who, like myself, are not historians may at times be somewhat rigid in approaching the past. If we are of a positivist persuasion, we may ravage history for "hard facts" and data, forgetting the truth spoken in the jest that *data* is the plural of *anecdote.* Like Leopold von Ranke and his fellow German historians of the last century, we may naïvely hope to reconstruct the past "exactly as it took place" *(wie es eigentlich gewesen war).*

Alertness to a second past, a perceived past, may temper our zeal; but more likely, it will lead us to ignore history because it challenges our settled categories of analysis.[11] Like the rich young man in the Gospel, we will go away sad because we have many possessions. If, however, we are willing to risk a departure from our accustomed professional ways, we may be able to learn from historians how to deal with a perceived past. Historians have made their peace with the past as something that they interpret. For example, in the Prologue to his recent book *The Uneasy State,* historian Barry Karl devotes several pages to a review of the literature on the New Deal period and its relationship to the Progressive era. He discusses more than a dozen major works. Some stress the connections between economic centralization, nationalism, and progress. Leftist historians reject this Progressive interpretation as an apology for American capitalism and concentrate instead on the conservative character of the New Deal as a form of "state capitalism." Still others see the New Deal as a period when Americans made a serious effort "to come to grips with the problem of how the functions of management and control, which are necessary in modern industrial society, can be performed without violating commitments to individualism and self-government."[12] Karl goes on to note several other interpretations of the same period before offering his own. He intones his litany of interpretations without any hint of embarrassment. Although he prefers some interpretations to others, he thinks all of them are worthy of serious comment.

This is not to say that Karl would let anything go. He would not suffer lightly a colleague who makes a president of Al Smith or Alf Landon in the name of interpreting a perceived past. There are limits to interpretation; the limits are no less real for being imprecise. In this sense, the historian lacks the freedom of the novelist and the playwright. Shakespeare could have had Romeo poison Juliet and run off with the batty old nurse. The historian does not enjoy that sort of freedom, but he is free to interpret within the generous bounds of prevailing critical scholarship. Although I am a political scientist, not a historian, I present my argument in an effort to imitate what historians do. I offer an interpretation of the constitutional tradition that departs from received positions. If careful readers should find my work defective, I would be neither surprised nor offended. What does worry me, however, is the critical reader who thinks that what I am doing is not worth doing at all. That reader is the object of my rhetoric. He is the one I ask to lower his customary threshold of acceptable evidence in view of the novelty of the argument I am making. In the spirit of W. H. Auden's elegy to President Kennedy, which is cited in the epigraph of this section, we are thinking in terms of how "the future of the past depends on us."[13] If I am no historian, I am even less a poet; but I would enter a plea for poetic license on the grounds of the novelty of what I am trying to do.

## *Founding the Republic in Argument*

The Anti-Federalists lost the debate over the Constitution not merely because they were less clever arguers or less skillful politicians but because they had the weaker argument.

—Herbert J. Storing

A second reason for lowering the threshold of acceptable evidence is that the very act of founding the American Republic was itself an act of public argument. Hannah Arendt, whose thoughts on authority I examined in the Introduction to this book, has argued that the source of authority of regimes is the founding act itself. Great founding documents, such as the Constitution or the Mayflower Compact, are authoritative because they express an act of founding. They are not themslves the act of founding, but result from that act. The authority of the document is a derived authority, derived from the act of founding. As Fustel De Coulanges noted in his great work on ancient cities, foundings were religious events that usually led to an annual ritual to reenact the founding, rather than to a charter or a covenant. When a conqueror captured a city that had already been built, he would order a new founding through religious ceremony, even though the roads and buildings were all in place. In antiquity to *be* a city meant to have a founding—a religious event in which new gods are installed to replace the conquered deities and to unite the people by showing themselves to be greater gods than the particularistic gods of family and tribe.[14]

Documents are dispensable; foundings are not. Where there is authority, there has been a founding. For Americans, however, documents are not dispensable because, as Arendt notes, American foundings are characterized by "mutual promise and common deliberation"; they rest on consensus and argument based on that consensus. The documents capture and crystallize, albeit imperfectly, the nature of the consensus and the outcome of the argument.

The Constitution of the United States expresses the consensus and the outcome of the argument of 1787/88. All serious participants in the debate shared a common commitment to some sort of popular government and to individual rights. It was this consensus that made argument possible. Argument can grow only in the fertile soil of consensus. Absent consensus, there is no argument. Politeness there may be or invective or sullen withdrawal, but not argument. As William Schambra has noted, it was a fundamental consensus that "made possible the Founding, and gave the ratification debates the air of a quarrel within the family rather than of a civil war."[15]

Thus, for Americans, the founding of the Republic was an acting out of a great public argument. The founding was in the argument. If Arendt is correct in saying that the authoritative norms of the regime are in the founding, then it follows that the norms are in the argument as well. I believe Arendt is correct, and that is why I ask the reader to examine carefully the criteria by which he or she judges the argument of this book. When we say that the administrative state is compatible with constitutional principles, we must remember that the principles in question were themselves the object of argument. The judgment on administrative compatibility cannot be made in the bright light of deductive reasoning from unassailable first principles; it must be made in the shadow of primordial controversy.

It is because the regime was founded in argument that I have emphasized argument throughout this book—the argument that Woodrow Wilson and Frank Goodnow had with the framers; the argument over the ICC; the New Dealers' argument with the conservative Court of the mid thirties; the argument within New Deal circles that surfaced in the tone of the Brownlow Report, as opposed to that of the Attorney General's Report. Because the founding was in argument, it was only fitting that the development of American politics should be in argument as well. And because the administrative state is part of American politics—a terribly important part today—it, too, should be part of the argument that is a projection in time of the act of founding. This is why I am partial to the New Dealers and am somewhat hard on Wilson and Goodnow. The New Dealers tried to legitimate the administrative state that they were founding with arguments that were, for the most part, plausible restatements of the founding argument. Wilson and Goodnow wanted to start a new argument and thereby suggested that an administrative state could not be reconciled either with the founding argument or, by implication, with the founding itself.

I ask the reader to temper his or her judgment of my position by recalling that the principles by which we judge the administrative state are somewhat unclear. There is some doubt about the principles, and I seek the benefit of that doubt. In seeking this indulgence, I assure the reader that I am not using doubt to render the Constitution nugatory. The doubts are not a Trojan horse, seeking admittance to the city only to destroy it from within. The doubts are rooted in the argument of 1787/88; but that argument was a "bounded" argument. Like the New Deal historians whom I discussed above, the framers and ratifiers of the Constitution carried on their argument within certain limits. Fortunately, they had the good sense not to aspire to be *rational*, in Herbert Simon's exaggerated sense of that term.[16] Some ideas would have been preposterous then as now—such as the abolition of private property or joining the Holy Roman Empire. They never considered such matters, not because they were "satisficing," but because they were part of a tradition that had long since closed off many possibilities that were open to other societies.

The criterion for judging the compatibility between the administrative state and constitutional principles is not simply a matter of logic. We do not *deduce* the Consumer Products Safety Commission from the text of the Constitution in the Euclidian spirit of Thomas Hobbes's *Leviathan*. The question is one of judgment rather than of logic: Does an administrative agency fall within the confines of the "bounded argument" of 1787/88? This question, of course, invites another: What are the bounds of the bounded argument? This second question recalls the infinite regress implicit in Juvenal's query "Who will guard the guards?" Such questions have been appropriately examined elsewhere when scholars have debated the relative value of comments from men like Benjamin Rush compared to those better-known authors of the founding period.[17] Interesting as such questions might be, an attempt to examine them here would take us too far afield. I shall rest my case in the hope that my plea for an adjusted criterion of acceptable argument will merit the reader's assent to the proposition that the administrative state is a plausible expression of the constitutional order envisioned in the great public argument at the time of the founding of the Republic.

## A CONSTITUTIONAL THEORY
## OF PUBLIC ADMINISTRATION

> It is constantly assured, especially in our Tolstoyian tendencies, that when the lion lies down with the lamb the lion becomes lamb-like. But that is brutal annexation and imperialism on the part of the lamb. That is simply the lamb absorbing the lion instead of the lion eating the lamb. The real problem is—can the lion lie down with the lamb and still retain his royal ferocity.
> —Gilbert K. Chesterton, *Orthodoxy*

If the administrative state is indeed compatible with constitutional principles, it is necessary to make some sort of statement on how we might expect administrative institutions to sustain these principles. In a word, there is need for a normative theory of Public Administration that is grounded in the Constitution. This section outlines such a theory. The theory proceeds, mindful of Chesterton's advice that when we summon the lion to lie down with the lamb, we should not expect the lion to become a lamb. That, as he says, would be imperialism on the part of the lamb. The administrative state must not forfeit its administrative character in order to achieve constitutional legitimacy. As Woodrow Wilson counseled, administration "must learn our constitutions by heart; must get the bureaucratic fever out of its veins; must inhale much free American air"; but—as Wilson insists—all this without ceasing to be administration.[18]

The statement of the theory that I propose brings together and elaborates certain normative considerations that have already been touched upon at several points in this book.[19] The role of the Public Administration is to fulfill the objective of the oath of office: to uphold the Constitution of the United States. This means that administrators should use their discretionary power in order to maintain the constitutional balance of powers in support of individual rights. This, of course, is what the Congress, the president, and the courts are supposed to do as well. This unity of purpose is as it should be, because the Public Administration, like Congress, president, and courts, is an institution of government compatible with the constitutional design of the framers. Congress, the president, and the judiciary, taken discretely, either constitute or head one of the three great "branches" of government.[20] Each contributes in its own peculiar way to the grand end of maintaining the constitutional balance of power in support of individual rights. The Public Administration neither constitutes nor heads any branch of government, but is subordinate to all three of them. Like Congress, president, and courts, the Public Administration makes its distinctive contribution in a manner that is consistent with its peculiar place, which is one of subordination.

The image of a balance wheel best captures the distinctive contribution of the Public Administration. The Senate, as it was originally intended by the framers (as opposed to the Senate of history), is the constitutional model for the Public Administration as balance wheel, because the Senate, like the Public Administration, was intended to exercise all three powers of government.[21] Unlike the Senate of the framers' intent, however, the Public Administration exercises all three powers in a subordinate capacity and must make its peculiar contribution in conformity with that subordination to the institutions of government created in the first three articles of the Constitution. It does this by choosing which of its constitutional masters it will favor at a given time on a given issue in the continual struggle among the three branches as they act out the script of *Federalist 51*, wherein ambition counteracts ambition and "the interest of the man . . . [is] connected with the constitutional rights of the place."

This, of course, is what the Public Administration has been doing ever since Alexander Hamilton's fascinating effort to position the Treasury Department he headed and himself, as secretary of the Treasury, as a buffer (or perhaps a conduit) between President Washington and the First Congress.[22] Hamilton knew that he and his department were subordinate both to the president and to Congress, but he had the statesmanlike vision to see in that dual subordination the opportunity to shape events. Examples as recent as the "Superfund" scandal point to the perennial practice of administrators choosing between constitutional masters struggling for control of a particular agency. Career civil servants at the Environmental Protection Agency (EPA) tilted toward Congress and away from the president in that newsworthy battle.[23] Without political support from Congress, EPA's career personnel could not have executed the agency's statutory responsibilities. Without an aggressive and cooperative civil service, Congress could not have uncovered the depth of the scandal.[24]

The normative theory that I am suggesting deals more directly with attitudes than with behavior. Administrative agencies often do choose among constitutional masters, but they usually do so as a matter of fact and seldom as a matter of constitutional principle. Their preoccupation with the low arts of organizational survival blinds them to the brighter angels of their nature. They should lift their vision to see themselves as men and women who "run a Constitution." The normative theory that I propose is intended to encourage administrators and the public to think about administrative behavior in constitutional terms. There is no need to ridicule as lackeys those administrators who zealously support the president; nor to condemn as obstructionists those who oppose him. Civil servants who provide Congress or the courts with vital but embarrassing information need not be "whistle blowers" to their friends and "leakers" to their enemies. By grounding our thinking about the Public Administration in the Constitution, we can transform erstwhile lackeys, leakers, obstructionists, and whistle blowers into administrative statesmen.

We can do this without substantive policy implications. The constitutional approach to Public Administration is suitable for administrators who think we do too little for the poor, as well as for those who think we do too much; for those who support a nuclear freeze and for those who oppose it; for supply-side economists and for advocates of industrial policy. The Constitution is permissive on these issues. Administrators will not be without firm, perhaps passionate, convictions on matters of this sort. They should certainly use their discretion to favor those policies that they think are most likely to promote the public interest; but they should assess the public interest against the broad background of constitutional principle.[25] The Constitution transcends a given tax policy, a weapons system, and food stamps. It cannot be confined to any such particulars. The constitutional word becomes flesh in statute, rule, and policy. Constitutionally motivated administrators, like lobbyists, may be policy advocates; but their advocacy, unlike that of lobbyists, should be tempered by the imperatives of the constitutional order. Administrators do not differ from lobbyists in the sense that lobbyists are committed to causes but administrators are not. Administrators differ from lobbyists because administrators take an oath to uphold the Constitution, but lobbyists do not. For public administrators, the Constitution is the cause above causes. In exercising discretionary authority to support this policy or that one, their judgment should be informed by the constitutional needs of the time, as well as by the needs of the poor, the environment, the Air Force, the housing industry, the economy, the Third World, and the myriad other matters that clamor for the attention of the Public Administration.

The link between subordination to constitutional masters and freedom to choose among them preserves both the instrumental character of Public Administration and the autonomy necessary for professionalism. In this way we can reinstate the great insight of the discredited dichotomy between politics and administration. This tired old war-horse still plays the mighty stallion, despite academic efforts to put him out to pasture. Every student of Public Administration denies the possibility of making a distinction between politics and administration; but everyone else continues to make that distinction. Although the attack on the dichotomy is well founded in social-science literature, it always fails to convince because the dichotomy holds the high ground from which administration can be seen both as subordinate to the political leadership of the day and as professionally exempt from political interference. By suggesting a theory of Public Administration that combines constitutional subordination and autonomy, I hope to preserve the enduring insight of the venerable dichotomy without succumbing to its naïve view of administration as apolitical. Administration is political; but like the judiciary, it has its own style of politics and its distinctive functions within the constitutional order.

The idea of having the Public Administration choose among competing constitutional masters may overstate the competitive relationship among the three great branches. The competition never ends, but it is not all consuming. The relationships can be harmonious in some policy areas, and often are. Louis Fisher's *Presidential Spending Power* convincingly describes a political world in which "moral understandings" and "gentlemen's agreements" penetrate the constitutional barriers between the legislative and executive branches.[26] Administrators facilitate these mollifying arrangements and are, at times, themselves parties to such understandings and agreements. This is but another way of maintaining the proper constitutional balance of powers. Rather than choose between the Congress and the presidency, the Public Administration may at times look for suitable means to bring them or keep them together.

When it does this, the Public Administration plays a crucial role in softening the harsh logic of separation of powers and proves itself a worthy successor to the courts and political parties that provided the same service in the nineteenth century.[27] Parties, courts, and agencies have emerged as the institutional expressions of Publius's caution against a doctrinaire interpretation of the principle of separation of powers. The theory that I suggest would teach us to view quite differently the independence of independent regulatory commissions, the formal accountability of inspectors general both to Congress and to the heads of their executive departments, and the clearly executive powers of Congress's Government Accounting Office. These institutions are exemplars, rather than aberrations, of American Public Administration. They present in dramatic form the pervasive administrative principle of responsibility, flowing upward simultaneously in two or three directions.

Thus far we have spoken of the role of the Public Administration in maintaining the appropriate balance of power. This is not an end in itself. Constitutional powers are separated, checked, and balanced to protect individual rights, which is the purpose of American politics. In discussing the appropriate balance, I have concentrated on the legislative and executive branches. The judiciary asserts its role in the constitutional balance through the doctrine of individual rights. This doctrine enables the courts to compete with the legislative and executive branches for the grand prize of contemporary politics: the control of the Public Administration.[28]

Because the administrative process affects individual rights in so many important ways, the Public Administration is no less subordinate to the courts than it is to the "political" branches. Judicial intervention in the administrative process can have profound and devastating effects on program management precisely because the intervention is made in the name of individual rights. Rights trump utility. Judicial intervention in defense of rights—for example, the rights of prisoners or patients in state mental hospitals—can irrevocably destroy the most careful long-term planning and the most elegant cost/benefit analysis. There is a natural and understandable tension between the courts, with their commitment to rights, and a managerial ethos of Public Administration that is deeply committed to utility.[29] A normative theory of Public Administration that is grounded in constitutional principle must not collapse into managerial utilitarianism. The courts must be considerd as serious competitors for the favorable exercise of administrative discretion. This is because the overwhelming majority of claims of individual rights begin and end in administrative agencies. It is not enough for public administrators to obey court orders; they should also take seriously the judicial values that are revealed in court opinions.[30] They should learn to think like judges, as well as like legislators and executives, because they are all three of these. In a regime of separation of powers, administrators must do the work of statesmen.

The claim for the important role of choosing one's constitutional master is grounded in the constitutional theory developed in chapter 6. The Public Administration is part of a constitutional *order* that was chosen by the people in the great ratification debate of 1787/88. The fact that administrators, like judges, are not elected in no way diminishes their constitutional stature. Popular election is simply one of at least twenty-two ways that have been or still are approved for holding office under the Constitution.[31]

To counteract our excessive reliance on election as the entitlement to office, we would do well to recall that the great constitutional scholar Edward S. Corwin once had to remind Franklin Roosevelt that the president has his powers, not from the people, but from the Constitution. It is only the Constitution that has power from the people. In his *Autobiography,* Theodore Roosevelt announced a "stewardship theory" of the presidency, by which he meant that "it was not only his [the president's] right but his duty to do anything that the needs of the Nation demanded unless such action was forbidden by the Constitution or by the laws."[32] Although this view of the presidency is not without support in some Supreme Court opinions, the threat that it poses to the rule of law is apparent.[33] If the American people have a "steward," the steward is their Constitution, not their president.

The Public Administration is no monolith. Throughout this book, I have often prefaced "Public Administration" with the definite article to underscore my effort to write about an institution of government and not about process and behavior.[34] When I speak of "the Public Administration" choosing among its constitutional masters, I do not envision every agency of the government rising as one man in support of, say, Congress against an overbearing president. The pluralism that dominates American politics is reflected in the Public Administration just as it is reflected in the Congress, the presidency, and the courts.[35]

I carry no brief for pluralism in its manifestation as the interest-group liberalism so soundly criticized by Theodore Lowi.[36] A legitimated Public Administration could be helpful in taming some unhappy pluralist excesses; but this is action at the margin of affairs. If pluralism is a problem and not the solution that some think it is, a prescription for political medicine much stronger than administrative reform is indicated.[37] The Public Administration, faithful to the prevailing pluralist structure of American politics, will choose its constitutional masters on an agency basis. It will do this only after bitter internal wranglings. At times it will make its choice in the lonely and desperate action of an alienated individual who is either a hero, a fanatic, or both.

The literature in public personnel management has at times called for an elite corps of unified, high-ranking senior career executives.[38] The Senior Executive Service (SES), which was created by the Civil Service Reform Act of 1978, is but a dim shadow of earlier suggested reforms. There is insufficient institutional support in this legislation to give the SES the kind of government-wide perspective that the literature envisioned. An important by-product of the widespread disappointment within the SES has been a marked increase in the tendency of senior career personnel to come together to protect their personal interests.[39] The SES remains a disappointment, because it has been all stick and no carrot, all risk and no reward.[40] Immediately after the passage of the Civil Service Reform Act, congressional support for bonuses and salary increments was reduced. This demoralized the senior executives and brought them together primarily for their financial self-interest. Now that they are increasingly organized, however, there is nothing to keep them from discussing issues of broader interest than their own finances. Indeed, they often do so in a public-spirited manner.[41] Perhaps these organizations will eventually develop into influential professional associations which will take positions on policy issues of the day in the name of nonpartisan managerial expertise.[42] Then, of course, it would be quite meaningful to speak of "the Public Administration" as an identifiable force, unified in its leadership and ready to influence public opinion on specific issues of current interest. Should such a formal embodiment of the Public Administration emerge, it would not be the first time that self-interest has planted the seed of high-minded public service. Publius would approve.

## THE OATH OF OFFICE

"When a man takes an oath, Meg, he's holding his own self in his hands. Like water. *(He cups his hands.)* And if he opens his fingers *then*—he needn't hope to find himself again. Some men aren't capable of this, but I'd be loathe to think your father one of them."

—Thomas More, in *A Man for All Seasons*

To bring our discussion to a close, let us turn to the oath of office. The oath not only reinforces the normative tone of this book, but it also captures nicely the tension between administrative autonomy and subordination, which I discussed in the preceding section. The oath justifies the administrator's claim to a certain professional autonomy in choosing among constitutional masters. The concept of "profession" necessarily implies some sort of independent judgment. This is true of physicians, attorneys, clergymen, teachers, engineers, musicians, and athletes. If Public Administration is in *any* sense a profession, administrators must *in some sense* be independent of their constitutional masters in carrying on their professional activities. A principled justification of some sort of independence is the great strength of the politics/administration dichotomy and explains its survival in the face of so much embarrassing evidence demanding its demise. This independence is heady wine. It sugggests rogue elephants, runaway bureaucracies, headless fourth branches, and so forth. In the final pages of this book, I shall argue that the oath to uphold the Constitution legitimates some kind of administrative independence; but precisely because it is an oath to uphold *the Constitution,* it has the potential to tame, channel, and civilize this independence in a way that will make it safe for and supportive of the founding principles of the Republic.

These, then, are the two major points that I make in this final section: (1) that the oath of office legitimates a degree of professional autonomy for the administrator and (2) that the object of the oath, the Constitution itself, can keep this autonomy within acceptable bounds.

## OATH JUSTIFYING AUTONOMY

> Each public officer who takes an oath to support the constitution swears that he will support it as he understands it and not as it is understood by others.
> —Andrew Jackson

The idea of the oath to uphold the Constitution as a source of independent judgment is nothing new. It was used by Chief Justice John Marshall in 1803 in *Marbury* v. *Madison.*[43] This was the case in which the Supreme Court discovered that it had the power to declare acts of Congress unconstitutional. The Constitution has no explicit language on this point. One of the arguments that Marshall used to justify the Court's power to nullify acts of Congress was that the justices are required to take an oath to support the Constitution. Marshall maintained that such an oath would be a "solemn mockery" if judges had to render decisions based on laws contrary to the Constitution they were sworn to uphold. Thus, for Marshall, the oath of office was woven into the fabric of an argument that interpreted the Constitution as conferring on judges a professional independence that permitted them to sit in judgment on at least some acts of Congress. Interestingly, Marshall ignored the fact that the

Constitution also imposes an oath "to support this Constitution" upon the president, all members of Congress, all state legislators, and "all executive and judicial Officers, both of the United States and of the several States."

This point was not lost on President Jackson. In his famous veto message against the renewal of the charter of the Second Bank of the United States, Jackson cited his oath of office as the basis for challenging the constitutionality of the bank, despite a Supreme Court ruling in support of the bank. "Each public officer," said Jackson, "who takes an oath to support the Constitution swears that he will support it as he understands it and not as it is understood by others."[44]

In citing these examples from Marshall and Jackson, I do not suggest that a parallel argument can be made to support such independence in constitutional matters for the civil service. State and federal employees take oaths that are based on statutes and administrative regulations, whereas the oath taken by presidents and judges is mandated by the Constitution itself. Indeed, the very words of the president's oath are prescribed in the Constitution. He must "preserve, protect and defend" the Constitution, which is a broader duty than that of the administrator who swears to "support and defend" it. Despite these important differences in the wording and source of their respective oaths, it is still true that both the president and the administrator take an oath to support the Constitution of the United States. If it is in the nature of an oath to confer independence, then administrators have some sort of independence in living out their oath in practice. To establish this point, we must look more closely at the nature of an oath.[45]

Early in the Reagan administration, the public was invited to reflect on this question when the president repeatedly referred to the public servant's oath in order to justify his firing of the striking members of the Professional Air Traffic Controllers Organization (PATCO). Under these circumstances the oath was invoked as an instrument to compel obedience. The president's position was that the air traffic controllers should be fired for violating their oath not to strike. He may well have been correct in firing the strikers; but if so, in relying on the oath not to strike, he was right for the wrong reason. The controllers had never taken an oath not to strike. They had taken an oath to uphold the Constitution and had made a promise not to strike. As we shall see below, there is an important difference between an oath and a promise. As far as the PATCO strikers were concerned, the president might well have justified his decision by arguing that termination is a just penalty for an open violation of law in a serious matter, after appropriate warnings have been given. In fact, the president sometimes made this argument, but he invariably embellished it with references to a nonexistent oath not to strike. In so doing, he trivialized the oath. He reduced a profound moral commitment to a shallow legalism.

An oath is a profound moral commitment, because its object is always something that is or should be of great significance to the juror. The playwright Robert Bolt captures this idea when, in *A Man for All Seasons,* he has Thomas

More explain to his daughter why he cannot violate his conscience by taking an oath that recognizes Henry VIII as head of the church in England: " 'When a man takes an oath, Meg, he's holding his own self in his hands. Like water. *(He cups his hands.)* And if he opens his fingers *then*—he needn't hope to find himself again. Some men aren't capable of this, but I'd be loathe to think your father one of them.' ''[46]

It is no coincidence that oaths, such as the oath to uphold the Constitution, usually call upon God to witness the swearing. The religious context of oaths is well known and suggests an appeal to someone or something transcendent.[47] The sacral language of oaths directs attention beyond the parties by whom and before whom the pledge or statement is made. For this reason, an oath can never be reduced to a question of subordinating the will of one human being to that of another. Such subordination would destroy the transcendent focus of the oath.

The same point can be put in more familiar secular terms. Many of us would find the violation of an oath morally offensive, because in terms of a secular ethic we believe that oaths bind in conscience. Perjury, for example, is often looked upon as a moral abomination, as well as a crime. A contemporary secularist might consider the invocation of the deity quaint verbiage, without retreating from the moral position that the oath itself binds in conscience. For such a person an oath cannot be simply a pledge of obedience by one person to another, because no one can resign his or her conscience to the safekeeping of another. An unqualified oath to obey is a contradiction in terms. Oaths, precisely because they are of moral significance, cannot be reduced to an abdication of one's will and judgment in favor of another human being.[48]

When President Reagan invoked the controllers' oath of office as a justification for firing them, he confused several issues. The act of firing a subordinate occurs within the context of the employer/employee relationship. This relationship, important as it is for putting bread on the table, does not rise to the level of the sort of activities that are worthy of an oath. An oath to obey the foreman at a GM plant is absurd. To the religious man or woman it would be a shocking example of taking the Lord's name in vain. At one level of analysis we can say that President Reagan was a boss firing some workers because they had failed to do what they were told. The argument over the justification of such an action can only be confused by references to an oath of office.

At another level we can view the president as the chief executive officer of the Republic, who fired the strikers for their lawlessness pursuant to his constitutional responsibility to attend to the faithful execution of the laws of the United States. At this level of argument, the oath of office is relevant, but it is the president's oath, not that of the strikers, that is at issue.

A third area of confusion is the mistake the president made in suggesting that the controllers had taken an oath not to strike. This is the oath that the controllers actually took:

I, _____, do solemnly swear (or affirm) that I will support and defend the Constitution of the United States against all enemies, foreign and domestic; that I will bear true faith and allegiance to the same; that I take this obligation freely, without any mental reservation or purpose of evasion; and that I will well and faithfully discharge the duties of the office on which I am about to enter, so help me God.

They also made this promise:

I am not participating in any strike against the government of the United States or any agency thereof, and I will not so participate while an employee of the government of the United States or any agency thereof.

In criticizing the controllers for breaking their oath not to strike, the president confused a promise with an oath. The confusion is understandable; oaths and promises are both commonly thought to bind in conscience. The difference between the two is that oaths are reserved for human activities of the highest order: marriage, citizenship, the healing arts, the pursuit of justice, divine worship, and so forth.[49] Promises can be serious or somewhat trivial. I can promise to sing at your wedding, to meet you for lunch, to send you a postcard, and so on. If at the last minute I should wantonly break my promise to sing at your wedding, I would be doing something wrong because I would needlessly cause you and the wedding party considerable inconvenience. Suppose, however, that my reason for doing this was that at the last minute I had discovered that your bride was your own sister. My refusal to sing at the incestuous nuptials would then be understandable. I could plausibly argue that my moral objection to incest overrides my moral commitment to keep my promise, that when I made the promise, I had not realized what it was that you were actually asking of me. Only a person with the morals of a Rumpelstiltskin would fault my decision.

Promises are morally binding, but they can always be reconsidered if unforeseen circumstances of a higher moral order intervene. Thus, if I break my promise to meet you for lunch because on the way to the restaurant I rescued a child from a burning building, no one would question the integrity of my decision. On the other hand, suppose that I told you the reason I missed the luncheon was that I had decided that the greatest good of the greatest number in the long run would be further advanced by my staying home to plant nasturtiums. You would then rightly look upon me as a singularly unreliable fellow who does not take his word very seriously. The purpose of the institution of promise keeping is precisely to impose cloture on utilitarian calculations about the greatest good. The utility of promise keeping in human affairs "trumps" any such calculation.[50] This is at least one reason why we are morally obligated to keep promises. The obligation, however, is subject to reappraisal when moral considerations of a higher order intervene—such as the incestuous nuptials or the child in the burning building.

Oaths, however, are not as easily reappraised. One reason for this is the religious origin of oaths. The believer who calls upon an omniscient, omnipotent, and benevolent deity to witness his oath would be well advised to concentrate on fidelity to that oath and not to worry about the consequences. Such a person has a powerful reason for saying, "Thy will be done." The secularist lacks the assurance of the believer, but he is also likely to be quite cautious in saying what circumstances, if any, would justify a physician's deliberately harming his patient or an attorney's suborning perjury. These questions raise intricate problems about absolute and relative moral principles which need not detain us here. My point has been simply to stress the difference between an oath and a promise and to suggest that when President Reagan confused the two in the PATCO case, he trivialized the oath.

The focus of this argument has been to present the moral significance of the oath of office as the reason for suggesting that it is a statement of professional independence, rather than subservience. The argument has been played off against President Reagan's reference to the oath as a commitment simply to obey. There is something unsettling about this argument, however. What kind of independence do we want in public administrators? Surely the oath to uphold the Constitution cannot be the basis for legitimating a runaway bureaucracy.

## OATH GUIDING AUTONOMY

> In the law beyond the law, which calls upon us to be fair . . . each of us is necessarily his own chief justice. In fact he is the whole Supreme Court from which there lies no appeal.
>
> —Earl Warren

The response to the concern over a runaway bureaucracy goes to the heart of the issue of professional autonomy. If professionalism necessarily implies some kind of independent judgment, it also implies restraint in the exercise of this independence. The restraint comes from the discipline of the professional community; the oath of office can be looked upon as the rite of initiation into that community. The moral character of the oath confers *professional* independence, not personal isolation. Ordinarily, oaths are social acts. They are recited publicly, and they bring the juror into some kind of relationship with others. Thus, the vertical relationship implied in an oath's invocation of the deity is supplemented by the horizontal relationship consequent upon entering the community of the sworn. This horizontal relationship is the basis of professional standards and mores by which the initiated can tutor and discipline neophytes in the hope of keeping the profession's independence within reasonable bounds. These standards and mores can be both altruistic and self-interested.

If Public Administration is a profession at all, it is a nascent one and therefore lacks the specific standards that one finds in the traditional professions. As a starting point, however, in our quest for self-restraining principles on professional independence, we would do well to begin with fidelity to the constitutional heritage to which the oath of office commits the juror.[51]

We may easily grow impatient with an expression such as "fidelity to the constitutional heritage." This is because we tend to think of the Constitution as law and of law as command. It is much simpler to say "Do what you are told" than to say "Be faithful to the constitutional heritage."

To obviate this problem, it is important to recall a point made earlier in this book. Although the Constitution is law, indeed "the supreme of the land," it is a very peculiar type of law. It is quite different from, say, a traffic law. The latter simply commands: Stop! Parts of the Constitution issue commands—the decennial census, the quadrennial presidential elections, and so forth; but at a deeper level the Constitution expresses and creates a community. It brings a political order into being and gives it formal definition. It is covenant, more than command. For this reason, the Constitution is a worthy object of an oath, whereas a traffic law is not—even though traffic laws save lives. The Constitution is the symbol of our common life as a people who are organized for action in history. It teems with majestic generalities such as "due process of law," "privileges and immunities," and "equal protection of the laws." Such language invites those who are banded together in civic friendship to join a great public argument over the meaning of the good life. It is an ongoing argument that has been graced by the likes of Publius and Lincoln. The document itself, drafted in 1787, can be looked upon as the conclusion of one great public argument that began in 1607 and the premise of another great argument that is still going on today.

If we can think in terms of the Constitution not simply as command but also as covenant, symbol, conclusion-and-premise-of-public-argument, expression-and-creation-of-community, and so forth, we may begin to make more sense out of "fidelity to the constitutional heritage" than the legal positivist would allow. The oath to uphold the Constitution can then be seen not simply as a pledge to obey but also as an initiation into a community of disciplined discourse, aimed at discovering, renewing, adapting, and applying the fundamental principles that support our public order. The task is to see the oath more as an act of civility than submission. The word *civility* suggests both the independence and the self-restraint we look for in professionals.

Let us now try to see what it might mean in practice for the professional administrator to look to the constitutional heritage for guidance in how to exercise his or her professional autonomy to choose responsibly among constitutional masters. Take the case of one whose administrative tasks bring to his attention presidential activities that are legally or even constitutionally questionable. It is clear to the administrator that if the president is to succeed in his dubious undertaking, he will need the support of a good number of reliable administrators and their staffs. The administrator's problem is whether the right thing for him to do is to resist, support, or ignore the questionable activity. If he reflects upon his oath of office for guidance, what is he likely to discover? Very little. The case as described is too general to yield a sensible answer. Suppose, however, that the case actually involves:

1. President Nixon establishing a system of warrantless wiretapping for purposes of national security; or
2. President Jefferson considering the Louisiana Purchase; or
3. President Lincoln suspending the writ of habeas corpus without congressional authorization; or
4. President Franklin Roosevelt planning during World War II to establish "relocation centers" for West Coast citizens of Japanese origin; or
5. President Truman seizing the steel mills during the Korean War.

Clearly the answer to the question of whether to resist, support, or ignore these constitutionally questionable activities is circumstantial, not doctrinaire. Quite literally, "It all depends." The oath to uphold the Constitution is not a talisman. Nor is it an abstract proposition from which one rigorously deduces correct behavior. It is, as suggested above, an initiation into a community of disciplined discourse in which one learns the ways of the constitutional heritage. The careful study of each of the situations given above will provide the administrator with the professional competence to have a *sense* of what is constitutionally appropriate. "Sense" is emphasized because it captures the movement toward the particular and the concrete and away from the universal and the abstract—a movement that is crucial for this argument. An example will help. In a deposition to a Senate committee investigating illegal intelligence activities, former President Nixon drew a parallel between his own national-security wiretapping activities and Lincoln's paying soldiers from Treasury funds without congressional appropriation. At an abstract level, Nixon had a good point. Both presidents had engaged in dubious activities for what they considered to be serious reasons of state. It is only when we look at the issues concretely—the men and the times involved—that we see how outrageous Nixon's comparison really was.

What I am suggesting is that among the skills and knowledge that we should look for in the public administrator is a professional competence in the constitutional heritage. This should not be confused with the lawyer's competence in constitutional law, which must be up-to-date and focused on advocacy. The case for the administrator as constitutionalist deals more with history than with the present, with insight rather than advocacy, with argument rather than law. A particularly instructive example is the debate in Lincoln's cabinet over the admission of West Virginia to the Union. Secretary of State William Seward, Secretary of War Edwin Stanton, and Treasury Secretary Salmon

Chase read papers defending the proposition that the loyal counties in the northwest section of secessionist Virginia could be established as a new state. The papers of Attorney General Edward Bates, Navy Secretary Gideon Welles, and Postmaster General Montgomery Blair denounced this as a violation of article 4 of the Constitution, which forbids the creation of a new state from part of an existing state without "the Consent of the Legislatures of the States concerned." Questions of military policy were nicely balanced against constitutional scruples over whether Virginia was still a state and, if so, where its legislature was to be found. Administrators who are steeped in constitutional traditions of this sort will have a profound sense of professional propriety. They will have a principled basis and, above all, a "sense" for when to bend and when to hold firm. They will know statesmanship when they see it.

# Appendix A

# The Constitution of the United States

We the People of the United States, in Order to form a more perfect Union, establish Justice, insure domestic Tranquility, provide for the common defence, promote the general Welfare, and secure the Blessings of Liberty to ourselves and our Posterity, do ordain and establish this Constitution for the United States of America.

ARTICLE. I.

Section. 1. All legislative Powers herein granted shall be vested in a Congress of the United States, which shall consist of a Senate and House of Representatives.

Section. 2. The House of Representatives shall be composed of Members chosen every second Year by the People of the several States, and the Electors in each State shall have the Qualifications requisite for Electors of the most numerous Branch of the State Legislature.

No Person shall be a Representative who shall not have attained to the Age of twenty five Years, and been seven Years a Citizen of the United States, and who shall not, when elected, be an Inhabitant of that State in which he shall be chosen.

Representatives and direct Taxes shall be apportioned among the several States which may be included within this Union, according to their respective Numbers, which shall be determined by adding to the whole Number of free Persons, including those bound to Service for a Term of Years, and excluding Indians not taxed, three fifths of all other Persons. The actual Enumeration shall be made within three Years after the first Meeting of the Congress of the United States, and within every subsequent Term of ten Years, in such Manner as they shall by Law direct. The Number of Representatives shall not exceed one for every thirty Thousand, but each State shall have at Least one Representative; and until such enumeration shall be made, the State of New Hampshire shall be entitled to chuse three, Massachusetts eight, Rhode-Island and Providence Plantations one, Connecticut five, New-York six, New Jersey four, Pennsylvania eight, Delaware one, Maryland six, Virginia ten, North Carolina five, South Carolina five, and Georgia three.

When vacancies happen in the Representation from any State, the Executive Authority thereof shall issue Writs of Election to fill such Vacancies.

The House of Representatives shall chuse their Speaker and other Officers; and shall have the sole Power of Impeachment.

Section. 3. The Senate of the United States shall be composed of two Senators from each State, chosen by the Legislature thereof, for six Years; and each Senator shall have one Vote.

Immediately after they shall be assembled in Consequence of the first Election, they shall be divided as equally as may be into three Classes. The Seats of the Senators of the first Class shall be vacated at the Expiration of the second Year, of the second Class at the Expiration of the fourth Year, and of the third Class at the Expiration of the sixth Year, so that one third may be chosen every second Year; and if Vacancies happen by Resignation, or otherwise, during the Recess of the Legislature of any State, the Executive thereof may make temporary Appointments until the next Meeting of the Legislature, which shall then fill such Vacancies.

No Person shall be a Senator who shall not have attained to the Age of thirty Years, and been nine Years a Citizen of the United States, and who shall not, when elected, be an inhabitant of that State for which he shall be chosen.

The Vice President of the United States shall be President of the Senate, but shall have no Vote, unless they be equally divided.

The Senate shall chuse their other Officers, and also a President pro tempore, in the Absence of the Vice President, or when he shall exercise the Office of President of the United States.

The Senate shall have the sole Power to try all Impeachments. When sitting for that Purpose, they shall be on Oath or Affirmation. When the President of the United States is tried, the Chief Justice shall preside: And no Person shall be convicted without the Concurrence of two thirds of the Members present.

Judgment in Cases of Impeachment shall not extend further than to removal from Office, and disqualification to hold and enjoy any Office of honor, Trust or Profit under the United States: but the Party convicted shall nevertheless be liable and subject to Indictment, Trial, Judgment and Punishment, according to Law.

Section. 4. The Times, Places and Manner of holding Elections for Senators and Representatives, shall be prescribed in each State by the Legislature thereof; but the Congress may at any time by Law make or alter such Regulations, except as to the Places of chusing Senators.

The Congress shall assemble at least once in every Year, and such Meeting shall be on the first Monday in December, unless they shall by Law appoint a different Day.

Section. 5. Each House shall be the Judge of the Elections, Returns and Qualifications of its own Members, and a Majority of each shall constitute a Quorum to do Business; but a smaller Number may adjourn from day to day, and may be authorized to compel the Attendance of absent Members, in such Manner, and under such Penalties as each House may provide.

Each House may determine the Rules of its Proceedings, punish its Members for disorderly Behaviour, and, with the Concurrence of two thirds, expel a Member.

Each House shall keep a Journal of its Proceedings, and from time to time publish the same, excepting such Parts as may in their Judgment require Secrecy; and the Yeas and Nays of the Members of either House on any question shall, at the Desire of one fifth of those Present, be entered on the Journal.

Neither House, during the Session of Congress, shall, without the Consent of the other, adjourn for more than three days, nor to any other Place than that in which the two Houses shall be sitting.

Section. 6. The Senators and Representatives shall receive a Compensation for their Services, to be ascertained by Law, and paid out of the Treasury of the United States. They shall in all Cases, except Treason, Felony and Breach of the Peace, be privileged from Arrest during their Attendance at the Session of their respective Houses, and in going to and returning from the same; and for any Speech or Debate in either House, they shall not be questioned in any other Place.

No Senator or Representative shall, during the Time for which he was elected, be appointed to any civil Office under the Authority of the United States, which shall have been created, or the Emoluments whereof shall have been encreased during such time; and no Person holding any Office under the United States, shall be a Member of either House during his Continuance in Office.

Section. 7. All Bills for raising Revenue shall originate in the House of Representatives; but the Senate may propose or concur with Amendments as on other Bills.

Every Bill which shall have passed the House of Representatives and the Senate, shall, before it become a Law, be presented to the President of the United States; If he approve he shall sign it, but if not he shall return it, with his Objections to that House in which it shall have originated, who shall enter the Objections at large on their Journal, and proceed to reconsider it. If after such Reconsideration two thirds of that House shall agree to pass the Bill, it shall be sent, together with the Objections, to the other House, by which it shall likewise be reconsidered, and if approved by two thirds of that House, it shall become a Law. But in all such Cases the Votes of both Houses shall be determined by yeas and Nays, and the Names of the Persons voting for and against the Bill shall be entered on the Journal of each House respectively. If any Bill shall not be returned by the President within ten Days (Sundays excepted) after it shall have been presented to him, the Same shall be a Law, in like Manner as if he had signed it, unless the Congress by their Adjournment prevent its Return, in which Case it shall not be a Law.

Every Order, Resolution, or Vote to which the Concurrence of the Senate and House of Representatives may be necessary (except on a question of Adjournment) shall be presented to the President of the United States; and before the Same shall take Effect, shall be approved by him, or being disapproved by him, shall be repassed by two thirds of the Senate and House of Representatives, according to the Rules and Limitations prescribed in the Case of a Bill.

Section. 8. The Congress shall have Power To lay and collect Taxes, Duties, Imposts and Excises, to pay the Debts and Provide for the common Defence and general Welfare of the United States; but all Duties, Imposts and Excises shall be uniform throughout the United States;

To borrow Money on the credit of the United States;

To regulate Commerce with foreign Nations, and among the several States, and with the Indian Tribes;

To establish an uniform Rule of Naturalization, and uniform Laws on the subject of Bankruptcies throughout the United States;

To coin Money, regulate the Value thereof, and of foreign Coin, and fix the Standard of Weights and Measures;

To provide for the Punishment of counterfeiting the Securities and current Coin of the United States;

To establish Post Offices and post Roads;

To promote the Progress of Science and useful Arts, by securing for limited Time to Authors and Inventors the exclusive Right to their respective Writings and Discoveries;

To constitute Tribunals inferior to the supreme Court;

To define and punish Piracies and Felonies committed on the high Seas, and Offences against the Law of Nations;

To declare War, grant Letters of Marque and Reprisal, and make Rules concerning Captures on Land and Water;

To raise and support Armies, but no Appropriation of Money to that Use shall be for a longer Term than two Years;

To provide and maintain a Navy;

To make Rules for the Government and Regulation of the land and naval Forces;

To provide for calling forth the Militia to execute the Laws of the Union, suppress Insurrections and repel Invasions;

To provide for organizing, arming, and disciplining, the Militia, and for governing such Part of them as may be employed in the Service of the United States, reserving to the States respectively, the Appointment of the Officers, and the Authority of training the Militia according to the discipline prescribed by Congress;

To exercise exclusive Legislation in all Cases whatsoever, over such District (not exceeding ten Miles square) as may, by Cession of Particular States, and the Acceptance of Congress, become the Seat of the Government of the United States, and to exercise like Authority over all Places purchased by the Consent of the Legislature of the State in which the Same shall be, for the Erection of Forts, Magazines, Arsenals, dock-Yards, and other needful Buildings;—And

To make all Laws which shall be necessary and proper for carrying into Execution the foregoing Powers, and all other Powers vested by this Constitution in the Government of the United States, or in any Department or Officer thereof.

Section. 9. The Migration or Importation of such Persons as any of the States now existing shall think proper to admit, shall not be prohibited by the Congress prior to the Year one thousand eight hundred and eight, but a Tax or duty may be imposed on such Importation, not exeeding ten dollars for each Person.

The Privilege of the Writ of Habeas Corpus shall not be suspended, unless when in Cases of Rebellion or Invasion the public Safety may require it.

No Bill of Attainder or ex post facto Law shall be passed.

No Capitation, or other direct, Tax shall be laid, unless in Proportion to the Census or Enumeration herein before directed to be taken.

No Tax or Duty shall be laid on Articles exported from any State.

No Preference shall be given by any Regulation of Commerce or Revenue to the Ports of one State over those of another: nor shall Vessels bound to, or from, one State, be obliged to enter, clear, or pay Duties in another.

No Money shall be drawn from the Treasury, but in Consequence of Appropriations made by Law; and a regular Statement and Account of the Receipts and Expenditures of all public Money shall be published from time to time.

No Title of Nobility shall be granted by the United States: And no Person holding any Office of Profit or Trust under them, shall, without the Consent of the Congress, accept of any present, Emolument, Office, or Title, of any kind whatever, from any King, Prince, or foreign State.

Section. 10. No State shall enter into any Treaty, Alliance, or Confederation; grant Letters of Marque and Reprisal; coin Money; emit Bills of Credit; make any Thing but gold and silver Coin a Tender in Payment of Debts; pass any Bill of Attainder, ex post facto Law, or Law impairing the Obligation of Contracts, or grant any Title of Nobility.

No State shall, without the Consent of the Congress, lay any Imposts or Duties on Imports or Exports, except what may be absolutely necessary for executing it's inspection Laws: and the net Produce of all Duties and Imposts, laid by any State on Imports or Exports, shall be for the Use of the Treasury of the United States; and all such Laws shall be subject to the Revision and Controul of the Congress.

No State shall, without the Consent of Congress, lay any Duty of Tonnage, keep Troops, or Ships of War in time of Peace, enter into any Agreement or Compact with another State, or with a foreign Power, or engage in War, unless actually invaded, or in such imminent Danger as will not admit of delay.

## ARTICLE. II.

Section. 1. The executive Power shall be vested in a President of the United States of America. He shall hold his Office during the Term of four Years, and, together with the Vice President, chosen for the same Term, be elected, as follows

Each State shall appoint, in such Manner as the Legislature thereof may direct, a Number of Electors, equal to the whole Number of Senators and Representatives to which the State may be entitled in the Congress: but no Senator or Representative, or Person holding an Office of Trust or Profit under the United States, shall be appointed an Elector.

The Electors shall meet in their respective States, and vote by Ballot for two Persons, of whom one at least shall not be an Inhabitant of the same State with themselves. And they shall make a List of all the Persons voted for, and of the Number of Votes for each; which List they shall sign and certify, and transmit sealed to the Seat of the Government of the United States, directed to the President of the Senate. The President of the Senate shall, in the Presence of the Senate and House of Representatives, open all the Certificates, and the Votes shall then be counted. The Person having the greatest Number of Votes shall be the President, if such Number be a Majority of the whole Number of Electors appointed; and if there be more than one who have such Majority, and have an equal Number of Votes, then the House of Representatives shall immediately chuse by Ballot one of them for President; and if no Person have a Majority, then from the five highest on the List the said House shall in like Manner chuse the President. But in chusing the President, the Votes shall be taken by States, the Representation from each State having one Vote; A quorum for this Purpose shall consist of a Member or Members from two thirds of the States, and a Majority of all the States shall be necessary to a Choice. In every Case, after the Choice of the President, the Person having the greatest Number of Votes of the Electors shall be the Vice President. But if there should remain two or more who have equal Votes, the Senate shall chuse from them by Ballot the Vice President.

The Congress may determine the Time of chusing the Electors, and the Day on which they shall give their Votes; which Day shall be the same throughout the United States.

No Person except a natural born Citizen, or a Citizen of the United States, at the time of the Adoption of this Constitution, shall be eligible to the Office of President; neither shall any Person be eligible to that Office who shall not have attained to the Age of thirty five Years, and been fourteen Years a Resident within the United States.

In Case of the Removal of the President from Office, or of his Death, Resignation, or Inability to discharge the Powers and Duties of the said Office, the Same shall devolve on the Vice President, and the Congress may by Law provide for the Case of Removal, Death, Resignation or Inability, both of the President and Vice President, declaring what Officer shall then act as President, and such Officer shall act accordingly, until the Disability be removed, or a President shall be elected.

The President shall, at stated Times, receive for his Services, a Compensation, which shall neither be encreased nor diminished during the Period for which he shall have been elected, and he shall not receive within that Period any other Emolument from the United States, or any of them.

Before he enter on the Execution of his Office, he shall take the following Oath or Affirmation:—"I do solemnly swear (or affirm) that I will faithfully execute the Office of President of the United States, and will to the best of my Ability, preserve, protect and defend the Constitution of the United States."

Section. 2. The President shall be Commander in Chief of the Army and Navy of the United States, and of the Militia of the several States, when called into the actual Service of the United States; he may require the Opinion, in writing, of the principal Officer in each of the executive Departments, upon any Subject relating to the Duties of their respective Offices, and he shall have Power to grant Reprieves and Pardons for Offences against the United States, except in Cases of Impeachment.

He shall have Power, by and with the Advice and Consent of the Senate, to make Treaties, provided two thirds of the Senators present concur; and he shall nominate, and by and with the Advice and Consent of the Senate, shall appoint Ambassadors, other public Ministers and Consuls, Judges of the supreme Court, and all other Officers of the United States, whose Appointments are not herein otherwise provided for, and which shall be established by Law: but the Congress may by Law vest the Appointment of such inferior Officers, as they think proper, in the President alone, in the Courts of Law, or in the Heads of Departments.

The President shall have Power to fill up all Vacancies that may happen during the Recess of the Senate, by granting Commissions which shall expire at the End of their next Session.

Section. 3. He shall from time to time give to the Congress Information of the State of the Union, and recommend to their consideration such Measures as he shall judge necessary and expedient; he may, on extraordinary Occasions, convene both Houses, or either of them, and in Case of Disagreement between them, with Respect to the Time of Adjournment, he may adjourn them to such Time as he shall think proper; he shall receive Ambassadors and other public Ministers; he shall take Care that the Laws be faithfully executed, and shall Commission all the Officers of the United States.

Section. 4. The President, Vice President and all civil Officers of the United States, shall be removed from Office on Impeachment for, and conviction of, Treason, Bribery, or other high Crimes and Misdemeanors.

## Article. III.

Section. 1. The judicial Power of the United States, shall be vested in one supreme Court, and in such inferior Courts as the Congress may from time to time ordain and establish. The Judges, both of the supreme and inferior Courts, shall hold their Offices during good Behaviour, and shall, at stated Times, receive for their Services, a Compensation, which shall not be diminished during their Continuance in Office.

Section. 2. The judicial Power shall extend to all Cases, in Law and Equity, arising under this Constitution, the Laws of the United States, and Treaties made, or which shall be made, under their Authority;—to all Cases affecting Ambassadors, other public Ministers and Consuls;—to all Cases of admiralty and maritime Jurisdiction;—to Controversies to which the United States shall be a Party;—to Controversies between two or more States;—between a State and Citizens of another State;—between Citizens of different States,—between Citizens of the same State claiming Lands under Grants of different States, and between a State, or the Citizens thereof, and foreign States, Citizens or Subjects.

In all Cases affecting Ambassadors, other public Ministers and Consuls, and those in which a State shall be Party, the supreme Court shall have original Jurisdiction. In all the other Cases before mentioned, the supreme Court shall have appellate Jurisdiction, both as to Law and Fact, with such Exceptions, and under such Regulations as the Congress shall make.

The Trial of all Crimes, except in Cases of Impeachment, shall be by Jury; and such Trial shall be held in the State where the said Crimes shall have been committed; but when not committed within any State, the Trial shall be at such Place or Places as the Congress may by Law have directed.

Section. 3. Treason against the United States, shall consist only in levying War against them, or in adhering to their Enemies, giving them Aid and Comfort. No Person shall be convicted of Treason unless on the Testimony of two Witnesses to the same overt Act, or on Confession in open Court.

The Congress shall have Power to declare the Punishment of Treason, but no Attainder of Treason shall work Corruption of Blood, or Forfeiture except during the Life of the Person attainted.


## ARTICLE. IV.

Section. 1. Full Faith and Credit shall be given in each State to the public Acts, Records, and judicial Proceedings of every other State. And the Congress may by general Laws prescribe the Manner in which such Acts, Records and Proceedings shall be proved, and the Effect thereof.

Section 2. The Citizens of each State shall be entitled to all Privileges and Immunities of Citizens in the several States.

A Person charged in any State with Treason, Felony, or other Crime, who shall flee from Justice, and be found in another State, shall on Demand of the executive Authority of the State from which he fled, be delivered up, to be removed to the State having Jurisdiction of the Crime.

No Person held to Service or Labour in one State, under the Laws thereof, escaping into another, shall, in Consequence of any Law or Regulation therein, be discharged from such Service or Labour, but shall be delivered up on Claim of the Party to whom such Service or Labour may be due.

Section. 3. New States may be admitted by the Congress into this Union; but no new State shall be formed or erected within the Jurisdiction of any other State; nor any State be formed by the Junction of two or more States, or Parts of States, without the Consent of the Legislatures of the States concerned as well as of the Congress.

The Congress shall have Power to dispose of and make all needful Rules and Regulations respecting the Territory or other Property belonging to the United States; and nothing in this Constitution shall be so construed as to Prejudice any Claims of the United States, or of any particular State.

Section. 4. The United States shall guarantee to every State in this Union a Republican Form of Government, and shall protect each of them against Invasion; and on Application of the Legislature, or of the Executive (when the Legislature cannot be convened) against domestic Violence.


## ARTICLE. V.

The Congress, whenever two thirds of both Houses shall deem it necessary, shall propose Amendments to this Constitution, or, on the Application of the Legislatures of two thirds of the several States, shall call a Convention for proposing Amendments, which, in either Case, shall be valid to all Intents and Purposes, as Part of this Constitution, when ratified by the Legislatures of three fourths of the several States, or by Conventions in three fourths thereof, as the one or the other Mode of Ratification may be proposed by the Congress; Provided that no Amendment which may be made prior to the Year One thousand eight hundred and eight shall in any Manner affect the first and fourth Clauses in the Ninth Section of the first Article; and that no State, without its Consent, shall be deprived of it's equal Suffrage in the Senate.

## ARTICLE. VI.

All Debts contracted and Engagements entered into, before the Adoption of this Constitution, shall be as valid against the United States under this Constitution, as under the Confederation.

This Constitution, and the Laws of the United States which shall be made in Pursuance thereof; and all Treaties made, or which shall be made, under the Authority of the United States, shall be the supreme Law of the Land; and the Judges in every State shall be bound thereby, any Thing in the Constitution or Laws of any State to the Contrary notwithstanding.

The Senators and Representatives before mentioned, and the Members of the several State Legislatures, and all executive and judicial Officers, both of the United States and of the several States, shall be bound by Oath or Affirmation, to support this Constitution; but no religious Test shall ever be required as a Qualification to any Office or public Trust under the United States.

## ARTICLE. VII.

The Ratification of the Conventions of nine States, shall be sufficient for the Establishment of this Constitution between the States so ratifying the Same.

## AMENDMENTS

### ARTICLE I.

Congress shall make no law respecting an establishment of religion, or prohibiting the free exercise thereof; or abridging the freedom of speech, or of the press; or the right of the people peaceably to assemble, and to petition the government for a redress of grievances.

### ARTICLE II.

A well regulated militia, being necessary to the security of a free State, the right of the people to keep and bear arms, shall not be infringed.

### ARTICLE III.

No soldier shall, in time of peace be quartered in any house, without the consent of the owner, nor in time of war, but in a manner to be prescribed by law.

## ARTICLE IV.

The right of the people to be secure in their persons, houses, papers, and effects, against unreasonable searches and seizures, shall not be violated, and no warrants shall issue, but upon probable cause, supported by oath or affirmation, and particularly describing the place to be searched, and the persons or things to be seized.

## ARTICLE V.

No person shall be held to answer for a capital, or otherwise infamous crime, unless on a presentment or indictment of a grand jury, except in cases arising in the land or naval forces, or in the militia, when in actual service in time of war or public danger; nor shall any person be subject for the same offense to be twice put in jeopardy of life or limb; nor shall be compelled in any criminal case to be a witness against himself, nor be deprived of life, liberty, or property, without due process of law; nor shall private property be taken for public use without just compensation.

## ARTICLE VI.

In all criminal prosecutions, the accused shall enjoy the right to a speedy and public trial, by an impartial jury of the State and district wherein the crime shall have been committed, which district shall have been previously ascertained by law, and to be informed of the nature and cause of the accusation; to be confronted with the witnesses against him; to have compulsory process for obtaining witnesses in his favor, and to have the assistance of counsel for his defense.

## ARTICLE VII.

In suits at common law, where the value in controversy shall exceed twenty dollars, the right of trial by jury shall be preserved, and no fact tried by a jury shall be otherwise reëxamined in any court of the United States, than according to the rules of the common law.

## ARTICLE VIII.

Excessive bail shall not be required, nor excessive fines imposed, nor cruel and unusual punishments inflicted.

## ARTICLE IX.

The enumeration in the Constitution of certain rights shall not be construed to deny or disparage others retained by the people.

## ARTICLE X.

The powers not delegated to the United States by the Constitution, nor prohibited by it to the States, are reserved to the States respectively, or to the people.

## ARTICLE XI.

Passed by Congress 5 March 1794. Ratified 8 January 1798.

The judicial power of the United States shall not be construed to extend to any suit in law or equity, commenced or prosecuted against one of the United States by citizens of another State, or by citizens or subjects of any foreign State.

## ARTICLE XII.

Passed by Congress 12 December 1803. Ratified 25 September 1804.

The electors shall meet in their respective States, and vote by ballot for President and Vice President, one of whom, at least, shall not be an inhabitant of the same State with themselves; they shall name in their ballots the person voted for as President, and in distinct ballots, the person voted for as Vice President, and they shall make distinct lists of all persons voted for as President and of all persons voted for as Vice President, and of the number of votes for each, which lists they shall sign and certify, and transmit sealed to the seat of the government of the United States, directed to the President of the Senate;—The President of the Senate shall, in the presence of the Senate and House of Representatives, open all the certificates and the votes shall then be counted;—The person having the greatest number of votes for President, shall be the President, if such number be a majority of the whole number of electors appointed; and if no person have such majority, then from the persons having the highest numbers not exceeding three on the list of those voted for as President, the House of Representatives shall choose immediately, by ballot, the President. But in choosing the President, the votes shall be taken by States, the representation from each State having one vote; a quorum for this purpose shall consist of a member or members from two thirds of the States, and a majority of all the States shall be necessary to a choice. And if the House of Representatives shall not choose a President whenever the right of choice shall devolve upon them, before the fourth day of March next following, then the Vice President shall act as President, as in the case of the death or other constitutional disability of the President. The person having the greatest number of votes as Vice President shall be the Vice President, if such number be a majority of the whole number of electors appointed, and if no person have a majority, then from the two highest numbers on the list, the Senate shall choose the Vice President; a quorum for the purpose shall consist of two thirds of the whole number of Senators, and a majority of the whole number shall be necessary to a choice. But no person constitutionally ineligible to the office of President shall be eligible to that of Vice President of the United States.

## ARTICLE XIII.

Passed by Congress 1 February 1865. Ratified 18 December 1865.

Section. 1. Neither slavery nor involuntary servitude, except as punishment for crime whereof the party shall have been duly convicted, shall exist within the United States, or any place subject to their jurisdiction.

Section. 2. Congress shall have power to enforce this article by appropriate legislation.

## ARTICLE XIV.

Passed by Congress 16 June 1866. Ratified 23 July 1868.

Section. 1. All persons born or naturalized in the United States, and subject to the jurisdiction thereof, are citizens of the United States and of the State wherein they reside. No State shall make or enforce any law which shall abridge the privileges or immunities of citizens of the United States; nor shall any State deprive any person of life, liberty, or property, without due process of law; nor deny to any person within its jurisdiction the equal protection of the laws.

Section. 2. Representatives shall be apportioned among the several States according to their respective numbers, counting the whole number of persons in each State, excluding Indians not taxed. But when the right to vote at any election for the choice of electors for President and Vice President of the United States, representatives in Congress, the executive and judicial officers of a State, or the members of the legislature thereof, is denied to any of the male inhabitants of such State, being twenty-one years of age, and citizens of the United States, or in any way abridged, except for participation in rebellion, or other crime, the basis of representation therein shall be reduced in the proportion which the number of such male citizens shall bear to the whole number of male citizens twenty-one years of age in such State.

Section. 3. No person shall be a senator or representative in Congress, or elector of President and Vice President, or hold any office, civil or military, under the United States, or under any State, who having previously taken an oath, as a member of Congress, or as an officer of the United States, or as a member of any State legislature, or as an executive or judicial officer of any State, to support the Constitution of the United States, shall have engaged in insurrection or rebellion against the same, or given aid or comfort to the enemies thereof. But Congress may by a vote of two thirds of each House, remove such disability.

Section. 4. The validity of the public debt of the United States, authorized by law, including debts incurred for payment of pensions and bounties for services in suppressing insurrection or rebellion, shall not be questioned. But neither the United States nor any State shall assume or pay any debt or obligation incurred in aid of insurrection or rebellion against the United States, or any claim for the loss or emancipation of any slave; but all such debts, obligations, and claims shall be held illegal and void.

Section. 5. The Congress shall have power to enforce, by appropriate legislation, the provisions of this article.

## ARTICLE XV.

Passed by Congress 27 February 1869. Ratified 30 March 1870.

Section. 1. The right of citizens of the United States to vote shall not be denied or abridged by the United States or by any State on account of race, color, or previous condition of servitude.

Section. 2. The Congress shall have power to enforce this article by appropriate legislation.

## ARTICLE XVI.

Passed by Congress 12 July 1909. Ratified 25 February 1913.

The Congress shall have power to lay and collect taxes on incomes, from whatever source derived, without apportionment among the several States, and without regard to any census or enumeration.

## ARTICLE XVII.

Passed by Congress 16 May 1912. Ratified 31 May 1913.

The Senate of the United States shall be composed of two senators from each State, elected by the people thereof, for six years; and each senator shall have one vote. The electors in each State shall have the qualifications requisite for electors of the most numerous branch of the State legislature.

When vacancies happen in the representation of any State in the Senate, the executive authority of such State shall issue writs of election to fill such vacancies: *Provided,* That the legislature of any State may empower the executive thereof to make temporary appointments until the people fill the vacancies by election as the legislature may direct.

This amendment shall not be so construed as to affect the election or term of any senator chosen before it becomes valid as part of the Constitution.

## ARTICLE XVIII.

Passed by Congress 17 December 1917. Ratified 29 January 1919.

After one year from the ratification of this article, the manufacture, sale, or transportation of intoxicating liquors within, the importation thereof into, or the exportation thereof from the United States and all territory subject to the jurisdiction thereof for beverage purposes is hereby prohibited.

The Congress and the several States shall have concurrent power to enforce this article by appropriate legislation.

This article shall be inoperative unless it shall have been ratified as an amendment to the Constitution by the legislatures of the several States, as provided in the Constitution, within seven years from the date of the submission hereof to the states by Congress.

## ARTICLE XIX.

Passed by Congress 5 June 1919. Ratified 26 August 1920.

The right of citizens of the United States to vote shall not be denied or abridged by the United States or by any State on account of sex.

The Congress shall have power by appropriate legislation to enforce the provisions of this article.

## ARTICLE XX.

Passed by Congress 3 March 1932. Ratified 23 January 1933.

Section. 1. The terms of the President and Vice President shall end at noon on the 20th day of January, and the terms of Senators and Representatives at noon on the 3d day of January, of the years in which such terms would have ended if this article had not been ratified; and the terms of their successors shall then begin.

Section. 2. The Congress shall assemble at least once in every year, and such meeting shall begin at noon on the 3d day of January, unless they shall by law appoint a different day.

Section. 3. If, at the time fixed for the beginning of the term of the President, the President-elect shall have died, the Vice President-elect shall become President. If a President shall not have been chosen before the time fixed for the beginning of his term, or if the President-elect shall have failed to qualify, then the Vice President-elect shall act as President until a President shall have qualified; and the Congress may by law provide for the case wherein neither a President-elect nor a Vice President-elect shall have qualified, declaring who shall then act as President, or the manner in which one who is to act shall be selected, and such person shall act accordingly until a President or Vice President shall have qualified.

Section. 4. The Congress may by law provide for the case of the death of any of the persons from whom the House of Representatives may choose a President whenever the right of choice shall have devolved upon them, and for the case of the death of any of the persons from whom the Senate may choose a Vice President whenever the right of choice shall have devolved upon them.

Section. 5. Sections 1 and 2 shall take effect on the 15th day of October following the ratification of this article.

Section. 6. This article shall be inoperative unless it shall have been ratified as an amendment to the Constitution by the legislatures of three-fourths of the several States within seven years from the date of its submission.

## ARTICLE XXI.

Passed by Congress 20 February 1933. Ratified 5 December 1933.

Section. 1. The Eighteenth Article of amendment to the Constitution of the United States is hereby repealed.

Section. 2. The transportation or importation into any State, Territory, or possession of the United States for delivery or use therein of intoxicating liquors in violation of the laws thereof, is hereby prohibited.

Section. 3. This article shall be inoperative unless it shall have been ratified as an amendment to the Constitution by conventions in the several States, as provided in the Constitution, within seven years from the date of the submission thereof to the States by the Congress.

## ARTICLE XXII.

Passed by Congress 24 March 1947. Ratified 26 February 1951.

Section. 1. No person shall be elected to the office of the President more than twice, and no person who has held the office of President, or acted as President, for more than two years of a term to which some other person was elected President shall be elected to the office of the President more than once. But this article shall not apply to any person holding the office of President when this article was proposed by the Congress, and shall not prevent any person who may be holding the office of President, or acting as President, during the term within which this article becomes operative from holding the office of President or acting as President during the remainder of such term.

Section. 2. This article shall be inoperative unless it shall have been ratified as an amendment to the Constitution by the legislatures of three-fourths of the several States within seven years from the date of its submission to the States by the Congress.

## ARTICLE XXIII.

Passed by Congress 16 June 1960. Ratified 29 March 1961.

Section. 1. The district constituting the seat of Government of the United States shall appoint in such manner as the Congress may direct:

A number of electors of President and Vice President equal to the whole number of Senators and Representatives in Congress to which the District would be entitled if it were a State, but in no event more than the least populous State; they shall be in addition to those appointed by the States, but they shall be considered, for the purposes of election of President and Vice President, to be electors appointed by a State; and they shall meet in the District and perform such duties as provided by the twelfth article of amendment.

Section. 2. The Congress shall have the power to enforce this article by appropriate legislation.

## ARTICLE XXIV.

Passed by Congress 27 August 1962. Ratified 23 January 1964.

Section. 1. The right of citizens of the United States to vote in any primary or other election for President or Vice President, for electors for President or Vice President, or for Senator or Representative in Congress, shall not be denied or abridged by the United States or any State by failure to pay any poll tax or other tax.

Section. 2. The Congress shall have the power to enforce this article by appropriate legislation.

## ARTICLE XXV.

Passed by Congress 6 July 1965. Ratified 10 February 1967.

Section. 1. In case of the removal of the President from office or of his death or resignation, the Vice President shall become President.

Section. 2. Whenever there is a vacancy in the office of the Vice President, the President shall nominate a Vice President who shall take office upon confirmation by a majority vote of both Houses of Congress.

Section. 3. Whenever the President transmits to the President pro tempore of the Senate and the Speaker of the House of Representatives his written declaration that he is unable to discharge the powers and duties of his office, and until he transmits to them a written declaration to the contrary, such powers and duties shall be discharged by the Vice President as Acting President.

Section. 4. Whenever the Vice President and a majority of either the principal officers of the executive departments or of such other body as Congress may by law provide, transmit to the President pro tempore of the Senate and the Speaker of the House of Representatives their written declaration that the President is unable to discharge the powers and duties of his office, the Vice President shall immediately assume the powers and duties of the office as Acting President.

Thereafter, when the President transmits to the President pro tempore of the Senate and the Speaker of the House of Representatives his written declaration that no inability exists, he shall resume the powers and duties of his office unless the Vice President and a majority of either the principal officers of the executive department or of such other body as Congress may by law provide, transmit within four days to the

President pro tempore of the Senate and the Speaker of the House of Representatives their written declaration that the President is unable to discharge the powers and duties of his office. Thereupon Congress shall decide the issue, assembling within forty-eight hours for that purpose if not in session. If the Congress, within twenty-one days after receipt of the latter written declaration, or, if Congress is not in session, within twenty-one days after Congress is required to assemble, determines by two-thirds vote of both Houses that the President is unable to discharge the powers and duties of his office, the Vice President shall continue to discharge the same as Acting President; otherwise, the President shall resume the powers and duties of his office.

## ARTICLE XXVI.

Passed by Congress 23 March 1971. Ratified 30 June 1971.

Section. 1. The right of citizens of the United States, who are eighteen years of age or older, to vote shall not be denied or abridged by the United States or by any State on account of age.

Section. 2. The Congress shall have power to enforce this article by appropriate legislation.

# Appendix B

# President Franklin D. Roosevelt's Message to Congress in Support of the Brownlow Report, 12 January 1937

I address this message to the Congress as one who has had experience as a legislator, as a subordinate in an executive department, as the chief executive of a State, and as one on whom, as President, the constitutional responsibility for the whole of the executive branch of the Government has lain for 4 years.

Now that we are out of the trough of the depression, the time has come to set our house in order. The administrative management of the Government needs overhauling. We are confronted not alone by new activities, some of them temporary in character, but also by the growth of the work of the Government matching the growth of the Nation over more than a generation.

Except for the enactment of the Budget and Accounting Act of 1921, no extensive change in management has occurred since 1913, when the Department of Labor was established. The executive structure of the Government is sadly out of date. I am not the first President to report to the Congress that antiquated machinery stands in the way of effective administration and of adequate control by the Congress. Theodore Roosevelt, William H. Taft, Woodrow Wilson, and Herbert Hoover made repeated but not wholly successful efforts to deal with the problem. Committees of the Congress have also rendered distinguished service to the Nation through their efforts from time to time to point the way to improvement of governmental management and organization.

The opportunity and the need for action now comes to you and to me. If we have faith in our republican form of government and in the ideals upon which it has rested for 150 years, we must devote ourselves energetically and courageously to the task of making that Government efficient. The great stake in efficient democracy is the stake of the common man.

In these troubled years of world history a self-government cannot long survive unless that government is an effective and efficient agency to serve mankind and carry out the will of the Nation. A government without good management is a house builded on sand.

In striving together to make our Government more efficient, you and I are taking up in our generation the battle to preserve that freedom of self-government which our forefathers fought to establish and hand down to us. They struggled against tyranny, against nonrepresentative controls, against government by birth, wealth, or class, against sectionalism. Our struggle now is against confusion, against ineffectiveness, against waste, against inefficiency. This battle, too, must be won, unless it is to be said that in our generation national self-government broke down and was frittered away in bad management.

Will it be said "Democracy was a great dream, but it could not do the job"? Or shall we here and now, without further delay, make it our business to see that our American democracy is made efficient so that it will do the job that is required of it by the events of our time?

I know your answer, and the answer of the Nation, because, after all, we are a practical people. We know good management in the home, on the farm, and in business, big and little. If any nation can find the way to effective government, it should be the American people through their own democratic institutions.

Over a year ago it seemed to me that this problem of administrative management of the executive branch of the Government should be a major order of business of this session of the Congress. Accordingly, after extended discussions and negotiations, I appointed a Committee on Administrative Management, to examine the whole problem broadly and to suggest for my guidance and your consideration a comprehensive and balanced program for dealing with the overhead organization and management of the executive branch as it is established under the Constitution.

The Committee has now completed its work, and I transmit to you its report, Administrative Management in the Government of the United States. I have examined this report carefully and thoughtfully, and am convinced that it is a great document of permanent importance. I think that the general program presented by the Committee is adequate, reasonable, and practical, and that it furnishes the basis for immediate action. The broad facts are known; the need is clear; what is now required is action.

The Committee on Administrative Management points out that no enterprise can operate effectively if set up as is the Government today. There are over 100 separate departments, commissions, corporations, authorities, agencies, and activities through which the work of the Government is being carried on. Neither the President nor the Congress can exercise effective supervision and direction over such a chaos of establishments, nor can overlapping, duplication, and contradictory policies be avoided.

The Committee has not spared me; they say, what has been common knowledge for 20 years, that the President cannot adequately handle his responsibilities; that he is overworked; that it is humanly impossible, under the system which we have, for him fully to carry out his constitutional duty as Chief Executive, because he is overwhelmed with minor details and needless contacts arising directly from the bad organization and equipment of the Government. I can testify to this. With my predecessors who have said the same thing over and over again, I plead guilty.

The plain fact is that the present organization and equipment of the executive branch of the Government defeats the constitutional intent that there be a single responsible Chief Executive to coordinate and manage the departments and activities in accordance with the laws enacted by the Congress. Under these conditions the Government cannot be thoroughly effective in working, under popular control, for the common good.

The Committee does not spare the Comptroller General for his failure to give the Congress a prompt and complete audit each year, totally independent of administration, as a means of holding the Executive truly to account; nor for his unconstitutional assumption of executive power; nor for the failure to keep the accounting system of the Government up to date to serve as the basis of information, management, and control.

The Committee criticizes the use of boards and commissions in administration, condemns the careless use of "corporations" as governmental instrumentalities, and points out that the practice of creating independent regulatory commissions, who perform administrative work in addition to judicial work, threatens to develop a "fourth branch" of the Government for which there is no sanction in the Constitution. Nor does the Committee spare the inadequacy of the civil-service system.

To meet this situation and bring our administrative management up to date, the Committee presents an integrated five-point program, which you will find set out in its report. It includes these major recommendations:

1. Expand the White House staff so that the President may have a sufficient group of able assistants in his own office to keep him in closer and easier touch with the widespread affairs of administration, and to make the speedier clearance of the knowledge needed for Executive decision.

2. Strengthen and develop the managerial agencies of the Government, particularly those dealing with the budget and efficiency research, with personnel and with planning, as management-arms of the Chief Executive.

3. Extend the merit system upward, outward, and downward to cover practically all non-policy-determining posts; reorganize the civil-service system as a part of management under a single, responsible administrator, and create a citizen board to serve as the watch dog of the merit system; and increase the salaries of key posts throughout the service so that the Government may attract and hold in a career service men and women of ability and character.

4. Overhaul the 100 independent agencies, administrations, authorities, boards, and commissions, and place them by Executive order within one or the other of the following 12 major executive departments: State, Treasury, War, Justice, Post Office, Navy, Conservation, Agriculture, Commerce, Labor, Social Welfare, and Public Works; and place upon the Executive continuing responsibility for the maintenance of effective organization.

5. Establish accountability of the Executive to the Congress by providing a genuine independent postaudit of all fiscal transactions by an auditor general, and restore to the Executive complete responsibility for accounts and current transactions.

As you will see, this program rests solidly upon the Constitution and upon the American way of doing things. There is nothing in it which is revolutionary, as every element is drawn from our own experience either in government or large-scale business.

I endorse this program and feel confident that it will commend itself to you also with your knowledge of government, and to the vast majority of the citizens of the country who want and believe in efficient self-government.

No important advance can be made toward the major objectives of the program without the passage by the Congress of the necessary legislation.

It will be necessary to provide for the establishment of two new departments, a Department of Social Welfare and a Department of Public Works, for the assignment by the President of all the miscellaneous activities to the 12 major departments thus provided, for reorganization of the civil-service system, for modernizng and strengthening the managerial agencies of the Executive, and for making the Executive more strictly accountable to the Congress. By the creation of two new departments nearly 100 agencies now not under regular departments can be consolidated as to their administrative functions under a total of 12 regular departments of the Government.

The remaining elements of the five-point program, though they must await your action on the basic legislation, may be initiated through appropriations and Executive orders.

In placing this program before you I realize that it will be said that I am recommending the increase of the powers of the Presidency. This is not true. The Presidency as established in the Constitution of the United States has all of the powers that are required. In spite of timid souls in 1787 who feared effective government the Presidency was established as a single strong Chief Executive Office in which was vested the entire executive power of the National Government, even as the legislative power was placed in the Congress, and the judicial in the Supreme Court. What I am placing before you is not the request for more power, but for the tools of management and the authority to distribute the work so that the President can effectively discharge those powers which the Constitution now places upon him. Unless we are prepared to abandon this important part of the Constitution, we must equip the Presidency with authority commensurate with his responsibilities under the Constitution.

The Committee on Administrative Management, after a careful examination of recent attempts to reorganize the Government and of State reorganizations carried out so ably by Gov. Frank O. Lowden in Illinois, Gov. Alfred E. Smith in New York, Gov. Harry F. Byrd in Virginia, Gov. William Tudor Gardiner in Maine, and by other governors, accepts the view held by my distinguished predecessors that the detailed work of reorganization is, as President Theodore Roosevelt said over 30 years ago, "essentially executive in its nature." The Committee accordingly recommends that reorganization should be a continuing duty and authority of the Chief Executive on the basis of standards set by the Congress. To make this safe, the Committee insists, however, that the Congress keep a watchful eye upon reorganization both through the annual budget and through the maintenance of strict executive accountability to the Congress under the independent audit of all financial transactions by an Auditor General. Under the proposed plan the Congress must by law establish the major departments and determine in advance the general principles which shall guide the President in distributing the work of the Government among these departments, and in this task the President is to act on the basis of careful research by the Bureau of the Budget and after conference with those primarily affected. Reorganization is not a mechanical task, but a human task, because government is not a machine, but a living organism. With these clear safeguards, and in view of our past muddling with reorganization, one cannot but accept the logic and wisdom of the recommendations.

I would not have you adopt this five-point program, however, without realizing that this represents an important step in American history. If we do this, we reduce from over 100 down to a dozen the operating executive agencies of the Government, and we bring many little bureaucracies under broad coordinated democratic authority.

But in so doing, we shall know that we are going back to the Constitution, and giving to the executive branch modern tools of management and an up-to-date organization which will enable the Government to go forward efficiently. We can prove to the world that American Government is both democratic and effective.

In this program I invite your cooperation, and pledge myself to deal energetically and promptly with the executive responsibilities of reorganization and administrative management, when you shall have made this possible by the necessary legislation.

# Notes

1. Charles T. Goodsell, *The Case for Bureaucracy: A Public Administration Polemic* (Chatham, N.J.: Chatham House, 1982) and "The Grace Commission: Seeking Efficiency for the Whole People," *Public Administration Review* 44 (May-June 1984): 196-204; Chester A. Newland, "The Reagan Presidency: Limited Government and Political Administration," *Public Administration Review* 43 (Jan.-Feb. 1983): 1-21, and "Crucial Issues for Public Personnel Professionals," *Public Personnel Management Journal,* 1984, pp. 15-45; H. George Fredrickson and Ralph C. Chandler, eds., "Citizenship and Public Administration," *Public Administration Review* 44 (special issue, Mar. 1984): 97-209; Marshall E. Dimock, "Centennials, Continuities and Culture," *Public Administration Review* 43 (Mar.-Apr. 1983): 99-107; H. Brinton Milward and Hal G. Rainey, "Don't Blame the Bureaucracy," *Journal of Public Policy* 3, pt. 2 (May 1983): 149-68; Bradley T. Patterson, "Managing in the Wilderness of Lost Consensus," *Public Administration Times,* 1 May 1984; Eugene B. McGregor, "Symposium: The Public Service as Institution," *Public Administration Review* 42 (July-Aug. 1982): 304-20; Paul Van Riper, "The American Administrative State: Wilson and the Founders—An Unorthodox View," *Public Administration Review* 43 (Nov.-Dec. 1983): 477-90; Henry J. Merry, *Constitutional Function of Presidential-Administrative Separation* (Washington, D.C.: University Press of America, 1978); Peter Woll, *American Bureaucracy,* 2d ed. (New York: Norton, 1977).

2. Supreme Court opinions are authoritative, but they sometimes lack legitimacy. *Dred Scott* v. *Sandford,* 19 How. 393 (1857), is, of course, the preeminent example. *Brown* v. *Board of Education of Topeka,* 347 U.S. 483 (1954) and 349 U.S. 294 (1955), the famous school-desegregation case, at first met with "massive resistance" but eventually gained popular support for the moral principle behind it. The Supreme Court decisions against the New Deal lacked legitimacy and eventually succumbed to a new court composed of New Dealers. Opponents of abortion on demand look forward to seeing *Roe* v. *Wade,* 410 U.S. 113 (1973), overruled. It is with examples of this sort in mind that I say legitimacy involves more than legality.

215

3. For a recent discussion of several meanings of legitimacy see Rayburn Barton, "Traditionalism as a Source of Administrative Legitimacy," Colloquium on the Status and Future of American Public Administration, region 9, American Society for Public Administration, in Spokane, Washington, Oct. 1984.

4. Throughout this book I refer to the authors of *The Federalist Papers* by their pseudonym "Publius." Only when I want to contrast one of the authors with another do I identify Madison, Hamilton, or Jay; but this is done quite sparingly. The reason I seldom identify the authors by their real names is that such identification weakens the force of *The Federalist* as a unified book. *The Federalist* is not simply a series of newspaper articles. There was careful planning and collaboration by the authors. There is a consistent argument sustained throughout the entire work that is blurred by giving more attention to the individual positions of the three authors than the authors themselves would have desired. I believe their preference to present themselves as Publius should be respected. *The Federalist* is one of those great books that we learn *from* rather than *about*. To do this, I try to meet the authors on their own terms. For a discussion of the booklike character of *The Federalist* see the introductory essay in Jacob Cooke's critical edition, published by Wesleyan University Press in 1982. See also David F. Epstein's *The Political Theory of "The Federalist"* (Chicago: University of Chicago Press, 1984); and Thomas S. Engeman, Edward J. Erler, Thomas B. Hofeller, eds., *The Federalist Concordance* (Middletown, Conn.: Wesleyan University Press, 1980), pp. xi–xiv. Contrary to customary usage, I cite *The Federalist* by number only, with no page reference to familiar editions such as those by Cooke or Clinton Rossiter. My reason for doing this is to discourage the use of *The Federalist* as a source for "proof texts" to support positions on issues of our own day. To lift a sentence from *The Federalist* out of its context contributes nothing to the understanding of the issues either of our day or of Publius's. I refer readers to the entire *Federalist* essay that I am citing to encourage them to see how the cited passage is integrated into the specific argument Publius is making and to judge for themselves whether I have caught the spirit of this argument as a whole.

5. Connections between legitimacy and performance appear frequently in social-science literature. James O. Freedman, *Crisis and Legitimacy: The Administrative Process and American Government* (Cambridge: Cambridge University Press, 1978), p. 10; Rexford Tugwell, *The Emerging Constitution* (New York: Harper's Magazine Press, 1974), pp. 573–74; Peter W. Colby and Patricia Ingraham, "Individual Motivation and Institutional Change under the Senior Executive Service," *Review of Public Personnel Administration* 2 (Spring 1982): 108; Kenneth Warren, *Administrative Law in the American Political System* (St. Paul, Minn.: West, 1982), p. 66; Louis Fisher, "Congress and the President in the Administrative Process: The Uneasy Alliance," in *The Illusion of Presidential Government,* ed. Hugh Heclo and Lester Salamon (Boulder, Colo.: Westview Press, 1981), pp. 21–24; Charles L. Black, *The People and the Court* (New York: Macmillan, 1960), p. 36.

6. I am writing these words in the middle of the fifth year of Ronald Reagan's presidency. Despite the campaign pledges of candidate Reagan in 1980, the Department of Education is still with us and will be with us after President Reagan leaves office.

7. Barry D. Karl, *The Uneasy State: The United States from 1915 to 1945* (Chicago: University of Chicago Press, 1983), pp. 180–81, 230; Stephen Skowronek, *Building A New American State: The Expansion of National Administrative Capacities, 1877–1920* (New York: Cambridge University Press, 1981), pp. 289–92; William West and Joseph Cooper, "The Congressional Veto and Administrative Rulemaking," *Political Science Quarterly* 98 (Summer 1983): 285–304; Theodore L. Becker, *American Government— Past—Present—Future* (Boston: Allyn & Bacon, 1976), pp. 272, 292.

8. This point is discussed critically with particular relevance to President Reagan's Office of Personnel Management by Chester A. Newland in "The Reagan Presidency." The best-known and most-far-reaching statement advocating political control of the career civil service appears in Stuart M. Butler, Michael Sanera, and W. Bruce Weinsod, *Mandate for Leadership II* (Washington, D.C.: Heritage Foundation, 1984).

9. A common error in political folklore is the strange belief that the framers of the Constitution were indifferent to matters of efficiency and effectiveness in government. This error is frequently made by persons who should know better. The most recent perpetrator to come to my attention is the distinguished former congressman Barber Conable. See his otherwise quite sensible remarks in "The Founding Fathers Didn't Want Efficient, Adventurous Government," *Bureaucrat* 12 (Fall 1984): 39–43. See also the dissenting opinion of Justice Brandeis in *Myers* v. *U.S.*, 272 U.S. 52 at 247, 293, and Chief Justice Burger's Opinion of the Court in *INS* v. *Chadha*, 462 U.S. 919 at 959. The chief justice is certainly correct when he says that "it is crystal clear from the records of the convention, contemporaneous writings and debates, that the framers ranked other values higher than efficiency." What is not crystal clear, however, is that the framers would have put the argument this way, especially in a debate on separation of powers, which was at issue in *Chadha*. Although efficiency was surely instrumental for higher values, there is little evidence to support the claim that the framers saw themselves as sacrificing efficiency through adherence to the principles of separation of powers. Separation of powers was intended to make the new government more, not less, efficient. For a sound criticism of Brandeis's oft-quoted dictum see Louis Fisher, *The Constitution between Friends* (New York: St. Martin's, 1978), p. 10.

10. Dwight Waldo, *The Administrative State* (New York: Ronald Press, 1948).

11. Although the term "administrative state" is commonplace, I could not find an adequate definition in the literature. There are references to Morstein Marx's book by that title as containing a definition; but, as Paul Van Riper has noted, Marx's definition is little more than an afterthought. Ralph Chandler, the coeditor of a distinguished Public Administration dictionary, graciously responded to my querulous prodding for a definition with the following: "The administrative state is that set of institutional arrangements which make a working system out of a regime's needs for hierarchical organization, rational decision making, rule of law, written procedures and records, and sufficient public funds to support a technology of public service."

Although I know of no better definition than Chandler's in the literature, I have some problems with his formulation. I think he may have defined the "state" rather than the "administrative state." What is missing from his definition is the positive character of the administrative state, its tendency (for weal and woe) to seize the initiative from individuals even when defending individual rights, and the broad discretionary powers conferred on administrative officers.

Rather than define the administrative state, Paul Van Riper (pp. 477–78) has offered ten criteria by which it can be recognized. The first six are Weberian: "(1) a workable organization in the classical hierarchical sense; (2) the recruitment of expertise by merit; (3) rational decision making; (4) the rule of law, with an emphasis on equality before the law; (5) written procedures and records; (6) and not only a money economy but sufficient public funds to support a complex administrative apparatus. From here one must go beyond Weber and add more criteria at best only implicit in his works: (7) Morstein Marx's requirement of a base in quantitative data and technique; (8) adequate supporting technology, especially pertaining to records, communications, and numeracy; (9) the enforcement of responsibility and ethical standards; and (10) all of the above in at least a moderately developed and mutually supporting arrangement."

12. Woodrow Wilson, "The Study of Administration," *Political Science Quarterly* 2 (1887): 197–222.

13. Letter of ASPA's President Bradley H. Patterson to members of the Committee on Three Centuries of Public Administration, 22 May 1984.


CHAPTER 1
INTRODUCTION

1. See note 9 of the Preface. The first four chapters of this book develop themes that I originally touched upon in my article "The Constitutional Foundations of the Administrative State," in *A Centennial History of the American Administrative State*, ed. Ralph C. Chandler (New York: John Wiley & Sons, forthcoming).

2. *Administration* is defined in *Federalist 72*. The frequency with which words appear in *The Federalist Papers* can be found in Thomas S. Engeman, Edward J. Erler, and Thomas B. Hofeller, eds., *The Federalist Concordance* (Middletown, Conn.: Wesleyan University Press, 1980).

3. It is unfortunate that so few contemporary political scientists follow Publius's example of integrating administrative matters into constitutional *structures* of government. One happy exception is Peter Woll's splendid *American Bureaucracy*, 2d ed. (New York: Norton, 1977).

4. *Federalist 72*.

5. Ibid.

6. *Federalist 77*.

7. Ibid.

8. Ibid.

9. Marvin Meyers, *The Jacksonian Persuasion: Politics and Belief*, 2d ed. (Stanford, Calif.: Stanford University Press, 1957), p. viii.

10. Consider the remarks of Congressman Jack Kemp: "Why in the world is the Federal Reserve trying to slow down the economy? On what mandate does the Fed decide the economy needs to be slowed down?" (*Washington Post*, 17 May 1984, p. C18).

11. A. C. Millspaugh, *Toward Efficient Democracy* (Washington, D.C.: Brookings Institution, 1949) and *Democracy, Efficiency, Stability* (Washington: Brookings Institution, 1942); Conley Dillon, "American Constitutional Review: Are We Preparing for the 21st Century?" *World Affairs*, Summer 1977, pp. 5–24; Charles M. Hardin, *Presidential Power and Accountability: Toward a New Constitution* (Chicago: University of Chicago Press, 1974); Rexford G. Tugwell, *Model for a New Constitution* (Santa Barbara, Calif.: Center for the Study of Democratic Institutions, 1970); Conley Dillon, "Recommendation for the Establishment of a Permanent Commission on Constitutional Review," *Bureaucrat*, July 1974, pp. 211–14; Herbert Croly, *Progressive Democracy* (New York: Macmillan, 1914).

12. Woodrow Wilson, "The Study of Administration," *Political Science Quarterly* 2 (1887): 197–222.

13. Woodrow Wilson, "Committee or Cabinet Government," *Overland Monthly*, 2d ser., 3 (Jan. 1884): 17–33. This article is reprinted in Arthur S. Link, ed., *The Papers of Woodrow Wilson*, 48 vols. (Princeton, N.J.: Princeton University Press, 1967), 2:614–40 (as of 1985 this edition of Wilson's papers had reached 17 July 1918). For a recent version of Wilson's thinking see Lloyd N. Cutler, "To Form a Government," *Foreign Affairs* 59 (Fall 1980): 140.

14. James O. Freedman mentions parties, committees, and judicial review as examples of extraconstitutional institutions that have attained legitimacy in American government (see his *Crisis and Legitimacy: The Administrative Process and American Government* [London: Cambridge University Press, 1978], pp. 127–29).

15. Paul Van Riper, "The American Administrative State: Wilson and the Founders—An Unorthodox View," *Public Administration Review* 43 (Nov.–Dec. 1983): 477–90.

16. Garry Wills, *Explaining America: The Federalist* (Garden City, N.Y.: Doubleday, 1981).

17. Theodore Bland, a staunch Anti-Federalist, reported that the Virginia Ratifying Convention was evenly divided—with "one-half of her crew hoisting sail for the land of *energy* and the other looking with a longing aspect on the shore of *liberty*" (Robert Rutland, *The Ordeal of the Constitution: The Anti-Federalists and the Ratification Struggle of 1787–88* [Norman: University of Oklahoma Press, 1966], p. 231). The sharp dichotomy that Bland draws between liberty and energy in government was precisely what Publius attacked (see *Federalist 1, 20, 25, 63,* and *85*). It is significant that the connection between vigorous government and individual rights is made quite explicitly in the first and last of *The Federalist Papers*. This point "frames" the argument of the essays as a whole.

18. Charles C. Tansill, ed., "Debates in the Federal Convention of 1787 as reported by James Madison," in *Documents Illustrative of the Formation of the Union of the American States* (Washington, D.C.: Government Printing Office, 1927), p. 43.

19. Ibid.

20. This comment applies more to *The Republic* than to Plato's *Laws*. The latter work puts considerable stress on the art of founding a regime, even though there is nothing in the *Laws* comparable to what Arendt describes as the Roman meaning of *auctoritas*.

21. Plato, *Republic*, bk. 10, 614a–618a.

22. Hannah Arendt, "What Is Authority?" in *Between Past and Present* (New York: Viking Press, 1961), p. 120.

23. Ibid., p. 123, citing Mommsen.

24. *Auctor* (author) is also from *augere* and is used synonymously with *conditor* (founder) for those who established the political order. Like literary authors, authors of regimes have their work live after them. "Authority" thus "augments" the work of political "authors."

25. See note 11 above.

26. Hannah Arendt, *On Revolution* (New York: Viking Press, 1963), p. 214. In stressing the "principle of mutual promise and common deliberation" as a founding principle, Arendt invites the reader to think of the Constitution more in terms of a covenant than a contract. That is, it creates a people, brings them into being, and to this day sustains them in being. Arendt's invitation is eloquently accepted by Milner S. Ball in *The Promise of American Law* (Athens: University of Georgia Press, 1981), pp. 7–15.

27. Herbert J. Storing, ed., *The Complete Anti-Federalist*, 7 vols. (Chicago: University of Chicago Press, 1981). Volume 1 of *The Complete Anti-Federalist* is Storing's thorough introduction to the writings that he edited so carefully. It is published in paperback under the title *What the Anti-Federalists Were FOR: The Political Thought of the Opponents of the Constitution*. The quotation in the text can be found on p. 3 of volume 1. Discussions of the seven-volume work can be found in Leonard J. Levy, "Against the Union," *New York Times Book Review,* 21 Feb. 1982; Edmund S. Morgan "The Argument for the States," *New Republic,* 28 Apr. 1983; my review essay of *The Complete Anti-Federalist* in *America* 148 (15 Jan. 1982). Professor Murray Dry has

compiled a one-volume abridged version of Storing's *Complete Anti-Federalist,* which is available in paperback from the University of Chicago Press under the title *The Anti-Federalist: Writings by the Opponents of the Constitution* (1985).

28. Ibid.

## CHAPTER 2
## SEPARATION OF POWERS

1. Herman Belz, "Separation of Powers," *Encyclopedia of American Government and Politics,* p. 46. I am grateful to Professor Belz for sharing with me his manuscript of this forthcoming publication.

2. *Annals of Congress,* 1:374.

3. Thomas K. McCraw, *Prophets of Regulation* (Cambridge: Harvard University Press, 1984), p. 215.

4. *Federalist 47.*

5. Herbert J. Storing, *The Complete Anti-Federalist,* 7 vols. (Chicago: University of Chicago Press, 1981), hereafter cited as *CAF.* References include the name or pseudonym of the Anti-Federalist author and three numbers, which indicate the volume number, the author's position in the volume, and the paragraph in the author's pamphlet or speech. References to volume 1 (Storing's introductory essay) and to Storing's notes will be by volume and page. Brutus, 2.9.197, 202; Mason, 2.2.7–8; Federal Farmer, 2.8.86, 175; Old Whig, 3.3.31; Officer of the late Continental Army, 3.8.3; DeWitt, 4.3.12–14; Agrippa, 4.6.73; Brutus, 5.15.1; Henry, 5.16.7–14; Cincinnatus, 6.1.26–32; Plebeian, 6.11.16. For a more relaxed Anti-Federalist stance on separation of powers see William Penn, 3.12.16–17; and Watchman, 4.22.4.

6. Since the vice-president of the United States is president of the Senate, it was essential to go outside of that body for a presiding officer at the impeachment trial of a president. Otherwise the vice-president would find himself in a severe conflict of interest.

7. In his remarks of 26 July, George Mason provided a nice summary of the convention's efforts to find a suitable way to elect a president (see Tansill, pp. 456–57). For a full reference to Tansill see note 18 of chap. 1

8. Tansill, pp. 662–63.

9. M. J. C. Vile, *Constitutionalism and Separation of Powers* (New York: Oxford University Press, 1967), p. 13.

10. *Federalist 47.*

11. Ibid.

12. For full discussions on the doctrine of separation of powers see Vile and see W. B. Gwyn, *The Meaning of the Separation of Powers* (New Orleans: Tulane University, 1965). The practical meaning of these doctrines in American politics is ably treated by Louis Fisher in *The Constitution between Friends* (New York: St. Martin's Press, 1978), pp. 7–15; and by Henry J. Merry in *Constitutional Function of Presidential-Administrative Separation* (Washington, D.C.: University Press of America, 1978), pp. 23–52.

13. For Rufus King's position see Tansill, p. 419; for James Wilson's position see Tansill, pp. 444–45.

14. Ibid., p. 396.

15. Ibid., p. 399.

16. Ibid., pp. 165, 423.

17. Ibid., p. 166.

18. Ibid.

19. Ibid.

20. Ibid., p. 422.

21. Ibid., p. 424.

22. Ibid., pp. 424–26.

23. Ibid., p. 548.

24. *Annals of Congress,* 1:591.

25. Ibid., p. 597.

26. Jennings Bryan Sanders, *Evolution of the Executive Departments of the Continental Congress* (Chapel Hill: University of North Carolina Press, 1935), pp. 3–5.

27. *Annals of Congress,* 1:597–98.

28. Tansill, p. 548 for Mercer, p. 424 for Gerry, p. 426 for Martin, p. 167 for Dickinson.

29. Ibid., p. 118.

30. Ibid., p. 117.

31. Ibid., p. 478.

32. Ibid., p. 567.

33. Ibid., p. 682.

34. The prohibition against having any officer of the United States serve as a member of Congress is unequivocal: "and no Person holding any Office under the United States, shall be a Member of either House during his Continuance in Office" (art. 1, sec. 6). Despite this clear language, many members of Congress hold commissions as reserve officers in the military. One can hope that members of Congress who treat so lightly their oath to uphold the Constitution would show considerable restraint in attacking the legitimacy of the administrative state (see *Schlesinger* v. *Reservists Committee to Stop the War,* 418 U.S. 208 [1974]).

35. Letter of President Washington to the "Chief Justice and Associate Justices of the Supreme Court of the United States," 3 Apr. 1790, in *John Jay's Correspondence and Public Papers,* 3:396.

36. I U.S. Stat. 49–50.

37. George C. Chalou, "St. Clair's Defeat, 1792," in *Congress Investigates,* ed. Arthur Schlesinger, 5 vols. (New York: Chelsea House Publishers, 1975), 1:10.

38. Ibid., p. 15.

## CHAPTER 3
## THE SENATE AS EXECUTIVE ESTABLISHMENT

1. *Federalist 65.*

2. Storing, *CAF,* Mason, 2.2.4 (for an explanation of *CAF* references see note 5 of chap. 2).

3. Storing, *CAF,* Monroe, 5.21.32, and Montezuma, 3.4.2. See also the comments of William Grayson on 14 June 1788 at the Virginia Ratifying Convention, in Jonathan Elliot, ed., *The Debates in the Several State Conventions on the Adoption of the Federal Constitution as Recommended by the General Convention at Philadelphia in 1787,* 5 vols., 2d ed. (Philadelphia: J. P. Lippincott, 1836; hereafter cited as Elliot), 3:375–77.

4. Storing, *CAF,* 5.21.37.

5. Tansill, p. 609 for Sherman, p. 319 for Morris, p. 324 for Madison, and p. 378 for King; see also the colloquy between Edmund Randolph and George Mason on pp. 528–29. for a full reference to Tansill see note 18 of chap. 1.

6. Ibid., p. 319.

7. Ibid., p. 468; see also art. 4, sec. 5, of the draft constitution submitted by the Committee of Detail on 6 Aug., in Tansill, p. 472.

8. Ibid., p. 474.

9. When this clause was eventually deleted, it was not because of any hesitation over the nonlegislative character of the Senate. The reason for deleting the clause was to *include* the executive functions of the Senate in the general congressional rule that a journal of proceedings should be published. Some framers wanted to exempt the Senate from this obligation when it was acting in a nonlegislative capacity (see Tansill, p. 519).

10. Tansill, p. 474.

11. A further discussion of the Senate's mobility can be found in Tansill, pp. 521–22.

12. Ibid., pp. 403, 430–32.

13. Ibid., p. 661.

14. Elliot, 3:491.

15. Ibid.

16. Storing, *CAF*, Cato, 2.6.45.

17. Ibid., 2.4.42 and 2.4.48 for Martin and 5.21.35 for Monroe; and Elliot, 3:220–22.

18. Some supporters of the Constitution shared this fear (see the remarks of James Wilson in Tansill, p. 674).

19. Storing, *CAF*, Federal Farmer, 2.8.170.

20. Ibid., Centinel, 2.7.23.

21. Ibid., Minority of Convention of Pennsylvania, 3.11.45. Several Anti-Federalists referred to the president as "president-general" because of his constitutional position as commander in chief of the army and navy. For a further discussion of the Anti-Federalists who favored a strong executive see Storing, *CAF*, 1:49 and note 5 on p. 94. Federal Farmer was one of the staunchest Anti-Federalist champions of a strong executive (see 2.7.128, where he follows Adams closely).

22. Some Federalists shared this concern (see comments of Wilson in Tansill, p. 684, and of Ellsworth, p. 537).

23. Elliot, 3:394.

24. Tansill, pp. 671, 686–87.

25. Richard Neustadt, *Presidential Power: The Politics of Leadership from FDR to Carter* (New York: Wiley, 1960, 1980), pp. 29–33.

26. Elliot, 3:493–94.

27. Storing, *CAF*, Lee, 5.6.5; and Elliot, 4:116–17.

28. *Federalist 62–65*.

29. Tansill, pp. 659–64 and 682–83. The office of vice-president was created to enable the electoral-college system to function, as Hugh Williamson notes on p. 682. Throughout the entire convention there was never any discussion of having the Speaker of the House succeed to the presidency. If the successor was to have any connection with Congress, that connection would only be with the Senate. The fact that the Presidential Succession Act of 1947 puts the Speaker of the House right after the vice-president and before the president *pro tempore* of the Senate is consistent with the democratic evolution of the office of the president and with the decline in awareness of the executive character of the Senate. It is interesting to note, however, that in the 1792 Succession Act, the president *pro tempore* of the Senate was placed ahead of the Speaker of the House and right after the vice-president of the United States. This suggests that the executive character of the Senate was quite clear to the members of the early sessions of Congress.

30. This point is also made by Rufus King in the Massachusetts Ratifying Convention (Elliot, 4:47–48) and by James Iredell in the North Carolina Ratifying Convention (Elliot, 4:41, 133).

31. Tansill, p. 275.

32. Ibid., p. 278.

33. Ibid., p. 281.

34. Ibid., p. 288.

35. Ibid., p. 378.

36. Storing, *CAF*, Centinel, 2.7.23.

37. Ibid., Brutus, 2.9.201.

38. Ibid., M. Smith, 6.12.27.

39. Tansill, pp. 222, 319, and 279.

40. Ibid., p. 117.

41. The fear of the Senate's treaty power was the basis of another Anti-Federalist argument. Article 6 of the Constitution provides that treaties shall be the Supreme Law of the land. The Anti-Federalists maintained that this could lead to *legislation* without concurrence from the House of Representatives. A generous definition of *treaty* could put the entire legislative power in the hands of the Senate. This danger was combined with the fear of the proposed "federal city," where the Senators would live all year round. Their distance from home and their six-year term would threaten republican virtue. On the dangers of the federal city see the following Anti-Federalist writings in Storing, *CAF*: Federal Farmer, 2.8.222–23; Aristocrotis, 3.16.2; Brutus, 2.9.200; Columbian Patriot, 4.28.8; Cato Uticensis, 5.7.7. The treaty argument is answered in *Federalist 64*.

42. Storing, *CAF*, Mason, 2.2.4.

43. Ibid., Martin, 2.4.42.

44. Ibid., Cato, 2.6.45.

45. Tansill, p. 499.

46. Ibid., p. 530 (emphasis added).

47. Ibid., p. 674.

48. Ibid., p. 278.

49. Ibid., p. 546.

50. See the colloquy between Madison and G. Morris in Tansill, p. 733.

51. Storing, *CAF*, Federal Farmer, 2.8.170.

52. *Federalist 66* and *76*.

53. *Federalist 66*. For further discussions of senatorial practice that confounds Hamilton's prediction see Louis Fisher, *The Constitution between Friends* (New York: St. Martin's Press, 1978), pp. 113–15.

54. Storing, *CAF*, Federal Farmer, 2.8.173.

55. George Mason is the leading Anti-Federalist on this point (see his remarks at the Virginia Ratifying Convention, in Elliot, 3:494–96).

56. *Federalist 65*. The quotation appears in the fifth paragraph. The references to the Senate in the two preceding paragraphs and the one following the quotation suggest that Publius was referring to the Senate, not to the entire Congress, when he speaks of "representatives of the nation."

57. Tansill, p. 222.

58. Ibid., p. 279. Edmund Randolph, Madison's fellow Virginian, went further. He looked to the second branch of the legislature "to guard the Constitution against encroachments of the Executive who will be apt to form combinations with the demagogues of the popular branch" (Tansill, p. 196).

59. Ibid., p. 285.

60. See chap. 6, pp. 80–82, for the Federalists' doctrine on checks and balances.

61. Per capita voting in the Senate received surprisingly little attention during the Philadelphia Convention. See Daniel Carroll's complaint that he "did not wish so hastily to make so material an innovation" (Tansill, p. 440).

62. Storing, *CAF*, A Farmer, 3.14.15.

63. Ibid., Livingston, 6.12.25.

64. Edgar A. Maclay, ed., *Journal of William Maclay* (New York, 1890), p. 110 (the entry for 14 July 1789 in *Maclay's Journal*).

65. The combination of powers in the Senate was discussed in chap. 2, pp. 16–18.

66. An excellent discussion of this literature can be found in Chester A. Newland, "Professional Public Executives and Public Administration Agendas," in *Professional Public Executives,* ed. Chester A. Newland (Washington, D.C.: American Society for Public Administration, 1980), pp. 1–29.


CHAPTER 4
REPRESENTATION AS A CONSTITUTIONAL DEFECT

1. Michael Lipsky, *Street Level Bureaucracy: Dilemmas of the Individual in Public Services* (New York: Russell Sage Foundation, 1980).

2. See Appendix A for the full text of article 1, section 2.

3. See the comments of James Wilson in Tansill, p. 160. For a full reference to Tansill see note 18 of chap. 1.

4. Storing, *CAF*, George Mason, 5.17.1. For an explanation of *CAF* references see note 5 of chap. 2.

5. Storing, *CAF*, Centinel, 2.7.22. Centinel weakens his argument by assuming that the Constitution required one representative for every thirty thousand persons. Article 1, section 2, provides that there cannot be *more* than one representative for every thirty thousand persons. Thus the situation, from Centinel's point of view, was even worse than he thought.

6. Ibid., Federal Farmer, 2.8.15.

7. Ibid., Brutus, 2.9.14. Obviously, Brutus would not be reconciled to the Constitution by adding a few more representatives to the House. His point is that republican principles cannot be satisfied in an extended republic—the point that Publius attacks so brilliantly in *Federalist 10*. George Mason makes a somewhat similar argument when he uses the impossibility of meeting republican standards as the basis for his position that the federal government should have less power in very important matters such as navigation (*CAF*, 5.17.1).

8. Ibid., Chase, 5.3.20.

9. Melancton Smith is perhaps the most effective Anti-Federalist spokesman on representation (see *CAF*, 6.12.1–40 passim; see also *CAF*, 5.14.27–34; Storing's introduction to "Essays by A Farmer," *CAF*, 5:6; for further statements by Federal Farmer see *CAF*, 2.8.97, 106–7, 114, 117–18). For statements by George Mason see *CAF*, 2.2.2 and 5.17.1; Tansill, p. 161; Elliot, 3:262, 265, 266. For a full reference to Elliot see note 3 of chap. 3.

10. Storing, *CAF*, Minority of Convention of Pennsylvania, 3.11.33.

11. For a recent discussion of Madison's views on representation see Garry Wills, *Explaining America: The Federalist* (Garden City, N.Y.: Doubleday, 1981), pp. 177–264. Wills argues that Madison looked to representation as the governmental institution that would refine not only public opinion but civic virtue as well.

12. At the Virginia Ratifying Convention, Patrick Henry offered the following *reductio ad absurdum* to Madison's filtering and refining: "If ten men be better than one hundred seventy, it follows of necessity that one is better than ten—the choice is more refined" (Elliot, 3:167).

13. Tansill, pp. 349–50, 694.

14. Ibid., p. 694. Hamilton's candid fears of presidential corruption may stand as a monument to the wisdom of secrecy in some forms of decision making.

15. Ibid., p. 349.

16. See *Federalist 10* and *55–58;* see also Tansill, pp. 162–63.

17. Tansill, pp. 160–61; see also statements by John Dickenson (Tansill, p. 168) and Hugh Williamson (Tansill, pp. 668, 694, 720). Williamson raised the issue of representation on three occasions at Philadelphia. He seems to have been more interested in increasing the size of North Carolina's delegation than in a theory of representation.

18. George Mason, Elbridge Gerry, and Edmund Randolph were the only members of the convention who stayed till the end but refused to sign the Constitution. All three were quite active participants during the convention, but after the convention, Mason was more effective than either Gerry or Randolph.

19. Tansill, p. 741.

20. Ibid.

21. Ibid.

22. Ibid.

23. For examples of Madison's emphasis on knowledge and information see *Federalist 10, 35, 36,* and *57;* see also his remarks at the Philadelphia Convention on 12 June, where he justifies his support for a three-year term for members of the House on the grounds that they will need a long time to acquire the requisite knowledge for their tasks (Tansill, p. 192).

24. *Federalist 58.*

25. Storing, *CAF,* M. Smith, 6.12.14.

26. To sample the arguments defending and attacking the idea of "representative bureaucracy" see Harry Kranz, *The Participatory Bureaucracy* (Lexington, Mass.: Lexington, 1976); Kenneth Meier, "Representative Bureaucracy: An Empirical Analysis," *American Political Science Review* 69 (June 1975): 526–42; Kenneth Meier and Lloyd Nigro, "Representative Bureaucracy and Policy Preferences," *Public Administration Review* 36 (July–Aug. 1976): 458–69; V. Subramaniam, "Representative Bureaucracy: A Reassessment," *American Political Science Review* 61 (Dec. 1967): 1010–19; Samuel Krislov and David H. Rosenbloom, *Representative Bureaucracy and the American Political System* (New York: Praeger, 1981); John W. Witherspoon, "The Bureaucracy as Representatives," in *Representation,* NOMOS X, ed. J. Roland Pennock and John W. Chapman (New York: Atherton, 1968), pp. 229–56.

27. Norton Long, "Bureaucracy and Constitutionalism," *American Political Science Review* 46 (Sept. 1952): 808–18.

28. Kenneth C. Davis, *Discretionary Justice: A Preliminary Inquiry* (Baton Rouge: Louisiana State University Press, 1969); Jeffrey L. Jowell, *Law and Bureaucracy: Administrative Discretion and the Limits of Legal Action* (Port Washington, N.Y.: Dunellen, 1975).

29. Storing, *CAF,* M. Smith, 6.12.16–17.

30. Further "healing" may come from congressional staff. By a judicious use of patronage a public-spirited congressman could come into close contact with those who think the way the people think and feel the way they feel. Further discussion of representation in the *Federalist* can be found in numbers *3, 10, 17, 27, 35, 36, 38, 46, 68, 72, 76, 77,* and *84.*

31. *Federalist 10*.

32. Vincent Ostrom, *The Intellectual Crisis in American Public Administration* (University: University of Alabama Press, 1973).

33. Our discussion of the Anti-Federalists' views on numbers of representatives would be incomplete if I failed to note an amusing coincidence, called to my attention by my colleague Charles Goodsell. Suppose that over the years, Congress had authorized seats in the House of Representatives in accordance with the constitutionally permitted maximum of one for every thirty thousand Americans. Assuming a present population of 235 million, we would have 7,833 congressmen. This is approximately the number of persons in the Senior Executive Service today!

34. For examples of literature on this topic see note 26 above. The idea of nonelected officials being representatives is not confined to "representative bureaucracy" literature. In her well-known philosophical treatment of the concept "representation," Hanna Pitkin notes that monarchs, titular heads of governments, courts, judges, and juries have all been considered representatives (*The Concept of Representation* [Berkeley: University of California Press, 1967], p. 227). In chapter 6, I will discuss more fully the idea of nonelected officials as "representatives."

35. Max Farrand, ed., *The Records of the Federal Convention of 1787*, 4 vols. (New Haven, Conn.: Yale University Press, 1937), 1:111.

36. Ibid.

37. For a fuller discussion of Mason's speech see Herbert J. Storing's Introduction to the 1969 reprint of Charles C. Thach, *The Creation of the Presidency, 1775–1789: A Study in Constitutional History* (Baltimore, Md.: Johns Hopkins University Press, 1923, 1969), pp. ix–xi.

38. Tansill, p. 131.

39. Ibid.

40. Ibid.

41. Ibid., p. 132.

42. Ibid., p. 131.

43. Stuart M. Butler, Michael Sanera, and W. Bruce Weinsod, *Mandate for Leadership*, vol. 2 (Washington, D.C.: Heritage Foundation, 1984).

44. Long, p. 816. It is unfortunate that this article of Norton Long's is not as well known as his earlier piece, "Power and Administration," *Public Administration Review* 9 (1949): 257–64. It seems to me that the two articles complement each other. The first article attacks (indeed demolishes) one normative base for public administration, while the second article provides a new one.

45. *Federalist 29*. In the quoted passage, Publius is summarizing his opponents' argument.

46. Ibid.

47. Ibid.

48. For a fuller discussion of the "select corps" in *Federalist 29* see David F. Epstein, *The Political Theory of "The Federalist"* (Chicago: University of Chicago Press, 1984), pp. 49–50.

49. This caveat is crucial. It would be a grievous error simply to assume that ordinary citizens will show appropriate sensitivity to constitutional norms and fair play without receiving instruction in these matters. The behavior of Vietnam-era draft boards—General Hershey's "little groups of neighbors"—should not be forgotten (see James W. Davis and Kenneth M. Dolbeare, *Little Groups of Neighbors: The Selective Service System* [Chicago: Markham Publishing Co., 1968]).

50. Bernard Bailyn, *The Ideological Origins of the American Revolution* (Cambridge: Harvard University Press, 1967), p. 74.

51. Federal Farmer's complaint was not in vain. The Sixth Amendment to the Constitution provides: "In all criminal prosecutions, the accused shall enjoy the right to a speedy and public trial, by an impartial jury of the State *and district* wherein the crime shall have been committed, which district shall have been previously ascertained by law . . ." (emphasis added).

52. On the relative independence from judges that was enjoyed by eighteenth-century juries see William E. Nelson, *Americanization of the Common Law: The Impact of Legal Change on Massachusetts Society, 1760–1830* (Cambridge: Harvard University Press, 1975).

53. Aristotle, *Politics*, bk. 3, chaps. 1–5, ll. 1274b–78b.

54. The quotations in the text are taken from Alexis de Tocqueville, *Democracy in America*, 2 vols. (New York: Random House, 1945), 1:295–96. The book was first published in Paris in 1835 and was translated into English in the same year by Henry Reeve. The Reeve translation was corrected by Francis Bowen in 1862 and further corrected and edited by Phillips Bradley for the Random House (Vintage Book) version that appeared in 1945. My discussion of Tocqueville originally appeared in John A. Rohr, "Civil Servants and Second-class Citizens," *Public Administration Review* 44 (Mar. 1984): 135–43.

55. It is not only the hearing officer, in the technical sense of the term, who has this opportunity. I have in mind as well those officers who listen to the public in rule-making proceedings and other administrative forums. These forums can be quite informal and can frequently be put together at the discretion of the administrator without specific legislative authorization. My comments are made in the spirit of Woodrow Wilson's advice that administrators take "constant public counsel" and of Carl Friedrich's noting of "popular sentiment" as a touchstone of administrative responsibility. See also Kenneth C. Davis's call for open hearings as a means of structuring administrative discretion. The administrator need not come to such hearings simply to learn, but to teach as well.

PART 2
FOUNDING THE ADMINISTRATIVE STATE
IN WORD, 1887–1900

1. On the utopian character of the *Republic* see Allan Bloom's interpretive essay in *The Republic of Plato*, trans. Allan Bloom (New York: Basic Books, 1968), pp. 305–435 (hereafter cited as Bloom).

2. *The Laws of Plato*, trans. Thomas L. Pangle (New York: Basic Books, 1980), p. 511 n. 2. Aristotle identifies the Athenian Stranger as Socrates. For a contemporary argument in support of Aristotle's position see Leo Strauss, *What Is Political Philosophy?* (Glencoe, Ill.: Free Press, 1959), pp. 31ff.

3. *Republic*, bk. 1, 328e–331d (Bloom, pp. 4–7, 312–16).

4. Ibid., 331d (Bloom, p. 7).

5. Woodrow Wilson, "The Study of Administration," *Political Science Quarterly* 2 (June 1887): 197–222. As noted in the Preface, the American Society for Public Administration is observing the one-hundredth anniversary of this essay. At least two collections of essays have been assembled in honor of this centennial: Jack L. Rabin and James S. Bowman, eds., *Politics and Administration: Woodrow Wilson and American Public Administration* (New York: Marcel Dekker, 1983); and Ralph C. Chandler, ed., *A Centennial History of the American Administrative State* (New York: Wiley, forthcoming). For a cogent argument that downplays the significance of Wilson's essay see Paul

Van Riper, "The American Administrative State: Wilson and the Founders—An Unorthodox View," *Public Administration Review* 43 (Nov.-Dec. 1983): 477–90.

6. Frank J. Goodnow, *Politics and Administration: A Study in Government* (New York: Russell & Russell, 1900, 1967).

## CHAPTER 5
## WOODROW WILSON AS CONSTITUTIONALIST

1. Woodrow Wilson, *Congressional Government: A Study in American Politics* (Boston: Houghton-Mifflin, 1885; references to *Congressional Government* herein are based on the Meridian Book edition [Cleveland, Ohio: World Publishing Co., tenth printing, 1967]); and Arthur S. Link, ed., *The Papers of Woodrow Wilson*, 48 vols. (Princeton, N.J.: Princeton University Press, 1966–85). Throughout this chapter there will be frequent references to Link's edition of the Wilson papers, especially volumes 5 through 10, which appeared between 1967 and 1971—hereafter cited as *Papers*. This chapter follows closely my essay "The Constitutional World of Woodrow Wilson," in *Politics and Administration: Woodrow Wilson and American Public Administration*, ed. Jack Rabin and James S. Bowman (New York: Marcel Dekker, 1983), pp. 31–49.

2. In limiting our examination to the years shortly before and after 1887, we must set aside an important book by Wilson, *Constitutional Government in the United States* (1908). This book presents quite a different interpretation of the Constitution from that of *Congressional Government*. The best discussion of the difference between the two books can be found in Christopher Wolfe's "Woodrow Wilson: Interpreting the Constitution," *Review of Politics* 41 (Jan. 1979): 121–42.

3. John M. Mulder, *Woodrow Wilson: The Years of Preparation* (Princeton, N.J.: Princeton University Press, 1978).

4. For a discussion of how the fragmented power in Congress contributed to the development of the administrative state see William E. Nelson, *The Roots of American Bureaucracy, 1830–1900* (Cambridge: Harvard University Press, 1982), chap. 5.

5. Wilson, *Congressional Government*, p. 214.

6. *Papers*, 2:614–40.

7. Ibid., p. 627.

8. Ibid., p. 628. For a discussion of proposals to enable cabinet members to sit in Congress see Leonard D. White, *The Republicans* (New York: Free Press, 1958), pp. 107–9. A contemporary discussion of Wilson's proposals can be found in the "Workbook" of the Committee on the Constitutional System. The "Workbook" includes a chapter of a forthcoming book by James L. Sundquist of the Brookings Institution (see "Workbook Supplement," pp. S16–S18).

9. *Papers*, 2:628.

10. *Federalist 51*.

11. *U.S. Constitution*, art. 5. The other provision that could not be amended is the prohibition against congressional interference with the importation of slaves prior to 1808.

12. Wilson, *Congressional Government*, p. 205. Walter Lippmann discusses Wilson's retreat from constitutional specificity in his Introduction to the Meridian Books edition of *Congressional Government*.

13. In tracing the origins of Wilson's constitutional thought, one finds in his unpublished essay "Government by Debate" (*Papers*, 2:159) some of the themes developed in "Committee or Cabinet Government," *Overland Monthly*, 2d ser., 3 (Jan. 1884): 17–33; and in *Congressional Government* (1885). The origins of the unpublished

essay can be traced to an article in *International Review* entitled "Cabinet Government in the United States" (1879; *Papers*, 1:493). Thence the trail leads to several contemporary articles on congressional reform in *The Nation* (*Papers*, 1:492–93). It ends with Walter Bagehot's *The English Constitution*. The American edition of this famous book appeared in 1873. Bagehot's influence on Wilson was profound. Wilson studied constitutional law under a Professor Southall at the University of Virginia. The only classroom notes on constitutional law printed in *The Papers of Woodrow Wilson* are found at 1:621 (9 Mar. 1880). They have nothing to do with congressional reform or cabinet governments, but they do illuminate Wilson's position on secession. The editors of *The Papers* note, however, that they have not printed all of Wilson's classroom notes (1:xv). Perhaps a further examination of Wilson's unpublished classroom notes might reveal some influence that Professor Southall had on Wilson's views on cabinet government. I do not think this likely, however, because Wilson's interest in cabinet government antedates his study of constitutional law at the University of Virginia.

14. Woodrow Wilson, *Division and Reunion, 1829–1889* (New York: Longman-Green, 1893).

15. Ibid., p. 211.

16. Ibid.

17. Ibid., p. 212.

18. Ibid., p. 211.

19. For a thorough discussion of Wilson's organic view of politics see Robert D. Miewald, "The Origins of Wilson's Thought: The German Tradition and the Organic State," in Rabin and Bowman, pp. 17–30.

20. Wilson, *Division and Reunion*, pp. 47–48.

21. *Papers*, 7:124.

22. Woodrow Wilson, *History of the American People*, 5 vols. (New York: Harper, 1901).

23. *Papers*, 7:212.

24. When circumstances required, Wilson was equal to a closely reasoned analysis of case law (see, e.g., his lectures at the New York Law School [*Papers*, 7:512] and *Division and Reunion*, p. 40).

25. Judging from the tone of Wilson's Preface to the fifteenth printing of *Congressional Government* in 1900, he seems to have been pleased with the general development of American institutions since the book first had appeared fifteen years earlier. The same tone is clear in *Constitutional Government in the United States* (New York: Columbia University Press, 1908), wherein Wilson makes his peace with separation of powers (see Wolfe, "Woodrow Wilson: Interpreting the Constitution"). For an explicit treatment of historicism and Wilson's thinking see Kent A. Kirwan, "Historicism and Statesmanship in the Reform Argument of Woodrow Wilson," *Interpretation* 9 (Sept. 1981): 339–51.

26. *Papers*, 7:127.

27. Ibid., pp. 127–28. In using materials from Wilson's lectures and classroom notes, I have ignored his prodigal use of italics because they may have been inserted to guide his eye rather than to emphasize a particular word or thought. In using his published materials, however, I have followed Wilson's lead.

28. Ibid., pp. 125–26.

29. A similar strategy was followed by the Brownlow Committee (see discussion below in chap. 9, p. 138).

30. Wilson, *Congressional Government*, pp. 181, 190 (emphasis in original), 191, 172–74. Although Wilson is uncertain about how to classify department heads, he is quite clear in assigning ambassadors and the "highest grades" of government officials

to the career side of the line that divides political from nonpolitical positions (pp. 159–60).

31. Ibid., p. 170.

32. In stressing the importance of administration, Wilson follows the teaching of Publius in *Federalist 17, 27, 46,* and *72.* He departs from Publius, however, when he suggests that administration is something other than politics. Publius makes a distinction between two levels of administration without suggesting that either level is apolitical (see Kent A. Kirwan, "The Crisis of Identity in the Study of Public Administration," *Polity* 9 (Spring 1977): 321–43.

33. Wilson, "Study of Administration," II. The centennial essay has been reprinted so often that it is more likely to be available to the reader in a collection of essays than in the 1887 volume of the *Political Science Quarterly* or in Wilson's *Papers.* Reprints of the essay usually indicate the three major sections of the essay by Roman numerals. I shall follow this usage and refer to the centennial essay by section rather than by page.

34. *Papers,* 7:125.

35. Ibid., p. 121.

36. For further examples of administration preceding constitutions see *Papers,* 7:518 and 128; see also Carl J. Friedrich, *Constitutional Government and Democracy,* 4th ed. (Waltham, Mass.: Blaisdell, 1968), p. 39; and Henry J. Merry, *Constitutional Function of Presidential-Administrative Separation* (Washington, D.C.: University Press of America, 1978), pp. 79–80. The close connection between constitution and administration in Wilson's thought was called to my attention by Herbert J. Storing, "American Statesmanship Old and New," in *Bureaucrats, Policy Analysts, Statesmen: Who Leads?* ed. Robert A. Goldwin (Washington, D.C.: American Enterprise Institute, 1980), pp. 88–113. For a lucid analysis of the centennial essay that discovers not one but three dichotomies (or discriminations) between politics and administration see Kirwan, "Crisis of Identity." The problem of democracy preceding bureaucracy in the United States is discussed by Michael Nelson in "A Short Ironic History of American National Bureaucracy," *Journal of Politics* 44 (Aug. 1982): 742–88.

37. Wilson, "Study of Administration," II; *Papers,* 7:138 (emphasis added).

38. *Papers,* 7:138.

39. Ibid., pp. 128–29.

40. Ibid., p. 129.

41. Wilson, "Study of Administration," II.

42. *Papers,* 7:130.

43. Ibid.

44. In relying on Wilson's 1891 lecture, I do not mean to confine the high profile of administration to Wilson's lecture for that one year. I have selected the 1891 notes because they integrate constitutional questions into an administrative lecture more clearly than any other section of his notes. I think it is fair to say that the high-profile model is thematic throughout the Johns Hopkins lectures. They begin in 1888 with Wilson telling his listeners he will "look at Administration from the very high ground of the inquiry—What are the functions of government." In 1898, the year after the final series of lectures on administration, Wilson returned to Johns Hopkins to lecture on Bagehot, Burke, and Maine. In the course of the Burke lecture he describes no less an issue than Parliamentary Reform as an administrative question!

It is interesting to note that after completing a decade of lecturing on administration at Johns Hopkins, Wilson returned to lecture on Bagehot, Burke, and Maine. It is as though his thought naturally took him from high-profile administration to the grand themes of these authors. The fact that he selects three English conservatives for his lectures suggests some of the unifying themes of his work over the previous decade.

Wilson's enthusiasm for Burke gives some insight into the nature of Wilson's organic view of politics. Burke is Wilson's model in this matter as Bagehot was his model in attacking separation of powers. Wilson once wrote, "If I should claim any man as my master, that man would be Burke" (*Papers*, 7:316). Wilson's lectures on Burke have a strong autobiographical flavor. Wilson presents the young Burke as a man who, like Wilson, neglected his formal studies to take his own education in hand through wide reading. Also like Wilson, Burke found the practice of law tedious and therefore turned his attention to philosophy, oratory, and statesmanship. Wilson's admiration for political orators was boundless. One of the reasons for Wilson's disdain for congressional government was that it put too little stress on oratory and debate (see, e.g., *Congressional Government*, pp. 141–42, 147, 72–75; and Henry W. Bragdon, *Woodrow Wilson: The Academic Years* [Cambridge: Harvard University Press, 1967], pp. 130, 241–42). Wilson's passion for oratory is linked to his admiration of "great men," which may possibly be traced to Carlyle's influence on him.

45. Arthur S. Link, *Wilson: The Road to the White House* (Princeton, N.J.: Princeton University Press, 1947), pp. 24, 34; see also Bragdon, p. 195.

46. My focus in this chapter is on Wilson's conservative political thought rather than his conservative stance on the issues of the day. For examples of the latter see Bragdon, p. 249.

47. *Papers*, 10:421.

48. Ibid., p. 355.

49. Ibid., p. 329; and Wilson, *Division and Reunion*, p. 21.

50. *Papers*, 7:352, 341, 354.

51. Ibid., p. 353.

52. Ibid.

53. Ibid., pp. 333–34.

54. Wilson, *Division and Reunion*, p. 80.

55. Ibid.

56. Ibid.

57. Bragdon, p. 157.

58. *Papers*, 6:231.

59. Ibid., p. 233.

60. Ibid., pp. 233–34.

61. Wilson's concern about the new immigrants is consistent with his abiding support for civil-service reform. He candidly acknowledged that "civil service reform is eminently wise and imperatively necessary for good government, but it is not democratic in idea—at least not in the modern idea of democracy. It substitutes for the average man or 'the man of the people,' the man of the schools; that is, the instructed and fitted man" (*Papers*, 7:81–82). Wilson's hope for solving the problem raised by the new immigrants was to turn to the nation's leaders:

> I believe that the only way in which we can preserve our nationality in its integrity and its old-time originative force in the face of growth and imported change is by concentrating it, by putting leaders forward vested with abundant authority in the conception and execution of policy. There is plenty of the old vitality in our national character to tell, if you will but give it leave. Give it leave and it will the more impress and mould those who come to us from abroad. I believe that we have not made enough of leadership.
>
> > A people is but the attempt of many
> > To rise to the completer life of one;
> > And those who live as models for the mass
> > Are singly of more value than they all.

We shall not again have a true national life until we compact it by such legislative leadership as other nations have. But, once thus compacted and embodied, our nationality is safe. An acute English historical scholar has said that "the Americans of the United States are a nation because they once obeyed a king": we shall remain a nation only by obeying leaders.

> Keep but the model safe
> New Men will rise to study it.

Wilson's gloomy prescription for the new immigrant population seems to be that obedience must do the work of character. For a discussion of Wilson's reliance on leadership as a departure from the views of the framers see Robert Eden, *Political Leadership and Nihilism: A Study of Weber and Nietzsche* (Tampa: University Presses of Florida, 1983), chap. 1.

62. William E. Gladstone, "Kin Beyond the Sea," *North American Review* (Sept. 1878).

63. *Papers*, 7:81-82.

64. Kirwan, "Crisis of Identity," p. 336.

65. The theme that bureaucratic structures serve as a defense of minority and individual rights in American history is developed skillfully by William Nelson in *The Roots of American Bureaucracy;* see especially chap. 5.

66. Wilson, "Study of Administration," III.

67. Ibid.

68. Morton Keller, *Affairs of State: Public Life in Late Nineteenth Century America* (Cambridge: Belknap Press of Harvard University Press, 1977), p. 296.

69. *Federalist 17, 27, 46;* see Introduction, pp. 1-3.

70. Although Publius and Wilson agreed on the importance of administration, it should be noted that Wilson's position is based on the belief that administration is ready to *replace* politics. For Publius, administration is an integral part of politics. If Wilson's ideas about the passing of the era of the high politics seems naïve, consider John F. Kennedy's remark that in the United States there would be no further need for "the great spirit of 'passionate movements' which have stirred this country so often in the past." Kennedy made this statement in 1962—virtually on the eve of the tumultuous era we have come to call "the sixties" (cited in Samuel P. Huntington, *American Politics: The Promise of Disharmony* [Cambridge: Belknap Press of Harvard University Press, 1981], p. 172).

71. *Papers*, 7:81-82. For a discussion of civil-service reform making room for "natural leaders" to assume their "rightful" place see David H. Rosenbloom, "Politics and Public Personnel Administration: The Legacy of 1883," in *Centenary Issues of the Pendleton Act of 1883: The Problematic Legacy of Civil Service Reform*, ed. David H. Rosenbloom (New York: Marcel Dekker, 1982), pp. 1-11.

72. Wilson was not the only American to favor some sort of parliamentary arrangement for the United States. For recent examples see Lloyd N. Cutler, "To Form a Government," *Foreign Affairs* 59 (Fall 1980): 126-43; and Theodore C. Sorensen, *A Different Kind of Presidency* (New York: Harper & Row, 1984). Perhaps the most interesting use of parliamentary language in recent years was President Nixon's explanation that he was resigning his high office because he had lost a "vote of confidence" when the House Judiciary Committee approved the articles of impeachment. By the use of parliamentary language, he tried to mask his disgrace as being a routine political defeat.

## CHAPTER 6
## FRANK J. GOODNOW AND THE FRAMERS

1. Frank J. Goodnow, *Politics and Administration: A Study in Government* (New York: Russell & Russell, 1900, 1967). Themes developed in this chapter appeared in my article "Professionalism, Legitimacy, and the Constitution," *Public Administration Quarterly* 8 (Winter 1985): 401–18.

2. Herbert J. Storing, "The 'Other' Federalist Papers: A Preliminary Sketch," *Political Science Reviewer* 6 (1976): 215–47. Political scientists have been fond of debating whether or not there is a theory underlying the Constitution. The best arguments that there is such a theory can be found in Martin Diamond, "Democracy and 'The Federalist': A Reconsideration of the Framers' Intent," *American Political Science Review*, Mar. 1959, pp. 52–68; and in chap. 5 of Herbert J. Storing, *What the Anti-Federalists Were FOR* (Chicago: University of Chicago Press, 1981); see also Martin Diamond, *The Founding of the Democratic Republic* (Itasca, Ill.: Peacock Press, 1981). The leading authors who deny such a theory are Max Farrand, *The Framing of the Constitution of the United States* (New Haven, Conn.: Yale University Press, 1913), and John Roche, "The Founding Fathers: A Reform Caucus in Action," *American Political Science Review*, Dec. 1961, pp. 799–816.

3. Gordon S. Wood, *The Creation of the American Republic* (Chapel Hill: University of North Carolina Press, 1969); Storing, *What the Anti-Federalists Were FOR* and "The 'Other' Federalist Papers."

4. Storing, *What the Anti-Federalists Were FOR*, p. 59.

5. A good comparison of the Whig and Republican positions can be found in Wood, chaps. 1 and 2.

6. For a discussion of the principle of legislative supremacy during the Philadelphia Convention (as opposed to the ratification debate) see Henry J. Merry, *Constitutional Function of Presidential-Administrative Separation* (Washington, D.C.: University Press of America, 1978), pp. 35–38.

7. See the report of the Pennsylvania ratification debate in John B. McMaster and Frederick D. Stone, *Pennsylvania and the Federal Constitution, 1787–1788*, 2 vols. (New York: Da Capo Press, 1970), 1:229. The Da Capo edition is a reprint. The book was originally published in one volume in Philadelphia in 1888.

8. Ibid., 1:302. Wilson's position is interesting. Since he was among the most democratic members of the 1787 Convention, it is not surprising that he should take the lead in developing a popular-sovereignty interpretation of the Constitution. During that convention he held a microcosm view of the legislature, but he had abandoned this position by the time of the ratification debate in Pennsylvania. For Wilson's microcosm statement during the convention see Tansill, p. 160 (for a complete reference to Tansill see note 18 of chap. 1). A discussion of Wilson's position on sovereignty at the time of the Revolution can be found in Bernard Bailyn, *The Ideological Origins of the American Revolution* (Cambridge: Harvard University Press, 1967), pp. 224–26. For a thorough critique of Wilson's political thought see Ralph A. Rossum, "James Wilson and the Pyramid of Government: The Federal Republic," in *The American Founding: Politics, Statesmen and the Constitution*, ed. Ralph A. Rossum and Gary L. McDowell (Port Washington, N.Y.: Kennikat Press, 1981), pp. 62–79.

9. McMaster and Stone, p. 229.

10. Wood, p. 547; see also p. 532: "Relocating sovereignty in the people by making them 'the fountain of all power' seemed to make sense of the entire system. Once the Federalists perceived 'the great principle of the primary right of power in the people,' they could scarcely restrain their enthusiasm in following out its implications.

One insight seemed to lead to another, until the Federalists were tumbling over each other in their efforts to introduce the people into the federal government, which they had 'hitherto been shut out of.' 'The people of the United States are now in the possession and exercise of their original rights,' said [James] Wilson, 'and while this doctrine is known and operates, we shall have a cure for every disease.' "

11. Storing, "The 'Other' Federalist Papers," p. 230 (emphasis added).

12. For the pertinent language used in the Pennsylvania debate over ratification see McMaster and Stone, 1970, 1:229, 250, 260, 270; see also *Federalist 27,* where Publius refers to "all officers legislative, executive and judicial," and *Federalist 28* and *46,* where all government officials are called representatives. Frank J. Goodnow refers to both elected and appointed personnel as "officers" in *Principles of the Administrative Law of the United States* (New York: Putnam, 1905), p. 257. He tends to blur the distinction by using the expression "the official relation" to describe both elected and appointed personnel (pp. 222–315 passim). During his presidency, Jefferson referred to both legislative and executive personnel as "officers" and to elected officials as "public functionaries" (see Paul Leicester Ford, ed., *The Writings of Thomas Jefferson,* 10 vols. [New York: G. P. Putnam, 1898], vol. 9). John Adams was the principal author of the Massachusetts Constitution of 1780, which includes members of the legislature within the term "officer." On James Wilson see Tansill, p. 126. See Tansill, p. 433, where both Williamson and Gerry include legislators in the term "officer." On Edmund Burke see Hanna F. Pitkin, *The Concept of Representation* (Berkeley: University of California Press, 1967), p. 172. Storing and Wood are not the only contemporary scholars who describe nonelected officials of the eighteenth century as "representatives." See Martin Diamond, *The Founding of the Democratic Republic,* p. 79, and "The Federalist," in *History of Political Philosophy,* ed. Leo Strauss and Joseph Cropsey (Chicago: University of Chicago Press), pp. 643 and 645. Matthew Crenson speaks of "the Republic's Administrative Representatives" in *The Federal Machine: Beginnings of Bureaucracy in Jacksonian America* (Baltimore, Md.: Johns Hopkins University Press, 1975), p. 6. This language is consistent with Hamilton's use of the term "representative democracy" to describe the government created by the Constitution. In using this expression, Hamilton was referring to the constitutional order as a whole and not just to its directly elected officials (Diamond, *Founding of the Democratic Republic,* p. 69).

13. Storing, "The 'Other' Federalist Papers," p. 230.

14. Emphasis added. Storing notes that for the Federalists, elections were "*merely* a method of choosing, not a method of authorizing" (emphasis added; see preceding paragraph on p. 80 and note 13).

15. A crude version of Adams's argument was stated by Gouverneur Morris at the Constitutional Convention in 1787 (see Tansill, pp. 319–21).

16. An argument affirming a mixed regime in the Constitution can be found in Paul Eidelberg, *The Philosophy of the American Constitution* (New York: Free Press, 1968).

17. Storing, "The 'Other' Federalist Papers," p. 231.

18. Tansill, p. 156.

19. Ibid., pp. 229, 240–41, 244, 275, 325.

20. Ibid., p. 206.

21. Ibid., pp. 226–34.

22. Ibid., p. 234.

23. Ibid., p. 240.

24. Ibid., p. 241.

25. Ibid.

26. For a discussion of *Federalist 78* see David F. Epstein, *The Political Theory of "The Federalist"* (Chicago: University of Chicago Press, 1984), pp. 186–90.

27. *Wilson Papers,* 7:352–54; for a full reference see note 1 of chap. 5.

28. William Blackstone, *Commentaries on the Laws of England,* 4 vols. (Chicago: University of Chicago Press, 1979). A facsimile of the first edition (1765) of Blackstone's *Commentaries* is provided in this reprint. For Blackstone's discussion of parliamentary supremacy see vol. 1, bk. 1, chap. 2, sec. 3; see also Stanley N. Katz's Introduction to vol. 1.

29. Ibid., p. 9.

30. Ibid., p. 79.

31. See chap. 5, pp. 61–62.

32. Goodnow, *Politics and Administration,* p. 17.

33. Ibid., chap. 2.

34. Ibid., pp. 17, 45, 85–87, 120–21, 131.

35. Ibid., p. 82.

36. Ibid., pp. 17, 23.

37. Ibid. Harmony between the executives and the legislature is a constant in Goodnow's thinking. It will be achieved through the extraconstitutional device of party government. In his later work, he repeated this point many times: see his *Principles of the Administrative Law of the United States,* pp. 232–33, and especially his congressional testimony on the "Establishment of a National Budget System," Hearings before the Select Committee on the Budget of the House of Representatives, 66th Cong., 1st sess. (Washington, D.C.: Government Printing Office, 1919), pp. 341–54.

38. Goodnow, *Politics and Administration,* p. 88. Woodrow Wilson, it will be recalled, considered including the heads of executive departments within the career civil service (see *Congressional Government,* p. 177, and chap. 5, p. 67 above).

39. Goodnow, *Politics and Administration,* pp. 40–43.

40. Ibid., p. 38.

41. Commentators on Goodnow's work have differed on just how sharply he distinguished politics from administration. I follow those who see a very sharp distinction—much sharper than the similar distinction drawn by Woodrow Wilson. For a contrary view see Paul Appleby, *Policy and Administration* (University: University of Alabama Press, 1975), p. 16.

42. Goodnow, "Establishment of a National Budget System," Hearings before the Select Committee on the Budget of the House of Representatives, pp. 351–54.

43. It is perhaps significant that in a later work, Goodnow claimed that the separation of powers was "theoretically a part of American public law" (*Principles of the Administrative Law of the United States,* p. 12). That *real* American public law was something quite different for Goodnow is abundantly clear from the topics he treated in this book. At the outset he maintained that administration and administrative law, in principle, should be studied independently of the study of constitutional law. "Constitutional law deals with the anatomy of government; administrative law and administration have to do with the functions, the physiology of government, so to speak" (p. 3). Under the influence of Taylorism, the biological metaphor yielded to management science. Goodnow and the scientific managers marched off into splendid isolation from constitutional norms and restraints. The apotheosis of this movement came in Leonard D. White's famous comment that "the study of administration should start from the base of management rather than the foundation of law, and is therefore more absorbed in the affairs of the American Management Association than in the decisions of the courts" (*Introduction to the Study of Public Administration* [New York: Macmillan, 1926], pp. vii–viii). After having had extensive practical experience in government, White changed his mind and turned to history to understand administration. This remarkable transformation is related by Herbert J. Storing in "Leonard D. White and the Study of Public Administration," *Public Administration Review* 25 (Mar. 1965): 38–51.

44. This is not to say the Constitution or its framers are above criticism. The legitimating force of the framers need not become ancestor worship. See Wood, *Creation of the American Republic*, pp. 562–64, for a discussion of how the framers' theory of the Constitution impoverished American political debate, and Storing, *What the Anti-Federalists Were FOR*, p. 63, for a discussion of the inadequate provisions for responsibility to the people in the Constitution. Such criticisms go beyond questions of legitimacy and examine the wisdom of the Constitution itself. As such they are outside the scope of this book.

## CHAPTER 7
## THOMAS M. COOLEY
## AND THE INTERSTATE COMMERCE COMMISSION

1. I. L. Sharfman, *The American Railroad Problem* (New York: Century, 1921), p. 31.

2. *Munn* v. *Illinois*, 94 U.S. 113 (1877).

3. *Wabash Railway Co.* v. *Illinois*, 118 U.S. 557 (1886).

4. The most comprehensive history of the ICC is I. L. Sharfman's *Administrative Law and Procedure*, 5 vols. (New York: Harper & Row, 1969). The Harper & Row edition is a reprint of the 1931 edition, which was published by the Commonwealth Fund. A critical history of railroad regulation can be found in Gabriel Kolko, *Railroads and Regulation: 1877–1916* (New York: Norton, 1965). For a brief but incisive history of the commission as a "captured agency" see Samuel P. Huntington, "The Marasmus of the ICC: The Commission, the Railroads, and the Public Interest," *Yale Law Review* 61 (1952): 467–509. More-recent treatments of the ICC and railroad regulation appear in Stephen Skowronek, *Building a New American State: The Expansion of National Administrative Capacities, 1877–1920* (New York: Cambridge University Press, 1982); Thomas K. McCraw, *Prophets of Regulation* (Cambridge: Harvard University Press, 1984), chaps. 1 and 2; and Ari Hoogenboom and Olive Hoogenboom, *A History of the ICC: From Panacea to Palliative* (New York: W. W. Norton, 1976).

5. "Railroad Commission of Massachusetts," *American Law Review* 22 (Sept.-Oct. 1888): 768–72; Charles C. Savage, "Constitutionality of Railroad Commissions," *American Law Review* 19 (Mar.-Apr. 1885): 223–33. Contemporary historians categorize the various state commissions somewhat differently (see McCraw, p. 57, and Hoogenboom, pp. 6–8). In general, the midwestern states tended to give more power to their commissions than did states in the East.

6. *Dartmouth College* v. *Woodward*, 4 Wheat. 518 (1819).

7. For a further discussion of Marshall's nation-building strategy see John A. Rohr, *Ethics for Bureaucrats: An Essay on Law and Values* (New York: Dekker, 1978), chap. 5.

8. "The Wisconsin Railroad Acts," *American Law Review* 9 (Oct. 1874): 50–73.

9. Ibid., p. 59.

10. Ibid., pp. 62–69.

11. "Legislative Control over Railway Charters," *American Law Review* 1 (1866): 451–77. In the landmark case, *Munn* v. *Illinois*, 94 U.S. 113 (1877), the Supreme Court upheld regulatory powers in certain carefully defined circumstances. The case did not involve a railroad commission. A commission was involved, however, in *Chicago, Milwaukee, and St. Paul Railway Co.* v. *Minnesota*, 134 U.S. 418 (1890). This case limited the holding in *Munn;* it is discussed below, p. 108.

12. Savage, "Constitutionality of Railroad Commissions." Savage devotes only one paragraph to delegation in a ten-page article. For him the issue is quite simple, because what has been delegated is not the power to make law but the power to execute it.

13. "Delegation of Powers and Trusts," *American Law Review* 21 (Nov.–Dec. 1887).

14. "The Status of a Railroad Corporation Established in Different States," *American Law Review* 7 (July 1873): 608–15.

15. Savage, p. 227.

16. 19 F. 679 (1884).

17. 19 F. 679, 697 (1884).

18. 144 118 U.S. 557 (1886).

19. Kolko, p. 33.

20. The railroad industry's eagerness for federal regulation is a major theme in Kolko's *Railroads and Regulation* (see especially his first two chapters).

21. *Congressional Record*, 49th Cong., 1st sess., vol. 17, pt. 7, p. 7285; remarks of Congressman O'Neill. In the remainder of this chapter, all references to the *Congressional Record* are from the first session of the 49th Congress, volume 17. Different parts of volume 17 will be cited. Subsequent references will be entered as *C.R.*, the part number, and the page number.

22. U.S., Senate, 95th Cong., 1st sess., "Study on Federal Regulation Prepared Pursuant to S. Res. 71," Committee on Governmental Affairs, vol. 5 of *Regulation Organization* (Washington, D.C.: Government Printing Office, 1977), pp. 25–27 (hereafter cited as U.S., Senate, "Study on Federal Regulation").

23. Act of 2 Mar. 1889, 25 Stat. L. 861 and following.

24. U.S., Senate, "Study on Federal Regulation," pp. 25–27.

25. Remarks by Congressman Reagan and Congressman Caldwell, *C.R.*, 7, 7281 and 7292–93.

26. Remarks of Congressman Reagan, *C.R.*, 7, 7283. In its early years, the ICC tried to rebut this criticism by holding hearings in different parts of the United States.

27. See note 23 of chap. 10.

28. See art. 3, sec. 2, of the Constitution and the Seventh Amendment. This point is discussed in chap. 10, pp. 162–63.

29. *Texas and Pacific Railway Co.* v. *Abilene Cotton Oil Co.*, 204 U.S. 426 (1907).

30. This is the same reasoning used by the federal circuit court in *Louisville and Nashville Railroad* v. *Tennessee Railroad Commission*.

31. 204 U.S. 426 (1907).

32. Louis L. Jaffe and Nathaniel L. Nathanson, *Administrative Law: Cases and Materials*, 4th ed. (Boston: Little, Brown & Co., 1976), p. 329.

33. This, of course, is the doctrine of primary jurisdiction. For the development of this doctrine after *Texas and Pacific Railway Co.* v. *Abilene Cotton Oil Co.* see *Texas and Pacific Railway Co.* v. *American Tie and Timber Co.*, 234 U.S. 138 (1914); *Great Northern Railway Co.* v. *Merchants Elevator Co.*, 259 U.S. 285 (1922); *U.S.* v. *Western Pacific Railroad Co.*, 352 U.S. 59 (1956); *Nader* v. *Allegheny Airlines, Inc.*, 426 U.S. 290 (1976).

34. John R. Dos Passos, *The Interstate Commerce Act: An Analysis of Its Provisions* (New York: Putnam, 1887), chap. 7; and Horace Stringfellow, "The Interstate Commerce Law," *American Law Review* 23 (Jan.–Feb. 1889): 84ff.

35. In the history of administrative law, judges have at times tended to look either to the quasi-legislative or to the quasi-judicial authority of agencies and to stress the one and ignore the other. In the famous *Morgan* cases, the judicial analogy dominated the

Supreme Court's thinking. This worked to the agency's disadvantage in the first two *Morgan* cases, 298 U.S. 468 (1936) and 304 U.S. 1 (1938), but to its advantage in *Morgan IV*, 313 U.S. 409 (1941). In *Bi-Metallic Investment Co.* v. *State Board of Equalization of Colorado*, 239 U.S. 441 (1915), Justice Holmes considered an administrative agency as merely an extension of a state legislature and needlessly restricted the right to a hearing. The most penetrating treatment of the nature of an administrative agency in a judicial opinion can be found, I believe, in Justice Felix Frankfurter's opinion of the Court in *Universal Camera Corp.* v. *N.L.R.B.*, 340 U.S. 474 (1951).

36. The exhaustive report of the Cullom Committee can be found in U.S., *Senate Report* no. 46, 49th Cong., 1st sess., 2 vols. (Washington, D.C.: Government Printing Office, 1886). The two volumes of the Cullom Report are published as part of an eleven-volume series of *Senate Reports* from the first session of the 49th Congress (1885/86). The Cullom Committee's report appears in volumes 2 and 3 of this series. Volume 2 is part 1 of the report, and volume 3 is part 2. References to the Cullom Report will be entered as "Cullom Committee Report," followed by part number and page number.

37. "Cullom Committee Report," 2:200.

38. Ibid.

39. Ibid., p. 201.

40. Ibid.

41. Ibid.

42. The need for an institution to mediate between corporations and the public was expressed with some regularity during the 1880s. Kolko (p. 26) cites the National Board of Trade as seeing itself in this manner. See also Kolko (p. 41) for a quotation from the *Railway Review* of 1886 in which the proposed Interstate Commerce Commission is commented upon favorably as standing between the railroad companies and the public. Comments along the same lines appear in Thomas Cooley's statement to the Cullom Committee on the role of the proposed commission (see below, pp. 104–5).

43. "Cullom Committee Report," 2:123.

44. Ibid., p. 124.

45. Ibid., p. 1202. Charles Francis Adams is one of the four "prophets of regulation" whom Thomas McCraw describes in his book by that title. McCraw discusses the relationship between Fink and Adams on pp. 47–55.

46. "Cullom Committee Report," 2:61.

47. *C.R.*, 4:307.

48. Ibid., p. 306.

49. Congressman Baker's comments were but a straw in the wind. Congressional debate revealed considerable confusion over the nature of the new institution of government. Congressman Dunham, e.g., hoped the proposed commission would emulate its predecessor in Illinois, which made rulings contrary to its statutory authorization and then appealed to the people for justification (*C.R.*, 8:463). Dunham championed a proactive—indeed hyperactive—agency (see his comments in *C.R.*, 8, at pp. 458, 460, 464, 465). Administrative rule making was another area of considerable uncertainty (see the remarks of Senators Cullom, Call, and Saulisbury in *C.R.*, 4:4223–27). The obscure contempt powers of the commission were discussed by Senator Platt in *C.R.*, 4:4319.

50. See the remarks of Congressman Johnson in *C.R.*, 4:314, and those of Congressman Dunham in *C.R.*, 4:459.

51. Ellis W. Hawley, *The New Deal and the Problem of Monopoly* (Princeton, N.J.: Princeton University Press, 1966), pt. 1.

52. Railroad man Albert Fink was an exception. Though both a believer in harmony and a proponent of the commission, Fink opposed giving the commission coercive authority on separation-of-powers grounds (see p. 97 above).

53. "Cullom Committee Report," 2:167 and 201; *C.R.*, 8:305–6, for remarks by Congressman Baker on 21 July 1886, and 4:3867, for the remarks of Senator Call on 27 Apr. 1886.

54. The most articulate spokesmen of this persuasion were C. F. Adams, Albert Fink, and A. T. Hadley (see "Cullom Committee Report," 2:1201, 89, 188). See also McCraw, chap. 1, pp. 4–7 and 43–44, for Adams's view of his circle of reform-minded friends as the "best men."

55. The conflict-of-interest provisions appear in section 2 of the ICA. They were quite strict for their time (see remarks by Senator Sewell, *C.R.*, 4:4366).

56. For a discussion of the late-nineteenth-century tendency to categorize and of the pertinence of this tendency to Public Administration see William E. Nelson, *The Roots of American Bureaucracy*, chaps. 4 and 5.

57. Published in Boston by Little, Brown & Co. in 1868.

58. Benjamin R. Twiss, *Lawyers and the Constitution: How Laissez-Faire Came to the Supreme Court* (Princeton, N.J.: Princeton University Press, 1942), p. 18.

59. Marver Bernstein, *Regulating Business by Commission* (Princeton, N.J.: Princeton University Press, 1955), pp. 32–33.

60. Cooley, *Treatise*, p. 356.

61. 13 N.Y. 432 (1856).

62. *Allgeyer* v. *Louisiana*, 165 U.S. 578 (1897).

63. Throughout this section, I follow Alan Jones's revisionist interpretation of Cooley in three of Jones's articles: "Thomas M. Cooley and the Interstate Commerce Commission: Continuity and Change in the Doctrine of Equal Rights," *Political Science Quarterly* 81 (Dec. 1966): 602–27; "Thomas M. Cooley and the Michigan Supreme Court: 1865–1885," *American Journal of Legal History* 10 (Apr. 1966): 97–121; and "Thomas M. Cooley and 'Laissez-Faire Constitutionalism': A Reconsideration," *Journal of American History* 53 (1967): 751–71. Jones includes the following legal historians among those who present a one-sided view of Cooley's jurisprudence: Clyde E. Jacobs, Benjamin Twiss, Sidney Fine, Edward S. Corwin, Charles G. Haines, Marver H. Bernstein, and Joel Francis Paschal. In a recent discussion of Cooley and the early years of the commission, Ari and Olive Hoogenboom follow closely Jones's assessment of Cooley, pp. 17–38.

64. The Supreme Court rejected this interpretation in *ICC* v. *Cincinnati, New Orleans, and Texas Pacific Railway Co.*, 167 U.S. 479 (1897).

65. Jones, "Thomas M. Cooley and the Interstate Commerce Commission," p. 622. A discussion with Senator Cullom on the topic of increasing the ICC's jurisdiction is reported in Cooley's diary for 27 September 1889. This diary is part of the Thomas M. Cooley Papers, which belong to the Michigan Historical Collections and are kept at the Bentley Historical Library of the University of Michigan at Ann Arbor (hereafter cited as Cooley Papers). In the Third and Fourth Annual Reports of the Interstate Commerce Commission, Cooley openly called for Congress to increase the power of his agency (see pp. 72–75 of the *Third Annual Report* and p. 56 of the *Fourth Annual Report*). These reports were required by statute and were submitted annually on 1 December. The first five reports (1887–91) appeared during Cooley's years on the commission. Hereafter they will be cited as ICCR, with report number and page number.

66. Cited by Jones, "Thomas M. Cooley and the Interstate Commerce Commission," p. 617; Cooley Papers, diary for 26 Apr. 1888.

67. Cooley Papers, scrapbook clipping from *Bismark Tribune* of 18 July 1889; *Federalist 23, 25,* and *31*.

68. Cooley Papers, diary for 26 Apr. 1888.

69. Cooley's strongest statement on the public character of corporations appears in his article "State Regulation of Corporate Profits," *North American Review* 138 (1883): 207–17. The public nature of corporations is mentioned often in the annual reports of the ICC prepared during Cooley's tenure as chairman (see ICCR, 1:4 and 84).

70. *Dartmouth College* v. *Woodward*, 4 Wheat. 518 (1819).

71. Cooley, *Treatise*, 2d ed. (1871), p. 335.

72. *Atkinson* v. *The Detroit Free Press*, 46 Mich. 383 (1881).

73. *People* v. *Salem*, 20 Mich. 473 (1870).

74. Ibid., at 478.

75. Jones, "Thomas M. Cooley and 'Laissez-Faire Constitutionalism,' " p. 758.

76. Railroad support for Cooley was unmistakably clear; but Brian Kolko errs when he says, "Cooley completely identified himself with the railroads' interests from at least 1882 on" (p. 47). Kolko emphasizes Cooley's position on "pooling" and the long-haul/short-haul clause of the ICA but neglects Cooley's jurisprudence, which explains his capacity to be supportive of the industry at times and at other times quite severe.

77. "Cullom Committee Report," 1:12.

78. Ibid.

79. Huntington, "Marasmus of the ICC."

80. E.g., see Alan Jones's discussion of Cooley's unwillingness to change his interpretation of the short-haul clause to meet railroad managers' demands, in "Thomas M. Cooley and the Interstate Commerce Commission," p. 619.

81. The expression is taken from the title of Marvin Meyers's fine book *The Jacksonian Persuasion: Politics and Belief* (Stanford, Calif.: Stanford University Press, 1957). William Leggett is the Jacksonian writer most readily associated with the equal-rights doctrine. Cooley was influenced by Leggett. Meyers discusses Leggett in chap. 9 of *The Jacksonian Persuasion*.

82. Thomas M. Cooley, *A Treatise on the Law of Torts or the Wrongs Which Arise Independently of Contract* (New York: Da Capo Press, 1972), pp. 5 and 6, cited by Jones, "Thomas M. Cooley and 'Laissez-Faire Constitutionalism,' " p. 763.

83. Thomas M. Cooley, "Labor and Capital before the Law," *North American Review* 337 (Dec. 1884): 503.

84. Cooley, *Treatise*, pp. 389–99.

85. Jones, "Thomas M. Cooley and the Interstate Commerce Commission," p. 605.

86. 94 U.S. 113 (1877).

87. Cooley Papers, "Addresses of Hon. T. M. Cooley, Chairman and Col. W. R. Morrison, Commissioner of the Interstate Commerce Commission, before the General Managers and General Passenger Agents of Lines in the Territories of the Central Traffic and Western States Passenger Associations," Rookery Building, Chicago, 11 Dec. 1888.

88. Jones, "Thomas M. Cooley and the Interstate Commerce Commission," p. 627.

89. *ICC* v. *Alabama Midland Railway Co.*, 168 U.S. 144 (1897); and *ICC* v. *Cincinnati, New Orleans, and Texas Pacific Railroad Company*, 167 U.S. 479 (1897).

90. Cooley, *Treatise*, p. 178. His principal judicial opinions on separation of powers are *Flint and Fentonville Plank Road Co.* v. *Woodhall*, 25 Mich. 104 (1872); *Sutherland* v. *The Governor*, 29 Mich. 320 (1874); and *Benjamin* v. *Manistee River Improvement Co.*, 42 Mich. 629 (1880).

91. James Bradley Thayer, "The Origin and Scope of the American Doctrine of Constitutional Law," *Harvard Law Review* 7 (1893), reprinted in Gary L. McDowell, ed., *Taking the Constitution Seriously* (Dubuque, Iowa: Kendall-Hunt, 1981), pp. 49–69. See Cooley Papers, letter from James B. Thayer of 24 Mar. 1885.

92. My surmise may rely excessively on the force of ideas to motivate action. There were powerful interests at stake for the courts as they beheld the creation of a national administrative agency that could threaten the role that courts and political parties had played in holding together the diversity of American government (see Skowronek, p. 19–47).

93. ICCR, 4:9 (1890).

94. *ICC* v. *Alabama Midland Railway Co.*, 168 U.S. 144 (1897).

95. Cooley, *Treatise*, pp. 356–57; see also p. 178.

96. *Flint and Fentonville Plank Road Co.* v. *Woodhall*, 25 Mich. 104 (1812), and *Weimar* v. *Bunbury*, 30 Mich. 203 (1874).

97. The "constitutional fact" issue in *Crowell* v. *Benson*, 285 U.S. 22 (1932), is one variation on this theme. Another is the arcane relationship between questions of law, questions of fact, and mixed questions (cf. *O'Leary* v. *Brown-Pacific-Maxon, Inc.*, 340 U.S. 504 [1951], and *O'Keefe* v. *Smith Associates*, 380 U.S. 359 [1965]).

98. *Johnson* v. *Robinson*, 415 U.S. 361 (1974), and *Ostereich* v. *Selective Service System Local Board No. 11*, 393 U.S. 233 (1968).

99. ICCR, 4:20–21.

100. Parts of Justice Blatchford's opinion in the *Minnesota Rate* case suggested that if the Railroad Commission had been required to follow a more elaborate procedure, its rate-making activities might have passed judicial muster.

101. Cooley calls for notice, hearing, representation by counsel, a written agency decision to be given to the parties, and, upon appeal to a circuit court, a judicial decision based on the record made before the ICC (ICCR, 4:20–21). As a matter of fact, the ICC had instituted some of these practices on its own. However, the *Minnesota Rate* decision served to put more stress on procedures commanded by statute than upon actual administrative behavior. At the outset of the commission's work, Cooley emphasized informal procedure. In the *First Annual Report* he stressed the connection between informal procedure and harmonious relationships among shippers, carriers, the commission, and the public. As relations became less harmonious, the ICC seems to have lost its initial enthusiasm for informality. On the advantages of informality see ICCR, 1:26–28; the initial procedures appear in app. D, pp. 128–30. See also the letter of Commission Secretary E. A. Moseley, p. 133.

102. ICCR, 1:27.

103. ICCR, 5:10.


PART 3

FOUNDING THE ADMINISTRATIVE STATE
IN DEED: THE NEW DEAL


1. Among New Deal practitioners, the most notable exception was Rexford Tugwell. He continued to criticize the Constitution in a most fundamental way long after the New Deal had come to an end (see his *Model for a New Constitution* [Santa Barbara, Calif.: Center for the Study of Democratic Institutions, 1970]). Academicians during the New Deal period were understandably less reluctant to raise fundamental issues: e.g., see William Y. Elliott, *The Need for Constitutional Reform: A Program for National Security* (New York: McGraw-Hill, 1935).

2. *Federalist Papers 23, 25, 31.*

3. In preparing for the Philadelphia Convention, James Madison diligently read the political authors of classical antiquity. He turned his study to good use both during the convention and in *The Federalist.* The frequent references to classical antiquity in eighteenth-century public argument were not simply vain displays of erudition. They were testimony to a belief in an abiding human nature that did not change over the millenia. Eighteenth-century man believed that he could learn *from* the ancients as well as about them. Twentieth-century man is less docile in such matters. His understanding of evolution and his belief in cultural relativism have made him suspicious of the idea of human nature. Hence he soon tires of the extensive discussion of lessons from classical antiquity that are so prevalent in *The Federalist,* e.g., *6, 18, 25, 38, 63* (see Ernest R. May, *"Lessons" of the Past: The Use and Misuse of History in American Foreign Policy* [London: Oxford University Press, 1973]).

4. Herbert J. Storing, "Political Parties and the Bureaucracy," in *Political Parties USA,* ed. Robert A. Goldwin (Chicago: Rand McNally, 1964), p. 158.

5. *Schechter Poultry Corporation* v. *United States,* 295 U.S. 495 (1935).

6. "Report of the President's Committee on Administrative Management," 74th Cong., 2d sess. (Washington, D.C.: Government Printing Office, 1937).

7. See, e.g., *U.S.* v. *Rock Royal Co-op, Inc.,* 307 U.S. 533 (1939), *Yakus* v. *U.S.,* 321 U.S. 414 (1944).

8. *Senate Document* no. 8, 77th Cong., 1st sess. (Washington, D.C.: Government Printing Office, 1941).


## CHAPTER 8
## NATIONAL SUPREMACY

1. C. Herman Pritchett, *The Roosevelt Court: A Study in Judicial Politics and Values* (New York: Macmillan, 1948), chap. 1; Robert H. McCloskey, *The American Supreme Court* (Chicago: University of Chicago Press, 1960), chap. 6; James Mac-Gregor Burns, *Roosevelt: The Lion and the Fox, 1882–1940* (New York: Harcourt Brace Jovanovich, 1956), chap. 15; and Alfred H. Kelly, Winfred A. Harbison, and Herman Belz, *The American Constitution: Its Origins and Development,* 6th ed. (New York: Norton, 1983), chaps. 24 and 25.

2. John D. Hicks and George E. Mowry, *A Short History of American Democracy,* 2d ed. (Boston: Houghton Mifflin Co., 1956), p. 760.

3. Chief Justice Hughes is often linked with Roberts in making "the switch in time." The change in Roberts's position in the few months between *Morehead* v. *New York ex rel. Tipaldo,* 298 U.S. 587 (1936), and *West Coast Hotel* v. *Parrish,* 300 U.S. 379 (1937), was more dramatic—and puzzling—than any of Hughes's changes.

4. Peter J. Irons, *The New Deal Lawyers* (Princeton, N.J.: Princeton University Press, 1982), p. 279; Peter Finley Dunne, *Mr. Dooley's Opinions* (New York: R. H. Russell, 1901), p. 26.

5. Alfred H. Kelly, "Clio and the Court: An Illicit Love Affair," *Supreme Court Review 1965* (Chicago: University of Chicago Press, 1966), pp. 119–58.

6. Robert L. Stern, "That Commerce Which Concerns More States Than One," *Harvard Law Review* 47 (1934): 1335–36.

7. Philip Kurland and Gerhard Casper, eds., *Landmark Briefs and Arguments of the Supreme Court of the United States: Constitutional Law* (Arlington, Va.: University Publications of America, 1975); see briefs for *Schechter* v. *U.S.* (ibid., vol. 28), *Carter* v. *Carter Coal Co.* (ibid., vol. 32), and *U.S.* v. *Darby* (ibid., vol. 37).

8. 9 Wheat. 1 (1824).

9. Stern, p. 1336.

10. Roosevelt Presidential Press Conferences, no. 209 (31 May 1935), vol. 5, p. 320, courtesy of Franklin D. Roosevelt Library, Hyde Park, N.Y.

11. Stern, p. 1337.

12. Ibid., p. 1338.

13. See Edward S. Corwin, "Some Probable Repercussions of 'NIRA' on our Constitutional System," *Annals of the American Academy of Political and Social Science* 172 (1934), reprinted in Richard Loss, ed., *Presidential Power and the Constitution: Essays by Edward S. Corwin* (Ithaca, N.Y.: Cornell University Press, 1976), pp. 54–63. In this essay, Corwin acknowledges the "solidarity of business" as a constitutional support for a broad interpretation of the commerce clause that will severely reduce any serious role for the states. Interestingly, Corwin quotes with approval Luther Gulick's comment that state government "is finished." Gulick was one of the authors of the Brownlow Report, discussed below.

14. Stern, p. 1339.

15. Ibid., p. 1340.

16. Ibid.

17. Ibid., p. 1341.

18. Ibid., pp. 1341–42.

19. Ibid., p. 1345. Here Stern anticipates the linguistic method that William W. Crosskey employs so skillfully in his *Politics and the Constitution,* 2 vols. (Chicago: University of Chicago Press, 1953). A third volume was published posthumously in 1980; William Jeffrey, Jr., was its coauthor. Crosskey's discussion of the commerce clause can be found in part 1 of volume 1, pp. 17–293.

20. See, e.g., the cautious tone in the remarks of Randolph and Madison on 31 May, in Tansill, p. 130. For a full reference to Tansill see note 18 of chap. 1.

21. Compare Stern's discussion of Bedford's 17 July amendment on p. 1339 with Tansill text (p. 389), which Stern follows. Note, in particular, the enumeration, which is imposed, and that the transcribed version of Madison's notes substitutes "severally" for "separately."

22. *Carter* v. *Carter Coal Co.,* 298 U.S. 238 (1936); *Schechter Poultry Corp.* v. *U.S.,* 295 U.S. 495 (1935); *Sunshine Anthracite Coal Co.* v. *Adkins,* 310 U.S. 381 (1940); *Panama Refining Co.* v. *Ryan,* 293 U.S. 388 (1935).

23. Tansill, p. 694.

24. Ibid., p. 706.

25. Max Farrand, *The Framing of the Constitution of the United States* (New Haven, Conn.: Yale University Press, 1913), p. 182.

26. The text of the address is presented by Robert H. Jackson in *The Struggle for Judicial Supremacy: A Study of a Crisis in American Power Politics* (New York: Knopf, 1941), app., p. 343.

27. In the same speech, FDR took liberties with the preamble to the Constitution. Consider the following paragraph: "'That, my friends, is what I honestly believe to have been the clear and underlying purpose of the patriots who wrote a Federal Constitution to create a National Government with national power, intended as they said, 'to form a more perfect union * * * for ourselves and our posterity.'" The Preamble of the Constitution does not say what FDR presents it as saying. The preposition preceding "ourselves and our posterity" is "to" not "for." This is because the reference to "ourselves and our posterity" occurs in the phrase that states that one of the purposes of the new government is to "secure the blessings of liberty to ourselves and our posterity." In an address intended to justify packing the Court, FDR was vulnerable on

the liberty issue. His conservative opponents presented themselves as the champions of liberty and used the Court-packing plan to illustrate their worst fears. As we shall see below in chapter 9, the Court-packing plan was linked to FDR's effort to reorganize the executive branch. His legislative initiative along this line was called "the dictator bill." To avoid reminding his listeners of the Preamble's statement on liberty, FDR stressed a "more perfect union" and changed "to" to "for" in order to accommodate his syntax.

28. 297 U.S. 1 (1936).

29. Ibid., at 64.

30. Ibid., at 87.

31. Kurland and Casper, 30:288–332. The *Butler* Court accepted the government's position that the spending power was coextensive with the taxing power.

32. Ibid., p. 301.

33. Ibid.

34. Ibid., p. 302.

35. Ibid., pp. 292 and 305.

36. Ibid., p. 292.

37. 9 Wheat. 1 (1824).

38. Kurland and Casper, 30:293–94.

39. Ibid., pp. 295–96.

40. Ibid., pp. 290–306.

41. *Coleman* v. *Miller*, 307 U.S. 433 (1939); *U.S.* v. *Pink*, 315 U.S. 203 (1942); *Steward Machine Co.* v. *Davis*, 310 U.S. 548 (1937); *U.S.* v. *Darby*, 312 U.S. 100 (1941).

42. The only brief in which I could find a reference to Madison's postratification writings was *Carter* v. *Carter Coal Co.*, 298 U.S. 238 (1936). I consulted the following briefs in addition to the four mentioned in note 41: *Schechter Poultry Corp.* v. *U.S.*, 295 U.S. 495 (1935); *Ex parte Quirin*, 317 U.S. 1 (1942); *Wickard* v. *Fillburn*, 317 U.S. 111 (1942); *U.S.* v. *Classic*, 313 U.S. 299 (1941); *Ashwander* v. *TVA*, 297 U.S. 288 (1936); *S.C.* v. *Barnwell*, 303 U.S. 177 (1938); *Graves* v. *O'Keefe*, 306 U.S. 466 (1939); *Humphrey's Executor* v. *U.S.*, 295 U.S. 602 (1935); *NLRB* v. *Jones-Laughlin*, 301 U.S. 1 (1937); *U.S.* v. *Belmont*, 301 U.S. 324 (1937).

43. Hamilton discusses the general welfare clause indirectly in *Federalist 30* and *34*. His position is predictably expansionist, but the discussion is too oblique to be useful for a legal brief.

44. It seems to me that a government has acted in a morally acceptable manner when it tells no lies, even though it does not tell the whole truth. Statutory protections of privacy and classification of certain forms of information as "confidential," "secret," or "top secret" suggest the futility of a "whole truth" standard. In addition to these legal matters, there is the more fundamental problem of how one knows that one has told the whole truth. What criterion of relevance would be employed? Interestingly, the United States Navy's Office of Information has as its motto: *"Nil nisi verum,"* which means "nothing but the truth." On the question of moral standards in government agencies see John A. Rohr, "The Problem of Professional Ethics," *Bureaucrat* 11 (Summer 1982): 47–50.

45. 4 Wheat. 316 (1819).

46. Kurland and Casper, 30:306–22.

47. *Steward Machine Co.* v. *Davis*, 310 U.S. 548 (1937).

48. The government's brief in *Butler* discussed other issues related to the intent of the framers. E.g., the brief argues that the framers were more concerned with where to locate the powers to tax and spend than with the extent of these powers. The

provisions in the Constitution that revenue bills must originate in the House and that the president can spend only appropriated funds suggest the main concern of the framers (see Kurland and Casper, 30:325-26). Other important discussions of the framers in the government briefs of this period can be found in (a) the *Steward Machine* v. *Davis* briefs, where the government defended the tax credits in the Social Security Act of 1935 as being a faithful expression of the founding generation's abhorrence of double taxation (see Kurland and Casper, 34:270-78); and (b) the *U.S.* v. *Darby* brief, where the original intent of the Tenth Amendment is discussed fully (see Kurland and Casper, 37:619-27).

49. Prior to the New Deal, there were two lines of cases interpreting the commerce clause; one was restrictive, and the other expansive. The restrictive line included *Kidd* v. *Pearson*, 128 U.S. 1 (1888), and *U.S.* v. *E. C. Knight and Co.*, 156 U.S. 1 (1895). These cases and their progeny stressed the distinction between commerce and manufacturing. The more expansive line included *Swift* v. *U.S.*, 136 U.S. 375 (1906), and *Chicago Board of Trade* v. *Olson*, 262 U.S. 1 (1923), where the doctrine of a "stream of commerce" was employed. Quite early in the New Deal period it became clear that the courts would tend to favor the restrictive line of cases (see Irons, pp. 46-54).

50. 4 Wheat. 316 (1819).

51. For further examples of Marshall's debt to Hamilton compare his opinions in *Marbury* v. *Madison*, 1 Cranch 137 (1803), and *Cohens* v. *Virginia*, 6 Wheat. 264 (1821), with *Federalist 78*.

52. Clinton Rossiter, *Alexander Hamilton and the Constitution* (New York: Harcourt, Brace & World, 1964), pp. 79-80.

53. A thorough discussion of this debate can be found in David H. Rosenbloom, *Federal Service and the Constitution* (Ithaca, N.Y.: Cornell University Press, 1971), pp. 26-33.

54. Harold C. Syrett, ed., *The Papers of Alexander Hamilton* (New York: Columbia University Press, 1969-79), vol. 8, p. 102 (hereafter cited as *Hamilton Papers*).

55. Ibid.

56. Article 2, section 3, provides that the president shall recommend to Congress "such Measures as he shall judge necessary and expedient." It is quite unlikely that the framers meant to restrict the president to recommending only those measures that are absolutely indispensable. This relaxed use of "necessary" in article 2 supports Hamilton's interpretation of the same word in article 1, section 8.

57. Ibid., p. 100.

58. Ibid.

59. Ibid.

60. Ibid.

61. Ibid., p. 121. It is interesting to contrast the ways in which Jefferson and Hamilton cite the necessary and proper clause. Jefferson quotes only part of the clause—that part which reads "The Congress shall have Power . . . To make all Laws which shall be necessary and proper for carrying into Execution the foregoing Powers." He omits the rest of the clause: "and all other Powers vested by this Constitution in the Government of the United States, or in any Department or Officer thereof." Jefferson's truncated version of the clause suggests that only laws that are necessary and proper to carrying out such "foregoing powers" as are mentioned in article 1, section 8, may be passed by Congress. Hamilton makes use of the full clause and correctly relates it to other parts of the Constitution as well. Specifically, he relates the necessary and proper clause to article 4, section 3, paragraph 2, which empowers Congress to "make all needful Rules and Regulations respecting the Territory or other Property belonging to

the United States." He argues that a bank is necessary to exercise the congressional power to make rules for the property of the United States (*Hamilton Papers,* 8:121).

62. Compare Hamilton's strategy in his 18 June speech at the Philadelphia Convention, in Tansill, pp. 215–25. There is a hint of the "resultant powers" doctrine toward the end of *Federalist 23.*

63. Plato, *The Republic,* trans. Allan Bloom (New York: Basic Books, 1968), bk. 2, 372a–374d, pp. 49–51. To defend the analogy between Adeimantus and Glaucon, on the one hand, and Jefferson and Hamilton, on the other, I would note the rough similarity between the agrarian ideal of Jefferson and Adeimantus's "healthy city," as well as the similarity between Glaucon's feverish city and the commercial empire that Hamilton envisioned. Once Socrates encourages Glaucon's ambition in book 2, the argument of *The Republic* never returns to Adeimantus's healthy city. So also, the ratification of the Constitution set in motion forces that eventually doomed the Jeffersonian dream. It should also be noted that Glaucon's feverish city is initiated with an act of injustice—an act of aggressive warfare against a neighboring city. Hamilton foresees that, for reasons of state, his commercial empire will need to wage offensive wars as well as defensive wars *(Federalist 34).* This is one reason why the Constitution provides for a navy. In the commercial republic, offensive wars for reasons of state will usually be naval wars. This position is attacked by the Anti-Federalist Brutus (see Storing, *Complete Anti-Federalist,* 2.9.86). Finally, we should note that in Hamilton's brief but exceedingly bold discussion of "resultant powers" (as opposed to expressed and implied powers), the only example he gives to illustrate his point is the telling example of sovereign power over territory conquered in war.

64. Gaillard Hunt, ed., *The Writings of James Madison,* 9 vols. (New York: Putnam, 1906), 6:33–34.

65. In *Federalist 44* Madison gives a more generous interpretation of the necesary and proper clause, but he stops far short of Hamilton's resultant powers.

66. Storing, *What the Anti-Federalists Were FOR,* p. 54; for a full reference see note 5 of chap. 2.

67. Ibid.

68. *Hamilton Papers,* 8:99.

69. Ibid., p. 107.

70. *McCulloch* v. *Maryland,* 4 Wheat. 316, at 421 (1819).

71. This was the argument in the elegantly crafted brief for the NLRB in *NLRB* v. *Jones-Laughlin Steel Co.,* 301 U.S. 1 (1937). Similar lines of reasoning with less elegance can be found in *Darby, Schechter,* and *Carter Coal Co.* Eventually the Court grew weary of following this elaborate chain of reasoning and simply expanded the meaning of commerce (see *Wickard* v. *Fillburn,* 317 U.S. 111 [1942]).

72. *Norman* v. *Baltimore and Ohio Railroad,* 294 U.S. 240 (1935); *Reconstruction Finance Corporation* v. *Bankers Trust Co.,* 294 U.S. 275 (1935); *Nortz* v. *U.S.,* 294 U.S. 317 (1935); *Perry* v. *U.S.,* 294 U.S. 330 (1935).

73. National Emergency Council Meeting of 28 Apr. 1934, in National Archives, Suitland, Md., RG44, box 10.

## CHAPTER 9
## EXECUTIVE SUPREMACY: THE BROWNLOW REPORT

1. "Report of the President's Committee on Administrative Management," 74th Cong., 2d sess. (Washington, D.C.: Government Printing Office, 1937). According to Brownlow, "Administrative Management" meant "top management" or "over-all

management." He drew a distinction between this kind of management and "departmental reorganization," which involved "the shifting and regrouping of bureaus and divisions in the departments and agencies" (*A Passion for Anonymity: The Autobiography of Louis Brownlow, Second Half* [Chicago: University of Chicago Press, 1958], p. 352).

2. Rowland Egger, "The Period of Crisis: 1933 to 1945," in *American Public Administration: Past, Present, Future,* ed. Frederick C. Mosher (University: University of Alabama Press, 1975), p. 71. Brownlow well knew the historic significance of his committee's work. His autobiography contains many examples of the committee members' self-conscious awareness of the significance of their project. Brownlow's description of an important meeting just prior to the release of the document captures nicely the mood of his autobiographical comments on the report. The meeting took place on Sunday 10 January 1937. In attendance were the president, the vice-president, the Speaker of the House, the majority leader of the Senate, the chairmen of the Senate Finance Committee and the House Committees on Appropriations and on Ways and Means, the president's son James, the three committee members, and four men from the committee's staff. The syntax is garbled, but Brownlow's assessment of the situation is quite revealing: "It was a Sunday afternoon in which—and I believe with the best will in the world—a representative of the executive branch, who can only be the President of the United States, and representatives of the legislative branch, who can only be the leaders of the majority party in the two houses of Congress, and the representatives of the students of political science and public administration met together to thresh things out" (p. 395).

3. James MacGregor Burns, *Roosevelt: The Lion and the Fox, 1882–1940* (New York: Harcourt Brace Jovanovich, 1956), pt. 4, pp. 291–406; Barry D. Karl, "Executive Reorganization and Presidential Power," *Supreme Court Review,* 1977, pp. 1–37, and *Executive Reorganization and Reform in the New Deal* (Chicago: University of Chicago Press, 1964; Midway reprint, 1979); Stephen Hess, *Organizing the Presidency* (Washington, D.C.: Brookings Institution, 1976), pp. 27–44; Richard Polenberg, *Reorganizing Roosevelt's Government: The Controversy over Executive Reorganization, 1936–1939* (Cambridge: Harvard University Press, 1966), pp. 211–66.

4. For a thoughtful view of the presidency immediately after Watergate see Frederick C. Mosher et al., *Watergate: Implications for Responsible Government* (Chicago: Basic Books, 1974).

5. Karl, *Executive Reorganization,* p. 27.

6. Brownlow, pp. 378–82.

7. Karl, *Executive Reorganization,* p. 270.

8. Brownlow, p. 392.

9. My evaluation of the constitutional principles in the Brownlow Report is somewhat negative. For this reason, I would urge readers to examine the entire report on their own. Unfortunately, the report is too long to be reproduced in its entirety as an appendix. I have included as an appendix, however, the full text of President Roosevelt's message to Congress supporting the Brownlow Report. This document accurately summarizes the main points of the report and offers a particularly insightful statement of its underlying constitutional principles. The president's message was written by Luther Gulick. Brownlow relates that Roosevelt told him to write it, but he delegated the task to Gulick. "Luther was rocked back on his heels," when Brownlow told him of his assignment. According to Brownlow, Gulick had considerable skill in imitating the writing style of others. Immediately after Gulick had completed the presidential message, Brownlow had dinner with Roosevelt's uncle Frederic A. Delano. When Delano read the message, he exclaimed: "The President wrote that himself.

These are his very words." As a matter of fact, there was only one word in the Gulick draft that Roosevelt changed. Gulick had the president describing the Brownlow Report as "a state document of permanent importance." Interestingly, Roosevelt changed "state" to "great." Brownlow maintains that the president consistently treated Gulick's words as his own—even quoting sentences from his message without notes. Throughout this chapter, I follow FDR's lead and treat the message as stating his own personal views.

10. The Brownlow Report is not the only effort during the New Deal to centralize power under the president. The National Industrial Recovery Act (NIRA) of 1933 had considerable potential for executive centralization, but the potential was frittered away through mismanagement by the National Recovery Administration (NRA) and by the excessive delegation of governmental authority to the private sector. A good discussion of the NRA can be found in Part 1 of Ellis W. Hawley, *The New Deal and the Problem of Monopoly* (Princeton, N.J.: Princeton University Press, 1966), and in section 1 of Peter H. Irons, *The New Deal Lawyers* (Princeton, N.J.: Princeton University Press, 1982). Hawley's book is helpful for understanding the NRA as an expression of the aspect of the early New Deal that ambitioned "a type of rationalized, government sponsored business commonwealth" (p. viii). Irons treats explicitly the management of the constitutional issues that plagued the NRA. The NIRA was declared unconstitutional by the Supreme Court in *Schechter Poultry Corporation* v. *U.S*, 235 U.S. 495 (1935). The main point of *Schechter* concerned the unconstitutional delegation of legislative authority to the president. An important minor theme in both the Court's opinion and in the oral argument was the delegation (or perhaps abdication) by the president of his authority to the private sector. One of the ironies of *Schechter* is that it can be read not only as holding that the president had too much power under NIRA but that he had given away too much of this power as well. In a somewhat unusual action, the Supreme Court found a second reason for declaring the NIRA unconstitutional; the wages and hours provisions of the statute were found to exceed the commerce power of Congress. At a press conference shortly after *Schechter* had been decided, President Roosevelt used extremely harsh language in criticizing the Court's decision. There were even some veiled threats of reprisals against the Court (press conference #209, of 31 May 1935, in *Published Press Conferences of FDR,* vol. 5, pp. 309-36). The fact that it was the Court's narrow reading of the commerce clause that provoked Roosevelt's anger suggests that he did not see the NRA as primarily a means of centralizing power in his own hands. He was less worried about the delegation doctrine of the *Schechter* court than about its position on commerce.

11. The origins of the contemporary administrative state are often traced to the Progressive Era (see Stephen Skowronek, *Building a New American State: The Expansion of National Administrative Capacities, 1877-1920* [Cambridge: Cambridge University Press, 1982]).

12. Brownlow Report, p. 2.

13. Ibid., p. 16.

14. The expression "Administrative Republic" is taken from Harvey Flaumenhaft, "Hamilton's Administrative Republic and the American Presidency," in *The Presidency in the Constitutional Order,* ed. Joseph M. Bessette and Jeffrey Tulis (Baton Rouge: Louisiana State University Press, 1981), pp. 65-112.

15. *Federalist 17, 27,* and *46.*

16. Brownlow Report, p. iv. Roosevelt was not the first president to concern himself with reorganization. What was distinctive about his approach was that he saw managerial control as the purpose of reorganization. His predecessors had stressed economy (see Polenberg, p. 7).

17. Brownlow Report, p. v.

18. Ibid., p. 33. FDR's message to Congress gave a bit more responsibility to Congress; it "may determine in advance the general principles which shall guide the President in distributing the work of government among these departments" (p. v). However, the actual reorganization will take place by executive order; FDR is explicit on this point (p. iv).

19. Ibid., p. 34 (emphasis added).

20. Ibid. p. 31.

21. Ibid., p. v.

22. The Brownlow Committee's managerial view of the presidency is particularly vulnerable in its extended discussion of "Fiscal Management." This section contains several hostile comments about the Government Accounting Office in general and the comptroller general in particular. One need not hold the Brownlow Committee's view of a managerial presidency to sympathize with FDR's frustration in trying to work with (or, more often, around) his obstreperous comptroller general, John R. McCarl. This interesting story is told in Frederick C. Mosher, *The GAO: The Quest for Accountability in American Government* (Boulder, Colo.: Westview Press, 1979), pp. 65–103; see also Brownlow, pp. 350–55. In discussing the anomalous position of the comptroller general, the committee gives no indication of any awareness of the peculiar position of the Treasury Department vis-à-vis Congress. Treasury has never been treated in the same way as other executive departments. At the Constitutional Convention, the report of the Committee of Detail (6 Aug. 1787) provided that "the Legislature" was "to appoint a Treasurer by ballot." To vest appointing power in the legislature as a whole (as opposed to the Senate alone) was a marked departure from the overall plan of the draft constitution that was submitted by the Committee of Detail (see Tansill, p. 475; for a full reference to Tansill see note 18 of chap. 1). The special relation between Congress and the Treasury Department is discussed above in chapter 2. Further, the very first Congress, quite significantly, designated only War and State as "executive" departments. Treasury was simply a department. Congress arranged the internal structure of Treasury in considerable detail but eschewed any such efforts with the "executive" departments—War and State. Finally, Hamilton's relationship with Congress as secretary of the Treasury was markedly different from that of Jefferson at State or Knox at War (see Leonard D. White, *The Federalists: A Study in Administrative History* [New York: Macmillan, 1948], chaps. 2, 3, 6, 7, and 10; Lynton Caldwell, *The Administrative Theories of Jefferson and Hamilton* [Chicago: University of Chicago Press, 1944], pp. 97–100; 1 Stat. 14 [1789]; 1 Stat. 12 [1789]; 1 Stat. 7 [1789]). The reason that Congress has always treated Treasury differently is because of congressional power over the nation's finances—i.e., the difference is grounded in the Constitution. The Brownlow Committee ignores this tradition in its discussion of fiscal management and treats its topic as though it were just another area of management. Later in the report, however, the good sense of the committee trumps its doctrine on scientific management. When reorganization is discussed, the committee spells out the major purposes of each department. Treasury is the *only* department that is to have any communication with Congress. This exception is not explained. It simply appears on a list of departmental functions. Treasury is to advise the Congress on revenue bills. No other department is to have any contact with Congress. The committee does not consider the possibility that this could be the camel's nose in the tent of the managerial presidency.

23. Emphasis added.

24. 12 Pet. 522 (1838).

25. Ibid., at 609.

26. Ibid., at 610.

27. Ibid.

28. Ibid. The *Kendall* Court recognized the distinction between ministerial and discretionary authority. The case at hand was an easy one for the Court, because the postmaster general's duties were merely ministerial. The Court left open the question of discretionary authority because it was not included in *Kendall*. The sweeping language of *Kendall*, however, leaves little room for an argument that Congress cannot impose discretionary duties on presidential subordinates.

29. The *Kendall* doctrine should not be confused with the managerial view of the presidency upheld in *Myers* v. *U.S.*, 272 U.S. 52 (1926), and modified in *Humphrey's Executor* v. *U.S.*, 295 U.S. 602 (1935), and in *Wiener* v. *U.S.*, 357 U.S. 349 (1958). These cases involved the removal powers of the president, whereas *Kendall* involved the statutory duties of presidential subordinates. For the story of President Jackson's clash with his Treasury secretary on removing deposits from the Bank of the United States see Edward S. Corwin, *The President: Office and Powers*, 4th ed. (New York: New York University Press, 1957).

30. Brownlow Report, p. 46.

31. The congressional language is ambiguous. It is not entirely clear whether Congress conferred the removal power on the president alone or discovered that the Constitution itself had already done this (see David H. Rosenbloom, *Federal Service and the Constitution: The Development of the Public Employment Relationship* [Ithaca, N.Y.: Cornell University Press, 1971], pp. 19–33).

32. Publius's call for career administrators is a point that has not received sufficient attention in Public Administration literature. An otherwise excellent book on high-ranking executives begins with the following comment: "The government of the United States is run not by career ministers but by amateurs. The Founding Fathers set up this system of citizen government in the spirit of Cincinnatus and it has thrived for 200 years" (John W. Macy, Bruce Adams, and J. Jackson Walter, *America's Unelected Government: Appointing the President's Team* [Cambridge, Mass.: Ballinger, 1983], p. xi). It is certainly true—all too true—that our government is run by amateurs, but it is doubtful that this practice can be traced to the founding fathers. In developing the argument of *Federalist 77*, Publius reiterates his fondness for a proto-merit system. He criticizes the practice of the state of New York, which allows the governor to appoint those "whose chief merit is their implicit devotion to his will" instead of those "men who are best qualified." See discussion of personnel management in chap. 3, pp. 35–37 above.

33. The Twenty-second Amendment makes the two-term tradition a constitutional mandate. This tradition was not anticipated in the debate over the ratification of the Constitution.

34. *Federalist 17, 27,* and *46* (see chap. 1 above).

35. Brownlow Report, p. 47.

36. *Federalist 72.*

37. For a discussion of the connection between the framers' debate on an executive council and the president's power to require written opinions see Charles C. Thach, *The Creation of the Presidency, 1775–1789: A Study in Constitutional History* (Baltimore, Md.: Johns Hopkins University Press, 1923, 1969), pp. 117–21. See also chap. 5, p. 62 above.

38. Storing, *CAF*. Richard Henry Lee's proposal can be found in 5.6.5; the minority of the Convention of Pennsylvania appears in 3.11.45; the Maryland Minority, in 5.4.7; George Mason's position, in 2.2.6; Cato's, in 2.6.26; Federal Farmer's, in 2.8.170; Federal Republican's, in 3.6.40. For a full reference to Storing's *Complete Anti-Federalist* see note 5 of chap. 2.

39. Tansill, p. 686. Mason's proposal for an executive council was proposed and defeated by a 3 to 8 vote on 7 September. The executive council was actually a fall-back position for Mason. At the outset of the convention he had favored a plural executive. When this failed, he looked to an executive council to limit the president.

40. Storing, *CAF*, 2.2.6. See discussion of antirepublican institutions in chap. 4, pp. 47–50 above.

41. In the *Schechter* case the Supreme Court agreed with Mason's view of how persons or agencies nominally subordinate to the president can *limit* rather than enhance his power. One of the faults the Court found with the NIRA was that it delegated authority to the president to create administraive agencies to assist him, but the recommendations and findings of these agencies "have no sanction beyond the will of the President. . . . Such recommendations and findings in no way limit the authority which Section 3 undertakes to vest in the President with no other conditions than those there specified" (295 U.S., at 539). This aspect of the *Schechter* case is frequently overlooked. The Court suggests that it would look more kindly on the delegation of legislative authority to the president if there were some way in which the agencies that the president himself could create to assist him would be able to limit his authority. The Court seems to be calling for some sort of procedure that the president would have to follow to reject the findings of an agency he himself had created pursuant to statute.

42. Brownlow Report, p. 33.

43. Ibid., p. v.

44. Two Whig Presidents, William Henry Harrison and Zachary Taylor, interpreted the president's office as being subordinate to Congress (see Leonard D. White, *The Jacksonians: A Study in Administrative History, 1829–1861* [New York: Macmillan, 1954], pp. 46–48). Presidential subordination was, of course, a major point in the constitutional thought of the civil-service reformers of the late nineteenth century. The Brownlow Committee's adherence to the politics/administration dichotomy was compatible with the effort to reconcile the principles of scientific management, on the one hand, and democratic government, on the other. The idea of an executive that was separate from the legislature but subordinate to it enjoyed considerable attention during the 1780s (see Herbert J. Storing's Introduction to Thach, p. vii).

45. For a discussion of "maladministration" as an impeachable offense see Raoul Berger, *Impeachment: The Constitutional Problems* (Cambridge: Harvard University Press, 1974).

46. Brownlow Report, p. 20.

47. White, p. 27.

48. Ibid., p. 28.

49. Brownlow Report, p. 2.

50. James Ceasar, *Presidential Selection: Theory and Development* (Princeton, N.J.: Princeton University Press, 1979), pp. 52–61. In his discussion of "leader" in *The Federalist*, Ceasar follows Robert Eden (see Eden's discussion in *Political Leadership and Nihilism: A Study of Weber and Nietzsche* [Tampa: University Presses of Florida, 1983], pp. 3–6). Eden compares *The Federalist*'s use of "leader" to the German *Verführer*, "tempter," "seducer," "deceiver." For examples of the pejorative use of "leader" or "leading individual" see *Federalist 6, 10, 43, 59, 62, 65, 66, 85*. Benign references to leaders of the Revolution appear in *Federalist 14* and *49*. For a complete list of "leader," "leaders," and "leading" see Thomas S. Engeman, Edward J. Erler, Thomas B. Hofeller, eds., *The Federalist Concordance* (Middletown, Conn.: Wesleyan University Press, 1980), p. 295.

51. Ceasar, p. 54.

52. Brownlow Report, p. 49.

53. The Declaration of Independence contains, of course, the classic statement of this proposition: "That to secure these Rights, Governments are instituted among Men." In my understanding of American history, this principle dominated the political thinking of the men of 1787 as well as the men of 1776. "The Constitution completes the work of the Declaration by actually establishing a government in order to secure rights" (see Richard G. Stevens's Introduction to *The Declaration of Independence and The Constitution of the United States* [Washington, D.C.: Georgetown University Press, 1984], p. v). For a utilitarian view of the idea of rights in *The Federalist* see Robert P. Burns, "The Federalist Rhetoric of Rights and the Instrumental Conception of Law," *Northwestern University Law Review* (forthcoming).

54. This theme is pervasive. It is stated at the beginning (p. iii), at the end (p. 53), and throughout the document.

55. Brownlow Report, p. iii.

56. Ibid.

57. This is not to say that Publius was silent on the purpose of government (see *Federalist 10*).

58. Brownlow Report, p. 1.

59. Ibid., p. 38 (emphasis added).

60. Ibid., p. 1.

61. I refer, of course, to Jefferson as author of the Declaration of Independence. Jefferson also espoused the principle of the sovereignty of the present generation. By this he meant that no generation could be bound by the decisions of a previous generation. This position would seem to be fundamentally at odds with the natural-rights doctrine announced in the Declaration of Independence. Jefferson's position on the sovereignty of the present generation appears frequently in his correspondence (to James Madison, 6 Sept. 1789, 7:454-62; to John Wayne Eppes, 24 June 1813, 13:269-79; to Samuel Kercheval, 12 July 1816, 15:32-44; to Governor Plumer, 21 July 1816, 15:46-47; to Thomas Earles, 24 Sept. 1823, 15:470-71; to Major John Cartwright, 5 June 1824, 16:42-52). Any discussion of what Jefferson "really" meant must take into consideration his famous letter to Henry Lee (8 May 1825, 16:117-19), in which he says that in writing the Declaration of Independence, he was expressing sentiments that were current at that time and that seemed to be called for on the eve of the Revolution. The letters mentioned above can be found in Andrew A. Lipscomb, ed., *The Writings of Thomas Jefferson*, 20 vols. (library ed.; Washington, D.C.: Thomas Jefferson Memorial Association, 1903). There is more than a hint of the "sovereignty of the present generation" position in the Brownlow Report. Henry Steele Commager's *Majority Rule and Minority Rights* (New York: P. Smith, 1943) presents a spirited defense of this position from the viewpoint of a scholar who was sympathetic to the New Deal. There is an important difference, however, between the majoritarianism of Jefferson and that of Commager. Jefferson believed there was a need to enlighten the majority; Commager did not. A good discussion of this matter appears in Morton J. Frisch, "The Theoretical Foundations of the American Regime"—a paper presented at the annual meeting of the American Political Science Association in Washington, D.C., in 1984.

62. Brownlow Report, p. 11. The committee's discussion of the relationship between the Civil Service Commission and the president is at odds with *Humphrey's Executor* v. *U.S.*, 295 U.S. 602 (1935).

63. Brownlow Report, p. 10.

64. The Brownlow Report seemed to borrow a page from the civil-service reformers of the 1880s. If the merit principle controls the entrance, there is no need to control the exit. This plan did not work. The exit was eventually controlled by executive order and later by the Lloyd-LaFollette Act of 1912.

65. Brownlow, pp. 378–82.

66. Ibid., p. 381.

67. Brownlow Report, p. 5.

68. Ibid., p. 13.

69. Ibid., p. 14.

70. The best discussion of honor in Public Administration literature is Lewis Mainzer's "Honor in the Bureaucratic Life," *Review of Politics* 26 (Jan. 1964): 70–90.

71. See chap. 5 above, pp. 73–75. There is an irony in comparing the Brownlow Report with the Civil Service Reform Act of 1978. The latter was rooted in part in an awareness of the inadequacy of the traditional dichotomy of politics and administration. It therefore proceeded to make the civil service more accountable politically while at the same time providing a reward system that was based on private-sector motivation—monetary bonuses. The Brownlow Report, on the other hand, accepted the politics/administration dichotomy but treated administrators like statesmen. The analogy between Congress and a board of directors is also used in the report of the Grace Commission (see Charles T. Goodsell, "The Grace Commission: Seeking Efficiency for the Whole People," *Public Administration Review* 44 [May–June 1984]: 201).

72. Brownlow Report, pp. 17, 18, 19, 28.

73. Ibid., p. iii; see also the opening paragraph of the Declaration of Independence and *Federalist 1*.

74. Brownlow Report, p. iii.

75. Ibid., pp. 2–3.

76. Ibid., p. 40.

77. The expression "fourth branch" is used to describe the bureaucracy in at least eleven introductory textbooks on American government (see the thorough survey of textbook statements on the bureaucracy in Henry J. Merry, *Constitutional Function of Presidential-Administrative Separation* [Washington, D.C.: University Press of America, 1978], app. A, pp. 107–17).

78. The intemperate language of the Brownlow Committee did not escape contemporary friends of the administrative state (see Louis Jaffe, "Invective and Investigation in Administrative Law," *Harvard Law Review* 52 [June 1939]: 1201–45).

79. Chap. 8, p. 132 above.

80. Storing, *What the Anti-Federalists Were FOR*, p. 54.

81. Ibid.

## CHAPTER 10
## INDIVIDUAL RIGHTS:
## THE ATTORNEY GENERAL'S REPORT

1. *Senate Documents*, no. 8, 77th Cong., 1st sess. (Washington, D.C.: Government Printing Office, 1941). An abridged version of the report has been reprinted under the title *Administrative Procedure in Government Agencies* by the University Press of Virginia, Charlottesville (1967), with a Preface by Charles K. Woltz (the unabridged version is hereafter cited as AGR).

2. AGR, app. A., pp. 251–52.

3. Ibid., p. 253.

4. *Monumental* and *prodigious* are words that should be used with considerable circumspection. They can be appropriately applied to the research that formed the background of AGR. The research staff that was headed by Walter Gellhorn produced twenty-seven monographs describing in detail the actual practices of administrative

agencies. Speaking of the high quality of the work that went into the report, Charles Woltz has observed: "Here for the first time in adequate fashion the administrative animal was studied scientifically, its corpus was dissected, its functions and structure were analyzed on the basis of knowledge rather than of hypothesis or previous ideas" (p. vii of Woltz's Preface to the 1967 reprinting of the AGR). The procedure followed by the staff is explained in the committee's "Interim Report" of 31 Jan. 1940. First, there were interviews with agency officials, employees, attorneys who had dealt with the agency, and members of the public who were affected by the agency. Staff members would then attend agency hearings and examine the files. A preliminary report was then prepared, which was sent to agency officials for comment. The committee members, without staff, would then meet with agency officials. Public hearings were then held on the draft monographs that had been prepared for each agency being studied (AGR, app. A).

5. AGR, pp. 25–33, 2, 63, 68, 102.

6. The expression "secret law" is Kenneth C. Davis's. Davis was a member of the AGR staff who later became a leading scholar in the field of administrative law. His book *Discretionary Justice: A Preliminary Inquiry* (Baton Rouge: Louisiana State University Press, 1969) has had a profound influence on the field of administrative law. The origins of many of the ideas that Davis weaves into the theme of discretion can be found in the AGR. This is particularly true of chapters 2 and 3 of the report. A hint of Davis's later controversial proposal for the use of "hypotheticals" in rule making can be found on pp. 99–100 of the AGR.

7. Storing, *CAF*, 2.4.7, 2.4.13, 2.6.8, and 2.7.30; for a full reference to *CAF* see note 5 of chap. 2.

8. Ibid., 4.23.3.

9. Ibid., 5.16.20; see also Edmund Randolph in support of secrecy, at 2.5.22; Federal Farmer on secrecy in commercial as opposed to diplomatic treaties, at 2.8.147; Deliberator opposes secret sessions in Congress, at 3.13.5; Wm. Summes does the same, at 4.5.2; Sydney attacks secrecy at the Constitutional Convention, at 6.9.2.

10. Sec. 3. of the Walter-Logan Act. The full title of Walter-Logan is "An Act to provide for the more expeditious settlements of disputes with the United States, and for other purposes" (H.R. 6324, 76th Cong., 3d sess., 1940).

11. Statement of Chairman Celler of the House Committee on the Judiciary, to accompany H.R. 6324, 76th Cong., 3d sess., report 1149, pt. 2, p. 3.

12. Jackson's comments were included in President Roosevelt's "Message from the President of the United States returning without approval H.R. 6324," 76th Cong., 3d sess., 18 Dec. 1940, p. 7 (hereafter cited as Walter-Logan veto message).

13. Ibid.

14. AGR, p. 35.

15. Kenneth C. Davis, *Discretionary Justice*, pp. 21–22, and *Administrative Law and Government*, 2d ed. (Minneapolis: West Publishing Co., 1975), pp. 215–17.

16. AGR, pp. 123, 62, 68, 46–50, and chap. 7 passim.

17. A strong emphasis on the character of administrators appears in Walter Gellhorn, *Federal Administrative Proceedings* (Baltimore, Md.: Johns Hopkins Press, 1941). The same is true of James M. Landis, *The Administrative Process* (Westport, Conn.: Greenwood Press, 1974), which was originally published by Yale University Press in 1938. A good discussion of Landis's important contribution to regulatory theory can be found in Thomas K. McCraw, *Prophets of Regulation* (Cambridge: Harvard University Press, 1984), pp. 153–221.

18. *Federalist 51.*

19. See, e.g., *Federalist 29, 31, 49, 55, 63,* and *76.*

20. Statement of Mr. Walter of the House Committee on the Judiciary to accompany H.R. 6324, 76th Cong., 3d sess., report 1149, p. 2.

21. Ibid.

22. Charles G. Haines, "The Adaptation of Administrative Law and Procedure to Constitutional Theories and Principles," *American Political Science Review* 34 (Feb. 1940): 14.

23. See Storing, *CAF*, 4.28.8, where A Columbian Patriot maintains that the people "wish for no *federal city* whose *'cloud cap't* towers' may screen the state culprit from the hand of justice; while its exclusive jurisdiction may protect the riot of armies encamped within its limits." See also the satirical letter of Aristocrotis to "his serenity the right respectable, most honourable highly renowned J[ame]s W[ilso]n, political hackney writer to the most lucrative order of the bank." Aristocrotis goes on: "I would entreat you, dear sir, that when you arrive at the summit of your desires, you would deign to look back to your former condition, and make some provision for the relief of your insolvent brethen in time to come: that you would procure congress to constitute the *ten miles square* into a Sanctum-Sanctorum, a place of refuge for well born bankrupts, to shelter themselves and property from the rapacity of their persecuting creditors" (*CAF*, 3.16.1 and 2).

24. Gellhorn, pp. 26–29, 35–37, 57, 70, 73, 97; Landis, pp. 28–29, 98–99, 62. New Dealers continued to stress reasoned decision making and fair play, even after they had been appointed to the Supreme Court (see the opinions of Justice Frankfurter in *SEC* v. *Chenery Corp.*, 318 U.S. 80 [1943], and Justice Jackson in *Wong Yang Sung* v. *McGrath*, 339 U.S. 33 [1950]). The need for reasoned decision making is a perennial theme in judicial review of administrative action. For a recent example see Justice White's opinion in *Motor Vehicle Manufacturers Association* v. *State Farm Mutual Insurance Co.*, 103 S.Ct. 2856 (1983).

25. Storing, *CAF*, 6.14.67.

26. Haines, p. 14; James Landis, "Crucial Issues in Administrative Law: The Walter-Logan Bill," *Harvard Law Review* 52 (May 1940): 1077–1102; Charles M. Wiltse, "The Representative Function of Bureaucracy," *American Political Science Review* 35 (June 1941): 510–16; Louis L. Jaffe, "The Report of the Attorney General's Committee on Administrative Procedure," *University of Chicago Law Review* 8 (Apr. 1941): 401–40.

27. Walter-Logan veto message, p. 2.

28. Landis, "Crucial Issues in Administrative Law," p. 1093.

29. Haines, p. 19.

30. Alexis de Tocqueville, *Democracy in America,* 2 vols. (New York: Random House, 1945), 1:295–96.

31. James H. Kettner, *The Development of American Citizenship: 1608–1870* (Chapel Hill: University of North Carolina Press, 1978), pt. 1.

32. Aristotle, *Politics,* bk. 3.

33. For a further discussion of this point see John A. Rohr, "Civil Servants and Second Class Citizens," *Public Administration Review* 44 (Mar. 1984): 135–40.

34. AGR, p. 194, title 1, sec. 7, par. 7.

35. Landis, "Crucial Issues in Administrative Law," p. 1093.

36. AGR, p. 216.

37. Storing, *What the Anti-Federalists Were FOR,* p. 64.

38. Storing, *CAF,* 4.17.22 and 2.7.44.

39. John B. MacMaster and Frederick D. Stone, *Pennsylvania and the Federal Constitution, 1787–1788,* 2 vols. (New York: Da Capo Press, 1970), 1:356–61.

40. In addition to James Wilson's arguments see *Federalist 83*. One of the Federalists' standard defenses of the Constitution's silence on jury trials in civil cases was to claim that Congress could provide for such trials should the need arise. The constitutional silence did not preclude discretionary action by Congress. A Farmer, an Anti-Federalist from Maryland, had a good rejoinder to this argument. He maintained that if Congress had such power, it was an implied power. If Congress had an implied power to take decisions away from judges and give them to juries, what other implied powers might Congress have as well? What happens to the independence of the judiciary if Congress can alter the distribution of judicial power so readily? A Farmer shrewdly turned the Federalists' soothing assurances about Congress providing for jury trials into an illustration of the danger of hidden powers in Congress (see Storing, *CAF*, 5.1.62).

41. AGR, pp. 104, 108.

42. Walter-Logan veto message, p. 8.

43. AGR, p. 92; *Federalist 83*.

44. It is ironic that administrative agencies are continually accused of thwarting efficiency through excessive "red tape." Red tape is the underside of the coin of procedural regularity. The New Dealers who wrote the AGR were partial to administrative discretion and informal procedure. Red tape was imposed upon the administrative process by the critics, not the friends, of the administrative state. They did so to preserve individual rights, just as the Anti-Federalists imposed the red tape of a jury trial in civil cases on the new government that they had criticized. For a recent example of the close connection between red tape and civil liberties see *Larkin* v. *Grendel's Den, Inc.*, 103 S.Ct. 505 (1982).

45. The formalism suggested by exquisite distinctions between various standards of review has not been taken too seriously by the courts in practice. Judicial practice is much more chaotic than the niceties of legal doctrine suggest. Nevertheless, the standards serve at least as a point of departure. An excellent discussion of the problem of the scope of review can be found in *Universal Camera Corp.* v. *NLRB*, 340 U.S. 474 (1951).

46. For a recent and thorough discussion of this matter see David O'Brien, "Marbury, the APA, and Science-Policy Disputes: The Alluring and Elusive Judicial/Administrative Partnership," *Harvard Journal on Law and Public Policy* (June 1984): 443–81.

47. The Supreme Court held that the NLRB's decision had settled a question of fact; but the publisher's argument that the NLRB had simply rendered a legal interpretation of the statutory word *employee* was surely not without merit (see *Hearst Publishing Co.* v. *NLRB*, 322 U.S. 111 [1944]).

48. AGR, p. 88, citing John Dickinson, *Administrative Justice and the Supremacy of Law in the United States* (New York: Russell & Russell, 1927), p. 55.

49. AGR, p. 92.

50. Robert H. Jackson, *The Struggle for Administrative Supremacy* (New York: Knopf, 1941).

51. Landis, "Crucial Issues in Administrative Law," p. 1093.

52. *Federalist 81;* see also William E. Nelson, *Americanization of the Common Law: The Impact of Legal Change on Massachusetts Society, 1760–1830* (Cambridge: Harvard University Press, 1975), pp. 165–71.

53. Storing, *CAF*, 2.8.194.

54. Ibid., 2.4.92.

55. Ibid., 2.7.25, 2.9.175, 3.2.7, 3.5.6, 3.11.38–39.

56. McMaster and Stone, p. 359.

57. Ibid., p. 377.

58. *Federalist 81.*

59. AGR, p. 97, citing 1 Stat. 137.

60. Ibid., p. 195.

61. Ibid., p. 228.

62. Storing, *CAF,* 5.17.1.

63. Transcript of National Emergency Council Meeting of 9 Jan. 1934, National Archives, Suitland, Md., RG44, box 12.

64. Ibid.; meeting of 23 Jan. 1934.

65. Ibid.; meeting of 17 Apr. 1934.

66. Secretary Perkins's reference to "police power" did not appear in a context that suggests that she was thinking in terms of the police power of the states in American constitutional law. What she had in mind was heavy-handed government.

67. In stressing the harmony between regulators and regulated, the New Dealers followed the lead of the architects of the Interstate Commerce Commission. There seems to be a strong bias in the administrative state toward stressing the harmony between government and industry. The opposite side of this coin is, of course, the discomfort of the administrative state with markets and competition.

68. AGR, p. 102.

69. Ibid., p. 109.

70. Ibid., p. 104.

71. Ibid., p. 105.

72. On the point of rule-making procedures that educate administrators see *Pacific Coast European Conference* v. *U.S.,* 350 F2d 197, 205 (1965), and Herbert Kaufman, "The Federal Administrative Procedure Act," *Buffalo University Law Review* 25 (1946): 479.

73. AGR, p. 101.

74. Chap. 6, p. 79; see also *Federalist 28* and *63;* Jean Yarborough, "Thoughts on *The Federalist's* View of Representation," *Polity* 12 (Fall 1979): 66; and Gordon Wood, *The Creation of the American Republic, 1779–1787* (Chapel Hill: University of North Carolina Press, 1969), pp. 596–600.

75. AGR, pp. 102, 103.

76. Ibid., p. 108.

77. Had the majority view of the AGR prevailed, the proposed Office of Federal Administrative Procedure would have been a major agency in United States government. A full chapter in the AGR is devoted to discussing this agency that was not to be. Some matters covered by statutory prescription in the APA would have been left to the judgment of the office proposed by the AGR. It would have been to administrative law what the Office of Management and Budget (OMB) is to budget and the Office of Personnel Management (OPM) is to personnel. Perhaps the managerial aspects of administrative law were not sufficiently clear to warrant the creation of such an agency. It would have been a peculiarly American version of *droit administratif.* A faint shadow of the AGR's Office of Federal Administrative Procedures appears in the Grace Commission's proposal for an "Office of Federal Management" (see Charles T. Goodsell, "The Grace Commission: Seeking Efficiency for the Whole People," *Public Administration Review* 44 [May–June 1984]: 201).

78. *Federalist 35;* see Yarborough, pp. 72–79.

79. *Federalist 51.*

## CHAPTER 11
## CONCLUSION

1. This decision was not made easily. I hold in high regard the profound, though unfashionable, constitutional scholarship of the late W. W. Crosskey. His exhaustive research into the lexical meaning of the text of the Constitution as of 1787 is a mighty bulwark against an intemperate use of the "living Constitution" metaphor. The organic metaphor is helpful, but it should not provide rhetorical cover for those who would render the language of the Constitution virtually meaningless. This includes justices of the Supreme Court, for it was from a member of that august bench that we heard the startling comment that the Constitution means what the Supreme Court says it means. Such judicial hauteur makes Crosskey's sophisticated linguistic inquiries quite attractive (see his *Politics and the Constitution,* 3 vols. [Chicago: University of Chicago Press, 1953, 1980]).

2. The Virginia Plan, submitted at the opening of the 1787 Convention, would have created a federal judicial system with a supreme and subordinate courts. On 5 June, Rutledge and Sherman took the lead in attacking this provision. They wanted state tribunals to be the courts of first instance under the new government—"the right of appeal to the supreme national tribunal being sufficient to secure the national rights and uniformity of Judgments." This position was opposed by Madison, Wilson, and Dickinson, but nevertheless was approved by a 5 to 4 vote, with two states divided. Madison and Wilson then moved "that the National Legislature be empowered to institute inferior tribunals." This motion carried by a vote of 8 to 2, with one state divided. This is the basis of Congress's discretionary power over the creation of inferior courts (see Tansill, pp. 157–59; for a full reference see note 18 of chap. 1 above).

3. Robert A. Goldwin, "Of Men and Angels: A Search for Morality in the Constitution," in *The Moral Foundations of the American Republic,* ed. Robert H. Horwitz (Charlottesville: University of Virginia Press, 1979), pp. 6–12.

4. Aristotle, *Nicomachean Ethics,* trans. David Ross (New York: Oxford University Press, 1925, 1984), bk. 1, 1094d, p. 3.

5. Edward Shils, *Tradition* (London: Faber & Faber, 1981), p. vii.

6. Ibid., p. 7.

7. Ibid., p. 326.

8. Ibid., p. 195.

9. Ibid.

10. Milner S. Ball, *The Promise of American Law: A Theological, Humanistic View of Legal Process* (Athens: University of Georgia Press, 1981), p. 20, commenting on Auden's "Elegy for JFK."

11. In the past decade or so, an "interpretist" mode of social science has come to the fore. *Sociological Paradigms and Organisational Analysis,* by Gibson Burrell and Gareth Morgan (London: Heinemann, 1979), discusses this development cogently (pp. 227–78). To date, it seems to me, the real strength of interpretism lies in its compelling polemic against an intemperate positivism. Interpretists are, of course, quite at home with the notion of a perceived past. However, I do not believe they have as yet a satisfactory norm for telling where interpretation ends and ideology or even propaganda begins. A particularly intriguing "interpretist" position can be found in Geoffrey Vickers's notion of "appreciation" (see his *Art of Judgment* [London: Chapman & Hall, 1966]).

12. Barry D. Karl, *The Uneasy State: The United States from 1915 to 1945* (Chicago: University of Chicago Press, 1983), p. 4.

13. See note 10 above.

14. Numa Denis Fustel De Coulanges, *The Ancient City,* trans. William Small (Garden City, N.Y.: Doubleday, n.d.), bk. 3, "The City," pp. 117–219. Although no date is given for Small's translation, the first French edition appeared in 1864.

15. William A. Schambra, "The Roots of the American Public Philosophy," *Public Interest* 67 (Spring 1982): 38.

16. Herbert A. Simon, *Administrative Behavior: A Study of Decision-Making Processes in Administrative Organizations* (New York: Macmillan, 1947). For a searching criticism of Simon's work see Herbert J. Storing, "The Science of Administration: Herbert A. Simon," in *Essays on the Scientific Study of Politics,* ed. Herbert J. Storing (New York: Holt, Rinehart & Winston, 1962). For a discussion of Storing's criticism of Simon see Kent A. Kirwan, "Herbert J. Storing and the Study of Public Administration," *Political Science Reviewer* 11 (1981): 194–219.

17. Michael Lienesch, "The Constitutional Tradition: History, Political Action, and Progress in American Political Thought, 1787–1793," *Journal of Politics* 42 (1980): 2–48.

18. Woodrow Wilson, "The Study of Administration," *Political Science Quarterly* 2 (June 1887): 197–222.

19. See the discussion at the end of chap. 6 and the treatment of *Kendall* v. *Stokes* in chap. 9, pp. 140–41.

20. Publius uses *department* where we use *branch* today. Contemporary usage is preferable for the present discussion in order to avoid confusion between the three great departments in the first three articles of the Constitution and the executive departments of article 2.

21. See the remarks of Senator William Maclay of Pennsylvania in the First Congress on 14 July 1789: "Mr. President, whoever attends strictly to the Constitution of the United States, will readily observe that the part assigned to the Senate was an important one—no less than that of being the great check, the regulator and corrector, or, if I may so speak, the balance of this Government" (Edgar S. Maclay, ed., *Journal of William Maclay* [New York, 1890], p. 110).

22. Lynton K. Caldwell, *The Administrative Theories of Hamilton and Jefferson* (New York: Russell & Russell, 1964), pp. 36, 99–100.

23. The story was literally front-page news for the first few months of 1983. A particularly insightful story about a central figure, Rita Lavelle, appeared in *Washington Post* of 5 Mar. 1983, p. C1.

24. During President's Reagan's first term, the superfund scandal was the most notable example of politically appointed officials trying to change administrative practice because of the results of the presidential election of 1980. It was not the only example. The "air bags" dispute over Department of Transportation regulations on passive restraints ended up before the Supreme Court of the United States, where Justice White gave a firm endorsement to the integrity of the administrative process against presidential claims of a popular mandate (*Motor Vehicle Manufacturers of the U.S.* v. *State Farm Mutual Automobile Insurance Co.,* 103 S.Ct. 2856 [1983]). Writing for the Court, Justice White reaffirmed the doctrine of the first *Chenery* case, 318 U.S. 80 (1943), namely, that the administrative process must be governed by reasoned decision making. For a discussion of the Reagan administration's efforts to change coal-surface-mining regulations see Donald Menzel, "Redirecting the Implementation of a Law: The Reagan Administration and Coal Surface Mining Regulation," *Public Administration Review* 43 (Sept.–Oct. 1983): 411–30.

25. Throughout this discussion the focus is on the *discretionary* authority of the Public Administration. Where ministerial functions are involved, administrators should execute legally correct commands. The rule of law demands nothing less. This

principle, however, is not terribly helpful, because the most important issues for administrators concern discretionary matters wherein the law empowers rather than commands. There may still be considerable administrative discretion even after a clear and legally correct command has been given, because such a command may contradict another clear and legal command from a competing institution of government. An executive order that is at odds with its alleged statutory foundation provides the classic case. For a good discussion of the impact of executive orders on the administrative process see Phillip J. Cooper, "By Order of the President: Administration by Executive Order and Proclamation," *Administration and Society* 18 (forthcoming, 1986).

26. Louis Fisher, *Presidential Spending Power* (Princeton, N.J.: Princeton University Press, 1975), pp. 73, 76. Fisher's discussion of impoundment under President Nixon shows the limitation of gentlemen's agreements when one of the parties to the agreement is no gentleman (see chap. 8). The discussion of "reprogramming" in chap. 4 suggests opportunities for the sort of administrative statesmanship envisioned in the theory of Public Administration that I have in mind.

27. Stephen Skowronek, *Building the New American State: The Development of Administrative Capacities, 1877–1920* (New York: Cambridge University Press, 1981), pp. 24–35.

28. An excellent discussion of the role of the judiciary in the administrative state appears in David H. Rosenbloom, *Public Administration and Law: Bench v. Bureau in the United States* (New York: Marcel Dekker, 1983), chap. 7.

29. John A. Rohr, "Public Administration and the Constitutional Bicentennial: An Essay on Research," *International Journal of Public Administration* 4 (1982): 349–80.

30. I have developed this point in chap. 2 of *Ethics for Bureaucrats: An Essay on Law and Values* (New York: Marcel Dekker, Inc., 1979).

31. The other twenty-one are: (1) selection of a president or a vice-president by the electoral college; (2) selection of a president by the House of Representatives voting as states; (3) selection of a vice-president by the Senate; (4) appointment by the president, with the advice and consent of the Senate; (5) appointment by the president alone, as provided by law; (6) appointment by the head of an executive department, as provided by law; (7) appointment by a court of law, as provided by law; (8) election to the Senate by a state legislature; (9) selection as a presidential elector in such manner as a state legislature shall choose; (10) selection by the House of Representatives as an officer of that body; (11) selection by the Senate as an officer of that body; (12) selection as an elector for the District of Columbia "in such manner as Congress may direct" (Twenty-third Amendment); (13) selection as vice-president upon nomination by the president and confirmation by both houses of Congress (Twenty-fifth Amendment); (14) discharge by the vice-president of presidential powers and duties as acting president upon the president's written declaration of his inability to discharge the powers and duties of his office (Twenty-fifth Amendment); (15) discharge by the vice-president of presidential powers and duties as acting president upon written declaration to the president pro tempore of the Senate and the Speaker of the House from the vice-president and a majority of the principal officers of the executive departments that the president is unable to discharge his powers and duties (Twenty-fifth Amendment); (16) discharge by the vice-president of presidential powers and duties as acting president upon written declaration to the president pro tempore of the Senate and the Speaker of the House from the vice-president and a majority of a body designated by law for this purpose that the president is unable to discharge the duties and powers of his office (Twenty-fifth Amendment); (17) congressional resolution of a dispute between the president and the vice-president over the president's ability to discharge the duties and powers of his office (Twenty-fifth Amendment); (18) accession by the vice-president to

the presidency upon the president's removal, death, resignation, or inability to discharge the powers and duties of his office; (19) accession to the position to act as president in such manner as Congress may by law provide in the case of the removal, death, resignation, or inability both of the president and the vice-president; (20) accession to office by presidential appointment when a vacancy has occurred during a recess of the Senate; (21) temporary appointment as senator by the governor of a state.

The provisions of the Twenty-fifth Amendment are particularly significant because this amendment was ratified in 1967, long after the president had been recognized as a man of the people. Despite the popular character of the office, the people are excluded from having any voice whatsoever in resolving whatever crisis might arise over presidential succession. Here is a legitimacy question of the first order that, as late as 1967, is left to the experts to settle. The Senate has an equal voice with the House in settling a dispute between the president and the vice-president, even though senators are chosen on the basis of state representation rather than by population. Nevertheless, the "malapportioned" Senate is the constitutional peer of the House in selecting the president. Other significant actors in resolving the crisis envisioned in the Twenty-fifth Amendment are the unelected heads of executive departments and the enigmatic "such other body as Congress may by law provide."

In all this, the spirit of the framers reasserts itself. The Twenty-fifth Amendment reaffirms Madison's "filtering" view of representation. If the people have chosen their congressmen and senators wisely, they have nothing to fear from letting these experts or those whom the experts designate decide the great matters of state that are anticipated in the amendment.

32. Edward S. Corwin, *The President: Office and Powers*, 4th ed. (New York: New York University Press, 1957), p. 153.

33. The leading cases are *In re Neagle*, 135 U.S. 1 (1890), and *In re Debs*, 159 U.S. 564 (1895). *Myers* v. *U.S.*, 272 U.S. 52 (1926), somewhat ironically supports Theodore Roosevelt's exuberant view of presidential authority. The irony comes from the fact that the opinion was written by Chief Justice Taft, whose own writings on the presidency were critical of Roosevelt's position.

34. The definite article is used in Gary L. Wamsley et al., "Refocusing the American Dialogue," in *A Centennial History of the American Administrative State*, ed. Ralph C. Chandler (New York: Wiley, forthcoming).

35. It has often been noted that the "Madisonian Model" of pluralism was intended to exist only in Congress, not in the executive branch. Among the delegates to the 1787 convention, George Mason was the strongest proponent of pluralism in the executive branch. He opposed the one-man executive. When he lost on this issue, he argued for an executive council to limit the president's power. His loss on this issue as well was one of the main reasons for his eventually joining the Anti-Federalist opposition to the Constitution. Publius, of course, speaks often of "unity in the executive." Care must be taken in interpreting his position in this matter. Unity in the executive does not always mean rigid hierarchy, as in the managerial textbook notion of unity of command. At times Publius's target was the plural executive favored by some Anti-Federalists. Unity in the executive at times means nothing more than a defense of a one-man presidency. Pluralism in the executive may be looked upon as a contemporary expression of the Anti-Federalist heritage.

36. Theodore J. Lowi, *The End of Liberalism* (New York: Norton, 1969).

37. Three recent books in administrative history bring out just how deeply the pluralist tradition is embedded in the American tradition: Barry D. Karl, *The Uneasy State;* Stephen Skowronek, *Building a New American State;* and William E. Nelson, *The Roots of American Bureaucracy, 1830–1900* (Cambridge: Harvard University Press,

1982). Nelson makes a provocative argument that traces the origins of American bureaucracy to the fundamental American commitment to pluralism. The connection between antislavery sentiment and civil-service reform has often been noted. The strength of Nelson's book lies in its explanation of how antislavery moral principles rallied to the support of bureaucratic structures. The deed was done in the name of pluralism (see, especially, Nelson's chap. 5, "Building Bureaucratic Authority Structures").

38. A good survey of this literature can be found in Chester A. Newland, "Professional Public Executives and Public Administration Agendas," in *Professional Public Executives,* ed. Chester A. Newland (Washington, D.C.: American Society for Public Administration, 1980), pp. 1–30.

39. Two particularly impressive organizations are the Federal Executive Institute Alumni Association and the Federal Executive and Professional Association. Their articulate newsletters provide considerable insight into the current mood among senior civil servants. Other groups include the Federal Managers Association, the American Foreign Service Association, the Federal Executive League, the Executive Women's Group, the Senior Executive Association, and Federally Employed Women, Inc. For an account of the formation of the Federal Employees' Roundtable see *Washington Post,* 9 Sept. 1982, p. C2. For examples of "Federal Workers . . . Fighting Back" see *U.S. News and World Report,* 29 Aug. 1983, pp. 53–54. A good overview of these organizations appears in Eileen Seidman, "Hanging Together: Federal Executive Associations," *Bureaucrat* (Winter 1983): 40–43.

40. Bernard Rosen, "Uncertainty in the Senior Executive Service," *Public Administration Review* 41 (Mar.–Apr. 1981): 203–7.

41. The survival of the Federal Executive Institute as a training facility for senior executives is due in no small part to organized pressure brought by career personnel in the SES (see David T. Stanley, "Civil Service Reform: Then and Now," in *Legislating Bureaucratic Change: The Civil Service Reform Act of 1978,* ed. Patricia W. Ingraham and Carolyn Ban [Albany: State University of New York Press, 1984], p. 282).

42. The need for the SES to develop a sense of community for public-spirited purposes is discussed by Norton Long in "The S.E.S. and the Public Interest," *Public Administration Review* 41 (May–June 1981): 305–12. The discussion of the oath of office develops more fully some points made in my earlier article "Administrative Decision-Making and Professionalism: The Role of the Constitution," *Review of Public Personnel Administration* 3 (Spring 1983): 61–70.

43. *1 Cranch* 137 (1803).

44. Mortimer J. Adler, ed., *The Annals of America,* vol. 5 (Chicago: Encyclopedia Britannica, Inc.), p. 528.

45. In concentrating on the oath taken by professional administrators, I set aside the implication of the fact that nearly all government employees take an oath to uphold the Constitution. The logic of my position would seem to compel me to hold that only those who exercise administrative duties should be required to take an oath of office. I am not ready to draw this conclusion. Suffice it to say that the discretionary character of administrative work requires an oath. This does not exclude the possibility that there may be other reasons for requiring an oath from nonadministrative personnel. Chief among these would be a certain esprit de corps within the public service. If questions of morale are set aside, it would seem that the oath should not be demanded of civilian personnel who carry out purely ministerial functions. An analogy might be drawn with the provisions for financial disclosure, which include some career personnel and exclude others. The analogy limps, however, because many more career personnel influence the constitutional balance of power than are likely to be influenced by the sorts of

financial matters that are pertinent to disclosure (see John A. Rohr, "Financial Disclosure: Power in Search of Policy," *Public Personel Management Journal* 10 [1981]: 29–40). On the matter of the relationship between an oath and an "officer," as opposed to an employee or a party to a contract, see Floyd R. Mechem, *A Treatise on the Law of Public Offices and Officers* (Chicago: Callaghan & Co., 1890), bk. 1, chap. 1, sec. 8.

46. Robert Bolt, *A Man for All Seasons* (New York: Random House, 1962), p. 81.

47. In some primitive religions, soldiers swore by their swords, but the swords were considered to be symbols of the power of the war god.

48. Members of some religious orders take vows of obedience, but these are always taken pursuant to the constitution of the order, the canon law of the Church, the teachings of scripture and tradition, and a variety of other safeguards against ecclesiastical arbitrariness. Those who take such vows do not see themselves as having abdicated their moral autonomy. Their vow pledges them to a dialogue with their religious superiors in which together they will seek to discern the will of God. The process is more properly mystical than simply authoritative (see "Obedienz," in *Theologisches Wörterbuch*, ed. Karl Rahner and H. Vorgrimler (Freiburg: Herder, 1961). According to the canon law of the Roman Catholic Church, a vow is a promise made to God (canon 1307). Since the vow of obedience is made to God, the ecclesiastical superior cannot invoke it to command something contrary to the will of God. Hence there is a limitation on authority built into the very definition of a vow of obedience.

49. It is difficult to get a precise understanding of *oath* today because of the two meanings of the word. Contemporary English usage allows *oath* to describe (1) the invocation of God to witness the truth of what one says and (2) that which one pledges to do. Thus I can take an oath to uphold the Constitution and also take an oath in the sense that I call upon God to witness the veracity of my intent to uphold the Constitution. This double meaning leads to some rather loose language. In the text I have offered a distinction between oath and promise that turns on the seriousness of the subject matter involved. Promises can be serious or trivial; oaths deal only with matters of great seriousness. Logically, I might have said that *oath* is a species of the genus *promise*. I resisted this formulation, however, because it would ignore the other meaning of oath—the invocation of God. To ignore the meaning of *oath* as an invocation of God would be a dreadful distortion of language. The invocation of God is precisely what most religious people mean by the word. Even in a secularist context, oath is used in the sense of invocation. For example, the current formulation of the oath of Hippocrates, as sworn by recent graduates of the University of Virginia's medical school, begins "I do solemnly swear by whatever I hold most sacred." In my discussion of *oath* I have used the word in both senses described above and have distinguished it from a promise, because it necessarily suggests something of the utmost seriousness. Because it deals with such serious matters, it is worthy of the invocation of God or "whatever I hold most sacred."

50. John Rawls, "Two Concepts of Rules," *Philosophical Review* 64 (1955): 3–32.

51. The Constitution is a particularly appropriate source of restraint on administrative exuberance, because constitutionalism stands, among other things, for limited government and procedural regularity. Its particular excellence is that it can check arbitrariness, an evil to which the administrative state is often prone. For a discussion of the word *constitution* in its twofold meaning of creating a political order and limiting power see Graham Maddox, "A Note on the Meaning of 'Constitution,'" *American Political Science Review* 76 (Dec. 1982): 805–9. It is interesting to note that the oath of office has not always been an oath to uphold the Constitution. During the Civil War,

workers in the Washington Navy Yard had to take an oath of loyalty, but not an oath to uphold the Constitution. Perhaps the reason for this was that the correct meaning of the Constitution was precisely the issue that led to the War (see J. Peck, *Roundshot to Rocket: A History of the Washington Naval Yard and U.S. Naval Gun Factory* [Annapolis, Md.: U.S. Naval Institute, 1949], pp. 142–49).

# Index

Adams, Charles Francis, 97–98
Adams, Henry Carter, 107
Adams, John: his *Defense of the Constitution of the United States of America*, 81; on jury trial, 51; on natural aristocracy, 81; on presidential power, 88; on representation, 80
Adeimantus (in Plato's *Republic*), 55, 131, 246 n. 63
Administration of government, 1–3; as basic governmental action, 68–69, 171; and change, 112; civil servants and, 36, 39; and constitutional theory, 77–84, 89; openness of, 155–56; as political activity, 60, 66–67, 79; Reagan administration, 188–91, 259 n. 24; setting of, 88. *See also* Administrative agencies; Administrative state; Executive departments
Administrative agencies: and adjudication of individual rights, 154–61; as captured, 168; judicial review of, 163–66, 175–76; powers of, 27, 259 n. 25; procedures of, 161–63 (*see also* Administrative Procedure Act); and rule making, 167–70; and senate function, 28–39, 171–94. *See also* Administrative state; Attorney General's Report; Interstate Commerce Act; Interstate Commerce Commission; Regulatory commissions
Administrative Procedure Act of 1946 (APA), 109, 155, 157, 163, 166
*Administrative State, The* (Waldo), xi
Administrative state, xi, 217 n. 11; and APA as Bill of Rights, 157; and citizenship, 161;

discretionary power of, 45, 68, 259 n. 25; founding of, 11, 112, 135–70 (*see also* Foundings); as healing constitutional defect, 40–53, 172–73; illegitimacy of, 4–5, 15, 68, 88; and ICC, 107–10; lawsuits in, 161, 175–76, 237 n. 35; legitimacy of, ix–xiii, 5, 7, 9, 39, 107–10, 130, 134, 171–94, 216 n. 5, 217 n. 9; on representation, 44, 45–48, 171; and *Schecter* case, 112. *See also* Administration of government; Administrative agencies; Administrative Procedure Act of 1946; Attorney General's Report; Brownlow report; Civil service; Executive departments
Administrators. *See* Civil service
Agricultural Adjustment Act of 1933, 122, 127. See also *U.S.* v. *Butler*
Amendments to the United States Constitution: no. 5, 92; no. 6, 227 n. 51; no. 7, 97, 109, 161, 162, 163, 166; no. 10, 126–28, 130; no. 14, 92, 93, 115; no. 17, 39; no. 22, 34, 142, 250 n. 33; and Woodrow Wilson, 61–63
American Association for Public Administration (ASPA), xi, xii, 59, 156
American Bar Association, 155
*American Law Review*, 93
American Political Science Association, 160
Annapolis Convention, 6, 118
Anti-Federalists: on aristocracy, 33; and Bill of Rights, 10; on checking president, 31–33, 35, 37; on civil servants, 36, 37, 158; and constitutional theory, 77–78; on executive senate, 22, 31–33, 35, 223 n. 41;